Marija Wakounig, Ferdinand Kühnel (Eds.)

Central Europe (Re-)visited

EUROPA ORIENTALIS

herausgegeben vom

Institut für Osteuropäische Geschichte
an der Universität Wien

Band 17

LIT

Central Europe (Re-)visited

A Multi-Perspective Approach To A Region

edited by

Marija Wakounig and Ferdinand Kühnel

LIT

Umschlagbild: Ferdinand Kühnel

Gedruckt mit Unterstützung des Bundesministeriums für Wissenschaft, Forschung und Wirtschaft in Wien

bmwfw
Bundesministerium für
Wissenschaft, Forschung und Wirtschaft

Bibliographic information published by the Deutsche Nationalbibliothek
The Deutsche Nationalbibliothek lists this publication in the Deutsche Nationalbibliografie; detailed bibliographic data are available on the Internet at http://dnb.d-nb.de.

ISBN 978-3-643-90738-7

Auslieferung/Verlagskontakt:
Fresnostr. 2
48159 Münster
Tel. +49 (0)251–62 03 20
Fax +49 (0)251–23 19 72
e-Mail: lit@lit-verlag.de
http://www.lit-verlag.de

LIT VERLAG
GmbH & Co. KG Wien 2015
Krotenthallergasse 10/8
A-1080 Wien
Tel. +43 (0) 1 / 409 56 61
Fax +43 (0) 1 / 409 56 97
e-Mail: wien@lit-verlag.at
http://www.lit-verlag.at

Auslieferung:
Österreich/Schweiz: Medienlogistik Pichler-ÖBZ GmbH & Co KG
IZ-NÖ, Süd, Straße 1, Objekt 34, A-2355 Wiener Neudorf
Tel. +43 (0) 2236/63 535 - 290, Fax +43 (0) 2236/63 535 - 243
e-Mail: mlo@medien-logistik.at

Deutschland: LIT Verlag Fresnostr. 2, D-48159 Münster
Tel. +49 (0) 2 51/620 32 - 22, Fax +49 (0) 2 51/922 60 99
e-Mail: vertrieb@lit-verlag.de

Contents

Preface

The eighth special volume of the 'Europa Orientalis' series contains reports and papers from the VIII. Annual Convention of the Centers for Austrian and Central European Studies, held in Minnesota (Minneapolis, USA) from 14 to 17 September 2014. These Centers were established to improve the cooperation between the host nations and Austria. They are also an opportunity for young researchers to connect with colleagues and to strengthen their international perspective during their respective scientific careers.

This special volume covers a wide range of topics compiled by current PhD students of the eight Centers for Austrian and Central European Studies. The focus of the contributions is on cultural, political, and modern Central European history. The annual reports of the Center Directors provide a comprehensive overview of the various activities of these institutions during the Academic Year 2014/2015.

It is one of the most important aims of the Austrian Federal Ministry of Science, Research and Economy not only to supply young scholars with research grants and scholarships, but also to encourage them to establish themselves in the international scientific community. While senior scholars usually benefit from their global network with partners and associates, the younger generation often has trouble getting in touch with their colleagues abroad. For this reason we decided in 2007 to bring together the best and most promising PhD students conducting their research at the various Centers for Austrian and Central European Studies. The present volume proves how important it was to implement the idea of regular annual meetings and to support it financially. Especially, as international experience and exchange continue to be fundamental for the success of future scientists. Therefore, events such as the VIII. Annual Convention of the Centers for Austrian and Central European Studies are a significant contribution to reach these targets.

Dr. Reinhold Mitterlehner

Vice Chancellor of Austria and Federal Minister of Science, Research and Economy

Editorial

The wide range of activities of the eight Austrian and Central European Centers and the working papers of the Center's current PhD students have culminated once more in a volume that is published in the Institute of East European History's prestigious 'Europa Orientalis' series. Each Center's director gave a brief report about his present engagement in this multilayered network and it could be shown how well the exchange within the centers works. The focus of this year's edition lies, as in previous years, in the research projects of the students. This year's title of the book "Central Europe (Re-)visited. A Multi-Perspective Approach to a Region" indicates that each new student's generation has a specific view on Central Europe and its history. The articles not only deal with Central Europe from a different perspective but also use different methodologies. In addition, the students come from different scientific disciplines such as history, political science, literary studies, or geography. The book is structured in three main parts, to bring the variety of topics under a common denominator: 'Concepts, Discourses & Methods', 'Ethnicity', and 'Identity' were chosen as the most appropriate categories.

On the occasion of the 70th birthday of the Austrian Center's former Director, we are also pleased to present Prof. Arnold Suppan's opus magnum "Hitler – Beneš – Tito: Konflikt, Krieg und Völkermord in Ostmittel- und Südosteuropa". The key messages of his book have been summarized in a special feature for this years' volume.

Each Center's director respective the thesis' supervisor were obliged to advise their PhD students in drafting their papers before these were sent to the editors. This has surely resulted in an even higher quality output of the research work presented within this volume. Besides different academic traditions, the editors have been again very keen to ensure that the guidelines are respected by all the authors in order to guarantee a certain level of coherence within the book. A style sheet is essential for the readability and comprehensibility of each article and, thus, an evidence for the scientific quality of this publication, although the strict adherence to the guidelines might often seem tedious.

Particular effort was made by both authors and editors in consistently translating foreign language titles within the text and in footnotes into the English language to make the volume even more accessible for the English speaking scientific community. These are included in square brackets, either within the text or – with regard to longer passages – in the footnotes. Nevertheless, we have decided – in accordance with the Ministry – to leave the authors the choice to write in either German or English. The dichotomy between being an international publication by using the *lingua franca* English and not to neglect the German language persists.

Abbreviations within the text are usually spelt out at their first mention. While the individual articles were formally streamlined following the guidelines of the 'Europa Orientalis' series and put into American English, the editors have tried to limit changes to the character of a text, where readability was an issue. Therefore, each text remains an expression of style and method of the individual author.

The editors would especially like to thank the Austrian Federal Ministry of Science, Research and Economy (Bundesministerium für Wissenschaft, Forschung und Wirtschaft BMWFW) and the Austrian Agency for International Cooperation in Education and Research (Österreichischer Austauschdienst, OeAD) for their support. Finally, the co-editor of the last two Center's volumes, Markus P. Beham, assisted this publication by offering his support as a native speaker in proof-reading the final manuscript as to language and expression.

Vienna, August 2015

Marija Wakounig, Ferdinand Kühnel

Feature Article

Arnold Suppan

Hitler – Beneš – Tito: Conflict, War, and Genocide in East-Central and South-East Europe[1]

Austrian Academy of Sciences

70 years after the end of World War II, the memories of political decisions, juridical acts, crimes against humanity, genocides, and expulsions in East Central and South East Europe in the first half of the 20th century are still alive. During the last decades these memories changed from the 'war generations' (*i.e.* generations who fought and suffered in World War II) to the generations of their children and grandchildren. Especially in the catastrophic decade between 1938 and 1948, the relationships between the 'Germans', 'Austrians', 'Magyars' and 'Italians' on the one hand, and the 'Czechs', 'Slovaks', 'Slovenes', 'Croats' and 'Serbs' on the other, were shattered and destroyed in a way that living together seemed impossible for the future.[2] It is the essential aim of this paper to present the historical, political, economic, social, psychological, and legal premises, contexts, and consequences of occupation, annexation, repression, war crimes, genocide, collaboration, resistance, revenge, displacement and expulsion in the Bohemian Lands and in Slovakia, as well as in Serbia, Croatia, Bosnia-Herzegovina, and Slovenia between 1938 and 1948. Beyond that, a comparison of the long period of repressed memories is important for an overall assessment.[3]

Hitler – Beneš – Tito

In the first half of the 20th century three political leaders dominated not only the political decision-making but also the political and ideological thinking in East

1 Arnold Suppan, Hitler – Beneš – Tito. Konflikt, Krieg und Völkermord in Ostmittel- und Südosteuropa, Internationale Geschichte/International History 1, 3 vols., Vienna [2]2014, XXXIV+2047 pp. with 140 illustrations and 13 maps. The following article was presented at the VIII Annual Convention of Austrian and Central European Centers in Minneapolis, 16 September 2014.

2 At a discussion in Rome, in April 2014, Gustavo Corni (Trento), spoke from second 'bloodlands' south of the Sudeten and Carpathian mountains and between the Adriatic and the Black Sea. *Cf.* Timothy Snyder, Bloodlands. Europe between Hitler and Stalin, London 2010.

3 Gerhard L. Weinberg, A World at Arms. A Global History of World War II, Cambridge 1994; I.C.B. Dear – M.R.D. Foot (Eds.), The Oxford Companion to the Second World War, Oxford/New York 1995; Richard J. Evans, The Third Reich at War, 1939–1945, London 2008; Tony Judt, Postwar. A History of Europe since 1945, London 2005.

Central and South East Europe. In 1945, they stood for the total break between the Germans and German Austrians on the one hand and the Czechs, Slovaks, Slovenes, Croats, and Serbs on the other hand: the German-Austrian Adolf Hitler (1889–1945), chief of the NSDAP (1921–1945) and German Reich chancellor and *Führer* (1933/1934–1945); the Czech Edvard Beneš (1884–1948), the Czechoslovak foreign minister (1918–1935) and president (1935–1938, 1940–1948); and the Croat-Slovene Josip Broz Tito (1892–1980), chief of the Communist Party of Yugoslavia (1937–1980), partisan warlord (1941–1945), prime minister (1945–1953), and president of Yugoslavia (1953–1980). Beneš, Hitler, and Tito had a common origin from Austria-Hungary, were baptized in the Roman Catholic Church and had a good knowledge of the German language. As members of the 'war generation' of World War I – Hitler and Tito as corporals, Beneš as national activist in the emigration – they developed strong anti-Habsburg, anti-Austrian, and anti-Catholic attitudes. After 1918, they represented totally different types of political leaders with different political conceptions: Hitler condemned 'Versailles', especially the war guilt of Germany and the reparations, agitated against 'Jewish Bolshevism', and demanded '*Lebensraum*' [living space] for the Germans in the East; Beneš defended the treaties of Versailles, Saint-Germain, and Trianon, and constructed an alliance system with Romania and Yugoslavia, the Little Entente, as well as bilateral pacts with France and the Soviet Union; and Tito agitated for the forbidden Communist Party of Yugoslavia (CPY) at home and within the Comintern. From 1933/1934 Hitler began to dominate policy in Central Europe and, from 1938, even European policy as an aggressive empire builder. Until September 1938, Beneš tried to resist this policy by planning. After his exile to London in October 1938, he continued this policy of resistance by negotiating with Churchill, Roosevelt and Stalin. Tito protested against the *Anschluss* of Austria and, after the April War in 1941, began to organize a Communist-led resistance movement against the German and Italian occupation. With the help of the Allies, Beneš and Tito survived the German occupation and shared the victory over Hitler and National Socialism. But there is no doubt: Hitler was – together with Stalin – the most cunning, unscrupulous and Machiavellistic politician of his era, and: He started World War II and was responsible for the worst genocide in history, the *Shoah*.[4]

4 Ian Kershaw, Hitler, 1889–1936: Hubris, New York 1999; Hitler 1936–1945: Nemesis, New York 2000; Hans-Ulrich Thamer – Simone Erpel (Eds.), Hitler und die Deutschen. Volksgemeinschaft und Verbrechen, Dresden 2010; Zbyněk A.B. Zeman, Edvard Beneš. Politický životopis, Praha 2002; Jindřich Dejmek, Edvard Beneš. Politická biografie českého demokrata, 2 vols., Praha 2006/2008; Vladimir Dedijer, Novi prilozi za biografiju Josipa Broza Tita, 3 vols., Zagreb 1980/1981; Stevan K. Pavlovitch, Tito – Yugoslavia's Great Dictator, London [2]2006; Raul Hilberg, The Destruction of the European Jews, New York 1961; Saul Friedländer, Nazi Germany and the Jews, 2 vols., New York 1997/2007; Mark Mazower, Hitler's Empire. How the Nazis Ruled Europe, New York 2008.

'Confrontational Communities' in the Habsburg Monarchy: Germans, Czechs, Jews, Slovaks, Magyars, Serbs, Croats, Slovenes, and Italians

Due to some language struggles and an increasing nationalist radicalism since the 1880s, the vast majority of the nationalities of Austria-Hungary were loyal to the Habsburg Monarchy until 1914. The cohabitation and coexistence of the Czech, German, Jewish, and Polish peoples in the Bohemian Lands (the present-day Czech Republic) and of the Slovak, Magyar, Ruthenian (Rusyn), Jewish, and German peoples in historical Upper Hungary (the present-day Slovakia and Carpatho-Ukraine), as well as of the Magyar, German, Romanian, Serbian, and Jewish peoples in historical Southern Hungary (the present-day Serb Vojvodina and Romanian Banat), the Croat, Serb, German and Jewish peoples in Croatia-Slavonia (the present-day Croatia) and the Slovene, Croat, Italian, and German peoples in Lower Styria, Carniola, and the Coastal region (the present-day Slovenia and Friuli-Venezia Giulia) were relatively free of insolvable conflict in the daily life of the Habsburg Empire until 1914. Many German-Bohemians, German-Moravians, German-Silesians, Germans in the Hauerland and Spiš, and the 'Swabians' in Banat, Bačka, Baranja, Syrmia, and East-Slavonia, along with the Germans in Lower Styria and Gottschee [Kočevsko] lived in their small towns and villages without any real contact with their Slavic neighbors; therefore, they spoke only their own German dialect and understood their Slavic neighbors little or not at all; if anything, they understood Hungarian in Upper and Lower Hungary or Italian in the Coastal region. This did not hold true for the Sudeten and Carpathian Germans in larger cities like Prague, Pilsen/Plzeň, Budweis/České Budějovice, Brünn/Brno, Olmütz/Olomouc, Mährisch Ostrau/Ostrava, Pressburg/Pozsony/Bratislava, and Kaschau/Kassa/Košice, the 'Swabians' in Temeschwar/Temesvár/Timişoara, Großbetschkerek/Nagybecskerek/Zrenjanin, Pantschowa/Pancsova/Pančevo, Semlin/Zemun, Neusatz/Újvidék/Novi Sad, Zombor/Sombor, and Esseg/Osijek, as well as the Germans in Agram/Zagreb, Fiume/Rijeka, Pola/Pula, Triest/Trieste, and Laibach/Ljubljana. These town-dwelling Germans lived in relatively close contact with their Czech, Slovak, Serb, Croat, or Slovene neighbors – as well as with Jews, Magyars, and Italians –, and had diverse economic (industries, crafts, shops, tourism), social (celebrations), and cultural (newspapers, theaters) interactions with them. Naturally, this was not possible without a certain command of the other languages, which they learned more in every day life than in school. In addition, there was an increasing number of ethnic and, to a lesser degree, denominational intermarriages.[5]

5 Helmut Rumpler – Martin Seger, Die Habsburgermonarchie 1848–1918, vol. IX/2: Die Gesellschaft der Habsburgermonarchie im Kartenbild. Verwaltungs-, Sozial- und Infrastrukturen. Nach dem Zensus von 1910, Wien 2010; Robert A. Kann, Das Nationalitätenproblem der Habsburgermonarchie. Geschichte und Ideengehalt der nationalen Bestrebungen vom Vormärz bis zur Auflösung des Reiches im Jahres 1918, 2 vols., Graz/Köln 1964; Carlisle A. Macartney, The Habsburg Empire, 1790–1918, London 1968; Robin Okey, The Habsburg Monarchy c. 1765–1918. From

After the defeat at Königgrätz/Hradec Králové in 1866, Emperor Francis Joseph I was convinced that the great-power status of the Habsburg Empire could only be guaranteed by dualism, with its acknowledgment of German and Magyar hegemony over the Panslavs. So, the 'Compromise' of 1867 became the basic law of a new entity, the 'Austro-Hungarian Monarchy' or Austria-Hungary. Both states were autonomous in their internal affairs, with separate parliaments and governments, and possessed full equality in common affairs, while the 'Emperor of Austria and Apostolic King of Hungary' decided upon war and peace, presided over the Crown Council, appointed the common ministers, the Austrian and Hungarian prime ministers and ministers, the governors of the provinces, the Croatian Banus, the mayors of Vienna and Budapest, the generals and admirals, and other high-ranking officials (even the university professors). The 'common affairs' were foreign policy, military affairs, and the finances needed for these, as well as the common currency, the national bank, customs barriers, and trade agreements. While Hungarian political leaders, in the words of Joseph Eötvös, were convinced 'that the existence of the empire is at the same time the preliminary condition of our existence', German-Austrian liberals recognized that dualism guaranteed them not only a constitution including a full listing of individual civil rights but also German-Austrian centralism.[6]

One positive aspect of the laws forming the Austrian December Constitution in 1867 was – in the eyes of the Czechs, Poles, Ruthenes (Rusyns), Romanians, Slovenes, Croats, Serbs, and Italians – a comprehensive bill of rights and above all a guarantee of the equal rights of languages 'customary' in a given land in schools and government agencies. In contrast to the famous Austrian article XIX/1867 which established equal rights for all nationalities [*Volksstämme*], the Hungarian Nationality Law XLIV/1868 established – along the lines of the French nation-state model (!) – only one 'unitary Hungarian political nation' (Ferenc Deák), and did not grant the 'nationalities' collective national rights or political institutions. Moreover, Hungarian became the state language to be used in parliament, the courts, and higher education. Other languages were permissible in churches, county and municipal governments, and in primary and some secondary schools. The only important concession of the Budapest government to national interests was the Hungarian-Croatian Compromise of 1868, 'an agreement unlike the Austro-Hungarian Compromise concluded not between political equals but unequals.'[7]

Enlightenment to Eclipse, Houndmills/London 2001; R.J.W. Evans, Austria, Hungary, and the Habsburgs. Central Europe, c. 1683–1867, Oxford 2006.

6 Éva Somogyi, Der gemeinsame Ministerrat der österreichisch-ungarischen Monarchie 1867–1918, Wien/Köln/Weimar 1996; Otto Urban, Die tschechische Gesellschaft 1848–1918, 2 vols., Wien/Köln/Weimar 1994; Helmut Rumpler, Eine Chance für Mitteleuropa. Bürgerliche Emanzipation und Staatsverfall in der Habsburgermonarchie, Wien 1997, 411–425.

7 Péter Hanák, Ungarn in der Donaumonarchie. Probleme der bürgerlichen Umgestaltung eines Vielvölkerstaates, Wien/München/Budapest 1984; Gerald Stourzh, Die Gleichberechtigung der Nationalitäten in der Verfassung und Verwaltung Österreichs 1848–1918, Wien 1985; László Péter, Die Verfassungsentwicklung in Ungarn, in: Helmut Rumpler – Peter Urbanitsch (Eds.),

The experiences of the non-German and non-Magyar 'nationalities' were diverse. Although the Czech-speaking (1910: 6.3 million) and German-speaking (1910: 3.5 million) populations in the Bohemian Lands developed more or less in parallel and high growth rates continued despite the steady increases in emigration quotas, there were some important differences. While the Czech-speaking population traditionally settled in the most fertile regions of the Bohemian and Moravian interior, the German speaking population lived mostly in the craft and manufacturing border regions with the most modern textile (around Reichenberg/Liberec) and chemical industries (around Aussig/Ústí nad Labem) in the monarchy. But this image changed profoundly during the second half of the 19th century due to the penetration of Czech capital into the engineering (Škoda) and leather (Baťa) industries. When after 1863 the Czech liberals in the Bohemian diet formed a coalition to restore the alleged historical-political autonomy of Bohemia, the German-speaking minority rejected the Bohemian state rights program, regarding the Bohemian Lands as 'German provinces'. Therefore, in 1866, Czech liberals accepted the end of the German Confederation with satisfaction. But in 1867, Czech politicians failed to achieve 'trialism', ignored the new Austro-Hungarian entity, and even failed to get the emperor's acceptance of the so-called 'Fundamental Articles'. On the other hand, the complex of constitutional laws of December 1867 also ensured the Czechs a wide range of civil and human rights and liberties with possibilities for self-governing institutions. When in 1878/1879 both the Old Czechs and the Young Czechs returned to the Bohemian diet and the Austrian parliament [*Reichsrat*], they switched from a struggle against the Austrian state to a struggle for the Austrian state, with the result that the 'confrontational community' (Jan Křen) of the Czechs and the Germans increased. With the newly active political engagement by the Czechs, the national-political situation was reversed: if the Czechs had been afraid of the Germanization of Bohemia during the previous decades, the Germans now feared Czechization. Czechs and Germans established 'national defense associations', aggressive formations of the national struggle. Czech-German relations became subject to constant conflicts and disagreements, especially in the so-called Badeni-crisis of 1897, the first time in history the *furor teutonicus* and the *furor bohemicus* clashed. On the other hand, national reconciliation was promoted by the so-called Moravian Compromise in 1905 and the introduction of universal suffrage in 1907, although the amount of tax contributions was still taken into account. But negotiations on a settlement of the language question recognizing Czech- and German-speaking zones in Bohemia and giving Czech full status as the 'inner language' of administration there failed. In July 1913, confronted with a budget crisis in Bohemia, Prime Minister Count Karl Stürgkh suspended the Bohemian constitution and

---

Die Habsburgermonarchie 1848–1918, vol. VII: Verfassung und Parlamentarismus, Wien 2000, 239–540.

a state commission took over the administrative functions of the standing committee of the diet.[8]

The differentiation between Catholics and Protestants held-up the Slovak nation-building process, because the Protestants (with the Kralice bible) favored the idea of a unitary Czecho-Slovak nation, while the Catholics preferred a Slovak identity. In the period of neo-absolutism, the Austrian government supported the extension of Slovak as the language of instruction in elementary and secondary schools. While old Hungarian magnate families represented the upper class, many Germans, Jews, and Magyars appeared in the entrepreneurial bourgeoisie. So the great majority of the Slovaks lived as owners and tenants of farms as well as small craftsmen and shopkeepers. As a result of the Austro-Hungarian Compromise, the Hungarian government started to introduce the Hungarian language in administration, jurisdiction, and education and abolished the three Slovak gymnasia. The traditionally strong county and town administrations were limited in favor of a Hungarian centralization. Nevertheless, Hungarian and Austrian capital established paper, iron and railway works, textile and tobacco factories, as well as gold and silver mines. Some Slovak intellectuals tried to oppose the increasing Magyarisation with the political idea of Czechoslovakism. They studied at the Czech part of the Charles-Ferdinand University in Prague, where they founded associations and periodicals. On the other hand, Slovak Catholic priests established the Slovak People's Party, which fought a confrontational policy against the *Lex Apponyi* for increased teaching of the state language. In 1907, at Černová, 15 villagers were killed and dozens more injured by police gunfire. While direct inter-ethnic contacts were part of the everyday experience of the 2.9 million Slovak (58 percent), Magyar (30 percent), German (7 percent), Rusyn (3.5 percent) and Jewish (0.5 percent) inhabitants of Upper Hungary, in 1914, about half a million Slovaks lived in the United States, which was about a quarter of the Slovak ethnic group.[9]

The Catholic Croats (1910: 2.9 million) and Orthodox Serbs (1910: 2.0 million) differed not only in their version of Christianity and in using different script – Latin and Cyrillic – while speaking almost the same Štokavian-based language, but for centuries they also belonged to different rulers. In 1848/1849, the

8 Otto Urban, Czech Society 1848–1918, in: Mikuláš Teich (Ed.), Bohemia in History, Cambridge 1998, 198–214; Karel Kazbunda, Otázka česko-německá v předvečer velké války, Praha 1995; Jan Křen, Die Konfliktgemeinschaft. Tschechen und Deutsche 1780–1918, München [2]2000; Gary B. Cohen, The Politics of Ethnic Survival. Germans in Prague, 1861–1914, West Lafayette [2]2006; Peter M. Judson, Guardians of the Nation. Activists on the Language Frontiers of Imperial Austria, Cambridge/London 2006; Jiří Kořalka, František Palacký (1798–1876). Der Historiker der Tschechen im österreichischen Vielvölkerstaat, Wien 2007; Tara Zahra, Kidnapped Souls. National Indifference and the Battle for Children in the Bohemian Lands, 1900–1948, Ithaca/London 2008; Robert Luft, Parlamentarische Führungsgruppen und politische Strukturen in der tschechischen Gesellschaft. Tschechische Abgeordnete und Parteien des österreichischen Reichsrats 1907–1914, München 2012.

9 Eva Mannová (Ed.), A Concise History of Slovakia, Bratislava 2000, 185–234; László Kontler, A History of Hungary, Houndmills/New York 2002; Dušan Kováč (Ed.), Na začiatku storočia 1901–1914, Bratislava 2004.

Habsburg's Croats and Serbs under the leadership of Banus Jelačić and Patriarch Rajačić took a stand against the Hungarian government and its anti-Habsburg policy. Although Vienna established a 'Serbian Vojvodina' [*Serbische Woiwodschaft und Temescher Banat*], from the 1850s the center of Serbian aspirations shifted to Belgrade, where Serbian political leaders like Ilija Garašanin started considering plans (*Načertanije* [Outline], 1844) for Serbian expansion in order to build a 'Serbo-Slavic empire'. In contravention to this ideology, but also to the Habsburgs, the Croat ideologist Ante Starčević demanded the old state's rights of the Croat people on the territory of medieval Croatia. Therefore, Starčević's Party of Right became the standard-bearer of Croat opposition to the 1867 *Ausgleich* and the 1868 *Nagodba*. Not surprisingly, the polarization between Croat and Serb ideas of the state reached a culmination over the question of Bosnia-Herzegovina.[10]

Since 1875, the 'Eastern Question' occupied the attention of Austro-Hungarian diplomacy. At the Congress of Berlin in July 1878, Count Gyula Andrássy achieved the occupation of the Ottoman provinces Bosnia-Herzegovina. A year later, he signed the Dual Alliance with Prince Bismarck, linking Austria-Hungary's security to Europe's strongest economic and military power. But when Foreign Minister Alois Lexa von Aehrenthal proclaimed the annexation of Bosnia-Herzegovina in October 1908, he provoked sharp protests by Russia, Serbia, the Entente powers, and the Ottoman Empire. Only Germany supported its ally openly, deepening the chasm between the alliance systems. Although the Carniola Diet welcomed the annexation, Slovene members of the *Reichsrat* declared their sympathies for the 'Serbian brothers' after the beginning of the First Balkan War. But the important writer of the Slovene *Moderna*, Ivan Cankar, critically rejected such romantic Yugoslav attitudes, for:

> 'By blood we are brothers, by language cousins, by culture, which is the fruit of centuries of the separate upbringing, we are less familiar to one another than the Upper Carniolan peasant is with the Tyrolean, or the Gorica vintner with the Friulian.'[11]

Despite negative aspects of the situation in the spring 1914, the Habsburg Empire – the census of 1910 recorded 51,390,649 inhabitants living on a territory of

10 Ivo Banac, The National Question in Yugoslavia. Origins, History, Politics, Ithaca 1984; Mirjana Gross, Die Anfänge des modernen Kroatien. Gesellschaft, Politik und Kultur in Zivil-Kroatien und -Slawonien in den ersten dreißig Jahren nach 1848, Wien/Köln/Weimar 1993; Holm Sundhaussen, Geschichte Serbiens 19.–21. Jahrhundert, Wien/Köln/Weimar 2007.

11 Peter Štih – Vasko Simoniti – Peter Vodopivec, Slowenische Geschichte. Gesellschaft–Politik–Kultur, Graz 2008, 304; Arnold Suppan (Ed.), Deutsche Geschichte im Osten Europas. Zwischen Adria und Karawanken, Berlin ^{2}2002; Vasilije Krestić, History of the Serbs in Croatia and Slavonia 1848–1914, Belgrade 1997; Solomon Wank, In the Twilight of Empire. Count Alois Lexa von Aehrenthal (1854–1912), vol. 1: Imperial Habsburg Patriot and Statesman, Wien/Köln/Weimar 2009; Luciano Monzali, The Italians of Dalmatia. From Italian Unification to World War I, Toronto 2009; Andrej Rahten, Ivan Šusteršič. Der ungekrönte Herzog von Krain, Wien 2012.

676,614 sqkm – was more or less successfully engaged in muddling through in time-honored fashion. Only alarmists thought that Austria-Hungary was drifting towards the abyss. When the *Times* correspondent Henry Wickham Steed returned home in 1913, he wrote that he had been unable during ten years of 'constant observation and experience' to perceive 'any sufficient reason' why the Habsburg monarchy 'should not retain its rightful place in the European community'.[12]

Nationalistic Tensions in Austria-Hungary during World War I

When Archduke Francis Ferdinand and his consort Sophie were assassinated in Sarajevo on 28 June 1914 by the young Bosnian Serb irredentist Gavrilo Princip – who was supported by colonel Dragutin Dimitrijević, the chief of the intelligence service of the general staff of the Serbian army (and the chief of a terrorist network) –, the diplomatic system left the governments in Vienna, Belgrade, Berlin, St. Petersburg, Paris, and London considerable room for political maneuver. But in all capitals the 'war party' succeeded and provoked a chain reaction: Emperor Francis Joseph, influenced by the chief of general staff General Conrad, decided very early to make war against Serbia; Berlin gave Vienna a *carte blanche*; the Ballhausplatz overreacted with an ultimatum to Belgrade; Russia's Imperial Council decided immediately to support Serbia; Serbia declined two points of the ultimatum and mobilized; Austria-Hungary declared war on Serbia; Russia – backed by France – ordered general mobilization; Germany demanded the end of Russian mobilization, and when it was refused, declared war on Russia; Germany demanded the neutrality of France, and when this was refused, declared war on France; partly because of the war-plan of General Schlieffen, which hurt Belgium's neutrality, Britain declared war on Germany; and Austria-Hungary declared war on Russia. The Emperor-King and his ministers in Vienna and Budapest failed to realize that they provoked a European war, mobilizing all enemies of the Dual Monarchy. But we should not forget the responsibility of the other state chancelleries in St. Petersburg, Berlin, Paris, and London: 'all of them fought because they decided that fighting was better than the alternative, and all were convinced that not going to war would risk their great-power status'.[13]

World War I, with its heavy mobilization of peoples, weapons, and ideologies increased ethnic tensions to a level beyond anything that had occurred prior to that point. In August 1914, there was 'an unfamiliar sensation that perhaps the

12 Henry Wickham Steed, The Hapsburg Monarchy, London 1919; *cf.* Oscar Jászi, The Dissolution of the Habsburg Monarchy, Chicago [2]1961.

13 James J. Sheehan, Where Have All the Soldiers Gone? The Transformation of Modern Europe, Boston/New York 2008, 58; Hew Strachan, The First World War, vol. I: To Arms, Oxford 2001, 64–102; Christopher Clark, The Sleepwalkers. How Europe Went to War in 1914, London 2012; Manfried Rauchensteiner, Der Erste Weltkrieg und das Ende der Habsburgermonarchie 1914–1918, Wien/Köln/Weimar 2013.

Monarchy was not going to die after all, but was instead experiencing a strange re-birth'. All its nations, as well as all classes, professions and creeds, initially shared this feeling. Massive pro-war demonstrations took place not only in Vienna, Graz and Innsbruck, but also in Budapest, Cracow, Zagreb, and Prague. On the one hand, the Austro-Hungarian armies fought heavy battles against the Russian armies in Volhynia, Galicia, Bukovina, and the Carpathian Rus', against the Serbian armies in Serbia and Montenegro, from May 1915 against the Italian armies at the Isonzo/Soča and in Trentino, and from August 1916 against the Romanian armies in Transylvania and Walachia. Because of the defeats of General Conrad in Galicia and General Potiorek in Serbia, the imperial-royal army needed German help, which it also required in 1916 against Romania, and in 1917 against Italy. Already in 1916, the German emperor took supreme command over all forces of the Central Powers and the German High Command encouraged its weaker ally with 'Nibelung loyalty'. At the end, all the military engagements of Austria-Hungary resulted in an 'overstretch' with heavy casualties (1.2 million soldiers killed in action, 3.5 million wounded, 2.5 million prisoners of war, 600,000 refugees, 400,000 dead civilians).[14]

On the other hand, war increased pressure within the monarchy: economic life, the administration and the judiciary itself were put under wartime absolutism. Even more problematic in the escalating ethnic fighting was the increasing coercion of Pan-Slavism, Pan-Serbianism, and Pan-Russianism by the German-Austrian and Magyar middle-classes. By the second half of 1914, this gave rise to mass persecutions of Serb, Croat, Slovene, Ukrainian, and Czech politicians, lawyers, journalists, professors, teachers, priests, and others who were nationally and politically active leading up to 1914; an interminable series of prosecutions for high treason were conducted, *e.g.* against the Czech leaders Karel Kramář and Alois Rašín. On the front, the main problem did not lie in consistent German and Magyar doubts about the 'reliability' of the Slavic regiments, because they suffered demonstrably heavy casualties on the Balkan, Galician – and later on the Italian fronts. Unfortunately, the emperor and the army high command sought the reasons for desertion not in poor leadership of the generals but in the personal failure of the soldiers and in nationalist agitation. But when the new Emperor Charles I wanted peace as quick as possible, the Germans and the British wanted a 'victorious conclusion'.[15]

---

14 Istvan Deak, Beyond Nationalism. A Social and Political History of the Habsburg Officer Corps, 1848–1918, New York 1990; Norman Stone, World War I. A Short History, London/New York 2007; Andrej Mitrović, Serbia's Great War 1914–1918, London 2007; Helmut Rumpler – Anatol Schmied-Kowarzik (Eds.), Die Habsburgermonarchie 1848–1918, vol. XI/2: Die Habsburgermonarchie und der Erste Weltkrieg. Weltkriegsstatistik Österreich-Ungarn 1914–1918. Bevölkerungsbewegung, Kriegstote, Kriegswirtschaft, Wien 2014; Manfried Rauchensteiner (Ed.), An Meine Völker! Der Erste Weltkrieg 1914–1918, Wien 2014.

15 Ivan Šedivý, Češi, české země a velká válka 1914–1918, Praha 2001; Dušan Kováč (Ed.), Prvá svetová vojna 1914–1918, Bratislava 2008; Richard Lein, Pflichterfüllung oder Hochverrat? Die tschechischen Soldaten Österreich-Ungarns im Ersten Weltkrieg, Wien 2011; Fritz Fellner – Do-

After Lenin and Wilson – partly for reason of war propaganda – had introduced the right to self-determination of the peoples in the international discussion, many nationalities of Austria-Hungary started to formulate their political demands. In May 1917, the Czech and South Slav deputies in the *Reichsrat* demanded federalization of the empire; in July 1917, the Serbs and Croats in exile signed the Korfu Declaration for a common Yugoslav kingdom. In the East, the revolting Bolsheviks accepted the Peace Treaty of Brest-Litovsk and a German domination in Eastern Europe for eight months. But the fate of Dual Monarchy was tied to the military fortunes of Germany. On 12 May 1918 in Spa, the emperors William II and Charles I signed a long-term treaty between the two empires, which prescribed a military union and maximum possible economic coordination. Now, the French, the British, the Italians and then the Americans intensified nationalist propaganda against the Habsburg Monarchy, although all of them had declared war on Austria-Hungary. So, the US Secretary of State, Robert Lansing, declared on 30 May 1918 that, because 'the Prussians will have to all intents won the war, [...]. Austria-Hungary must be practically blotted out as an empire. It should be partitioned among all nationalities of which it is composed.'[16]

When the morale of the German army began to crumble in August 1918, it was clear that Germany could no longer win the war. Therefore, when the Germans offered an armistice to President Wilson, the Joint Council of Ministers in Vienna did the same, asking for peace negotiations based on the 14 points. But on 18 October 1918, Wilson stated he would be

> 'no longer at liberty to accept the mere "autonomy" of these peoples as the basis for peace, but is obliged to insist that they, and not he, shall be the judges of what action of the Austro-Hungarian government will satisfy their aspirations and their conception of their rights and destiny as members of the family of nations.'

A year later, the Czech historian Josef Pekař characterized this answer as the 'death sentence' for the Habsburg monarchy.[17]

After the last Italian attack at Vittorio Veneto, the Austro-Hungarian army fell apart through the retreat of many regiments, which simply decided to go home, refusing further resistance. The armistice of Padova, signed in the villa Giusti on

---

ris A. Corradini (Eds.), Schicksalsjahre Österreichs. Die Erinnerungen und Tagebücher Josef Redlichs, 1869–1936, 3 vols., Wien/Köln/Weimar 2011.

16 University of Zagreb – British Academy (Eds.), R.W. Seton-Watson and the Yugoslavs. Correspondence 1906–1941, 2 vols., Zagreb/London 1976; Josef Kalvoda, The Genesis of Czechoslovakia, Boulder 1986, 294f.; *cf.* Frank Hadler (Ed.), Weg von Österreich! Das Weltkriegsexil von Masaryk und Beneš im Spiegel ihrer Briefe und Aufzeichnungen aus den Jahren 1914 bis 1918, Berlin 1995.

17 Jan Opočenský, Umsturz in Mitteleuropa. Der Zusammenbruch Österreich-Ungarns und die Geburt der Kleinen Entente, Hellerau bei Dresden 1931; Leo Valiani, La dissoluzione dell'Austria-Ungheria, Milano 1966; Alan Sked, The Decline and Fall of the Habsburg Empire 1815–1918, London/New York 1989.

3 November 1918, determined the withdrawal of the Austro-Hungarian troops not only from all occupied territories in Northern Italy, the Balkans, and Eastern Europe but also back to the Brenner. On the home-front, everyone was claiming their national independence: Poland (7 October), Czechoslovakia (28 October), the State of the Slovenes, Croats, and Serbs (29 October), German-Austria (30 October), and Hungary (31 October). Emperor-King Charles and more than 600 years of Habsburg rule became irrelevant overnight.[18]

The Paris Peace Order: Saint-Germain and Trianon

All nationalities of the former Habsburg monarchy hoped for decisions of the Peace Conference in Paris in their favor. While the German-Austrian government demanded all Austrian crownlands and districts with a German majority as well as the German districts in the West Hungarian counties, the Hungarian government offered autonomy to all nationalities while still demanding all lands of the historical Hungarian kingdom except Croatia-Slavonia. The Czechoslovak government demanded not only the historical provinces of Bohemia, Moravia, and Austrian Silesia but also the inclusion of Slovakia with the strategic border at the Danube from Bratislava until the river Ipoly/Ipel' and Carpatho-Russia as well as a corridor to Yugoslavia; the Polish government demanded the whole crownland of Galicia and the duchy of Cieszyn; the Romanian government demanded Transylvania, Maramureş, Crişana, the Banat, and the Bukovina; the Yugoslav government demanded the Banat, Bačka, Baranja, Croatia-Slavonia, Medjimurje, Prekmurje, Lower Styria, Lower Carinthia, Carniola, Gorica, Trieste, Istria, Rijeka, Dalmatia, and Bosnia-Herzegovina; and, last but not least, the Italian government demanded Trentino, South Tyrol, Gorizia-Gradisca, Trieste, Istria, Fiume, parts of Dalmatia and some Adriatic islands. Comparing all these demands, only the core regions of Austria, Hungary, Bohemia, Moravia, Serbia, Croatia, Bosnia-Herzegovina, and Slovenia remained undisputed, all 'borderlands' stood in discussion.[19]

Although the German Bohemian spokesmen sent a note of protest against the 'imperialistic encroachments of the Czech State' to President Wilson, the French foreign minister rejected a plebiscite and arbitration, as proposed by the Austrian government: 'The Czecho-Slovak State has for its boundaries, at least until the decision of the Peace Conference is reached, the boundaries of the historic provinces of Bohemia, Moravia and of Austrian Silesia.' While the Czechoslovak Foreign Minister Edvard Beneš warned the Prague government to 'avoid all struggles and bloody riots in the German parts of Bohemia', he initiated a policy of *faits accom-*

18 Richard G. Plaschka – Horst Haselsteiner – Arnold Suppan, Innere Front. Militärassistenz, Widerstand und Umsturz in der Donaumonarchie 1918, 2 vols., Wien 1974.

19 Mária Ormos, From Padua to the Trianon, 1918–1920, Boulder 1990; Arnold Suppan, Jugoslawien und Österreich 1918–1938. Bilaterale Außenpolitik im europäischen Umfeld, Wien/München 1996; Ignác Romsics, Der Friedensvertrag von Trianon, Herne 2005; Peter Haslinger, Nation und Territorium im tschechischen politischen Diskurs 1880–1938, München 2010.

plis in order to secure the territories claimed by the new state. In November and December 1918, Czech troops penetrated the German Bohemian, Moravian, and Silesian borderlands without any major incidents. From 4 March 1919, the German Social Democratic Party organized demonstrations of workers demanding the right of the Germans in the Bohemian lands to take part in election of the Viennese parliament. On that occasion, however, the Czechoslovak government did not hesitate to use armed force; 54 demonstrators were killed. But in the meantime, Beneš required a strategically defensible and economically strong Czechoslovakia from the Council of Ten to help the Allies replace German and Austrian influence in the area. Since the French government wanted to weaken Germany, the Allies tacitly tolerated the inclusion of the German borderlands into Czechoslovakia.[20]

When the armistice agreement between the Allies and Hungary, signed at Belgrade on 13 November 1918, stated explicitly that all Hungarian territory, with the exception of Croatia-Slavonia, was to remain under Hungarian civil administration, the Prague government denied the Hungarian sovereignty over the Slovak counties, appealed to the right of self-determination for the Slovaks and threatened military action 'to prevent violence and anarchy'. With the help of the French and Italian military missions, the Czechoslovak army tried to establish its authority in Slovakia. But the situation became dangerous when the Communist-led government of Béla Kun in Budapest conducted a successful campaign against Eastern Slovakia. In June 1919, the Council of Four decided the new borders of Hungary and the Hungarian Red Army was forced to retreat. Because of the early occupation of Southern Hungary by Serbian troops, there were not many discussions at the Peace Conference on the new border between Hungary and Yugoslavia; only the possessions of Pécs and the Banat stood in debate. While the Serbian troops had to retreat from Pécs, the Banat was divided between Romania and Yugoslavia.[21]

---

20 Hugo Hassinger, Die Tschechoslowakei. Ein geographisches, politisches und wirtschaftliches Handbuch, Wien/Leipzig/München 1925; Nina Almond – Ralph H. Lutz (Eds.), The Treaty of St. Germain. A Documentary History of Its Territorial and Political Causes, Stanford/London 1935; Hermann Raschhofer (Ed.), Die Tschechoslowakischen Denkschriften für die Friedenskonferenz von Paris, 1919–1920, Berlin 1937; Jan Rychlík – Thomas D. Marzik – Miroslav Bielik (Eds.), R.W. Seton-Watson and His Relations with the Czechs and Slovaks. Documents 1906–1951, Praha/Bratislava 1995; Kalvoda, Genesis, 435–442; Jindřich Dejmek – František Kolář (Eds.), Československo na pařížské mirové konferenci 1918–1920, Praha 2001; Klaus Koch – Walter Rauscher – Arnold Suppan (Eds.), Außenpolitische Dokumente der Republik Österreich 1918–1938 (ADÖ), vol. 1, Wien 1993, doc. 33, 36, 62, 74, 75, 96, 104, 126, 180, 182, 184–186; vol. 2, Wien 1994, doc. 226, 226 A–F.

21 Magda Ádám – György Litván – Mária Ormos (Eds.), Documents diplomatiques français sur l'histoire du bassin des Carpates 1918–1932, 2 vols., Budapest 1993/1995, vol. I, doc. 33, 204; Andrej Mitrović, Razgraničenje Jugoslavije sa Mađarskom i Rumanijom 1919–1920, Novi Sad 1975; Márian Hronský, The Struggle for Slovakia and the Treaty of Trianon, 1918–1920, Bratislava 2001; Margaret MacMillan, Paris 1919. Six Months that Changed the World, New York 2002.

After regional battles between South Slav and Carinthian, as well as Styrian, troops in Southeastern Carinthia and Lower Styria at the turn of 1918/1919, a US field mission toured through the Slovene-German-mixed Southeastern Carinthia and reported: 'there are many Slovenes who do not wish to join Yugoslavia [...] – we strongly recommend that the final frontier between Austria and Yugoslavia in the province of Carinthia be drawn along the watershed of the Karawanken mountains'. But the Yugoslav delegation in Paris protested at the Council of Ten, and on 18 February demanded a demarcation line including the German cities of Klagenfurt and Villach. Marshal Ferdinand Foch told the Yugoslavs: 'Whatever you have occupied shall remain in your possession'. Nevertheless, the *Commission des Affaires Roumaines et Yugoslaves* recommended to the Council of Four a plebiscite in Lower Carinthia, and on 12 May Clemenceau, Lloyd George, and Wilson accepted this advice. In the plebiscite on 10 October 1920, supervised by British, French, and Italian officers, 59 percent of the population decided to remain in Austria.[22]

Soon after the Carinthian plebiscite, the Belgrade government had to negotiate an agreement with the new Italian government. In the Treaty of Rapallo, signed on 12 November 1920, Italy kept the whole Littoral, Trieste, Istria, the islands of Cres and Lošinj, but in Dalmatia only the city of Zadar and the islands of Lastovo and Palagruža; Rijeka was to become a buffer state between the two countries, but in 1924 it was divided between Italy and Yugoslavia. However, half a million Croats and Slovenes became new minorities in Italy without minority rights; the same happened with the 220,000 Germans in South Tyrol.[23]

Therefore, on the substance of the peace treaties of Saint-Germain, Trianon and Neuilly Zara Steiner judged very clearly:

> 'The treaties with Austria, Hungary, and Bulgaria were far harsher and more vindictive than the one with Germany. The Austrian and Hungarian settlements were punitive in the extreme; the former was left in a perilous economic state, and the latter, if economically viable, was so stripped of territories and people as to guarantee its revisionist status.'[24]

22 Sarah Wambaugh, Plebiscites since the World War. With a Collection of Official Documents, 2 vols., Washington 1933; Suppan, Jugoslawien, 523–558; Christine M. Gigler, Die Berichte der Coolidge-Mission im Jahre 1919. Die mitteleuropäischen Interessen der USA nach dem Ersten Weltkrieg, Klagenfurt 2001, 68–129; Ernest Petrič (Ed.), The Slovenes in the Eyes of the Empire. Handbooks of the British Diplomats attending the Paris Peace Conference of 1919, Ljubljana 2007. In the Lower Styrian town of Marburg/Maribor Yugoslav soldiers shot against German demonstrators, killed 8 and wounded 20 persons, including children.

23 Marina Cattaruzza, L'Italia e il confine orientale, 1866–2006, Bologna 2007, 124–134; Luciano Monzali, Italiani di Dalmazia 1914–1924, Firenze 2007.

24 Zara Steiner, The Lights That Failed. European International History 1919–1933, Oxford 2005, 99; *cf.* Adam Tooze, The Deluge. The Great War. America and the Remaking of the Global Order, 1916–1931, New York 2014.

Czechoslovakia and Yugoslavia as Nation-States between the Wars

Czechoslovakia and Yugoslavia with their German and Magyar minorities and with Germany, Austria and Hungary as neighbors suffered repeated setbacks after 1918 due to a variety of factors. These included conflicts over border-demarcations; the politics of 'de-Germanization', 'de-Austrianization', and 'de-Magyarisation'; the 'nostrification' of foreign companies; the land reform to confiscate estates; the lack of political participation by national minorities until 1923/1925; and discriminatory trade restrictions between the 'winning' and 'losing' countries. Here, above all, the psychological factor of humiliation must not be underestimated. It is for this reason that the large majority of the 3.2 million Sudeten Germans did not regard Czechoslovakia as their country – by definition, the nation state of the 'Czechoslovak nation', with 'Czechoslovak' as the official state language. The same was true of the scattered minorities of the 450,000 Danube Swabians and the 40,000 Germans in Slovenia, who did not develop an allegiance to the nation state of the Serbs, Croats, and Slovenes, with Serbo-Croatian as the official state language. Incidentally, neither of the two German minority groups was allowed to play a role in the shaping of the new constitutions and administrations.[25]

Against the propaganda slogans in Prague and Belgrade: 'Away from Rome, away from Vienna!', the development of Austrian and Hungarian secondary and higher education in the final decades before World War I left a manifold legacy to the monarchy's successor states. Czechoslovakia found itself well supplied with educated Czech public officials, professors, teachers, physicians, and lawyers; but, as Slovaks had no academic secondary or higher education in their own language during the final decades of rule from Budapest, nearly 22,000 Czech bureaucrats, educators, and professionals came to take up positions in Slovakia during the 1920s. The northern parts of Yugoslavia (Slovenia, Croatia-Slavonia, and the Vojvodina) showed some parallels to Czechoslovakia with respect to regional differences in the supply of educated professionals and public officials after 1918. Although the Slovenes had no university under the Austrian regime, they still enjoyed higher levels of education than did the Serbs, Bosnians, Montenegrins, Albanians, and Macedonians; therefore, Slovenes were able to find positions in Yugoslavia's central bureaucracy during the interwar period far in excess of their small share of population.[26]

---

25 Elizabeth Wiskemann, Czechs and Germans. A Study of the Struggle in the Historic Provinces of Bohemia and Moravia, London/New York 1938; Jaroslav Kučera, Minderheit im Nationalstaat. Die Sprachenfrage in den tschechisch-deutschen Beziehungen 1918–1938, München 1999; Jozo Tomasevich, Peasants, Politics, and Economic Change in Yugoslavia, Stanford/London 1955, 344–382; Suppan, Jugoslawien, 709–732.

26 Bohumila Ferenčuhová – Milan Zemko (Eds.), V medzivojnovom Československu 1918–1939, Bratislava 2012, 126–143; Gary B. Cohen, Education and Middle-Class Society in Imperial Austria, 1848–1918, West Lafayette/Indiana 1996, 266–268; Vodopivec, Slowenische Geschichte, 333–337.

With the rich heritage of Austria-Hungary, Czechoslovakia organized huge productive forces, gained an important body of knowledge, created enormous material wealth, and enriched its natural surroundings. Therefore, Beneš feared a customs union with Austria and Hungary, as he explained to *Delnické Listy* in 1920:

> 'The Czechs had fought not for political freedom – for this they had enjoyed to a certain extent before the war [sic!, A.S.] – but for their economic independence, and therefore the scheme for a confederation of the Danubian States, or even of a "Customs Union", is out of question for the Czechoslovak Republic. A political union with Austria and Hungary would mean that these countries would gain influence in our internal affairs: Austria by the way of the Germans living in our State, Hungary through the Magyars in Slovakia. The unfavourable economic conditions of Austria and Hungary form an obstacle to an economic union [...].'[27]

Foreign minister Beneš fought against both, the danger of an *Anschluss* of Austria to the German Reich as well as the danger of a restoration of the Habsburgs in Vienna or Budapest. On 21 March 1931, when the Austrian and the German foreign minister announced their plan of a customs union France and Czechoslovakia sharply protested, accompanied by Romania and Yugoslavia. Great Britain demanded a screening by the Council of the League of Nations and by the Permanent International Court in The Hague. But Charles Fenwick, the editor of the *American Journal of International Law* criticized:

> '[T]he Governments of Great Britain and France were singularly lacking in statesmanship when they set their hands not only against the political union of Austria and Germany, but even against a restricted customs union which might have brought economic relief to Austria without necessity of closer political ties. [...] the withdrawal of prohibitions against it would have eased the political situation and would have greatly strengthened the democratic forces both in Austria and in Germany.'[28]

Because the German Reich not only became a member of the League of Nations, but also the League Council following the Locarno Pact in October 1925, its im-

27 Frederick Hertz, The Economic Problem of the Danubian States. A Study in Nationalism, London 1947, 64–66; Manfred Alexander (Ed.), Deutsche Gesandtschaftsberichte aus Prag. Innenpolitik und Minderheitenprobleme in der Ersten Tschechoslowakischen Republik, 1918–1932, 3 vols., Wien/München 1983, München 2004/2009; Alice Teichova, An Economic Background to Munich. International Business and Czechoslovakia, Cambridge 1974; György Ránki, Economy and Foreign Policy. The Struggle of the Great Powers for Hegemony in the Danube Valley, 1919–1939, Boulder/New York 1983; Christoph Boyer, Nationale Konkurrenten oder Partner? Studien zu den Beziehungen zwischen Tschechen und Deutschen in der Wirtschaft der ČSR 1918–1938, München 1999.

28 Charles Fenwick, Editorial Comment: Fuit Austria, in: American Journal of International Law 32, Washington 1938, 312.

portance to Czechoslovakia and Yugoslavia was reinforced, as it now had a voice in the evaluation of minority treaties. On the other hand, the global economic crisis divided the Sudeten Germans, regardless of their political 'activism' after 1926, even more strongly from Czechoslovakia. The drop in exports in Sudeten German light industry and the decrease in spa tourism resulted in large-scale unemployment – as many as 600,000 men and women, *i.e.* 37.5 percent of the people able to work. In their view, these developments were not opposed strongly enough by the Prague government. When Milan Hodža's government accepted demands of the younger generation of German 'activists' in February and March 1938 (public works contracts for local contractors and labor in the border regions, proportional minority representation in the civil service), it was too late. Many Sudeten Germans had begun to look to Nazi Germany and Hitler in the fight against the mass unemployment.[29]

In January 1919, the Harvard professor Archibald C. Coolidge, head of the US field mission in Austria-Hungary, sent Lieutenant Le-Roy King to Zagreb, Belgrade, and Ljubljana. In April, he gave his 'impressions of the Yugoslavs in general':

> 'The Serbs are the one South Slav people who have really held off their external oppressors and gained their freedom as a political organism by their own continuous and determined fighting. Neither the Slovenes nor the Croatians have won their freedom; it has been given to them; [t]hey feel this themselves, and often try to establish an historical struggle for themselves out of the fact that they have been suppressed. [...]
>
> The Slovenes are superior to the Croatians, and their peasants show a higher percentage of literacy owing to the influence of the Roman Church, which in Slovenia is seen at its best. It has created the peasants' or popular party, and its priests have instilled a national idealism into the Slovenes which does not exist among the Croats. [...]
>
> The Croatians are opportunists, show the childlike indirectness and superficiality of the Slav [sic! A.S.], corrupted by a sinister residuum left by Magyar contact [...]. Having little practical ambition, they are always talking about the superiority of their civilization to that of the Serbs, and saying that their only hope is America. [...]

29 Anonym [Edvard Beneš], Germany and Czechoslovakia. By an active and responsable Czechoslovak Statesman, Prague 1938; Hertz, Economic Problem, 177; Ferdinand Seibt, Deutschland und die Tschechen. Geschichte einer Nachbarschaft in der Mitte Europas, München/Zürich 1993; Rudolf Jaworski, Vorposten oder Minderheit? Der sudetendeutsche Volkstumskampf in den Beziehungen zwischen Weimarer Republik und der ČSR, Stuttgart 1977; Ronald M. Smelser, Das Sudetenproblem und das Dritte Reich 1933–1938, München/Wien 1980; Reiner Franke, London und Prag: Materialien zum Problem eines multinationalen Nationalstaates, München 1981; Jiří Kovtun, Republika v nebezpečném světe, Éra prezidenta Masaryka 1918–1935, Praha 2005; Martin Zückert, Zwischen Nationsidee und staatlicher Realität. Die tschechoslowakische Armee und ihre Nationalitätenpolitik 1918–1938, München 2006.

> The Serbs, of course, are essential as they are the only element of real strength that exists in Yugoslavia today. Serbia's strength is military and does very well while the foundations are being laid. Military orders take the place of legislation and courts; but what is going to happen when the Serbs demobilize their army, tuck in their shirts again, and start making laws, administering civil justice, developing mines and forests and water power, sending ambassadors abroad, founding universities, and organizing the thousand and one instruments of a normal civilized state? [...] The Croats and Slovenes know much more about this sort of thing than the Serbians, and although they have never created any of them for themselves, they are used to railroads, books, and hotels.'[30]

The different parties in the Yugoslav parliament struggled over the constitution, the land reform, the unification of administration and public instruction. There were four democratic elections, and governments changed from time to time – always under the leadership of Serbian prime ministers, foreign ministers and ministers of the army and the navy. But, when on 20 June 1928, a Montenegrin deputy of the Belgrade parliament shot two Croat deputies and wounded three more, among them the Croat peasant leader Stjepan Radić, who died some weeks later, a total political break between Belgrade and Zagreb occurred. Even King Alexander I was shocked: 'We cannot stay together with the Croats. Since we cannot, it would be better to separate. The best way to do this would be to effect a peaceful separation, like Sweden and Norway did.' But in 1929, King Alexander abolished the 1921 constitution, introduced a royal dictatorship, changed the name of the kingdom to the Kingdom of Yugoslavia and strengthened the centralist administration by dividing the land in nine provinces (*banovine*) and the district of Belgrade; six of these regions and the capital had a Serbian majority.[31]

The severe agricultural crisis beginning in the late 1920s forced Yugoslavia to look for new export markets and led to a rapprochement with Nazi Germany. Another reason for the Yugoslav approach to Germany was the Balkan policy of Benito Mussolini, who proposed in March 1933 a Four Power Pact, a cooperation of Britain, France, Italy, and Germany to regulate all European problems, including the revision of some German and Hungarian borders. In the meantime, the Zagreb lawyer Ante Pavelić, between September 1927 and January 1929 a member of the Yugoslav parliament, had organized the Ustasha-Movement as a terrorist organization and found support by émigrés in Italy, Austria, Germany, Hungary, and Bulgaria. On 9 October 1934, a Macedonian revolutionary, supported by three Ustashe, killed King Alexander and the French Foreign Minister Louis

30 Report King to Coolidge, Ragusa/Dubrovnik, 19 April 1919, in: Gigler, Coolidge-Mission, 224–226.

31 Branko Petranović – Momčilo Zečević (Eds.), Jugoslavija 1918/1988. Tematska zbirka dokumenata, Beograd 1988; Memorandum R.W. Seton-Watson, May 1930, in: R.W. Seton-Watson and the Yugoslavs II, 193–200; Živko Avramovski (Ed.), Britanci o Kraljevini Jugoslaviji. Godišnjij izveštaji Britanskog poslanstva u Beogradu 1921–1938, 2 vols., Zagreb 1986; N.A., Gor čez izaro, *Slovenec*, Ljubljana 1932 February 15th, s.p.

Barthou in Marseille. In debates before the League of Nations Yugoslavia accused Hungary of partial responsibility for the assassination, because the criminals had been trained in Hungary. The Italian government ordered the disarming of all 500–600 Ustashe in Italy and sent most of them to camps on the Lipari Islands; Pavelić was kept under surveillance in Siena and in Florence.[32]

Until the German-Austrian agreement in July 1936, Belgrade and Prague feared a restoration of the Habsburgs in Vienna more than the *Anschluss*. As a result of the new foreign policy of Prince Regent Paul and Prime Minister Milan Stojadinović to the Axis powers, on 25 March 1937, Italy and Yugoslavia signed a treaty of friendship and nonaggression. Foreign Minister Conte Galeazzo Ciano thought that the alliance between the Italians and the South Slavs could smoothen a possible *Anschluss* of Austria to Germany. Indeed, when Stojadinović visited Hitler in Berlin, in January 1938, the Reich chancellor was only interested in Yugoslavia's attitude towards the *Anschluss*. Hitler convinced Stojadinović: Germany has no territorial but only economic interests at the Adriatic Sea and the Balkans; Germany would not accept a restoration of the Habsburgs in Austria; and Germany would respect the Yugoslav borders. Stojadinovic answered very concretely: 'Yugoslavia does see the Austrian question as an interior question of the German people.'[33] – Hitler was very content.

Hitler's Occupation of Czechoslovakia

Hitler's occupation policy vis-à-vis Czechoslovakia did not originate from consistent strategic planning, but developed gradually as part of Hitler's military-political-economic objectives. When he formulated a policy of conquest by 5 November 1937 for dismembering Czechoslovakia and dominating the Bohemian-Moravian-Silesian region, Hitler's main goal was to incorporate the rich industrial potential of the Bohemian Lands into the German war economy, and not the 'freeing' of the Sudeten Germans.[34] Following the *Anschluss* of Austria in March 1938, the Sudeten German Party began to support National Socialism publicly and called for

32 Birgit Farley, Aleksandar Karađorđević and the Royal Dictatorhip in Yugoslavia, in: Bernd J. Fischer (Ed.), Balkan Strongmen. Dictators and Authoritarian Rulers of South-East Europe, West Lafayette, Indiana 2007, 50–86; Jacob B. Hoptner, Yugoslavia in Crisis 1934–1941, New York/London 1962; Bogdan Krizman, Ante Pavelić i ustaše, Zagreb 1983, 156–224; Vuk Vinaver, Jugoslavija i Francuska izmedju dva svetska rata, Beograd 1985; Richard J.B. Bosworth, Mussolini, London 1998. In late July 1934, after the Nazi Putsch in Austria, Yugoslavia absorbed over 2,000 emigrant Austrian National Socialists into Slovenia and Croatia, before sending them to Germany by ship, in November 1934. See Dušan Nećak, Die österreichische Legion II. Nationalsozialistische Flüchtlinge in Jugoslawien nach dem misslungenen Putsch vom 25. Juli 1934, Wien/Köln/Weimar 1996.

33 Minutes of Foreign Minister Neurath and Prime Minister Stojadinović, Berlin, 17 January 1938, Arhiv Jugoslavije, Beograd, zbirka Stojadinovića, F-24; *cf.* Milan Stojadinović, Ni rat ni pakt. Jugoslavija izmedju dva rata, Buenos Aires 1963.

34 Adam Tooze, The Wages of Destruction. The Making and Breaking of Nazi Economy, New York 2008.

the recognition of the Sudeten German ethnic group as a legal entity and for compensation 'for the injustices inflicted upon Sudeten Germandom since the year 1918'. After the party won 90 percent of the German vote in the local elections held in May and June 1938, Henlein systematically refused the proposals for autonomy by the Prague government and President Beneš. And Hitler threatened at the *Parteitag* of the NSDAP in Nuremberg to help the Sudeten Germans, and many of the Sudeten Germans understood Hitler's speech as a signal for an uprising. But when the Prague government declared a state of emergency, Prime Minister Chamberlain got on a plane to visit Hitler at the Berghof. There, Chamberlain accepted Hitler's demand of the secession of the *Sudetenland*, meaning all regions of Czechoslovakia with a German majority. As the British and the French government demanded this secession from Beneš and the Czechoslovak government, Prague accepted the demand on 21 September 1938. But when Hitler added new demands, also for Poland and Hungary, Chamberlain left Bad Godesberg without result, and the new Prague government ordered the general mobilization. On the one hand, Hitler threatened war; on the other hand, he promised that 'once this problem is solved, there will be no further territorial problem for Germany in Europe'. To keep peace, the Foreign Office as well as the *Auswärtige Amt* gave Mussolini the role of mediator, and Hitler agreed. In the afternoon of 29 September 1938, Hitler, Mussolini, Chamberlain and Daladier met at Munich. They negotiated the modalities of the secession of all Bohemian-Moravian-Silesian territories with a 51 percent German-Czech ratio based on the last Austrian pre-war census of 1910. Now, Beneš had to suffer the humiliating experience of having his country's destiny decided without his consultation.[35]

Despite an overwhelming majority of the British and the French parliaments voting for the Munich Agreement, Hitler signed a military directive on 21 October 1938 for the *Wehrmacht*, including the liquidation of the remainder of the Czech state. While Poland took the Cieszyn region, the German-Italian arbitration on 2 November 1938, signed in the Vienna Belvedere, gave Hungary the southern strip of Slovakia and Ruthenia, including Komarno and Košice. Already on 6 October 1938, Hlinka's Slovak People's Party had declared the autonomy of Slovakia, and the Catholic priest Jozef Tiso became the head of the Slovak government. When the central government struggled with the autonomous government on positions in the administration, the police and the army, the new Czecho-Slovak President Emil Hácha dismissed the Slovak prime minister. Now, Hitler in-

35 Bernd-Jürgen Wendt, Großdeutschland. Außenpolitik und Kriegsvorbereitung des Hitler Regimes, München 1987; Peter Glotz *et al.* (Eds.), München 1938. Das Ende des alten Europa, Essen 1990; Igor Lukes – Erik Goldstein (Eds.), The Munich Crisis 1938. Prelude to World War II, Portland 1999; Roland J. Hoffmann – Alois Harasko (Eds.), Odsun. Die Vertreibung der Sudetendeutschen. Dokumentation zu Ursachen, Planung und Realisierung einer "ethnischen Säuberung" in der Mitte Europas 1848/1849–1945/1946, vol. 1, München 2000; Stanislav Biman – Roman Cílek, Der Fall Grün und das Münchner Abkommen, Berlin [no date]; Detlev Brandes, Die Sudetendeutschen im Krisenjahr 1938, München 2008; Zara Steiner, The Triumph of the Dark. European International History 1933–1939, Oxford 2011, 579–657.

vited Tiso to Berlin and gave him an unambiguous choice: an immediate declaration of independence, or the prospect of the division of Slovakia between Hungary, Poland, and Germany. On the next day, 14 March 1939, Tiso presented a report on his talks in Berlin to the Slovak Parliament, and the Parliament declared the origin of the independent Slovak State. Hitler immediately invited Hácha to Berlin and, in the night of 14–15 March 1939, forced him to accept the rule of the Reich. The next morning, German troops entered Prague and Brno; the following day, Hitler proclaimed the creation of the Protectorate of Bohemia and Moravia at the Prague castle. US diplomat George F. Kennan reported on the German invasion in Prague, on 15 March:

> 'About ten o'clock, word came that the German troops had already reached the palace. [...] A crowd of embittered but curious Czechs looks in silence. [...] For the rest of the day, the motorized units pounded and roared over the cobblestone streets; hundreds and hundreds of vehicles plastered with snow, the faces of the occupants red with some thought was shame but what I fear was in most cases merely the cold.'[36]

Hitler's Occupation of Yugoslavia

After Hitler's occupation of Bohemia and Moravia and Mussolini's occupation of Albania, the Axis Powers divided spheres of influence in East Central and South East Europe. In May 1939, National Socialist functionaries in Yugoslavia began to replace the hitherto authoritative, predominantly Catholic *Kulturbund* higher-ups, but Hitler pursued no grievances against Yugoslavia relating to its German minorities and did not call the Danube Swabians 'heim ins Reich'. When Hitler explained to the Italian Foreign Minister Galeazzo Conte Ciano on 12 August 1939, that Poland represented an acute danger for Germany that had to be eliminated, Ciano suggested that Yugoslavia represented a similar danger for Italy. Hitler answered: 'Italy should grasp the first favorable opportunity to dismember Yugoslavia and occupy Croatia and Dalmatia.' The Italians began preparing for military action against Yugoslavia, but Italy's entry into the war against France in June 1940 brought the planned Italian invasion of Yugoslavia to a temporary halt.[37]

---

36 Magda Ádám – Gyula Juhász – Lajos Kerekes (Eds.), Allianz Hitler – Horthy – Mussolini. Dokumente zur ungarischen Außenpolitik 1933–1944, Budapest 1966; George F. Kennan, From Prague After Munich. Diplomatic Papers, 1938–1940, Princeton 1971, 86f., 103; Peter A. Toma – Dušan Kováč, Slovakia. From Samo to Dzurinda, Stanford 2001, 109–120; Michal Schvarc – Martin Holák – David Schriffl (Eds.), "Tretia ríša" a vznik Slovenského štátu. Das "Dritte Reich" und die Entstehung des Slowakischen Staates, dokumenty I, II, Bratislava 2008/2010.

37 Galeazzo Ciano, L'Europa verso la catastrophe, 2 vols., Milano 1963, vol. 2, 43–45, 83f.; Dušan Biber, Nacizem in Nemci v Jugoslaviji 1933–1941, V Ljubljani 1966; Geza Ch. Paikert, The Danube Swabians. German Populations in Hungary, Rumania and Yugoslavia and Hitler's Impact on their Patterns, The Hague 1967; Hans-Ulrich Wehler, Nationalitätenpolitik in Jugoslawien. Die deutsche Minderheit 1918–1978, Göttingen 1980; Militärgeschichtliches Forschungsamt (Ed.),

Until 27 March 1941, Hitler believed that Yugoslavia, with its metal and agricultural products and a valuable source of raw materials, would be able to keep out of the conflict. To secure Germany's influence on the Balkans, Hitler demanded that Yugoslavia to join the Tripartite Pact as Slovakia, Hungary, Romania and Bulgaria had done before. But the Belgrade government still tried to defend Yugoslavia's neutrality. So, in February 1941, Hitler invited first Prime Minister Dragiša Cvetković and Foreign Minister Alexander Cincar-Marković, and then, in March, Prince Regent Paul to the Berghof and made clear that Yugoslavia had to decide on a position in the future conflict in Greece: with Germany or against Germany. Under this direct threat, the Crown Council in Belgrade decided to join the Tripartite Pact. But two days after Cvetković and Cincar-Marković had signed the pact in the Vienna Belvedere, on 25 March 1941, an officers' coup in Belgrade under the direction of General Dušan Simović – at some British urging – forced the government and Prince Paul to resign. Fearing any threat of British air force operations against the southern flank of the German armies, which would soon invade the Soviet Union, Hitler decided on the same day on 'Operation 25', the invasion and destruction of Yugoslavia.[38]

In the conquest of Yugoslavia, Italy, Bulgaria, and Hungary played second fiddles. First, the Germans tried to enlist the Croat peasant leader Vladko Maček to proclaim an 'independent' Croatia and call in German troops to effect the separation from the rest of Yugoslavia. When Maček refused to play the role of a German agent, and German troops were nearing Zagreb, SS Colonel Edmund Veesenmayer convinced the most prominent Ustasha in Zagreb, the former Austro-Hungarian Lieutenant Colonel Slavko Kvaternik, to proclaim the independence of Croatia over the radio station. In the evening of 10 April, German tanks were greeted in Zagreb by a crowd of people. On 12 April 1941, Hitler gave a Preliminary Directive on the partition of Yugoslavia: Croatia within its ethnic frontiers would become an independent state; the Dalmatian coast including Bosnia-Herzegovina and Montenegro should be left to the Italian political decision. Mussolini received Pavelić at the Palazzo Venezia and ordered the return of the Ustashe to Croatia in Italian uniforms. But they arrived in Zagreb on 15 April without fanfare and through empty streets. The conquest of Yugoslavia ended with the capitulation of the Yugoslav army on 17 April.[39]

Das Deutsche Reich und der Zweite Weltkrieg, 10 vols., Stuttgart/München 1979–2008; Gerald D. Feldman, Die Creditanstalt-Bankverein in der Zeit des Nationalsozialismus, 1938–1945, in: Gerald D. Feldman – Oliver Rathkolb – Theodor Venus – Ulrike Zimmerl (Eds.), Österreichische Banken und Sparkassen im Nationalsozialismus und in der Nachkriegszeit, vol. 1: Creditanstalt-Bankverein, München 2006, 423–444.

38 Dragiša Cvetković, Ili rat ili pakt. Unutarnja i spoljna politika Namesništva, Paris 1965 (unpublished), Hoover Institution Archives (HIA), Stanford, Cvetković papers, box 2; Memoari Dušana Simovića, HIA, Simović papers, box 1; Institute for Contemporary History (Ed.), The Third Reich and Yugoslavia 1933–1945, Belgrade 1977.

39 Jozo Tomasevich, War and Revolution in Yugoslavia, 1941–1945: Occupation and Collaboration, Stanford 2001, 50–53; Branko Petranović, Srbija u drugom svetskom ratu 1939–1945, Beograd

The Nazi Occupation Policy in the Protectorate of Bohemia and Moravia

The Nazi command structure in Czechoslovakia acted under differing titles and had both direct and indirect control: German civil administrations in *Sudetenland* (*Reichsstatthalter* Konrad Heinlein), Southern Moravia, and Southern Bohemia; a Czech government in Prague headed by President Emil Hácha and led by General Alois Eliáš (1939/1941), Jaroslav Krejčí (1942/1944) and Richard Bienert (1945) under German protectorate (*Reichsprotektor* Konstantin Freiherr von Neurath; SS generals Reinhard Heydrich and Kurt Daluege; the former Reich Minister of Interior Wilhelm Frick); a Slovak government in Bratislava (President Jozef Tiso; Prime Minister Vojtech Tuka) under the control of German envoys and advisers. This illustrates the different levels of the Czechs and the Slovaks in the hierarchy of the new National Socialist Europe.[40]

In the first months of occupation, Czech intellectuals were shocked. They needed some memorial events like the memorial day of Jan Hus on 6 July to remember specific Czech traditions. Exactly twelve days before the German attack against Poland, George Kennan gave his thoughtful concluding report from Prague:

> 'The German camp continues to reflect all the current manifestations of National Socialism. Herr Frank the real leader, sits at his desk in the Czernin Palace, the perfect image of the German 'Halbgebildeter' whom National Socialism raised to power. […] Behind him stand his forces: the dignified but inactive Baron von Neurath, the careerist intellectuals of the party, the underworld figures of the Gestapo, the correct and impassive officers of the Reichswehr. […]
>
> Perhaps the main reason for German willingness to let the Czech "autonomous" authorities vegetate in peace is the increasing preoccupation with the preparation of Bohemia and Moravia as a military hinterland for the event of war.'[41]

The perfidious occupation policy of the SS, and eventually the Gestapo and the security forces in the Protectorate of Bohemia and Moravia, mostly managed by the Sudeten German Higher SS- and Police Leader Karl Hermann Frank, held the

---

1992, 63–75.

40 Alice Teichova, The Protectorate of Bohemia and Moravia (1939–1945) The Economic Dimension, in: Teich, Bohemia in History, 267–305; *cf.* Raphael Lemkin, Axis Rule in Occupied Europe. Laws of Occupation. Analysis of Government Proposals for Redress, Washington 1944; Václav Král (Ed.), Acta occupationis Bohemiae et Moraviae. Die Deutschen in der Tschechoslowakei 1933–1945, Prag 1964; Eagle Glassheim, Noble Nationalists. The Transformation of the Bohemian Aristocracy, Cambridge/London 2005; Pavel Maršalek, Pod ochranou hákového kříže. Nacistický okupační režim v českých zemích 1939–1945, Praha 2012.

41 Kennan, From Prague, 217–225.

Czech people captive – forcefully managing the workers with a carrot and stick policy and punishing the intellectuals. Many isolated acts and waves of terror followed. Demonstrations on 28 October 1939 accompanied the closing of all Czech universities and technical colleges and the deportation of 1,200 students to concentration camps. Mass-shootings and mass-arrests at the end of September 1941 took place following SS General Heydrich's ascension to power as Deputy *Reichsprotektor*. The assassination of Heydrich on 27 May 1942, which was ordered by Beneš and his intelligence service chief Moravec, was followed by mass-executions and the total destruction of the small villages Lidice and Ležáky, as well as the execution of all men and a part of the women living within the villages, and the deliberate execution of Czech intellectuals: between 27 May and 3 July 1942 3,188 persons were arrested, 1,357 of them sentenced to death and shot or hanged.[42]

On 27 November 1940, the Soviet consul general in Prague, Vasilij Kulikov, visited the secretary general of the Third International, Georgij Dimitrov, in Moscow and told him astonishing details from the situation in the Protectorate:

- 'The Baťa, Škoda, and other plants are working at full capacity making arms and equipment for the German army.
- In the environs of Prague an enormous aviation factory is being built, which is to produce up to a thousand aircraft a month.
- The patriotic, anti-German spirit of the Czechs has not been broken.
- Terrible hatred of the Czechs for the National Socialist of Germany. In that atmosphere one finds national solidarity among the Czechs. A very thin stratum of society has deliberately gone over to serve the Germans.
- The chief director of 'Baťa' in the city of Zlín – Glavnička, Josef – is pro-Soviet. So are the chief director of 'Škoda' Gromadko and his deputy Škvor.'[43]

Nevertheless, from this view the occupying policy of the SS General Frank, since 1943 also *Staatsminister*, was 'successful'. This can be measured by the achievement of the immediate goal of the National Socialists in making the greatest possible demands on Bohemia and Moravia for the German wartime economy. This certainly exacerbated the short-comings of the Czech resistance and the longtime blockage of any possible insurgence. Although Frank's policy could without a doubt be categorized as inhumane and, was considered a war crime, it was more lenient in light

42 Detlev Brandes, Die Tschechen unter deutschem Protektorat, 2 vols., München/Wien 1969/75, I, 83–95, 251–267; Vojtěch Mastný, The Czechs under Nazi Rule: The Failure of National Resistance, 1939–1942, New York 1971; Miroslav Kárný – Jaroslava Milotová – Margita Kárná (Eds.), Deutsche Politik im "Protektorat Böhmen und Mähren" unter Reinhard Heydrich 1941–1942. Eine Dokumentation, Berlin 1997; Peter Demetz, Prague in Danger. Scenes from the Life of a European City, New York 1997, 78–82; Derek Sayer, The Coasts of Bohemia. A Czech History, Princeton 1998, 25–27; *cf.* Ruth-Bettina Birn, Die Höheren SS- und Polizeiführer. Himmlers Vertreter im Reich und in den besetzten Gebieten, Düsseldorf 1986; Peter Longerich, Heinrich Himmler. Biografie, München 2008.

43 Ivo Banac (Ed.), The Diary of Georgi Dimitrov 1933–1949, New Haven/London 2003, 138f.

of the situation than the more brutal occupation policies of other Nazi functionaries in Serbia or Slovenia.[44]

In August 1943, a very informative report from Moravská Ostrava reached the Czechoslovak exile government in London via Stockholm. Written in correct German, the report obviously came from a German member of the multi-ethnic Communist Party of Czechoslovakia:

- Munich: the Czech population is criticizing the capitulation; Beneš and Syrový should have fought together with the Soviet Union;
- the Protectorate-government is not seen as a traitor; Hácha didn't have another choice; the Czech population is thankful that the Czech men must not fight;
- Beneš does have fellows in Prague, not so much in Bohemia, even lesser in Moravia (Brno and Ostrava) and in Slovakia; many people do not wish his return to power;
- the Czech population is hearing more radio Moscow than London;
- good relationship of the Czech to the Slovak population; they had not other choice than to collaborate with the Germans;
- although there is no anti-Semitism, the Czech population doesn't want to restitute Jewish ownership in mines and steel works;
- the Sudeten Germans lost many soldiers; therefore, they are hating the Czechs who are not obliged to fight and are living relatively well in the German industry and as peasants;
- the Czech population is hating the Germans, especially the Nazis; the attitude towards the German workers is more tolerant.
- panic-stricken fear from bombing [by the Allies, A.S.]; many refugees of the Ruhrgebiet who are sleeping in hotels, camps, and even in the open air.[45]

In October 1941, SS General Heydrich ordered the deportations of the Bohemian and Moravian Jews first to Theresienstadt [Terezín], then to Auschwitz [Oświęcim] and other death camps for extermination; therefore, the number of victims resulted especially large: Almost 80,000 native Jews died in Nazi concentration camps and thousands of others died on the front-lines.[46]

44 René Küpper, Karl Hermann Frank (1898–1946). Politische Biographie eines sudetendeutschen Nationalsozialisten, München 2010; *cf.* Jaromír Balcar, Panzer für Hitler – Traktoren für Stalin. Großunternehmen in Böhmen und Mähren 1938–1950, München 2014; Chad Bryant, Prague in Black. Nazi Rule and Czech Nationalism, Cambridge/London 2007.

45 Zpráva 2, 8. srpna 1943, Archiv Ústavu T.G. Masaryka, Praha, fond Edvard Beneš II, 38-16-1.

46 Livia Rothkirchen, The Jews of Bohemia and Moravia Facing the Holocaust, Lincoln/Jerusalem 2005; Jörg Osterloh, Nationalsozialistische Judenverfolgung im Reichsgau Sudetenland 1938–1945, München 2006.

The German Reich and Slovakia

Although the Slovak State had to sign a 'defense treaty' with Nazi Germany on 23 March 1939, and the Slovak government had to follow Nazi 'advisers', who were sent from Berlin to Bratislava, the Slovak regime became less oppressive and less regimented than its German role model. Nevertheless, Slovakia had to enter the Anti-Comintern-Pact and declared war on the Soviet Union. Germany's war industry stimulated the Slovak industrial and mining expansion, every year about 40,000 Slovak citizens left to work in Germany, the sale of agricultural products increased, and the *Hermann Göring Werke* controlled large industrial enterprises and acquired large sections of forest all over Slovakia. On the 'offer' of the SS, in the spring of 1942 the Tiso regime with the Hlinka Guard sent 60,000 Slovak Jews to the 'eastern territories', where most of them were murdered.[47]

By far the largest and most violent resistance act against the Nazi regime in Czechoslovakia was the Slovak National Uprising from the end of August until the beginning of November 1944. At the end of 1943, representatives of the Citizens Bloc (Catholics, Lutherans, Social Democrats) and communists formed the Slovak National Council to start a general armed surrection in two cases: 1) the entrance of Slovakia by the Soviet Red Army, or 2) the invasion of Slovakia by the German army; Lieutenant Colonel Ján Golian, the Chief of Staff of the Slovak army at home, prepared the military uprising. But at the end of August 1944, while the German military mission from Romania was shot in Martin, two battle-worthy Slovak divisions were disarmed by German troops in Eastern Slovakia and taken prisoners of war. When the Tiso government accepted Germany's offer of military intervention, the Germans started attacks from Hungary, the General Gouvernement, the Protectorate and Lower Austria. While the Soviets sent 24 partisan groups with 404 men from Ukraine, General Rudolf Viest flew from London through Moscow to Banská Bystrica to take over the command of the resistance military operations. Beneš told the British and Americans that in Slovakia it was the Czechs who revolted and were fighting for freedom. The Americans sent military aid in a B-17 from Bari, two other missions came from Britain and the Soviet Union. But on 18 October, the German units under SS General Hermann Höfle began their final onslaught with seven divisions; on 3 November, Viest and Golian were captured, also members of the US and British military missions. In

47 Jörg K. Hoensch, Die Slowakei und Hitlers Ostpolitik, Köln 1965; Peter Witte – Michael Wildt [et alii] (Eds.), Der Dienstkalender Heinrich Himmlers 1941/1942, Hamburg 1999; Toma – Kováč, Slovakia, 122–148; Tatjana Tönsmeyer, Das Dritte Reich und die Slowakei 1939–1945. Politischer Alltag zwischen Kooperation und Eigensinn, Paderborn 2003; Walter Brandmüller, Holocaust in der Slowakei und katholische Kirche, Neustadt an der Aisch 2003; Ivan Kamenec, On the Trail of Tragedy. The Holocaust in Slovakia, Bratislava 2007; István Deák, The Worst of Friends. Germany's Allies in East-Central Europe – Struggles for Regional Dominance and Ethnic Cleansing, 1938–1945, in: Marina Cattaruzza – Stefan Dyroff – Dieter Langewiesche (Eds.), Territorial Revisionism and the Allies of Germany in the Second World War, New York/Oxford 2013 17–29.

the uprising, both sides committed war crimes – against prisoners of war, civilians, and minorities. But the general plan, to open the way for the Red Army was not successful.[48]

The Nazi Occupation Policy in Serbia

At mid-April 1941, Belgrade correspondent Ray Brock sent a report to the *New York Times* from Budapest:

> 'German army of occupation in Serbia is conducting systematic campaign of looting, confiscation and unauthorized seizure of property belonging to Serbians and Foreigners including Americans. Homes, Apartments and Villas throughout Belgrade and Northern and Central Serbia at Vrnjačka Banja, Kovilača Banja, Han Pijesak in Bosnia and scores of similar resorts have been sacked by Germans down to last stick of furniture, last shred of clothing, last potato and last loaf of bread.'[49]

The Nazi command structure in Serbia was divided into four branches: military-administrative, diplomatic, economic, and police, with the plenipotentiary and commanding general in Serbia at the head. The German Army High Command outlined his basic duties: safeguarding the railroad line between Belgrade and Salonika as well as the Danube shipping route; executing the economic orders issued by Reich Marshal Göring as the plenipotentiary for the Four-Year Plan; guarding Yugoslav prisoners of war; and maintaining peace and order. For garrisoning purposes, the Germans brought to Serbia, in early June 1941, three garrisoning divisions, also a division in the eastern parts of the Independent State of Croatia. These garrisoning divisions came partly from Austria, with many overage soldiers and poor armaments. As the Germans recognized the need for a unified command over their forces in South East Europe, on 9 June 1941, Hitler appointed Field Marshal Wilhelm List as armed forces commander in South East Europe (*Wehrmachtsbefehlshaber Südost*), with headquarters in Salonika. The district command in the Banat became an independent command under the direct control of the commanding general in Serbia and the government of the Banat Swabians, whose community became a public law entity.[50]

---

48 Vilém Prečan (Ed.), Slovenské národné povstanie. Nemci a Slovensko 1944. Dokumenty, Bratislava 1965; Jozef Jablonický, Povstanie bez legiend, Bratislava 1990; Toma – Kováč, Slovakia, 132–148; *cf.* James Ward, No Saint. Jozef Tiso, 1887–1947, PhD Diss. Stanford 2008.

49 Telegram Ambassador Thomsen to Auswärtiges Amt, 12 May 1941, HIA Stanford, Tomasevich papers, box 3 (Benzler collection).

50 Hans Umbreit, Auf dem Weg zur Kontinentalherrschaft, in: Militärgeschichtliches Forschungsamt (Ed.), Das Deutsche Reich und der Zweite Weltkrieg, vol. 5/1, Stuttgart 1988, 3–345; Tomasevich, Occupation, 64–78; Hamburger Institut für Sozialforschung (Ed.), Verbrechen der Wehrmacht. Dimensionen des Vernichtungskrieges 1941–1944. Ausstellungskatalog, Hamburg 2002.

When the Serbian Chetniks and the Communist Partisans started the uprising in July 1941, the local gendarmerie and police forces could not secure peace and order anymore. Therefore, in September 1941, the German headquarters in Salonika dispatched an Infantry Regiment from Greece with an artillery unit and the German Army High Command sent the 342nd Infantry Division from France to Serbia. On 16 September 1941, Hitler appointed the commanding general in Greece, General Franz Böhme, a former Austrian general, as plenipotentiary commanding general in Serbia, and gave the directive for drastic measures against Communist-led resistance in all German-occupied areas. This order stipulated that up to 100 people were to be executed for each German soldier or official killed and up to 50 for each one wounded. The two most terrible outrages that the Germans committed in Serbia on the basis of this decree were the executions in mid-October 1941 of about 1,755 people in Kraljevo and about 2,300 people in Kragujevac. Before Böhme was transferred to Finland, on 5 December 1941, he gave a summary of the casualties: German losses – 160 killed in action, 378 wounded; 'enemy losses' – 3,562 killed in action, 11,164 hostages shot (among them thousands of Jews).[51]

The followers of Böhme could consolidate the partisan warfare, because the Partisans were driven out by the Germans from Southwest Serbia to Southeast Bosnia, and the occupation regime with the puppet government of General Milan Nedić was confronted now with resistance actions of the Chetniks. At the same time, on 11 January 1942, the Yugoslav government in exile appointed General Draža Mihailović as Minister of War and 'High Commander of the Yugoslav Army in the homeland'. The former Yugoslav foreign minister Momčilo Ninčić, a Serb, accused the Germans and the Ustashe in *The Times*:

> 'My people are living, in this war, through terrible times. [...] The cold-blooded cruelty of the German army's punitive expeditions in Serbia; the massacres, unknown in history, of Serbs in Bosnia, Herzegovina, and Croatia, where Pavelich's regime is proceeding according to plan, in connivance with the German forces, to wipe out 2,000,000 Serbs who were living on the territory of the so-called 'Independent State of Croatia', [...] all this clearly confirms that there is a plan for a systematic extermination of the Serbian people. [...] Despite all this, General Draža Mihailović with his comrades continues to struggle. We shall once more be a free nation. But after our common victory, which is beginning to mould into a more and more definite shape, we shall have to demand that the punishment of the bloodthirsty offenders shall spare nobody, because only if it is severe will it be just and serve as a reminder to future generations.'[52]

---

51 Plenipotentiary commanding general in Serbia, Belgrade, 20 December 1941, Bundesarchiv/Militärarchiv Freiburg im Breisgau (BA/MA), RW 40/23a; Jozo Tomasevich, War and Revolution in Yugoslavia, 1941–1945: The Chetniks, Stanford 1975; Milovan Djilas, Der Krieg der Partisanen. Memoiren 1941–1945, Wien 1978, 116–120.

52 N.A., *The Times*, London 1942 June 15th, s.p.

From 8 August 1942 to 25 August 1943, Air Force Colonel General Alexander Löhr, the former commander of the Austrian air force, acted as commander in chief in South East Europe (*Oberbefehlshaber Südost*). He demanded the dissolution of the Chetnik units (although in 1941 several thousand Chetniks were transferred to the Serbian gendarmerie), the arming of the Banat Swabians, the dispatch of the SS Mountain Division Prinz Eugen to Croatia as well as the defense of the Bor copper mines and the Trepča iron mines. After the landing of the Allies in Sicilia, Hitler reorganized anew the senior command of German forces in the Balkans, and when Italy capitulated, German troops took over Sandžak, Kosovo, Montenegro, Dalmatia, and Istria, with heavy battles against the Partisans in Dalmatia. Concurrently the Bulgarian 1st Occupation Corps occupied most of Serbia on German's behalf. The 'Concluding Report on the Military Administration in Serbia', completed in April 1945, stressed the negative effects of the multiplicity of power in the occupation regime. The situation was especially problematic for General Nedić, who found that arrangements made with one German agency were often countermanded by another, usually to the detriment of his government. But, as Jozo Tomasevich summarized rather cleverly: 'In spite of its many inherent problems, however, Germany's occupation policy in Serbia worked reasonably well until the spring of 1944.'[53]

Total Warfare in the Independent State of Croatia

Most of the Croat population was pleased at the defeat of Yugoslavia and the establishment of the 'Independent State of Croatia'. But the new state was neither a nation state nor independent: from the 6.3 million inhabitants only 3.25 million were Croats, 1.725 million Serbs, 950,000 Bosnian Muslims, 150,000 Germans, 75,000 Magyars, 60,000 Czechs and Slovaks, 40,000 Jews, 30,000 Slovenes, and 10,000 Roma. Until mid-1943 Croatia became a satellite state of Germany and Italy, afterwards one of Hitler's last surviving allies. Although Croatia did not possess political and military independence, the Ustasha-regime under the leadership of Ante Pavelić gained the freedom to maneuver against the ethnic and religious minorities – especially against the Serbs, Jews, and Roma – and made the regime responsible for war crimes, crimes against humanity, and genocide.[54]

53 Milan Ristović, General M. Nedić – Diktatur, Kollaboration und patriarchalische Gesellschaft Serbiens 1941–1944, in: Erwin Oberländer (Ed.), Autoritäre Regime in Ostmittel- und Südosteuropa 1919–1944, Paderborn/München/Wien/Zürich 2001, 633–688; Tomasevich, Occupation, 82.

54 Statistics made by the German Auswärtiges Amt, pol. IV/2444g, Berlin, 21 May 1941, HIA Stanford, Tomasevich papers, box 3 (Benzler collection); Ivo Goldstein, Croatia. A History, London 1999, 133f.; *cf.* Ladislaus Hory – Martin Broszat, Der kroatische Ustascha-Staat 1941–1945, Stuttgart 1964; Slavko Goldstein, 1941: Godina koja se vraća, Zagreb 2007; Alexander Korb, Massengewalt der Ustaša gegen Serben, Juden und Roma in Kroatien 1941–1945, Hamburg 2013.

From October 1941 until August 1944 most military operations in occupied Yugoslavia were directed, or undertaken, by the Germans against the Partisans. Since the beginning of 1942, Tito, the high commander of the Partisan troops, sent telegrams to Moscow for help. The situation of Tito's High Command [*Vrhovni štab*] detoriated, when after 15 April 1942 German, Italian and Croat troops began to attack. On 24 May, Tito sent a new telegram to Dimitrov in Moscow:

> 'Since 22 May I have been in the Montenegrin sector of the front with [my] chief of staff. The situation here is critical. Italian troops, together with Draža Mihailović's Chetniks [...] are advancing from all sides against our Partisan troops. The Chetniks are coming through forests and over mountains, while the Italians are motorized. The Chetniks possess enormous quantities of automatic weapons, mortars, and ammunition. They are mobilizing peasants by force; resisters are either killed or driven en masse into concentration camps in Albania. Our Partisan bataillons are completely exhausted from continuous fights; we are also out of ammunition. We must withdraw the majority of our bataillons from Montenegro to prevent their destruction.'[55]

At the same time, the Yugoslav government in exile sent a statement to Stalin and Molotov, which exaggerated the military strength of the Chetniks:

> 'General Mihailović, who enjoys great popularity with the Serbian populace and throughout Yugoslavia, commands a well-organized army, the only one of its kind, numbering (depending on the character of partisan warfare) from 80 to 150 thousand Chetniks fighting under the command of regular Yugoslav army officers. [...] Mihailović's troops have rendered a valuable service not only to Yugoslavia but also to Russia.'[56]

But the Germans calculated the military strength of the Partisans higher than that of the Chetniks. At the end of 1942, Hitler ordered a common offensive of German, Italian, Croat, and some Chetnik troops, altogether 80,000 men, against approximately 30,000 Partisans in Western Croatia and Northwestern Bosnia. On 20 January 1943, the main attack started from Karlovac to Bihać, then over Drvar and Livno to Mostar, led by the 7th SS Mountain Division Prinz Eugen, recruited most from the Swabians in the Yugoslav Banat, under the command of the SS-General Arthur Phleps, himself born a Transylvanian Saxon. The retreat of the partisans during February left many dead or wounded. In March 1943, between the German forth and fifth offensive, Tito tried to exchange prisoners of war with

55 Banac, Dimitrov, 218; Tomasevich, Chetniks, 210f.

56 Banac, Dimitrov, 239f.; Franklin Lindsay, Beacons in the Night. With the OSS and Tito's Partisans in Wartime Yugoslavia, Stanford 1995; Alexander Dallin – F.I. Firsov (Eds.), Dimitrov and Stalin 1934–1943. Letters from the Soviet Archives, New Haven/London 2000, 210–225.

the Germans. After the breakthrough, in June 1943, of the partisans from Montenegro to Bosnia (in the Sutjeska-gorge) with heavy losses, Stalin applauded: 'Well done, Yugoslav heroes.'[57]

Indeed, the National Liberation War of the Partisans had two objectives: a struggle for national liberation from National Socialism and Fascism and a struggle against the oppression of the old regime, meaning the Chetniks of General Mihailović, the Ustasha of Pavelić, and the Slovene *Domobranci* of General Leon Rupnik. This liberation war should bring 'true freedom, equality, and brotherhood for all nations of Yugoslavia'. But some Partisan methods did not coincide with these goals and the Hague convention:

> 'The burning of "enemy" villages and the confiscation of "enemy" property were commonplace during the Left Error. Partisan units were given quotas of "fifth columnists" to be shot. [...] Partisan newspapers printed the names of executed "kulaks" [...]. Churches were desecrated and such anti-Western jingles as "Partisans, prepare your machine guns to greet the king and Englishman" were quite popular.'[58]

The Nazi and Fascist occupation policy in Slovenia

In April 1941, Slovenia (the former *Dravska banovina*) was divided between Germany, Italy, and Hungary. The Germans established civil administrations in Lower Styria and Upper Carniola, administered by the Styrian and Carinthian district leaders Siegfried Uiberreither and Friedrich Rainer (from 16 December 1941). Hitler ordered his officials 'to make these lands German again', and Himmler issued a directive on the removal of 'foreign elements', meaning 260,000 Slovenes, especially the intelligentsia including the clergy. Until mid-1942, an estimated 80,000 Slovenes were expelled to Serbia, Croatia, the Italian-annexed *Provincia di Lubiana* (Ljubljana, Dolenjska, and Notranjska), and the Reich. Even Nazi Party officials worried about the damaging effects on the supply of labor for war industries.[59]

While the former ruling elite in the Italian province attempted to find a modus vivendi with the occupier and did not risk active and armed resistance, some leftist circles (Communists, Christian Socialists, *Sokoli*) established a 'Liberation

57 Banac, Dimitrov, 281; Klaus Schmider, Der Partisanenkrieg in Jugoslawien 1941–1944, Hamburg/Berlin/Bonn 2002; Thomas Casagrande, Die volksdeutsche SS-Division "Prinz Eugen". Die Banater Schwaben und die nationalsozialistischen Kriegsverbrechen, Frankfurt am Main 2003, 242–244.

58 Ivo Banac, With Stalin against Tito. Cominformist Splits in Yugoslav Communism, New York 1988, 82; Peter Broucek (Ed.), Ein General im Zwielicht. Die Erinnerungen Edmund Glaises von Horstenau, vol. 3: Deutscher Bevollmächtigter General in Kroatien und Zeuge des Untergangs des "Tausendjährigen Reiches", Wien/Köln/Graz 1988.

59 Tone Ferenc (Ed.), Quellen zur nationalsozialistischen Entnationalisierungspolitik in Slowenien, 1941–1945. Viri o nacistični raznarodovalni politiki v Sloveniji 1941–1945, Maribor 1980, 231–332.

Front' under the leadership of Boris Kidrič. They claimed its exclusive right to represent the nation against the occupiers and accepted the leading rule of the Communist Party of Yugoslavia under Tito. When the Liberation Front started partisan warfare in the fall of 1941 against the Germans and the Italians, the occupiers reacted with sharp repression and the shooting of hostages. Threatened by some partisan successes in the spring of 1942, the conservative elite around the Roman Catholic Bishop Gregorij Rožman slipped into collaboration with the Italian High Commissioner Emilio Grazioli and into civil war. The Partisans did not hesitate to kill prominent members of the non-communist elite and destroyed several village guards. After the capitulation of Italy, the Liberation Front organized a major assembly in Kočevje/Gottschee and elected 120 members to the Slovene National Liberation Committee, and at the end of 1943, the Slovene partisan army was acknowledged to be an Allied military force as part of the Yugoslav partisan army.[60]

In September 1943, the German occupiers included the land between Ljubljana, Gorica, Trieste, Pula and Rijeka into the *Operationszone Adriatisches Küstenland* under the leadership of the Carinthian *Reichsstatthalter* Rainer. SS and Wehrmacht units executed brutal 'cleansings' in the hinterland of Trieste, in Istria, and in Dolenjska. Under German advice, the former Yugoslav general Leon Rupnik became head of the administration in Ljubljana and organized the Slovene Home Guard units (*Domobranci*). When the exiled Royal government in London reached an agreement with the AVNOJ ([*Antifašističko Vijeće Narodnog Oslobođenja Jugoslavije*], Anti-Fascist Council for the National Liberation of Yugoslavia) government, the Slovene counterrevolutionary camp was left out of any support by the Allies. Quite to the contrary, at the end of the war, the British surrendered the members of the Home Guard to the Partisans and the majority was executed.[61]

Revenge and Retribution

President Beneš and Defense minister Sergej Ingr ordered from exile in London that revenge and retribution be visited upon all Germans. This was also how the Czech and Slovak resistance saw the situation in their respective countries. In the middle of April 1945, the Czechoslovak Košice government called on the Czech and the Slovak people not to have any mercy on the German enemy. The Czech people, during the Prague insurrection between 5 May and 8 May, experienced German fire-bombings of the city center and the use by SS units of women and

60 Janko Prunk, A Brief History of Slovenia, Ljubljana 1996, 99–105; Vodopivec, Slowenische Geschichte, 356–373; Tamara Griesser-Pečar, Das zerrissene Volk. Slowenien 1941–1946. Okkupation, Kollaboration, Bürgerkrieg, Revolution, Wien/Köln/Graz 2003, 46–204; Davide Rodogno, Il nuovo ordine mediterraneo. Le politiche di occupazione dell'Italia fascista in Europa, 1940–1943, Torino 2003; H. James Burgwyn, Empire on the Adriatic. Mussolini's Conquest of Yugoslavia, 1941–1943, New York 2005.

61 Prunk, History, 106f.; Vodopivec, Slowenische Geschichte, 374–387; Griesser-Pečar, Volk, 296–424; Maurice Williams, Gau, Volk und Reich. Friedrich Rainer und der österreichische Nationalsozialismus, Klagenfurt 2005.

children as hostages for protection against insurgents' barricades. After Soviet tank commanders reached the city, the National Assembly on 9 May demanded of the people: 'Capture the German murderers, and if they offer any resistance, kill them'. And President Beneš stated seven days later in Prague: 'It will be necessary [...] to liquidate out especially uncompromisingly the Germans in the Czech lands and the Hungarians in Slovakia, in whatever way this liquidation can further the interest of a united state of Czechs and Slovaks.'[62]

Not only were revenge and retribution demanded, but at the same time, the creation of a 'revolutionary climate' that would rid the countries of Germans and Magyars, preferably in the framework of military operations. Members of the Czechoslovak army, armed revolutionaries, freed prisoners, and Soviet soldiers handed out justice, either alone or in lynch mobs, to known or suspected National Socialists and collaborators. On the morning of 31 May 1945, 26,000 German women, children, and elderly were put on the road out of Brno and force-marched towards the Austrian border. Of these, almost 1,000 people did not survive the sadistic displacement. At the end of May 1945, soldiers of the 1st Czechoslovak division executed almost 800 Germans at Postoloprty. A mass murder of Germans also happened at Ústí nad Labem, on 31 July 1945, after an explosion in an ammunition depot. Meanwhile, tens of thousands of Germans were detained in barracks, movie-theater auditoriums, and guesthouses as the prisons, penitentiaries, and camps filled up. Forced-labor, violence, rape, starvation, and disease caused mass-deaths and often led to suicides. After a year-long detailed study, Tomáš Staněk estimated the number of deaths in the camps at between 4,000 and 5,000 people.[63]

The first great acts of revenge against the Germans in Yugoslavia directly followed after the capture of Vojvodina by the Red Army, which advanced from Romania and Bulgaria into Serbia and Southern Hungary in October 1944. In the wake of the Russian soldiers, who raped countless numbers of women, Yugoslav partisans killed over 7,000 German civilians in the Banat, the Bačka, and Syrmia. These civilians could not be evacuated in time, nor did they have the chance to flee. The Communist led Organisation for the Protection of People (OZNA) especially executed industrialists, affluent businessmen, rich farmers, professionals, teachers, and clergymen; rich Magyars and Serbs were not spared from the killings. Germans and Magyars were arrested and imprisoned as 'persons of suspicion to the state'. However, the Communist military administration began to differentiate

---

62 N.A., *News Chronicle*, London 1944 November 4th, s.p.; N.A., *Svobodné slovo*, Praha 1945 May 17th, s.p.

63 Kulturstiftung der deutschen Vertriebenen (Ed.), Vertreibung und Vertreibungsverbrechen 1945–1948. Bericht des Bundesarchivs vom 28. Mai 1974. Archivalien und ausgewählte Erlebnisberichte, Bonn 1989; Tomáš Staněk, Verfolgung 1945. Die Stellung der Deutschen in Böhmen, Mähren und Schlesien (außerhalb der Lager und Gefängnisse), Wien/Köln/Weimar 2002; Tomáš Staněk, Internierung und Zwangsarbeit. Das Lagersystem in den böhmischen Ländern 1945–1948, München 2007; Norman M. Naimark, Fires of Hatred. Ethnic Cleansing in Twentieth-Century Europe, Cambridge/London 2001, 115f.; Collegium Bohemicum – Antikomplex (Eds.), Tragická místa paměti. Tragische Erinnerungsorte, Praha 2010, 131–156, 246–249, 334–338, 415–447.

between the two ethnic groups after 1 December 1944. Beginning at Christmas 1944, 27,000 women and men were taken from the Danube Swabian camps and villages and deported to the Soviet Union for purposes of forced labor. After January 1945, the mass-confinement of around 170,000 Danube Swabian men, women, and children in work and starvation camps occurred in Bačka and Banat. Over 50,000 of these people did not survive this internment because of hunger, epidemics, torture, and shootings.[64]

The Corps of the National Defense of Yugoslavia (KNOJ) enforced 'the liquidation of Chetnik, Ustasha, White Guard and other "anti-people gangs"'. Following the end of the war, partisan fighters executed whole lists of Croat, Slovene, and Serb 'collaborators' (*Ustaše*, *Domobrani*, *Domobranci*, and *Četnici*), those mass-graves in Slovenia, Croatia and Serbia only began to be discovered in the 1990s. But the OZNA-chief Aleksandar Ranković was unsatisfied with the work of his men: 'During 10 days in liberated Zagreb only 200 bandits were shot. [...] You work contrary to our orders since we have told you to work quickly and efficiently and to finish all in the first days.'[65]

On Saturday, 26 May 1945, when Marshal Tito was received with ovations by a huge crowd at the Kongresni Trg in Ljubljana, he threatened revenge with clear words:

> 'Regarding those traitors who were within the country itself, and in every particular people, this is now the matter of the past. The hand of justice, the avenging hand of our nation has already reached a great majority; only a minority of traitors has managed to escape and be taken under the wing of patrons abroad. This minority will never again gaze upon our lovely mountains, our blooming fields. Should this happen, it will last but for a very brief time.'[66]

From the 'Lawless Displacement' to the 'Orderly and Humane Transfer'

Resettlement plans had already been developed during the interwar period. Not only Hitler and Stalin, but also Churchill, considered ethnic cleansing to be a tolerable political instrument in order to align future political and national borders. The example of the 1922/1923 'population exchange' between Turkey and Greece

---

64 Donauschwäbische Kulturstiftung (Ed.), Leidensweg der Deutschen im kommunistischen Jugoslawien 1944–1948, 4 vols., München/Sindelfingen 1993–1997; Zoran Janjetović, Between Hitler and Tito. The Disappearance of the Vojvodina Germans, Belgrade 2000; Tibor Cseres, Titoist atrocities in Vojvodina 1944–1945. Serbian Vendetta in Bacska, Toronto 1993.

65 Hrvatski institut za povijest (Ed.), Partizanska i komunistička represija i zločini u Hrvatskoj 1944.–1946. Dokumenti, Slavonski Brod 2005, dok. 110; Vladimir Geiger – Ivan Jurković, Što se dogodilo s Folksdojčerima? Sudbina Nijemaca u bivšoj Jugoslaviji, Zagreb 1993.

66 Drago Jančar (Ed.), The Dark Side of the Moon. A Short History of the Totalitarianism in Slovenia 1945–1990, Ljubljana 1998, 5; Jera Vodušek Starič, Prevzem oblasti 1944–1946, Ljubljana 1992.

was widely known and carried no negative stigma. Beneš was also an advocate of 'ethnic engineering'. Under the impact of the German repression, first under Heydrich, and then after his murder – particularly evident in the liquidation of the village of Lidice – Beneš attained on 6 July 1942 the public rescission of the Munich Agreement by the British government, as well as the secret approval for the general principle of the transfer of German minorities from Central and Southeastern Europe after the war. In the spring of 1943, US President Roosevelt agreed, followed in December 1943 by Generalissimo Stalin. Directly following the end of the war the 'lawless displacement' from Czechoslovakia of Germans and Magyars happened. Germans and Magyars were declared 'enemies of the state' and whole segments of the population were arrested, interned, and chased from their land, while their property was confiscated without compensation. German civilians were singled-out by having *Swastikas* drawn on their backs, or, following the example for the Jews, were forced to wear an 'N' for 'German' [*Němec*] sewn onto their clothes. Part of the German population was placed in concentration camps, while others were used as forced labor, while still others were transported in freight cars over the border. Few Germans were able to escape the Czech militias, revolutionary soldiers, or security forces still in possession of their belongings. In this manner, from the beginning of May to the beginning of August 1945, 450,000 Sudeten Germans were expelled to the Soviet-controlled German sector, 200,000 to the American-controlled German sector, and 150,000 to Austria.[67]

After all, neither the Red Army in Moravia, Eastern and Central Bohemia, nor the US Army in Western and Southern Bohemia were interested in any more chaos. But it was not until the Potsdam Conference on 2 August 1945 that they put an end to these illegal displacement campaigns and arranged for the 'orderly and humane transfer' of German people out of Czechoslovakia, Poland, and Hungary. With that, the Allies met the basic demands of the Czech, Slovak, and Southern Slav nationalists who wanted the land – but without its German population, regardless of whether it had constituted a majority or a minority. Parallel to the Potsdam article XIII, on 2 August 1945, a Beneš Decree was issued which denied Germans and Magyars, with the exception of the 'antifascists', citizenship. It was the legal basis for coerced resettlement. The Prague government explained to the Allied Control Council for Germany that there were still 2.5 million Germans left to evacuate – a number which was surely exaggerated. On 20 November 1945, the Allied Control Council agreed to the dispersion of displaced persons to oc-

---

67 Friedrich Prinz (Ed.), Wenzel Jaksch – Edvard Beneš. Briefe und Dokumente aus dem Londoner Exil 1939–1943, Köln 1973; Detlev Brandes, Der Weg zur Vertreibung 1938–1945. Pläne und Entscheidungen zum "Transfer" der Deutschen aus der Tschechoslowakei und Polen, München [2]2005; Emilia Hrabovec, Vertreibung und Abschub. Deutsche in Mähren 1945–1947, Frankfurt am Main 1995; Roland J. Hoffmann – Kurt Heissig – Manfred Kittel – Gudrun Heissig – Anne Rohstock (Eds.), Odsun. Die Vertreibung der Sudetendeutschen. Dokumentation zu Ursachen, Planung und Realisierung einer "ethnischen Säuberung" in der Mitte Europas 1848/1849–1945/1946, vol. 2, München 2010.

cupied zones in Germany: 1.75 million Germans from Czechoslovakia would be deported to the US zone, and 750,000 to the Soviet zone. The transports started in January 1946, and on 1 November 1946, Interior Minister Nosek reported to President Beneš that 2,170,598 Germans had been deported.[68]

Clearly, there was no comparable master plan for the displacement and resettlement of the Yugoslav ethnic Germans in Marshall Tito's closest staff (in any case, none has been made known to date). However, plans among Serb intellectuals existed for achieving a Serb majority in the Vojvodina through the resettlement of the Danube Swabians and Magyars. The most famous of these plans came from one of the seven assassins responsible for the death of Archduke Franz Ferdinand in Sarajevo, Vaso Čubrilović, who became the Yugoslav Minister for Agriculture and Land Reform in March 1945. In Yugoslavia, mass expulsion and imprisonment in camps of certain ethnic groups – especially Germans – was not only a revenge for their real or presumed support for the Nazi ideology and the Nazi occupation policy but also a way to change the national structure of population in specific territories (mainly in the Vojvodina, in Slavonia, and in Slovenia) and an attempt to solve social problems. The new government was aware of the fact that confiscation of property of real and supposed enemies opened the possibility for realisation of land reform and colonisation.[69]

'AVNOJ Resolutions' and 'Beneš Decrees'

The 'AVNOJ Resolutions' and 'Beneš Decrees' and the fate of the Danube Swabians and Slovenian Germans, as well as the Sudeten and Carpathian Germans are for the most part – though not completely – to be understood as political and legal reactions to the German occupation forces in Serbia (including Vojvodina), Slavonia, and Slovenia as well as in the Protectorate of Bohemia and Moravia. While the idea of revenge for the German occupation policy existed among the AVNOJ leadership, among Czechoslovak exiles in London around President Beneš the idea of 'revenge against Munich' played the most important role. What should particularly not be overlooked is that both the Belgrade and Prague governments deprived the Germans of any available possibility for livelihood through their resolutions of expropriation.[70]

---

68 Ray M. Douglas, "Orderly and Humane". The Expulsion of the Germans after the Second World War, New Haven 2012; Alfred M. de Zayas, Nemesis at Potsdam: The Anglo-Americans and the Expulsion of the Germans – Background, Execution, Consequences, London 1979.

69 Aleksa Djilas, The Contested Country: Yugoslav Unity and the Communist Revolution, 1919–1953, Cambridge 1991; Michael Portmann, Die kommunistische Revolution in der Vojvodina 1944–1952. Politik, Gesellschaft, Wirtschaft, Kultur, Wien 2008.

70 Karel Jech (Ed.), Němci a Maďaři v dekretech prezidenta republiky. Studie a dokumenty 1940–1945. Die Deutschen und Magyaren in den Dekreten des Präsidenten der Republik. Studien und Dokumente 1940–1945, Brno 2003; Benjamin Frommer, National Cleansing. Retribution against Nazi Collaborators in Postwar Czechoslovakia, Cambridge 2005.

Confiscation of 'public enemies' property was anticipated by the decision of the Presidium of the AVNOJ on 21 November 1944 to transfer 'enemy property' (German, Magyar, *etc.*) and the property of absent persons under state administration. Despite the clear content of this AVNOJ resolution, international historiography continues to contain speculation, that the Yugoslav Germans and Magyars lost their earlier citizenship with this resolution. But the law on confiscation on property and implementation of confiscation of 9 June 1945, disqualified all potential enemies and at the same time allowed higher communist officials to acquire material benefits. The intention of the new communist authorities was obviously to destroy economically all social classes, which were considered enemies of the new social order.[71]

The AVNOJ Resolutions and Beneš Decrees had numerous consequences. Due to the AVNOJ Resolution of 21 November 1944, the Danube Swabians and Slovene Germans lost all of their real estate, and the larger part of their moveable property: a total of 96,874 individual possessions with 636,847 hectares of agriculture and forestry land, all industrial concerns, 8,268 handicraft enterprises, commercial operations, houses, apartments, banks, insurance policies, hotels, treatment facilities, medical practices, attorney's offices, libraries, theaters, museums, *etc.* The total loss of assets is equivalent to a loss of 15,589 billion German marks. Over and above that, in Slovenia was confiscated from so-called enemies of the state: 24,000 confiscations of property, 69 percent of capital invested in industry, 682 trading companies and around 8,474 rural properties.[72]

Using the Beneš Decrees Nr. 12 and 108, the Sudeten and Carpathian Germans (and Magyars) were stripped, without compensation, of a total of 1.62 million hectares of arable land and 1.3 million hectares of forest, or more than 29,000 km^2 (a total land area larger than Moravia!), in addition to nearly 3,900 industrial concerns, 34,000 handicraft enterprises, hundreds-of-thousands of commercial operations, homes, and apartments, as well as banks, insurance policies, hotels, treatment facilities, medical practices, attorney's offices, libraries, theaters, museums, and 120,000 motor vehicles. The Sudeten Germans estimated the total loss to 33.516 billion Reich marks.[73]

71 Slobodan Nešović (Ed.), Zakonodavni rad Pretsedništva AVNOJ-a i Pretsedništva Privremene narodne skupštine DFJ (19 novembra 1944–27 oktobra 1945) po stenografskim beleškima i drugim izvorima, Beograd 1951.

72 Leopold Egger, Das Vermögen und die Vermögensverluste der Deutschen in Jugoslawien, Sindelfingen 1983; Jančar, The Dark Side, 37.

73 Eduard Kubů – Jan Kuklík jun., Ungewollte Restitution. Die Rückerstattung jüdischen Eigentums in den böhmischen Ländern nach dem Zweiten Weltkrieg, in: Constantin Goschler – Philipp Ther (Eds.), Raub und Restitution. "Arisierung" und Rückerstattung des jüdischen Eigentums in Europa, Frankfurt am Main 2003, 184–204.

The Death Toll of War

A summary also requires a description of the death toll of war. According to the 1930 population census, the population of Czechoslovakia before the Munich Agreements equaled at least 15 million. Between October 1938 and December 1946, nearly 600,000 (= 4 percent) of these people violently lost their lives: in NS death and concentration camps, as soldiers on the frontlines, in guerilla warfare, by military and police executions, as victims of bombings, by forced labor, and by expulsion. The greatest number of victims were Jews, of which all told 270,000 were murdered, predominately in Auschwitz; 6,000 Roma also fell prey to racist persecution. The Sudeten and Carpathian Germans counted roughly 190,000 soldiers killed in action and 30,000 victims of displacement. The Czechs suffered a death toll of 40,000–45,000, the Slovaks of approximately 30,000 victims. The number of Czechoslovak Magyars, Rusyns, and Poles who violently lost their lives has never been statistically recorded.[74]

In March 1941, the population of Yugoslavia, which continued to increase into the 1930s, consisted of almost 15.9 million. Between April 1941 and March 1948, over 1.2 million (= 7.5 percent) of these people violently lost their lives: in mass persecutions by the Ustasha against Serbs, Jews, and Roma; in partisan and Chetnik wars against the occupying forces, as well as against the Ustasha, Muslims, and each other; in German, Italian, Hungarian, and Bulgarian hostage shootings and executions; in Croat and German death and concentration camps during the war; in Yugoslav concentration camps after January 1945; as soldiers on the frontlines, from forced labor, and by expulsion. The Serbs had the largest number of victims, of which a total of 530,000 lost their lives; the Croats suffered 240,000 deaths, both the Slovenes and the Bosnian Muslims around 100,000, and the Montenegrins nearly 30,000. Among the minorities, the Jews had the highest relative number of victims with 50,000. The Yugoslav Germans lost nearly 60,000 civilians and more than 25,000 soldiers killed in action. The Yugoslav Magyars claimed around 20,000 soldiers and civilians killed, while both the Yugoslav Albanians and Roma suffered 18,000 violent deaths.[75]

Until the breakup of Yugoslavia in 1991/1992 it remained largely unclear whether the total death tolls among the South Slavic people were due more to the occupying powers or the different fratricidal wars. Generally, it is believed that the fratricidal wars – initiated, naturally, by the occupation – caused considerably more deaths than the occupying powers. No doubts, in the 'Independent State of Croatia', fratricidal wars between the *Ustaše*, *Domobrani*, partisans, *Četnici*, and

---

74 Miroslav Kárný, Die tschechoslowakischen Opfer der deutschen Okkupation, in: Jörg K. Hoensch – Hans Lemberg (Eds.), Begegnung und Konflikt. Schlaglichter auf das Verhältnis von Tschechen, Slowaken und Deutschen, Essen 2001, 137–146.

75 Vladimir Žerjavić, Population Losses in Yugoslavia, 1941–1945, Zagreb 1997; Bogoljub Kočović, Nauka, nacionalizam i propaganda. Između gubitaka i žrtava Drugog svetskog rata u Jugoslaviji, Paris ^{2}1999.

Muslims claimed the majority of the victims. In this manner the Slovene fratricidal war between the Communist-led 'Liberation Front' and the *Domobranci* cost 14,000–18,000 Slovene victims on the non-Communist side, particularly in May and June 1945. Even in Serbia, the mutual revenge campaigns by the *Četnici* and partisan fighters exceeded the brutal persecution measures of the NS occupation in terms of mass executions of hostages.[76]

Memory and Historization

An examination of the German/Austrian-Czechoslovak and German/Austrian-Yugoslav history of conflict in the 20th century reveals – in addition to a wealth of positive economic, social, technical, cultural, academic, and scientific connections – a long list of discrimination, injury, degradation, oppression, warlike actions, destruction, persecution, expulsion, and genocide. Therefore, it is understandable that different, at times very contradictory, historical understandings still exist at the beginning of the 21st century. In order to overcome the divide that exists in East Central European comparative history, it is absolutely necessary for each side to incorporate a deeper understanding not only of the pain and injustices they suffered, but also of those crimes they perpetrated. The remembrance of a perpetrated injustice, and the public acknowledgement of the victim, is the litmus test for the internal transformation of a country and its society; it is the necessary symbol of its denunciation of terrible, historical consistencies.[77]

Since 1989, a new generation, less familiar with the people and countries east of the fallen 'Iron Curtain', wants to discover and explore Eastern Europe, with its many different languages, religions, and cultures – without the ballast of the National Socialist and Soviet Communist past. Naturally, with that also come the German, Austrian, and Jewish histories of Eastern and Southeastern Europe, including the violent chapters. In the course of two totalitarian dictatorships, and of National Socialist, imperialist, racist, nationalist, and Communist motivated wars and acts of repression, over forty million people violently lost their lives in Eastern and Southeastern Europe in the decade between 1938 and 1948. Amplified knowl-

76 Drago Jančar (Ed.), Temna stran meseca. Kratka zgodovina totalitarizma v Sloveniji 1945–1990, Ljubljana 1998; Tomasevich, Occupation, 751–778.

77 Reinhart Koselleck, Der 8. Mai zwischen Erinnerung und Geschichte, in: Carsten Dutt (Ed.), Reinhart Koselleck, Vom Sinn und Unsinn der Geschichte, Berlin 2010, 254–265; Monika Flacke (Ed.), Mythen der Nationen. 1945 – Arena der Erinnerungen. Eine Ausstellung des Deutschen Historischen Museums, 2 vols., Berlin 2005; Christoph Cornelißen – Roman Holec – Jiří Pešek (Eds.), Diktatur–Krieg–Vertreibung. Erinnerungskulturen in Tschechien, der Slowakei und Deutschland seit 1945, Essen 2005; Václav Havel, Fassen Sie sich bitte kurz. Gedanken und Erinnerungen zu Fragen von Karel Hvížďala, Reinbek bei Hamburg 2007; Mitja Velikonja, Titostalgia – A Study of Nostalgia for Josip Broz, Ljubljana 2008; Ljiljana Radonić, Krieg um die Erinnerung. Kroatische Vergangenheitspolitik zwischen Revisionismus und europäischen Standards, Frankfurt am Main/New York 2010; Marc Halder, Der Tito-Kult. Charismatische Herrschaft im sozialistischen Jugoslawien, München 2013; David Schriffl, Tote Grenze oder lebendige Nachbarschaft? Österreichisch-slowakische Beziehungen 1945–1968, Wien 2012.

edge of the complicated history of this region, the exploration and interpretation of this past as 'learned history', and the 'historicization of events' could perhaps help to make comprehensible the old and new prejudices and fears, the inherited images of 'the enemy', and national sensitivities, or at least to make known the difficulties in creating a politically, economically, socially, and emotionally united Europe. In any case, any sort of moral arrogance in the unilateral assignment of blame is therefore wholly misplaced. Only with a shared reconsideration of the past, borne from a European spirit of reconciliation, can the history of Europe's ethnic groups during that dark decade interlink; and with that, contribute to the development of a shared European culture of remembrance.[78]

78 Aleida Assmann – Ute Frevert (Eds.), Geschichtsvergessenheit, Geschichtsversessenheit. Vom Umgang mit der deutschen Vergangenheit nach 1945, Stuttgart 1999; Harald Welzer, Der Krieg der Erinnerung. Holocaust, Kollaboration und Widerstand im europäischen Gedächtnis, Frankfurt am Main 2007.

Center Reports

Marija Wakounig

Nothing New in the Institute of East European History at the University of Vienna: Activities Report on the Academic Year 2014/2015

University of Vienna

Personnel, Teaching, and Other Matters

In a modified way referring to the title of Erich Maria Remarque's novel "Im Westen nichts Neues" [In the West Nothing New], it may be said that the Academic Year 2014/2015 for the Institute of East European History did not undergo significant modifications. The activities of the Institute's staff also seem to be untouched by the occassion of the 650th Anniversary of the University of Vienna, which otherwise determined University's everyday life.

In personnel, research, and teaching matters there is only little news to report: Ten scholars (three full professors, three extraordinary professors, one assistant professor, one *post-doc*, and two *prae-doc* assistants) are representing the Institute's academic staff and are supported by four secretaries. The limited four year contract of Markian Prokopovych ended in March 2015, after which he was employed as guest lecturer at the Institute during the summer term 2015. The same position was also held by Per Anderson Rudling from Sweden, who was our guest professor for the still vacant professorship for Russian History (since 2011). But we have successfully insisted on the new application (announcement) for this professorship of Russian History; the announcement process is currently already under way. Our *prae-doc* assistent Ulrich Hofmeister defended his doctoral thesis in November 2014, which received the Grete-Mostny doctoral prize in June 2015. It is a great pleasure to announce that our colleague Philipp Ther is one of the award winners of the Leipzig Book Fair Prize [Preis der Leipziger Buchmesse] 2015. His monograph "Die neue Ordnung auf dem alten Kontinent. Eine Geschichte des neoliberalen Europa" won in the category of non-fiction.

During the Academic Year 2014/2015 the Institute's staff was – business as usual – obligated to teach, to research, to publish, and last but not least to organize and host (respectively sometimes also participate in) international conferences, symposia, workshops, and other events. The following professional and scientific events were held especially under the patronage and with the financial support of the Viennese Austrian and Central European Center:

- The international symposium 'Altösterreichischer Adel zwischen Nation – Nationalismus – Faschismus/Nationalsozialismus (1870–1938/1945)' was held from 1 to 3 December 2014. While the welcoming remarks and the opening discussion (moderated by Marija Wakounig) between Oliver Rathkolb (Institute of Contemporary History/Institut für Zeitgeschichte) and Václav Horčička and Jan Županič from the Charles University Prague were given at the Institute lecture hall, the conference venue was the Old Chapel [Alte Kapelle] on the University Campus. Both the opening and all events of the symposium were very well attended, which demonstrated the timelessness of this topic and the scientific need to research and discuss the so-called nobility theme. The event was honoured by the presence of Ari Rath, the former editor in chief of the *Jerusalem Post*.
- On the occasion of the presentation of the famous biographer Constantin Wurzbach (1818–1893) and his historical situatedness in Galicia by the guest speaker Isabel Röskau-Rydel from Krakow, Marija Wakounig acted as co-speaker. The event took place in the Vienna Polish Academy of Science (Polnische Akademie der Wissenschaften – Wissenschaftliches Zentrum in Wien) on 19 March 2015.
- The conference 'Ozeane: Grenzen, Interaktionen, Konflikte, Interdisziplinäre Zugänge', organized and coordinated by Friedrich Edelmayer, Margarete Grandner, Hermann Mückler, and Gerhard Pfeisinger and financially supported by the Viennese Austrian and Central European Center, took place at the Old Chapel on the University Campus from 17 to 18 April 2015. 14 international and national scholars provided new insights into the very ambitious, global, and mainstream topic; Marija Wakounig served as the chairwoman as well as the speaker.
- The presentation of the monograph "Grenze(n) und Herrschaft(en) in der kleinpolnischen Stadt Sandomierz 1772–1844" gave a delightful occassion for an event on 17 June 2015. The presenters Kerstin S. Jobst and Marija Wakounig expressed their pleasure that the author Christoph Augustynowicz had succeeded in preparing and finishing his book for printing despite the heavy responsibilities of his administrative positions, followed by the author's witty and inspired remarks on the contents of his book. The monograph is the 16th volume in the Institute's series 'Europa Orientalis' and was published with the financial support of the Austrian Federal Ministry of Science, Research and Economy (Bundesministerium für Wissenschaft, Forschung und Wirtschaft) via the Viennese Austrian and Central European Center.
- A highlight of the Academic Year 2014/2015 was the international symposium 'Die Neuordnung (Ostmittel-)Europas. Vom Wiener Fürstentag zum Wiener Kongress 1515–1815'. The opening was made by Alfred Kohler's innovative keynote speech in the Institutes lecture hall on 1 July 2015. New insights, per-

spectives and perceptions (to the meaning of the term 'Neuordnung') were given by 17 international and national scholars on the following two days (2–3 July 2015). The symposium was organized by Marija Wakounig in collaboration with Christian Lackner (Institute of History of the University of Vienna). This symposium was one of the kick-off events of the eight Austrian and Central European Centers for the closing conference in Vienna on 25 and 26 October 2015.

The so-called First Congress of Vienna on ocassion of the doubble marriage [Doppelhochzeit] between the Habsburg and Jagiellonian dynasties 1515, being the initial decision for the Habsburgs to gain the Crowns of Saint Wenceslas and Saint Stephen after the Battle of Mohacs 1526, when the young King Louis II was killed, can be interpreted as the date of the founding of the Habsburg Monarchy. This constellation acts as the historic legitimation of the Austrian and Central European Centers. The aim of the before-mentioned kick-off symposium as well as of the closing conference is mainly to remember the 500th Anniversary of the First Congress of Vienna and its consequences for Central Europe.

Publications

The following anthologies and monographs were published between October 2014 and June 2015:

- Christoph Augustynowicz, Grenze(n) und Herrschaft(en) in der kleinpolnischen Stadt Sandomierz 1772–1844, Europa Orientalis 16, Wien 2015;
- Kerstin S. Jobst, Geschichte der Ukraine, Reclam Sachbuch, Stuttgart ^{2}2015;
- Andreas Kappeler, Kleine Geschichte der Ukraine, C.H. Beck Paperback 1059, München 2014;
- Gherardo Ortalli – Oliver Jens Schmitt – Ermanno Orlando (Eds.), Il *Commonwealth* veneziano tra 1204 e la fine della Repubblica. Identità e peculiarità, Venezia 2015;
- Oliver Jens Schmitt – Michael Metzeltin (Eds.) Das Südosteuropa der Regionen, Sitzungsberichte der philosophisch-historischen Klasse 858, Wien 2015;
- Philipp Ther, Die neue Ordnung auf dem alten Kontinent. Eine Geschichte des neoliberalen Europa, Berlin 2014;
- Marija Wakounig – Markus Peter Beham (Eds.), Mind and Memory in Discourse. Critical Concepts and Constructions, Europa Orientalis 15, Wien/Berlin 2014.

A message on one's own account: Ferdinand Kühnel, the co-editor of this anthology, became a doctoral candidate after his successful presentation of his doctoral proposal to the faculty doctoral advisory board in March 2015. His exceptional theme 'DE DIFFUGIO – Vom lautlosen Verschwinden ethnischer Minderheiten von Grabsteinen. Ethnische Homogenisierung am Beispiel Kärntens seit 1918' and the outstanding written research proposal convinced several internal and external peer-reviewers to choose him as one of 26 candidates for the prestigious and coveted three-year uni:docs fellowship. The co-editor of the last years' anthologies, Markus Peter Beham, pursued an LL.M. degree at Columbia University in New York through a Fulbright scholarship. Both, present and former co-editor attended the last Annual Conventions of the Austrian and Central European Centers. It is evident from their achievements and activities that their participation in the work of the Austrian and Central European Centers has been an essential pillar in their astonishing academic progress.

Joseph F. Patrouch

The Wirth Institute for Austrian and Central European Studies, Faculty of Arts, University of Alberta: Active in Edmonton and Beyond in 2014/2015

University of Alberta

The Wirth Institute, in addition to its ties to and support from Austria, also enjoys the recognition of a number of other Central European countries, including Croatia, Czech Republic, Hungary, Poland, Slovakia, and Slovenia. The Institute sponsors programs and hosts scholars either from these countries, or working on topics relating to them or their shared histories. Wirth Institute activities can include exhibitions relating to history or contemporary art, concerts, lectures, workshops, recordings, and publications. The Wirth Institute has a national mandate: it is the only such institute in Canada. In the period under review in the following report, the Wirth Institute sponsored activities across the country, from Cape Breton in the east, to Banff in the Rocky Mountains in the west, with two conferences in between, in the national capital, Ottawa. In addition, the Institute hosted an international meeting of its alumni association, the Wirth Alumni Network (WAN), in Prague.

As always, one of the central activities of the Institute was to host a cadre of guest researchers, mostly doctoral students enrolled at various Central European institutions. These doctoral fellows are selected after national competitions in their respective countries. The governments of Austria, Croatia, Czech Republic and Hungary support these programs financially, as do contributions from the local Austrian, Croatian, Czech and Slovak, Hungarian, and Polish communities in Edmonton and across Canada. During Academic Year 2014/2015, the Wirth Institute hosted five doctoral researchers, one each from Austria, Croatia, Czech Republic, Hungary, and Poland.

This year's BMWFW-sponsored Austrian fellow was Agata Joanna Lagiewka, a literary scholar enrolled in the Institut für Germanistik at the Universität Graz. In addition to participating in Wirth Institute activities in Edmonton, Ms Lagiewka delivered papers at the German Studies Association meeting in Kansas City, Missouri (USA) and at the German Studies Association of Australia (GSAA) Conference 'The Foreign and the Self in German literature, society and culture' at the University of Sydney. Her PhD research examines transcultural German and English literature in the context of diaspora, migration and autobiographical writing.

Jana Maresova, a PhD Candidate in the Department of Anglophone Literatures and Cultures at the Faculty of Arts at Charles University, Prague, pursues research on contemporary Canadian Aboriginal literature, with a special focus on storytelling and myth as used in particular novels. Noémi Nagy, a PhD candidate at the Faculty of Law, University of Pécs, participated in the annual Austrian Centers and Institutes meeting in Minneapolis, Minnesota (USA). She also delivered a paper at the annual meeting of the Hungarian Studies Association of Canada which was held in Ottawa. Ms Nagy's research focuses on the issue of language rights. Marjeta Šinko is a Research and Teaching Fellow and PhD Candidate in Comparative Politics in the Faculty of Political Science, University of Zagreb. Her dissertation is titled 'Formation of Gender Equality Policies in Croatia and Slovenia from 1990 until 2008'. Michał Wiącek is a PhD Candidate at the Faculty of Social Sciences, University of Wrocław. He also participated in the Minneapolis meeting highlighted in this volume, as well as at the workshop 'National Revival in the Shadow of European Unity' at the Hebrew University in Jerusalem in January, 2015. Mr. Wiącek's research focuses on the visions of a united Europe in the Polish exile press after World War II.

Various other researchers have been affiliated with the Wirth Institute over the past year. These include our new Senior Research Associate, the literary and cultural critic Peter Swirski of the Sun Yat-sen University in Guangdong, China. Professor Swirski is one of the primary organizers of the Wirth Institute's planned May 2017 conference on Central European popular culture to be held in conjunction with the Silesian University in Katowice, Poland. Professor Mária Czellér of the Institute of Business Communication and Professional Language Studies at the University of Debrecen researched at the Wirth Institute in summer 2014 with the support of the Campus Hungary program of the Balassi Institute. Adam Chrobak continued his research at the Institute on the topic of the Hungarian migration to Alberta with the support of the Kőrösi Csoma State Fellowship Program, a Hungarian initiative. Mr. Chrobak will return to the Institute in 2015 to continue this project. The Italian researcher Jaro Stacul also continued as a Research Associate at the Institute. His activities included the public lecture 'Demolishing and Redeveloping History in Post-Socialist Poland' at the Institute of Ethnology and Cultural Anthropology of the University of Warsaw in May 2015.

The Wirth Institute sponsored or co-sponsored four conferences during Academic Year 2014/2015. These included an international conference dedicated to the topic of the internment of Austro-Hungarians and other 'enemy aliens' by the Canadian government during World War I, which was organized with the Canadian Institute for Ukrainian Studies. This conference was held at the Cave and Basin National Historic Site in Banff National Park from 17–18 October 2014. It brought together 17 researchers from Canada, Austria, Italy, and Turkey to discuss the plight of the approximately 8,500 internees who were held in a system of 20 camps across Canada from 1914–1920. The primary funding for the conference came from the Canadian First World War Internment Recognition Fund.[1] The proceedings of the conference are to be published and distributed across Canada.

From 31 October until 1 November, the Institute sponsored a conference at Carleton University in Ottawa titled 'The US, Canada, the Great Recession, and Austrian Monetary Theory'. This meeting was part of the ongoing series of conferences sponsored every other year by the Wirth Institute on topics relating to the Austrian School of Economics. The papers from the conference, as from previous conferences in the series, are to be published by Emerald Group Publishing as part of their series "Advances in Austrian Economics". Articles from the 2012 conference, which was held in Lake Louise, Alberta, were recently released.[2]

As part of the celebrations marking the twentieth anniversary of the Austrian Canadian Council, the Wirth Institute sponsored a day-long conference at the University of Ottawa on 23 May 2015. The topic was 'Reconsidering *Heimat*: Transcultural Identities and Relations'. Organized by Helga Mitterbauer, the BMWFW Visiting Professor of Austrian Studies at the University of Alberta, this conference included scholars from Austria and Germany, as well as presentations by Wirth Institute Founding Director Franz Szabo and Alfred Wirth, one of the Institute's primary benefactors. Institute Director Joseph F. Patrouch introduced the life and accomplishments of the Austro-Canadian mountain guide Conrad Kain. All in attendance at the conference received complimentary copies of the new book of correspondence by Cain.[3] The Wirth Institute helped sponsor a book launch party for this collection on 21 October 2014.

The fourth Wirth Institute conference of the past year was held in Prague in June 2014. This was the third biannual meeting of the Wirth Alumni Network (WAN). Every two years, the alumni of the various Wirth fellowship programs come together in a different Central European location to socialize, reinvigorate personal and scholarly contacts, and discuss their research and professional progress. The first such meeting was held in Vienna in 2010, and the second in Budapest in 2012. The alumni of the Czech program organized the Prague 2014 meeting, and many alumni from the programs in Austria, Croatia, Hungary, and Poland joined them for a number of days full of presentations and field trips. His Excellency Ferdinand Trauttmansdorff, the Austrian ambassador to Czech Republic, hosted a reception at his residence for the participants, and His Excellency Otto Jelinek, the Canadian Ambassador to the Czech Republic, delivered the introductory remarks to the conference participants. The Czech government also recognized the contributions of Franz Szabo and Alfred Wirth, as well as of Pavel

1 For more information about this conference, see Joseph F. Patrouch, Conference on Canadian Camps in World War I, in: Austrian Studies Newsmagazine 27/1, Minneapolis 2015, 24–25, here 31.

2 Steven Horwitz – Roger Koppl (Eds.), Entangled Political Economy. Advances in Austrian Economics 18, Bingley 2014.

3 Zac Robinson (Ed.), Conrad Kain. Letters from a Wandering Mountain Guide, 1906–1933, Edmonton 2014.

Jelen, the President of the Edmonton Chapter of the Czechoslovak Society for Arts and Sciences (SVU), a major supporter of the Wirth Institute, by awarding the three men medals in conjunction with this meeting.[4]

In addition to these four conferences, the Wirth Institute also was involved with the organization of a number of other lectures, exhibitions, and musical performances. The lectures included 'Comparing the 1815 and 1919 Settlements: Can Anything Useful be Learned?' by Paul W. Schroeder, Professor Emeritus, University of Illinois, Urbana-Champagne (USA) on 11 September 2014. This lecture kicked off a series of interrelated events among the various Austrian centers and institutes around the world dealing with the anniversaries of the Vienna Congresses of 1515 and 1815. On 29 September Andrzej Nowak of the Jagiellonian University (Krakow, Poland) delivered the lecture 'The Russian Imperial Strategy: Targets and Instruments'. The annual Toby and Saul Reichert Holocaust Lecture was held on 16 October by Robert Jan Van Pelt of the University of Waterloo (Canada). It was titled 'Auschwitz, Summer 1944: The Destruction of the Hungarian Jews'. On 19 March 2015 Matthew Rampley of the University of Birmingham (UK) delivered the lecture 'Museums and Politics in Austria-Hungary'.

Two alumni of the Wirth Fellowship programs returned to Edmonton to deliver public talks. On 21 October, Ignacy Józwiak of the Graduate School for Social Research in Warsaw delivered the talk 'Central-EU-rope and the Oriental-Occidental Tug of War: Studying State Borders and Cross-Border Mobility'. On 27 May 2015 Josef Svéda, a post-doctoral Fulbright Fellow at the University of California, Berkeley (USA), gave the lecture 'Land of Wealth and Prosperity, or Exploitation and Poverty? Images of the USA in Czech Literature and Culture'.

The Wirth Institute helped to organize two exhibitions over the last year. The first, titled 'Face to Face: Works from Slovakia', featured student and faculty art from the Fine Arts Academy in Banská Bystrica. It was on display in the University of Alberta's Fine Arts Gallery June and July 2014. The second exhibition was titled 'Bertha von Suttner: A Life for Peace' and concentrated on the life and works of the first woman to win the Nobel Peace Prize. This exhibition was displayed in the Rutherford Library at the University of Alberta in August and September 2014. Joseph F. Patrouch and Helga Mitterbauer delivered talks introducing the exhibition, which was provided by the Austrian Cultural Forum in Ottawa.

Since the foundation of the Wirth Institute in 1998, music and its performance and study have played a major role. 2014/2015 was no exception. For example, in October, two gusle specialists, Jure Miloš of Bosnia and Herzegovina and Joško Ćaleta of Croatia, were flown in to participate in the conference 'Singing Storytellers: The Lives, Music, and Verbal Artistry of Bards in Our World' held at Cape Breton University (Sydney, Nova Scotia, Canada). The Wirth Institute co-sponsored the Edmonton concert of the Czech musicians Ivan Ženatý and Martin Ka-

4 'Szabo, Wirth, awarded Medals at WAN', in: Austrian Studies Newsmagazine 26/2, Minneapolis 2014, 26.

sík on 29 October. On 7 December, the Institute sponsored its annual Christmas concert, a fundraiser for the University of Alberta's Student Food Bank. As has become tradition, choirs from the local community sang Advent and Christmas songs in various Central European languages. This year, the concert was also the occasion for the release of the Wirth Institute's latest CD: 'Stille Nacht: Christmas Carols from Austria'. This CD features live recordings from various Wirth Institute Christmas concerts held between 2002 and 2013.

The Edmonton Opera performed 'Die Zauberflöte' this season, and the Wirth Institute was involved when Cameraon MacRae of the production team presented some 'behind-the-scenes' information at one of the Institute's monthly 'Central European Cafés' on 9 January. Institute Director Patrouch also gave a public lecture on the spatial and historical contexts of the work on 14 January. The Wirth Institute helped sponsor a performance of Slavic liturgical pieces at the St. Josephat Ukrainian Catholic Cathedral in Edmonton on 27 January. They were performed by the 'Kappella Kyrie Slavic Chamber Choir'. The annual 'Johann Strauss Ball' was held on 28 February and featured honored guests His Excellency Arno Riedel, Austrian ambassador to Canada, and Alfred Wirth. The ball raises money for scholarships to help music students from Alberta to study in Austria. This year, two Edmonton students will travel to Austria to study in Eisenstadt and Salzburg. On 19 April the Institute helped sponsor the Alberta Baroque Ensemble's concert 'Hayden and Company.'

The ongoing collaboration with the 'Franz-Schubert-Institut in Baden bei Wien' continued. The institute's director, Deen Larsen, visited Edmonton twice to audition musicians, lecture, and hold master classes. A public celebration of the renewal of the agreement between the University of Alberta and the Schubert Institute which provides support for Larsen's visits and scholarships for University of Alberta voice and piano students to participate in the summer institute was held on 19 March. Larsen delivered lectures at both the main campus of the University of Alberta and its Liberal Arts campus in Camrose. Professor Alexander Carpenter from that campus taught a study abroad course in Vienna in spring 2015 which focused on the musical heritage of the city. The Wirth Institute provided financial support for the students who participated.

The study of the Holocaust in Central Europe is an important aspect of the Wirth Institute's programs. In addition to the annual 'Reichert Holocaust Lecture' mentioned above, plans call for the establishment of a Holocaust Reading Room at the Institute. This small library will be based around the donation of Holocaust-related materials made last year by Dr. William Pearce, a long-time member of the Reichert Holocaust Lecture Advisory Committee. The Wirth Institute also supported the showing of the docu-drama 'O Consul de Bordeaux' on 27 January, film about the heroic efforts of a Portuguese consul in France who helped many people escape the German Nazi regime and its allies.

The Wirth Institute continued to cooperate closely with the European Union Centre of Excellence (EUCE) at the University of Alberta. As part of the university's International Week activities, the Institute and EUCE sponsored a panel on de-mining activities in Croatia and Bosnia and Herzegovina on 26 January. The panel featured Her Excellency Koviljka Špirić, the Bosnian ambassador to Canada, together with Mark Minenko, a retired Canadian military officer who served in Croatia and Bosnia, and Wirth Fellow Marjeta Šinko. On 24 March, the new Hungarian ambassador to Canada, His Excellency Bálint Ódor, delivered a public lecture on the topic of Hungary and the EU. He also participated in a Political Science undergraduate class on the politics of Central Europe.

BMWFW Visiting Austrian Professor Mitterbauer taught an undergraduate class on Austrian Culture in Fall Term 2014. Wirth Institute Director Patrouch taught an undergraduate lecture course on the Habsburg Dynasty in Winter Term, 2015. He also led an undergraduate seminar on comparative early modern cities, with particular emphasis on Brussels, Madrid, Vienna, Bratislava, and Prague. In December, Director Patrouch taught an intensive graduate course at the Hebrew University in Jerusalem on the topic of the Habsburg Dynasty.[5] On 24 December he delivered the public lecture 'The First Vienna Congress of 1515: Dynastic, Intellectual, Physical, and Meteorological Contexts' in Jerusalem before attending Christmas Mass at the Austrian Hospice in the city. On 10 April, Director Patrouch gave a public presentation on the same topic in Edmonton as part of the monthly 'Central European Cafés' sponsored by the Institute. In November 2014 he travelled to Budapest to participate in the international review of the Doctoral College at the Faculty of Central European Studies of the Andrássy University.

Future plans for the Wirth Institute include continued study of Central European migration to Canada. An international workshop discussing the cultural ties between Brussels and Vienna in the decades around 1900 is also being organized by Helga Mitterbauer together with University of Alberta faculty members Piet Defraeye and Christian Reynes. Activities marking the twentieth anniversary of the Dayton Accords in Bosnia and Herzegovina are also in the planning stages, as is the fourth Wirth Alumni Network meeting, which will be held in Wrocław, Poland in June 2016 in connection with an international conference there. The annual month-long faculty exchange program with the Universität Innsbruck, which saw Christian Quendler from that university visit Edmonton in September, 2014 and Srilati Ravi of the University of Alberta visit Innsbruck in May 2015, will continue. A new agreement signed with the Silesian University in Katowice, Poland in May 2015 sets up a similar program of faculty exchange between Alberta and Silesia. This program is scheduled to begin in May 2016, continuing and expanding the wide-reaching activities of the Wirth Institute.

5 Joseph F. Patrouch, Austrian Studies in Jerusalem. A Wide-Reaching Endeavor, in: Austrian Studies Newsmagazine 27/1, Minneapolis 2015, 31.

Georg Kastner

Jahresbericht der Fakultät für Mitteleuropäische Studien Budapest

Andrássy Universität Budapest

Das Studienjahr 2014/2015 brachte für die Andrássy Universität Budapest eine Reihe von Veränderungen mit sich, die in der Folge auch für den Fachbereich Mitteleuropäischen Studien sehr wesentliche Auswirkungen hatten. Auch wenn es im personellen Bereich im vergangenen Jahr keine besonderen Änderungen gab – solche stehen uns im kommenden Jahr noch bevor – gab es vor allem im strukturellen Aufbau der Universität geradezu einen Umbruch. Mit Ende des Jahres 2015 soll es an der Universität keine Fakultäten mehr geben, die wissenschaftlichen Mitarbeiterinnen und Mitarbeiter sollen dadurch von Verwaltungsaufgaben entlastet werden, womit die Forschungsquote mittelfristig erhöht werden soll. Die entsprechenden Umgestaltungsmaßnahmen banden jedoch im abgelaufenen Jahr zahlreiche Ressourcen, um dieses von den Trägern vorgegebenes Ziel zu erreichen. Hinkünftig wird der mitteleuropäische Fachbereich daher nicht mehr in einer Fakultät, sondern in einem Zentrum organisiert sein. Zur Zeit laufen Gespräche mit den Vertretern der anderen Fachbereiche der Universität, in wie weit im Zuge der nötigen Profilbildung eine intensivere Zusammenarbeit möglich sein wird. In Folge der Neuprofilierung wird es aller Wahrscheinlichkeit nach auch zu einer fachlichen Neudefinition von Lehrstühlen kommen, wobei der historisch-kulturwissenschaftlichen Ausrichtung durchaus Rechnung getragen wird.

Im Bereich der Lehre gab es nach dem sehr langwierigen Akkreditierungsprozess der vergangenen beiden Jahre keine wesentlichen Veränderungen. Nach der Neuakkreditierung des kulturdiplomatischen Studienprogramms 'Mitteleuropäische Studien – Diplomatie' im Jahr 2014 widmete sich die Fakultät der Umsetzung dieses Programms. Im September 2014 starteten elf Studierende aus Ungarn, Österreich, Deutschland und der Ukraine ihre Ausbildung, die Nachfrage für das kommende Studienjahr liegt um einiges höher, endgültige Zahlen für das Studienjahr 2015/2016 werden aber erst mit Ende September 2015 feststehen. Die neuen Studierenden sind höchst motiviert, die Studienleistungen teilweise herausragend. Im nun folgenden dritten Semester werden alle einen praktischen Ausbildungsteil an einer kulturdiplomatischen Institution absolvieren. Die Anbahnung entsprechender Kontakte zu diversen Organisationen, wie den österreichischen Kulturforen, dem Collegium Hungaricum in Wien bzw. in Berlin oder aber auch zu einer polnischen Organisation war daher ein wesentliches Anliegen, das in den letzten Monaten erfolgreich umgesetzt werden konnte.

Im Bereich Mitteleuropäische Geschichte wurde das Doktoratskolleg einer internationalen Evaluierung unterzogen, deren Ergebnisse im organisatorischen Bereich zu Veränderungen führen werden. Im Herbst 2014 bzw. Frühjahr 2015 wurden zwei neue Kollegiatinnen und ein neuer Kollegiat aufgenommen. Besonders erfreulich ist, dass mit MMag. Béla Mattias Teleky ein Absolvent des Instituts für Osteuropäische Geschichte an der Universität Wien den Weg nach Budapest gefunden hat, es also hier zu einer intensiveren Zusammenarbeit mit einem der anderen Zentren kommen wird. Für Herbst 2015 läuft noch eine Ausschreibung, die mit 31. August 2015 enden wird.

Derzeit wird an einer Anpassung des Masterstudiums 'Mitteleuropäische Geschichte' gearbeitet. Eine solche ergibt sich einerseits auf Grund der Erkenntnisse des ständigen Evaluierungsprozesses, andererseits aber auch aus einer Änderung der vom ungarischen Ministerium vorgegebenen Rahmenbedingungen. Wir hoffen, den Anpassungsprozess bis zum Beginn des Studienjahres 2016/2017 abschließen zu können.

Im vergangenen Studienjahr war die Fakultät Gastgeberin zahlreicher wissenschaftlicher Veranstaltungen, die teilweise mit Gedenktagen in Zusammenhang standen. So starteten wir am 10. September 2014 mit der eintägigen Konferenz 'Kriegserinnerung zwischen Vergangenheitsbewältigung und Zukunftsgestaltung' in das neue Studienjahr. Referenten waren u. a. Rolf Wernstedt vom Volksbund Deutsche Kriegsgräberfürsorge und Gerald Lamprecht vom Zentrum für jüdische Studien der Universität Graz. Umrahmt wurde die Konferenz von einer Ausstellung mit dem Titel: 'Der Alltag an der österreichisch-ungarischen Ostfront in den Augen von László Moholy-Nagy'.

In den Bereich 'Science to Public' fiel ein gemeinsam mit dem Österreichischen Kulturforum (ÖFK) Budapest am 5. November 2014 organisierter Filmabend mit anschließender Podiumsdiskussion unter dem Titel: 'Sissi – Kult und Kitsch'. Neben einer Vorführung des ersten Teils der in Ungarn bis heute höchst populären Sissi-Trilogie von Ernst Marischka mit Romy Schneider in der Titelrolle im Uránia Filmpalast, sollte die Bedeutung des Films für die Rezeption der franzisko-josephinischen Epoche in Ungarn, Österreich und Deutschland analysiert werden. Die Beschäftigung mit der Frage, welches Bild besonders der österreichische Nachkriegsfilm von der untergehenden Habsburgermonarchie zeichnet, gehört seit langem zum ständigen Forschungsbereich der Fakultät, zu dem auch schon mehrere Master-Arbeiten verfasst wurden. An der erwähnten Diskussion nahm u.a. auch der international anerkannte Kulturwissenschaftler Frank Stern (u.a. ehemaliger Professor am Institut für Zeitgeschichte der Universität Wien) teil.

Einen letzten großen Höhepunkt im Kalenderjahr 2014 bildete die dreitägige Konferenz 'Von Desintegration zu Integration? Österreich und Ungarn von der Monarchie zur Europäische Union 1914–2014' (11. bis 13. November 2014), die von Richard Lein gemeinsam mit Maximilian Graf (Österreichische Akademie der Wissenschaften, ÖAW) organisiert wurde. Neben international arrivierten Kollegen wie Arnold Suppan, Wolfgang Mueller, Stefan Malfèr (ÖAW), Peter Haslinger (Universität Marburg/Gießen), Miroslav Šepták (Nationalarchiv, Prag) oder Róbert Fiziker (Ungarisches Nationalarchiv) konnten auch junge Kolleginnen und Kollegen, besonders aus dem Doktoratskolleg eingebunden werden. Die Beiträge werden gemeinsam mit den Vorträgen anderer Tagungen des Jahres 2014 sowie aktuellen Forschungsergebnissen im Jahrbuch 2014 des Mitteleuropa-Zentrums gegen Jahresende erscheinen. Den Abschluss des Jahres bildete am 3. und 4. Dezember die schon traditionelle Doktoranden-Tagung, die vom vierten Jahrgang des Doktoratskollegs organisiert wurde und unter dem Motto 'Raum und Identität im Wandel. Mitteleuropäische Geschichte(n) im 20. Jahrhundert' stand. Neben Dissertantinnen und Dissertanten aus Österreich, Ungarn und Deutschland nahmen diesmal auch eine Kollegin von der dänischen Universität Sønderborg sowie ein Kollege vom Deutschen-Historischen Institut Paris teil.

Das Sommersemester 2015 wurde zunächst mit einem von Orsolya Lénárt organisierten Vortrag mit anschließender Diskussion unter dem Titel: 'In der Mundart bleiben wir zu Hause' eröffnet, der sich mit der Frage der sprachlichen Identität der Ungarndeutschen auseinandersetze. Zu Gast war die junge Historikerin, Journalistin und Repräsentantin der ungarndeutschen Gegenwartsliteratur Angela Korb. Unwesentlich später war auf einem von Ursula Mindler-Steiner organsierten Veranstaltung Volker Benkert von der Arizona State University zu Gast. Er sprach zum Thema 'Neue Dimensionen der generationellen Auseinandersetzung mit dem DDR-Staatssozialismus'.

Wiederum in den Bereich 'Science to Public' fiel ein am 11. Mai 2015 gemeinsam mit dem ÖKF-Budapest organisiertes Symposium zum Eurovision Song Contest. Anlass war der wenige Tage später in Wien ausgetragene Musikwettbewerb. Auch hier konnte ein Vortragender des Instituts für Osteuropäische Geschichte der Universität Wien begrüßt werden, nämlich der Marie-Curie Fellow Dean Vuletic. Neben mehreren Referaten zum Thema fand auch eine Podiumsdiskussion statt, an der auch zwei Musiker teilnahmen: András Kállay-Saunders aus Ungarn (Teilnehmer am ESC 2014 in Kopenhagen) sowie Nadine Beiler aus Österreich (Teilnehmerin am ESC 2011 in Düsseldorf). Ein höchst beeindruckender Live-Aufritt von Nadine Beiler beschloss die Veranstaltung.

Höhepunkt des Sommersemesters war schließlich die zweitägige Konferenz 'Österreich 1945–1955–1995' vom 20. Mai bis 21. Mai 2015. Auch hier gelang es, zahlreiche Experten aus Österreich, Ungarn und Deutschland zu versammeln. Diese Veranstaltung wurde ebenfalls mit Unterstützung des ÖKF organisiert.

Den Abschluss des wissenschaftlichen Programms des Sommersemesters 2015 bildete ein von Ursula Mindler-Steiner organisierter Gastvortrag von Anna Cichopek-Gajraj von der Arizona State University. Sie sprach über 'A Comparative Approach to the Postwar History of Jews in Poland'. Vortrag und Diskussion wurden von András Kovács (CEU) moderiert.

Besonders erfreulich war die Intensivierung der Zusammenarbeit mit den anderen Österreich- und Ostmitteleuropa Zentren (Austrian and Central European Centers). Großer Dank gilt dabei Ingeborg Fialová-Fürst für die Einladung zu einer Konferenz im Oktober 2014 und Marija Wakounig für die Einladung zu einer Konferenz im Dezember 2014. Das Sommersemester 2015 durfte Georg Kastner als Gastprofessor an der Universiteit Leiden (Niederlande) verbringen.

Mit Ende des Sommersemesters schied Prof. Arnold Suppan als Professurleiter aus und trat in den wohlverdienten Ruhestand. Für die jahrelange Unterstützung der Aufbauarbeit von Fachbereich, Fakultät und Universität gebührt ihm ganz besonderer Dank.

Ruth Fine

Center for Austrian Studies: Activities Report 2014

Hebrew University of Jerusalem

Last year has indeed been a very active and fruitful period of academic and cultural and activities for the Center for Austrian Studies at the European Forum, the Hebrew University of Jerusalem, thanks to the ongoing support of the Austrian Ministry of Foreign Affairs, the Austrian Ministry of Education, Science and Culture, and the Friends of the Hebrew University in Austria. We have organized symposia, lectures, conferences, and workshops on Austrian issues, promoting the academic contact between Austrian and Israelis scholars and students. In the following pages, I will summarize the broad spectrum of our activities and achievements.

Research Grants

The Center for Austrian Studies provides various individual research grants so as to encourage young scholars and students to actively participate in research projects. After a call for papers was issued, the scholarship committee of the center assessed the research proposals. The research-grant recipients are required to submit the results of their year-long work in a paper to be published in the Working Paper Series of the European Forum.

Three research grants were provided by the City of Vienna:

- Aaron Menczer Fund
  Translation and publication of the book Joanna Nittenberg – Benjamin Kaufmann (Eds.), Trotz allem ... Aron Menczer und die Jugendalijah to Hebrew.
- Gilad Sharvit, PhD candidate, Department of Philosophy 'Freud and the Critic of Religion: Therapy and Religious Practice'
- Prof. Yoav Rinon, Department of German Language and Literature 'Karl Kraus: translation and Publication of Selected Writings'

One research grant was granted jointly by the Center for Austrian Studies and the IWM (Institut für die Wissenschaften vom Menschen [Institute for Human Sciences], Vienna): Assaf Ashkenazi, post-doctoral fellow, Program in European Studies, 'Hebrew Translations and Adaptations of Iberian Literature'.

Student Stipends

- Omri Ben-Yehuda, PhD candidate at the European Forum at the Hebrew University
  Research topic: Analysis of Voice and Voices. Kafka and Agnon; Supervisors: Hanan Hever (Department of Hebrew Literature, The Hebrew University of Jerusalem) and Galili Shahar (Department of Comparative Literature, Tel Aviv University);
- Susi Cohen-Weisz, Post-doctoral fellow at the European Forum at the Hebrew University
  Research topic: Strengthening Jewish Group Identity and European-Jewish Identity in Germany and Vienna; Supervisor: Peter Medding (Department of History of the Jewish People and Contemporary Jewry);
- Moran Pearl, PhD candidate at the European Forum at the Hebrew University
  Research topic: Books and Libraries as Witnesses of the Holocaust. Monuments in Vienna, Berlin and Jerusalem; Supervisor: Bianca Kühnel (Department of the History of Art, The Hebrew University of Jerusalem);
- Shimrit Shriki, PhD candidate at the European Forum at the Hebrew University
  Research topic: National-religious commemorative practice within the context of Jerusalem emulations in Germany and Austria; Supervisor: Bianca Kühnel (Department of History of the Jewish People and Contemporary Jewry, The Hebrew University of Jerusalem);
- András Sziklai, PhD studies at the European Forum at the Hebrew University
  Research topic: Shaping Jewish Public Opinion in Hungary at the Turn of the 20th Century. The Weekly Egyenlőség (Equality) and Its Editor Miksa Szabolcsi; Supervisor: Michael K. Silber (Department of History of the Jewish People and Contemporary Jewry, The Hebrew University of Jerusalem)
- Ofer Waldman, PhD candidate at the European Forum at the Hebrew University
  Research topic: Encountering the Diachronic Neighbors. Historical Archaeology in North-Western Bohemia; Supervisor: Yfaat Weiss (Department of History of the Jewish People and Contemporary Jewry, The Hebrew University of Jerusalem)
- Sara Yanovsky, Post-doctoral fellow at the European Forum at the Hebrew University
  Research topic: Facing the Challenge of Jewish Education in the Metropolis. A Comparative Study of the Jewish Communal Organizations of Budapest and Vienna, from 1867 until World War II; Supervisor: Michael K. Silber (Department of History of the Jewish People and Contemporary Jewry, The Hebrew University of Jerusalem)

Travel Scholarship

- Yuval Lubin, MA student, Department of English, The Hebrew University of Jerusalem (The University of Salzburg and the Stefan Zweig Center, Salzburg, Austria, 24–25 January 2014)
  Presentation: 'Knowing the Unknown. A Comparison between the Short Story and the Movie "Letters form and Unknown Woman" Austria and America: Cross-Cultural Encounters 1933–1955'

Language Scholarship

The Center for Austrian Studies grants 30 students from the Hebrew University scholarships for a two-month intensive language course at the University of Vienna. These scholarships include flight cost as well as dormitory and tuition fees. The scholarships are funded by the Austrian Foreign Ministry, the Austrian Ministry of Science, Research and Economy, the Austrian Friends of the Hebrew University and the Center for Austrian Studies, the Helmut Zilk Fonds für internationale Beziehungen Wien, and the University of Vienna.

In addition, the center grants 19 students from the Hebrew University scholarships for two- or three-week intensive language courses at different Austrian universities: Graz, Klagenfurt, Salzburg, Innsbruck, and Linz. Theses scholarships are funded by the hosting universities and the Austrian Friends of the Hebrew University and the Center for Austrian Studies, and cover the dormitory and tuition fees.

The language scholarships are granted to students from different faculties and departments of the Hebrew University who need an extensive knowledge of German for their academic work. Many of these students also deal directly with Austria or the Austrian legacy in Central Europe.

Conferences, Workshops and Guest Lectures

- Annual Convention der Österreich-Zentren, Leiden, NL, 23–27 October 2013.
  This year's annual convention, organized by the Austrian Ministry for Science, Research and Economy was held in Leiden (The Netherlands). The Center for Austrian Studies was represented by its director, Prof. Ruth Fine, and two of its MA students, who presented their research projects:Ofer Waldman ('Ich wollte zeigen, wir sind da – Searching for Traces in the Former Sudetenland') and Paz Zvick ('On the Rise of Extreme-Right Parties in Post-Communist Countries in Central and Eastern Europe').
- International Conference, 'Freud and the Humanities Revisited: Literature and Literary Criticism in Freuian Context Today', 9–10 October 2013.
  In cooperation with the Mandel Institute of Jewish Studies, the Center for Research on the History and Culture of Polish Jewry, Leo Baeck Institute Jerusalem, the Institute for the History of Polish Jewry and Israel-Poland Re-

lations, Tel Aviv University, the Project of the Jews in Galicia and Bukovina, Herzl Institute, University of Haifa, and Jewish Galicia and Bukovina Association. Although Freud's main aim was aiding human beings by means of psychoanalysis, his lifelong interest in literature is a constant presence in his writing. In fact, as Freud himself confessed more than once, his understanding of the human psyche was sometimes based on, and often reflected in, the literary works of the authors he so admired. Whether it is Goethe's Faust, frequently quoted in his writing, or Jensen's "Gradiva" serving as a model of psychotherapy, his discussion of Dostoevsky or his analysis of the uncanny, all attest to Freud's unabashed admiration for the humanities in general and literature in particular. The aim of the conference was to utilize Freudian insights in order to shed new light on literary works and literary criticism. Freud's prolific and fertile thought, so exquisitely manifest in his varied fields of interest and research, served as the basis of the papers in this conference. We believe that this Freudian reconsideration enriched both theoretical investigations and understanding of literary works, renewing our apprehension of Freud's relevance to contemporary thinking about literature.

- International Conference, 'Revealers of Secrets – 200 Years of Galician Haskalah', 22–25 December 2013.

  The year 2013 marked the bicentennial of two initiatives that were the beginning of the Haskalah movement in Galicia: the establishment of a modern Jewish school and the composition of a Hebrew maskilic journal by one of the leaders of the movement, Joseph Perl. Galicia was one of the three major centers of the Haskalah, along with Germany and the Russian Empire. The center in Galicia led the Haskalah in the first half of the 19th century, paving new paths in Jewish culture and Jewish thought, 'Wissenschaft des Judentums', Hebrew and Yiddish literature, and Jewish nationalism. Despite the central role of the Galician Haskalah in shaping the face of modern European Judaism and the image of the modern Jew, its place in Haskalah historiography is less prominent than that of the other two centers. The conference focus was a renewed discussion and a comprehensive consideration of the Galician Haskalah.

- 1st meeting of the Austria-Israel Salon, 'The Challenges of Austrian-Israeli Relations', 4 March 2014, in cooperation with the forum 'Young Israelis Meeting Austria'.

  The economic crisis, rising right wing extremism, coping with the memories of the *Shoa*, the Arab-Israeli conflict, and the implications of these developments on the Jewish community in Austria are topics that were discussed. Speakers: H.E. Aviv Shir-On, Former Ambassador of Israel to Austria, and H.E.Dr. Franz Josef Kuglitsch, Ambassador of Austria to Israel. Respondent: Dr. Ben Segenreich, Journalist, expert for the Arab-Israeli conflict for Austrian Broadcasting ORF and the Austrian newspaper *Der Standard*.

- 'Europe Day', 12 May 2014, in cooperation with the Delegation of the European Union to the State of Israel.

  Celebrating Europe Day at the Hebrew University is a well-established tradition initiated and organized by the European Forum. Throughout the years, Europe Day was commemorated with a strong emphasis on reaching to the general public, bringing key speakers from academia and the policy arena to speak and debate at the Hebrew University. Europe Day 2014 furthered this tradition by blending together academic excellence with a festive celebration of the European spirit. Europe Day comprised of two events: an academic conference and a Eurofest, featuring Café Europe, Prize winning contest, live music and more. All events were free and open for students and the general public.
- Eurofest, 12 May 2014

  Information stands of EU member states and cultural institutes at the 'Forum' of Mount Scopus campus.

  Europe Day Colloquium: Prof. Enrique Barón Crespo, Jean Monnet Chair, Universidad de Castilla la Mancha; Former President of the European Parliament, H.E. Ambassador Lars Faaborg-Andresen, Head of the European Union Delegation to the State of Israel, Prof. Alfred Tovias, Jean Monnet Chair, the Hebrew University of Jerusalem.
- 2nd meeting of the Austria-Israel Salon, 'The Role of Culture in Foreign Policy', 12 June 2014, in cooperation with the forum 'Young Israelis Meeting Austria'.

  Speaker: H.E.Dr. Martin Eichtinger, Director General for Cultural Policy at the Austrian Federal Ministry for European and International Affairs.

- International Conference in Salzburg, 'Perceptions and Translations of Jerusalem in German and Italian Speaking Areas', 3–8 August 2014, in cooperation with SPE©TRUM | Visual Translations of Jerusalem and the University of Salzburg.

Publications

Monograph

- Neta Bodner, Walking to 'Jerusalem' from Vienna: A Seventeenth-Century Way of the Cross, Jerusalem 2014. (In cooperation with SPE©TRUM | Visual Translations of Jerusalem)

  Neta Bodner is a PhD candidate at the European Forum and a research fellow in the project SPE©TRUM | Visual Translations of Jerusalem.

Working papers

- Nir Cohem, Department of Musicology, 'Gideon Klein: Life and Music'.
- Lotem Pinchover, Program in European Studies, 'Tradition and Innovation in the Former Cathedral of Gurk'.

Teaching

Visiting Lecturers

During the previous Academic Year, the Center for Austrian Studies hosted two guest lecturers, who taught intensive courses which discussed Austrian issues:

Paul Michael Lützeler, Washington University in St. Louis, Rosa May Distinguished University Professor in the Humanities, Director of the Max Kade Center for Contemporary German Literature, 9–13 March 2014, 'Exiled and Cosmopolitan Authors on Europe (1933–2012)'

The course dealt with essays written by German and Austrian authors who either were exiled writers during the Nazi period of the 1930s and 1940s (Thomas Mann, Klaus Mann, Hilde Spiel, and Manès Sperber) or were part of the inner emigration and resistance (Reinhold Schneider). In addition, contemporary cosmopolitan essayists like Hans Magnus Enzensberger, Adolf Muschg, and Robert Menasse were included. What these writers have in common is their conviction that there exists a common multifaceted European culture that is worth to be defended against racism, chauvinism, totalitarianism and consumerism. What they are concerned about is less the political institutionalization of a united Europe but rather the awareness of a cultural heritage that is based on the dialogic relation of its components (Antiquity, Judaism, Christianity, and Enlightenment).

Günter J. Bischof, Marshall Plan Professor of History, Director, CenterAustria, University of New Orleans, 15–18 June 2014, 'Building Bridges Across the Cold War Abyss: The Vienna Summit of 1961'

The course covered the history of a special moment in the Cold War when détente seemed a possibility. The issues discussed by President Kennedy and Chairman Khrushchev were vital Cold War crisis points in the early 1960s – Berlin/the German Question, Cuba, Laos/Vietnam & Decolonization, nuclear disarmament. We studied these Cold War crises along with the leaders of the two superpowers and their respective views on these issues. Both Cold War Summitry and the Vienna summit venue as well as Austrian neutrality in the Cold War will also be covered.

Study Trip

- Prof. Israel Yuval and Prof. Michael Toch, the Hebrew University of Jerusalem
  'A Town in the Country: Vienna and its Satellites'
  In cooperation with the Teddy Kollek Chair for the Study of Cultural Aspects of Vienna and Jerusalem

This year the Center for Austrian Studies, together with the Teddy Kollek Chair for the Study of Cultural Aspects of Vienna and Jerusalem, conducted a one-week study tour to Vienna, Nikolsburg (Mikulov), Regensburg and Munich. We discussed the encounter between Jewish and non-Jewish history in Vienna and its surrounding towns in Medieval Ages and in Modern Times. The Vienna program included a visit to the old city center, its churches and synagogues, the Jewish Museum, and two Holocaust memorials. Most of the tours were guided by scholars from the Institut für Geschichte der Juden in Österreich, specializing in the history of Vienna and its Jews. Nikolsburg, a small town on the Czech-Austrian border, is an example for a number of Moravian towns that served as a staging point for massive Jewish emigration to Vienna at the turn of the 19th century from east to west, which changed the Jewish demography profoundly, and created cultural phenomena in the cities of Western metropolis, Vienna, Berlin, London, and New York. We toured the Jewish Quarter, the oldest synagogue (though not medieval), the fortress, and the Jewish cemetery, which served all the communities in Moravia from the 17th century. In Regensburg, we met students from Ludwig-Maximilians-University of Munich led by Professor Eva Haverkamp, a historian of the Middle Ages. The two groups toured together in the new archaeological excavations, which uncovered parts of the Jewish Quarter of the city extant until the expulsion in the year 1519. We also visited the monastery and the church of Sankt Emmeram and the Scottish church – two sites that were probably the source of inspiration for the Pietistic movement known as 'Ashkenazi Hasidism' and the legend of Rabbi Amnon of Mainz. In Munich, we visited the Pinakothek, concentrating on works related to the history of the Jews, primarily the monumental drawing by Wilhelm von Kaulbach 'The Destruction of Jerusalem'. In addition, we visited a number of buildings relevant to the city's Nazi past. The academic goal of the tour was to make history present at its occurrence and to draw attention to the importance of the acquaintance with the physical environment in understanding the history of ideas. This issue is of crucial importance to Israeli students studying Jewish history in general and German history in particular. The purpose of the tour was to point out the constant symbiosis between the history of the Jewish minority and majority groups.

Austrian Film Forum

For several years, the Austrian Film Forum has offered the opportunity to view a selection of Austrian films at the Hebrew University of Jerusalem. It has been established by the Center for Austrian Studies, in cooperation with the Austrian Library at the Hebrew University and is open and accessible for the general public. The viewers shall get acquainted with various aspects of Austrian history, society, and culture, in addition to several courses and lectures at the university, which deal specifically with those issues.

This year's Film Forum was launched by screening the expressionist epos 'The City Without Jews' (1924) by Hans Karl Breslauer, which can be valued as a satirical response to the primitive Anti-Semitism in Austria before World War II. Anat Varon, a PhD student at the department of History at the Hebrew University, presented the film by giving a lecture, discussing the historical background and cultural context in the film.

During the second semester, the Austrian Film Forum presented a series of films about Austria after World War II. Each film told a different story and delivered a different image of the Second Austrian Republic, as well as the Nazi era. One of the principal purposes of this year's Film Forum was to give its viewers an impression of how Austria's popular picture has changed throughout the decades after World War II. For example, while many Austrian film productions of the 1940s, 50s and 60s only made shy references to the events of World War II, Austrian mainstream cinema from the 1980s onwards put a stronger focus to the Nazi era. Again, Anat Varon agreed to give another interesting lecture in the framework of the Film Forum, presenting the cinematic adoptions of the history and the fate of the Trapp Family whose story became famous through the musical 'The Sound of Music'.

At our closing event we will have the great pleasure of welcoming an another special guest, Prof. Walter Manoschek from the University of Vienna (Deartment of Government), who will present his latest documentary 'Dann bin ich ja ein Mörder'. This film has been prised by Nobel Prize laureate Elfride Jelinek for delivering a highly valuable and objective portrait of the perpetrators and the victims of the so-called 'Deutsch Schützen massacre', a 1945 mass killing of approximately 60 Jewish forced laborers at the Austrian-Hungarian border. This event was supported and sponsored by the Culture Forum of the Austrian Embassy in Tel Aviv.

Each screening included a brief introduction by Martin Stechauner, this year's research fellow at the Center for Austrian Studies, providing some historical, social, and political context. At the end of each screening there was an optional debate on questions raised by the films. Not all of the featured films in our program were exclusive Austrian productions; however, each film dealt with Austria or Austrian history in its own cinematographic way.

These are the movies that were shown:

- Die Stadt ohne Juden [The City without Jews, 1924], 12 January 2014
  Lecture by Ms. Anat Varon, PhD candidate, Department of History, the Hebrew University of Jerusalem, Director: Hans Karl Breslauer
- Der Dritte Mann [The Third Man, 1949], 18 February 2014
  Director: Carol Reed
- Der Hofrat Geiger [Hofrat Geiger, 1947], 4 March 2014
  Director: Hans Wolff

- Die Trapp-Familie in Amerika [The Sound of Music II, 1958], 25 March 2014
  Lecture by Ms. Anat Varon, PhD candidate, Department of History, the Hebrew University of Jerusalem, Director: Wolfgang Liebeneiner
- Im weißen Rößl [The White Horse Inn, 1960], 29 April 2014
  Director: Werner Jacobs
- Der Bockerer [Bockerer, 1981], 13 May 2014
  Director: Franz Antel
- Die Fälscher [The Counterfeiters, 2007], 27 May 2014
  Director: Stefan Ruzowitzky
- Dann bin ich ja ein Mörder [So I Am a Murderer, 2012], 10 June 2014
  Presented by the director, Prof. Walter Manoschek, Department of Government, University of Vienna, in cooperation with the Culture Forum of the Austrian Embassy in Tel Aviv, Director: Walter Manoschek

Austrian Library

The Austrian Library, incorporated into the Bloomfiled Library for the Humanities and Social Sciences, contained in 2009 3687 books. Since it is a reference library, it is not easy to estimate how often and how many of these books are used. However 520 of these books have been borrowed in 2009.

The Center for Austrian Studies has organized its own reference library for students and scholars and has set up working space for its students and research fellows. With these steps, the Center became a vivid point of intellectual exchange.

Jeroen Duindam

The Leiden Austria Center in 2014: Towards a Wider Horizon?

Leiden University

After the successful 2013 Annual Convention in Leiden, plans to broaden the scope of the activities of the Leiden Foundation for Austrian Studies [*Stichting Oostenrijkse Studiën*] took shape rapidly. In a series of meetings with Hugo Weiland, Patrick Dassen, and Jeroen Duindam with Prof. Dr. Petr Kopecky (Leiden Political Science Department) and Dr Antoaneta Dimitrova, (Leiden-related The Hague Campus), a plan for a Center for Central and Eastern European Studies has been developed. Ideally, this Leiden-based center will form a meeting point for colleagues from other Dutch universities dealing with Central European history and culture. Now, almost a year later, the Center is approaching its inauguration. The Center will start a speakers' series, while the long-established activities of the Foundation, notably the visiting professorship in the second semester of every Academic Year, will continue. In this new constellation, the Leiden contribution to the Annual Conventions will probably become more interdisciplinary.

The planning of the 2014 Minneapolis Annual Convention in late September rather than in late October prevented the Leiden Center to contribute this year: these weeks are a critical moment in the start of the Dutch semester, and leave no space for travel. We deplore our absence, but understand from various reports that it in no way undermined the Convention, which again was productive and successful intellectually as well as socially – the hallmark of our meetings.

The ongoing activities of the Leiden History Institute related to Central Europe, soon to be fitted into the larger context of the Center for Central and Eastern European Studies, can be summarised in the names of several researchers. Jovan Pešalj's dissertation on borders, migration and state control in the 18th century Habsburg monarchy, co-supervised by Leiden and Vienna colleagues, approaches completion. Dr. Felicia Rosu, likewise, currently finishes the final chapters of her comparative study of the Polish and Transylvanian elective monarchies in the 16th century. Dr. Patrick Dassen's newly published major study on Germany and the First World War "Sprong in het duister. Duitsland en de Eerste Wereldoorlog"[1] was widely praised in Dutch media and acclaimed by a wide reading public. Profiting from a sabbatical in the second semester of 2013/2014 and the outstanding support of

1 Patrick Dassen, Sprong in het duister. Duitsland en de Eerste Wereldoorlog [Leap in the Dark. Germany and the First World War], Amsterdam 2014.

the Netherlands Institute of Advanced Studies in Wassenaar, I was able to finish a global comparative study of dynastic rule, to be published by Cambridge University Press in 2015: "Dynasties. A Global History of Power 1300–1800."[2] The work on this book entailed lectures in, among others, Trinity College Dublin, Bern University Switzerland, and the German Historical Institute in Rome.

In the first months of 2015, the Leiden History Department had several job openings; our expectation now, after a series of job interviews with relevant candidates, is that Central Europe will become a stronger presence in our staff, in terms of personnel and publications. Further details will follow in our next report. The renewal of the special chair for Central European Studies, temporarily left vacant upon the retirement of Prof. Dr. Nicolette Mout, occupies an important position among the plans of the Foundation. In the coming two years we hope to convince the university board that renewal of this special chair will provide a better basis for the Austrian and Central European connections at Leiden University. The activities of the Center for Central and Eastern European Studies, ideally under the aegis of a future special chair, may also lead to a change in responsibilities of the Foundation board – we hope it will allow our venerable but ever-active chair Hugo Weiland to gradually leave some of his responsibilities to others.

Following the successful visiting professorship of the Vienna musicologist Prof. Dr. Marie-Agnes Dittrich in 2013/2014, we were happy to find another outstanding candidate. Prof. Dr. Georg Kastner, known to all of us as director of the Budapest Austria Center based at the Andrássy University, is the Foundation's visiting professor to Leiden in the summer semester of 2014/2015. He has been teaching two courses, a lecture course on 'Central Europe 1713–1914: The Habsburg Empire between the Pragmatic Sanction and World War I', and a seminar titled: 'A Spontaneous National Uprising. The Hungarian Revolution 1956'. At this moment, it already has become clear that the Leiden students appreciate the themes as well as the excellent teaching of Georg Kastner, who thus amply confirms the reputation of his predecessors in our visiting professorship.

On another note, we need to consider that the Austrian *Universitätsgesetz* of 2002 makes it more difficult to invite professors from Austria to Leiden according to the Foundation's standard practice. In the past, Institutes were able and willing to gracefully allow their faculty members to teach at Leiden, without expecting financial compensation for their absence. Recent experiences show this may no longer be the case. Increasingly, institutes expect full compensation of teaching tasks (*i.e.* money for replacement) before endorsing the leave of faculty.

Our ambitions and efforts would not have been possible without the help of our Viennese friends and sponsors Florian Gerhardus and Dr. Christoph Ramoser as well as the support of the Austrian ambassador Dr. Werner Druml whose cordial presence remains a cornerstone of our activities.

---

2 Jeroen Duindam, Dynasties. A Global History of Power 1300–1800, Cambridge 2015.

Daniel Pinkerton and Gary B. Cohen

The Center for Austrian Studies at the University of Minnesota

University of Minnesota

Founded in 1977, the Center for Austrian Studies at the University of Minnesota (CAS) serves as an international leader in promoting new scholarship about Austria and Central Europe across disciplines in the humanities, the social sciences, international business management, and the fine arts. The Center also connects scholars, students, and an international community to resources in Minnesota, Austria, Central Europe, and the EU, and enriches the teaching mission of the university and the College of Liberal Arts by connecting its research and outreach programs with classroom opportunities for students.

From July 2010 through June 2014, Klaas van der Sanden served as interim director with great dedication and energy, while still attending to other significant duties in our Institute for Global Studies. A new permanent director for the Center, Howard Louthan, was named in late spring 2014. Since Howard cannot begin his duties until late summer 2015 and Klaas needed to get back to full-time service in the Institute for Global Studies, Gary Cohen agreed to return to CAS as interim director for 2014/2015.

In 2014/2015, the CAS had a busy and productive year. We started it by hosting the annual meeting of the Austrian and Central European Centers from around the world. The first meeting was held in 2007 at the University of Minnesota – a fitting choice, since our CAS was the first such center outside of the Austrian Republic and is North America's oldest interdisciplinary center for Habsburg and post-Habsburg study. It was hosted subsequently by each of the other institutions except Olomouc before returning to the University of Minnesota in 2014. The 2014 meeting was a wonderful combination of stimulating scholarly presentations by graduate students from Andrássy University in Budapest, the Wirth Institute in Canada, Hebrew University in Jerusalem, CenterAustria in New Orleans, the Institute of East European History of the Vienna University, and Palacký University in Olomouc, the Czech Republic; opportunities to connect again with friends and colleagues; and, as is usual at these meetings, an opportunity to see some of the host city. CAS took the attendees on a Mississippi River cruise and gave them some free time to go to museums and musical and theatrical performances. Arnold Suppan, well-known historian of modern East-Central and Southeast Europe, gave a scholarly lecture. We are most grateful to Barbara Weitgruber, Christoph Ramoser, and everyone at the Bundesministerium für Wissenschaft, Forschung, und Wirtschaft (BMWFW) for continuing this important tradition.

Including Suppan's lecture, the Center for Austrian Studies presented eleven lectures representing a range of disciplines during the 2014/2015 Academic Year.

- Tuesday, 16 September: Arnold Suppan, history, University of Vienna and Austrian Academy of Sciences. 'Hitler – Beneš – Tito. Conflict, War, and Genocide in East-Central and South-East Europe.' Cosponsored by the BMWFW.
- Wednesday, 8 October: John Deak, history, University of Notre Dame. 'The Unraveling of the Habsburg Empire: New Perspectives on Austria-Hungary's Internal War in 1914.'
- Tuesday, 28 October: Kimberly Zarecor, architecture and architectural history, Iowa State University. 'Why Ostrava Is Not Detroit: Communist Legacies in a Post-Communist Industrial City.' Cosponsored by the Department of Geography, the University of Pittsburgh Press, and the Andrew M. Mellon Foundation.
- Wednesday, 19 November: The 30th Annual Robert A. Kann Memorial Lecture. James Tracy, history, University of Minnesota. 'Habsburg-Ottoman Wars, 1526–1606: A Clash of Civilizations.'
- Wednesday, 11 February: Christian Karner, sociology and social policy, University of Nottingham. 'Signs of the Nation: Resisting Globalization?'
- Wednesday, 25 February: Jeffrey Chipps Smith, Kay Fortson Chair in European Art, University of Texas, Austin. 'Emperor Rudolf II and the Mysterious Obsession of Collecting.' Cosponsored by the Department of Art History.
- Wednesday, 11 March: Larry Silver, Farquhar Professor of Art History, University of Pennsylvania. 'Maximilian I, Charles V, and the Formation of the Habsburg Monarchy.' Cosponsored by the Department of Art History.
- Friday, 13 March: Jessica Keating, art history, Carleton College: 'Collecting Exotica at Early Modern Habsburg Courts.' Cosponsored by the Center for Early Modern History.
- Wednesday, 1 April: Eike D. Schmidt, James Ford Bell Curator of Decorative Arts and Sculpture, Minneapolis Institute of Arts. 'Empire & Enlightenment: Sculpture and Decorative Arts in 18th Century Vienna.' Cosponsored by the Department of Art History.
- Wednesday, 22 April: Irmgard Wetzstein, communication studies, University of Vienna. 'Debating Alternative Gender Identities in Austria: The Case of the Viennese Life Ball 2014.'
- Friday, 24 April: Lecture. Thomas Wallnig, history, University of Vienna, Visiting Fulbright Scholar, Stanford University. 'Critical Monks: The German Benedictines, 1680–1740.' Cosponsored by the Center for Early Modern History.

- Thursday, 30 April: Lecture. Carl Neumayr, sociology, Karl-Franzens University, Graz, BMWFW Fellow. 'Professor as Profession: A Review of Faculty Surveys, 1960s-Present.'

The lectures by Smith, Silver, Keating, and Schmidt were held in conjunction with the exhibit 'The Habsburgs: Rarely Seen Masterpieces from Europe's Greatest Dynasty', which the Kunsthistorisches Museum Wien sent to the Minneapolis Institute of Arts from 15 February to 10 May. These lectures were extremely popular, filling a large lecture room with faculty, students, and community members. The Kann Memorial Lecture, as has been the case in recent years, also attracted a full house.

Other cosponsored events included musical performances, workshops, and lectures:

- Thursday, 5 February: Concert. The Bakken Trio. Performance of Arnold Schönberg's 'Verklärte Nacht' [Transfigured Night] in the original string sextet version. Schönberg scholar Michael Cherlin, School of Music, gave introductory remarks and led a post-performance discussion. Cosponsored by the Institute for Advanced Study.
- Friday, 20 February: Concert. The Schubert Trio and Friends: 'A Schubertiade' featuring works of Schubert, Albrechtsberger, and Brahms.
- Tuesday, 14 April: Lecture. Yehudit Shendar, retired deputy director, Museum, Yad Vashem, Jerusalem. 'The Insatiable Pursuit of Art: Nazi Art Looting – Perpetrators, Victims, Provenance Researchers.' Cosponsored with the Centers for Holocaust and Genocide Studies, Jewish Studies, and German & European Studies; the Weisman Art Museum, the Department of Art History; and Hillel: The Jewish Student Center.
- Saturday, 25 April: Teacher Workshop: 'World War I and the Armenian Genocide.' Heller Hall. Cosponsored by the Center for Holocaust and Genocide Studies.
- Friday–Sunday, 15–17 May: Symposium. 'Gender and Global Warfare in the 20th Century.' Cosponsored by the Departments of History and Gender, Women's, & Sexuality Studies; Institute for Advanced Studies: African Studies Initiative; and the Interdisciplinary Center for the Study of Global Change.

The Center continued to support research by scholars and graduate students:

- The generosity of David and Rosemary Good enabled us to continue the CAS book and dissertation prize competitions. The 2014 CAS prizes, awarded in the fall, went to Dominique K. Reill for her book "Nationalists Who Feared the Nation" (Stanford University Press, 2012) and to Anita Kurimay for her dissertation, 'Sex in the 'Pearl of the Danube': The History of Queer Life, Love, and Its Regulation in Budapest, 1873–1941' (defended at Rutgers University, 2012).

- The Center once again awarded summer research grants to University of Minnesota graduate students for 2015. They went to Jeffrey Martin (School of Music) and Dylan Mohr (Cultural Studies and Comparative Literature).
- The Voices of Vienna Scholarship, created and funded by Kathryn and the late Wilbur C. Keefer in honor of William E. Wright, founding director of CAS, is awarded to graduate students from the College of Liberal Arts and the School of Music in alternating years. In 2015, it was awarded to Jeffrey Martin (School of Music).

The Austrian government continued to support CAS in many ways. One of the most important was the continuation of the BMWFW/CAS Fellowship, which sends an Austrian graduate student to the Center each year for ten months to do doctoral research and writing. The 2014/2015 Fellow was Carl Neumayr, from the Institute of Sociology at the Karl-Franzens University of Graz. His PhD thesis concerns quantitative approaches to surveys of professors in the United States and Austria. Carl also gave a presentation in the lecture series (see above) and assisted the Center in the areas of social networking and new media.

On 10 August 2001, the University of Minnesota's College of Liberal Arts (CLA) and the Austrian Fulbright Commission signed an agreement creating the Fulbright Visiting Professorship (FVP) at the University of Minnesota. CLA students and colleagues benefit, as the FVP creates expanded course offerings with fresh points of view and fosters new transatlantic research collaborations. This collaboration continued in 2014/2015. This year's FVP, the twelfth in the series, was Irmgard Wetzstein, a senior lecturer at the University of Vienna's Department of Communication. She was in residence in the School of Journalism and Mass Communication for spring semester 2015. Her research interests include societal and discursive potentials as well as technological implications of social media, political communication, conflict communication, journalism, social research methods, and advertising. She taught a graduate seminar in communications theory and gave lectures at the Center and the School of Journalism.

The publications of the Center for Austrian Studies last year continued our strong traditions. 'The Austrian Studies Newsmagazine', edited by Daniel Pinkerton, continued to appear twice a year. Copies were mailed out to over 2,700 subscribers, primarily (but not exclusively) in North America and Europe. Volume 45 of the peer-reviewed scholarly journal, 'The Austrian History Yearbook', edited by Pieter Judson, came out in April. It was one of the richest volumes the Center has produced; its 447 pages contained a revised version of James Tracy's Kann Memorial Lecture, 13 articles, and forty-two book reviews. The R. John Rath Article Prize for 2014 went to Michael O'Sullivan for 'A Hungarian Josephinist, Orientalist, and Bibliophile: Count Karl Reviczky, 1737–1793.' No new volumes came out in 2014/2015 in our book series with Berghahn Books, Austrian and Habsburg Studies, but several volumes are under consideration.

The Center had some staffing changes for 2014/2015. Mollie Madden, the longtime assistant editor of the 'Austrian History Yearbook', completed her PhD in medieval history, and Sharon Park took her position. Christopher Flynn started as a graduate assistant, worked on an edited volume, and was chief copyeditor for the 'Austrian Studies Newsmagazine'. Finally, Dr. Kevin Mummey did splendid work both as an editorial assistant and as a program director until January, 2015. He was replaced by Jennifer Hammer, and we welcome her to the CAS staff.

Finally, the Center benefits each year from the generosity of a number of private donors. We are grateful for every one of them. For 2014/2015, we wish to acknowledge in particular the gifts of David and Rosemary Good; of Peter Kann, son of the late Robert A. Kann; and especially of Bruce Pauley, retired professor of Habsburg and Austrian history. The support of these donors was most welcome and, in the case of Dr. Pauley, completely unsolicited. We thank them heartily for their contributions.

Günter Bischof

CenterAustria: 2014 Annual Report

University of New Orleans

Student and Faculty Exchanges

Incoming and outgoing student exchange programs with the University of Innsbruck are continuing with considerable success. Incoming to UNO were 59 Innsbruck students taking courses at UNO, most of them for a semester (42 in the fall of 2013, 17 in the spring of 2014), a few stayed for the entire Academic Year of 2013/2014. Three students spent a year at UNO on scholarships. Katrin Lisa Voggenberger, a business education major from the University of Innsbruck held the CenterAustria fellowship and contributed to our regular office work. Martina Prugger, a PhD candidate in the Applied Mathematics at the University of Innsbruck, was the 2013/2014 Nick Mueller Fellow (she found most of her professional contacts at Tulane University). Markus Habermann, a PhD candidate in Political Science from the University of Vienna, was the Austrian Ministry of Science Fellow. He worked on his Vienna dissertation on the topic of "Emotion in Political Communication: Can Austrian Politicians Learn from American Politicians?".

24 students from universities all over Austria (including Graz and Vienna) participated in the 'Austrian Student Program' – a *Schnupperstudium* at an American university during their semester break in February and took 'American Studies' courses in History, Political Science, Sociology, and Economics. 2014 was the last

Innsbruck Students Welcome, Aug. 2014.

time this program was organized. After more than 30 years of its existence, the University of Innsbruck is coming up with a new format, namely some type of graduate student conference on specific themes, a kind of 'winter school' at UNO.

Given the numerous University of Innsbruck student cohorts who have studied at UNO in past years, a UNO-Austrian Alumni Association Chapter Innsbruck was founded some years ago; they organize regular student orientation meetings and reunions in Innsbruck, usually in late June before the UNO-Innsbruck Summer School Program begins its session.

The UNO International Summer School in Innsbruck is organized by the Division of International Education at UNO. Attending the 39th Summer School in Innsbruck were 270 American students from all over the South (about a dozen UNO students among them) and 24 faculty members from more than 20 universities; Günter Bischof directed the summer school in 2014 (beginning of July to mid-August 2014). Some 50 Innsbruck students enrolled in summer school classes too. Moreover, a dozen students attended our 'Academic Year Abroad' semester/year-long program in Innsbruck.

Conferences/Workshops

Center Austria organized with Professor Klaus Franz of the University of Innsbruck's Department of Geography the Annual UNO – Innsbruck Conference. The March 2014 meeting was on the topic of 'Enduring Cultures: Indigenous Responses to Changing Environments in the 21st Century'. Speakers from the US, Finland, Sweden, and Russia explored the difficult environmental challenges of native American tribes and European indigenous people, especially the Sami of Scandinavia and Russia.

The speakers of the 'Indigenous Peoples' conference went on a field trip to explore the Houma native American tribe of Louisiana.

German Instruction

In a unique cooperation between UNO's CenterAustria, Benjamin Franklin High School, Deutsches Haus of New Orleans, Tulane University, and Louisiana State University the 'Deutsche Samstagsschule' was continued in the spring of 2014. This new initiative of a German School in New Orleans teaching Saturday morning classes for adults and German immersion instruction for kids ages 4+ comes out of the American Association for German Teachers, Louisiana Chapter. During one of the regular fall meetings at UNO's CenterAustria, the idea was born to enhance the instruction in the German language in the City of New Orleans with the 'Samstagsschule' and to promote German language instruction in area high schools. CenterAustria also hosted again the annual fall meeting of the Louisiana Chapter of the American Association for German Teachers. Berthold Molden, the visiting Marshall Plan Chair of Austrian and European Studies, served as the keynote speaker for the meeting with a lecture on Friedrich Torberg.

Cooperations

Next to its partnerships with the Universities of Innsbruck and Graz, CenterAustria continued its cooperations with the Austrian Marshall Plan Foundation, the 'Ludwig Boltzmann Institut für Kriegsfolgenforschung' in Graz, and the Botstiber Foundation in Media, PA, and especially its Institute for Austrian-American Studies. The cooperation with the Universities of Innsbruck and Graz covers the routine of regular administrative organization meetings (UNO and UI have binannual Business Meetings – one in New Orleans in February, and one in Innsbruck in July of every year), student exchanges, faculty contacts, symposia, and guest lectures. Brendon Keene, a history graduate student in Global and International Studies, spent a year at the University of Graz taking history courses and serving as an intern in the 'Ludwig Boltzmann Institut für Kriegsfolgenforschung'.

UNO administers the Marshall Plan Chair of Austrian and European Studies in cooperation with the Austrian Marshall Plan Foundation. The 2013/2014 chairholder was once again Dr. Bertold Molden, an adjunct lecturer in the Department of History at the University of Vienna. He taught courses in the History Department on Latin America, the Holocaust, and a Graduate Seminar. The Marshall Plan Foundation also administers a scholarship program for Austrian and American students for mid-term research visits. University of Graz and Villach University of Applied Sciences students spending the spring semester at Louisiana State University in Baton Rouge under the mentorship of geography professor Michael Leitner came to CenterAustria for a workshop presenting their research in April 2014. The papers delivered in the October 2013 Workshop on 'Regional Economic Development', co-sponsored by the Austrian Marshall Plan Foundation, were published in the spring of 2014 by innsbruck university press: Günter Bischof,

(Ed.), Regional Economic Development Compared: EU-Europe and the American South, Innsbruck 2014.

CenterAustria continued its work in the 'Quiet Invaders Project', funded by the Botstiber Foundation. This project works on the prosopography (collective biography) of Austrian immigrants to the United States in the 20th Century from the Burgenländers to Schwarzenegger. 2012/2013 Ministry Fellow Dominik Hoffman-Wellenhof finished his dissertation at the University of Graz on "Identity Crises in Austrian Jewish Refugees' Autobiographies", written under the auspices of the 'Quiet Invaders' project. Eva Maltschnig is continuing her dissertation research on "Austrian War Brides" and conducting interviews with Austrian war brides across the United States for her Vienna dissertation. Günter Bischof continues to sit on the board of the Botstiber Institute for Austrian-American Studies, which has become a major funding agency for research in the field of Austrian-American Relations. Bischof also served as a panelist in the Annual Bostiber Lecture at the Austrian Embassy in Washington, D.C., in late May 2014: 'Espionage and Intelligence in the 21st Century: How did we get here and where do we go from here? – An Austrian American Discussion.'

CenterAustria also continued its unofficial cooperation with the Wirtschaftsunversität Wien and Günter Bischof has been giving special seminars and lectures there.

CenterAustria's cooperation with the 'Ludwig Boltzmann Institut für Kriegsfolgenforschung' (BIK) in Graz is expanded in the joint project '1989: The End of the Cold War in Eastern Europe'. BIK has become a premier platform in Cold War Studies in Europe with its vast network of scholars in Eastern and Western Europe built since its 'Red Army in Austria' and 'Prague Spring 1968' research projects. BIK has become a bridge builder within the Cold War scholarly community in the Russian Federation and Eastern East/Central Europe, building and promoting a network of scholars working on the international history of the Cold War. This has allowed access to Russian and Eastern European/East Central European archives and has richly informed our knowledge of 'the other' side in the Cold War. A smaller English version of the massive volume on the "Vienna Summit of 1961", which appeared in German in 2012, was published in 2014: Günter Bischof – Stefan Karner – Barbara Stelzl-Marx, (Eds.), The Vienna Summit and Its Importance in International History (The Harvard Cold War Studies Book Series, ed. Mark Kramer) with Lexigton Books. Next to Dr. Mark Kramer of Harvard University's Project of Cold War Studies in the Davis Center of Russian and Eurasian Studies, CenterAustria serves as the American node in this '1989: The End of the Cold War in Eastern Europe' research collaborative project. BIK's Peter Ruggenthaler is coordinator of the ambitious 1989 project. From October 23–25, the BIK, organized a major conference at Vienna's Diplomatic Academy on the occasion of the 25th anniversary of the fall of the Berlin Wall and the End of the Cold War.

BIK Conference in Vienna.

Prizes

CenterAustria initiated and sponsored a new scholarly prize in conjunction with the American Friends of the 'Dokumentationsarchiv des Österreichischen Widerstandes (DÖW)', on whose board Bischof sits. This major new prize in studies related to Austria and Czechoslovakia in the World War II Era is dedicated to the scholarly work and legacy of Radomir Luža, the late scholar of Central Europe who taught at Tulane University in New Orleans for three decades. Luža published major works on Czechoslovakia, Austro-German relations in the Anschluss Era, as well as the Austrian and the Czech resistance during World War II. Luža was a refugee from Communist Czechoslovakia (he slipped across the border into Austria during the Czech Coup of February 1948). The prize is organized by the American Friends of DÖW and is sponsored by CenterAustria. No prize was bestowed in 2014.

Art Exhibitions

As part of the art exchange program between the Cultural Office of the City of Innsbruck and the Department of Fine Arts at UNO, two art exhibits were organized. UNO fine arts students Peter Hoffmann and Wendell Brunious exhibited their work in the Andechs Gallery in Innsbruck's old city in July 2014. Innsbruck artists Nicole Weniger and Katharia Zibulka presented their work in an exhibit at UNO St. Claude Gallery in New Orleans in September 2014. These exhibits allow young artists to display their work for the first time overseas and visit and get to know the art world in these cities (the Innsbruck artists also visit New York City for a few days and stay at the Austrian Cultural Forum). The artists were present during the openings of both shows and used their stays for 'artists in residence' appointments.

Publications

CenterAustria Book Series

- Contemporary Austrian Studies Series (UNO Press/innsbruck university press):

  Günter Bischof – Ferdinand Karlhofer – Samuel R. Williamson, Jr. (Eds.), 1914. Austria-Hungary, the Origins, and the First Year of World War I, CAS 23, New Orleans/Innsbruck 2014.

TRANSATLANTICA

- Günter Bischof – Jason Dawsey – Bernhard Fetz (Eds.), The Life and Work of Gűnther Anders. Émigré, Iconoclast, Philosopher, Man of Letters, TRANSATLANTICA 8, Innsbruck 2014.

Books

- Günter Bischof (Ed.), Regional Economic Development Compared. EU-Europe and the American South, Innsbruck 2014.
- Günter Bischof – Coleman Warner (Eds.), Museum Man: Essays in Honor of Gordon H. 'Nick' Mueller [= *Festschrift* for the Founding Director of UNO's CenterAustria on the occasion of his 75th birthday], New Orleans 2014.

Cover, Contemporary Austrian Studies 23.

Cover of Anders Volume.

Cover of Museum Man.

Networking and Research Platform

In an effort to increase cooperation between Austrian Centers worldwide Dr. Ruth Fine of the European Forum at Hebrew University in Jerusalem invited Günter Bischof to teach a one-week Seminar on Cold War Summitry 'Building Bridges across the Cold War Abyss: The Vienna Summit of 1961'. He also gave a public lecture on 'The Acceleration of History in 1989: The Bush Administration and the

End of the Cold War in Eastern Europe'. As a result of this visit Bischof continues to mentor European Forum students on their projects dealing with contemporary Austrian history.

Günter Bischof presented his book "Relationships/Beziehungsgeschichten: Austria and the United States in the Twentieth Century, TRANSATLANTICA 4, Innsbruck 2014" in book talks at the Austrian Embassy in Washington (with Ambassador Hans Peter Manz and James Carafano/Heritage Fooundation), at the America House in Vienna (with Ambassador Peter Moser and Lonnie Johnson/ Fulbright), and in the American Corner in Innsbruck.

Günter Bischof is regularly providing leads to American and Austrian researchers from the worlds of media and academic who work on topics of 20th century Austrian history, US – Austrian relations, and/or contemporary New Orleans. For the 70th anniversary conference of D-Day at the National World War II Museum in New Orleans, Günter Bischof participated in a panel on D-Day Memories (talking about German and Austrian D-Day Memory), which was taped and aired on C-Span. Bischof also consulted with many scholars individually on their research projects. This kind of 'service' to the international research and media communities is increasingly becoming a function of Austrian Centers in the US and elsewhere.

Summary

I. Lectures – Spring 2014

- Günter Bischof, CenterAustria, University of New Orleans
  'The Acceleration of History in 1989: The Bush Administration and the End of the Cold War in Eastern Europe'
- Michael Freund, Webster University of Vienna & *Der Standard*
  'Satire, Comedy and a Century of Wars: A Comparison of the Critical Methods of Karl Kraus and Jon Stewart'
- Berthold Molden, Marshall Plan Chair, UNO, Annual Marshall Plan Chair Lecture
  'Friedrich Katz: A Transatlantic Life Through the Fault Lines of the 20th Century'
- Andrea Grisold, Harvard University/Vienna University of Economics and Business Administration
  'What keeps you up at night? Creative Destruction and the Rise & Fall of Media Industries'
- CenterAustria Research Fellows 2013–2014 Presentations
  Martina Prugger, Nick Mueller Fellow, University of Innsbruck (Applied Mathematics)
  'A Short Introduction to Mathematical Fluids'
  Markus Habermann, Austrian Ministry of Science Fellow, University of Vienna (Political Science)

'Emotion in Political Communication: Can Austrian Politicians Learn from American Politicians?'

- Workshop with LSU Marshall Plan Foundation Fellows (in cooperation with Prof. Michael Leitner, Department of Geography and Anthropology, LSU)

II. Lectures – Fall 2014

- Hans Petschar, Director, Picture Archives of the Austrian National Library
  'The Visual Record of World War I: Gathering War -- The Austrian National Library's Collections on World War I'
- Samuel F. Williamson, Jr., President Emeritus, University of the South
  'Austria-Hungary and the Origins of World War I'
  (incl. Presentation of Günter Bischof – Ferdinand Karlhofer – Samuel R. Williamson, Jr. (Guest Editor) (Eds.), 1914. Austria-Hungary, the Origins, and the First Year of World War I, CAS 23, New Orleans/Innsbruck 2014.)
- Wilhelm Kohler, University of Tübingen & Harvard University
  'Recent Developments in Global and Transatlantic Trade Policy'
- Victoria I. Zhuravleva, Russian State University for the Humanities (RGGU), Moscow
  'Russia and the United States: An Image of Each Other in the Context of the Ukrainian Crisis'

Ingeborg Fialová-Fürst

Österreich-Zentrum Olmütz 2014/2015

Palacký Universität Olmütz

Nach dem 'Anlauf-Jahr' 2013, das vor allem der Festlegung organisatorischer Strukturen (Arbeitsteam, Kompetenzen, Aufgabenbereiche) und der Vorstellung des Österreich-Zentrums dem hiesigen akademischen sowie breiteren Publikum (Werbebroschüre, Einrichtung der Web-Seiten http://www.oezentrum.cz/, informative Aufsätze in der Uni- und Regionalpresse) gewidmet war, hat das Olmützer Österreich-Zentrum im Jahre 2014 alle geplanten Aktivitäten in allen Sparten voll entfaltet.

Ein großer Vorteil des Olmützer Österreich-Zentrums liegt darin, dass es bereits bestehende und bewährte Einrichtungen und Projekte (mit verwandten thematischen Schwerpunkten) überdacht, bündelt und dadurch Synergie-Effekte erzielen und nutzen kann. Es sind dies: Die Arbeitsstelle für deutschmährische Literatur, der Lehrstuhl der Stiftungsprofessur der BRD, die Österreich-Bibliothek und das Österreich-Lektorat im Lehrstuhl für Germanistik, das Postdoc-Programm des tschechischen Schulministeriums und der EU sowie das CEEPUS-Programm (Partnerschaft mit der Grazer Germanistik). Außerdem arbeitet das Olmützer Österreich-Zentrum aufs engste mit der österreichischen Botschaft in Prag und dessen Österreichischem Kulturinstitut (ÖKI) zusammen; heuer erfuhr es ideelle Stärkung durch das Programm der Internationalisierung der Palacký-Universität, das der neue Rektor, der Historiker, Prof. Miller, bei seinem Amtsantritt proklamierte und betonte, dass nicht nur die englischsprachigen Aktivitäten gemeint sind.

Arbeitsstelle für deutschmährische Literatur: Grundlagenforschung, Sicherung der Archivbestände

In der Arbeitsstelle (AS) konnte dank dem Postdoc-Programm des tschechischen Schulministeriums und der EU die bis Juni 2015 finanzierte Stelle eines/einer Geschäftsführers/Geschäftsführerin eingerichtet werden, die Dr. Lukáš Motyčka besetzte. Unter seiner Leitung wurden Recherchen unternommen, das Archiv und die Bibliothek der Arbeitsstelle durch Neuzugänge (auch durch Schenkungen von Teilnachlässen – Schaukal, Krywalski) aufgefüllt, Archivbestände sukzessive elektronisch gespeichert, gesichert und übersichtlich geordnet, so dass einzelne Forscherinnen und Forscher einen Überblick über sowie Zugriff auf das Material haben. Aus urheberrechtlichen Gründen kann das elektronische Archiv der AS aber nicht ins Netzt gestellt werden, so dass Forschung nur 'im Hause' betrieben werden kann. Die informativen Web-Seiten der AS werden durchgehend aktualisiert.

Im Jahre 2013 wurde eine neue interaktive Datenbank entworfen, in welche 2014/2015 die Daten zur deutschmährischen Literatur eingespeichert wurden, so dass sie nach weiteren Programmier-Verfeinerungen Ende 2015 versuchsweise gestartet werden kann. Zugleich werden Sponsoren (österreichische/deutsche Firma mit Sitz in Tschechien) für die Finanzierung weiterer Programmier- und Auffüll-Arbeiten gesucht. Die mährische Niederlassung der Firma Siemens hat bereits die Schenkung eines kleineren Geldbetrags zugesichert.

Dank wissenschaftlicher Projekte der einzelnen Leiterinnen und Leiter der Arbeitsstelle/Lehrstuhlmitglieder (Krappmann, Fiala-Fürst, Rinas) hat die Arbeitsstelle eine Ausweitung um und Konzentration auf drei thematische Schwerpunkte erfahren: Forschung zur Rezeption des 1. Weltkriegs in der deutschböhmischen Literatur (Krappmann), Erforschung der romantischen Epoche in der deutschböhmischen und deutschmährischen Literatur (Fiala-Fürst), das Böhmakeln (Rinas – in Zusammenarbeit mit der Universität Bamberg)

Wissenschaftliche Auswertung und Bearbeitung des Materials, Erträge: Publikationen, Konferenzen

Konferenzen

2014 wurden unter Teilnahme österreichischer Kolleginnen und Kollegen zwei internationale wissenschaftliche Konferenzen veranstaltet:

- Franz Spunda im Kontext (3.–4. Oktober 2014)
- Kulturtransfer am Beispiel (Post)Kakaniens (16.–17. Oktober 2014)

Die Referate beider Konferenzen werden in Buchform im Universitätsverlag 2015 publiziert.

Publikationen

e-book-Reihe

2014 erschien der erster Band der e-Buch-Reihe des Österreich-Zentrums: Ingeborg Fialová-Fürst (Hg.), Prager deutsche, deutschböhmische und deutschmährische Literatur. Eine Neubestimmung. Die e-Buch-Reihe wird 2015 mit einem Band von Jörg Krappmann, Religiöse Sinnsuche am Vorabend des 1. Weltkriegs am Beispiel von Wissenschaftlern aus Böhmen und Mähren fortgeführt.

Reihe Beiträge zur deutschmährischen Literatur:

- Sabine Eschgfäller, Antroposofové na Moravě (a v Čechách). Příspěvek ke kulturním dějinám a orální historii antroposofického hnutí 1911–1992, Band 27, Olomouc 2015;

- Jörg Krappmann – Jaromír Czmero (Hgg.), Kurt Krolop, Ludwig Winder. Sein Leben und sein erzählerisches Frühwerk. Ein Beitrag zur Geschichte der Prager deutschen Literatur, Band 28, Olomouc 2015;
- Eine Monographie über Kurt Gröger befindet sich im Druck.

Reihe *poetica moraviae:*
- Roman Karl Scholz, Výbro z díla/Auswahl aus dem Werk. Übersetzt von Lucy Topolská und Radek Malý, Band 6, Olomouc 2014,
- Lukáš Motyčka – Barbora Veselá (Hgg.), Anthologie der deutschmährischen Literatur (zweisprachig), Band 7, Olomouc 2014;
- Katja Kernjak (Hg.), "Milá pampeliško" – "Lieber Hugo". Die Korrespondenz zwischen Hugo (sowie Bibi) Haas und Friedrich Torberg, Band 8, Olomouc 2014;
- Eugen Schick, Z tichých uliček a o malých lidech, Band 9, Olomouc 2015;
- Karl Hans Strobl, Podivuhodné příběhy, Band 10, Olomouc 2015.

Außerdem publizierten die Mitglieder der Arbeitsstelle und des Lehrstuhls diverse Zeitschriftenstudien zu österreichischen Themen und hielten Vorträge auf diversen Konferenzen – im Ausland und in Tschechien.

Lehre und studentisch-wissenschaftliche Tätigkeit

Im Sommer- und Wintersemester 2014/2015 wurden sieben Kurse (Vorlesungen und Seminare) zur österreichischen Kultur, Geschichte und Literatur angeboten. Fünf Magisterarbeiten zum österreichischen Schwerpunkt konnten fertiggestellt und erfolgreich verteidigt werden, sieben Dissertationen zu österreichischen Schwerpunkten befinden sich im Entstehungsstadium.

Die drei bereits genannten Projekte (1. Weltkrieg, Romantik, Böhmakeln) entwickeln sich unter der Mitarbeit zahlreicher studentischer Hilfskräfte, so dass die Studierenden aller Studienabschnitte im Forschungsprozess die Techniken und Methoden wissenschaftlichen Arbeitens lernen.

Das Angebot österreichischer Themen bereicherten Gastvorträge österreichischer Wissenschaftlerinnen und Wissenschaftler (Grazer Kollegen aus dem CEEPUS-Programm: Alice Le Trionnaire-Bolterauer, Christian Neuhuber, Günter Höfler, Christopher Ebner, Robert Vellusig) sowie weiterer Gäste: Helmut Lethen (IFK Linz), Karl Hohensinner, Bertold Voss (Linz), Sophie Zimmermann (Wien).

Im April 2015 wurde eine studentische Exkursion nach Wien unternommen.

Öffentlichkeitsarbeit – Kulturelle Aktivitäten für ein breiteres Publikum ('Ö-Events')

In Zusammenarbeit mit dem Professoren-Klub der Olmützer Universität 'Societas cognitorum' wurde im Sommersemester 2015 den Studierenden und der interessierten Öffentlichkeit ein interdisziplinärer 'Vorlesungszyklus 1815' angeboten. Die einzelnen elf Vorträge behandelten die bildende Kunst – Goya (Ladislav Daniel), die Geschichte der Olmützer Universität (Jiří Fiala), die Literatur der tschechischen nationalen Widergeburt (Dalibor Tureček), die Literatur der deutschen Romantik (Ingeborg Fialová-Fürst), die Musik zwischen Klassizismus und Romantik (Marek Keprt), die Entwicklung der Naturwissenschaften um 1815 (Tomáš Opatrný), die Entstehung der historischen und vergleichenden Linguistik (Jiří Černý), die Napoleonischen Kriege (Miloš Trapl), die amerikanische Literatur der Ära Good Will (Michal Peprník), die Lage Lateinamerikas um 1815 (Ivo Barteček) und den Wiener Kongress als Wendepunkt in den Internationalen Beziehungen und im Völkerrecht (Stephan Wendehorst)

In Zusammenarbeit mit der österreichischen Botschaft in Prag wurde die 'Reihe Olmützer Deutschgespräche' geplant und durchgeführt: Gespräche mit hervorragenden Persönlichkeiten des tschechischen öffentlichen Lebens, die eine Affinität zur deutschen Sprache haben und durch ihre Erfahrungen junge Menschen zum Erlernen der deutschen Sprache animieren können. Es wurden bereits Gespräche geführt mit: Karel Schwarzenberg (ehemaliger Außenminister der ČR), Magda Vášáryová, (ehem. Botschafterin der ČSFR/ČR in Österreich), Peter Brod (ehem. Redakteur der BBC und Free Europe), Ivana Oborna (Prorektorin für Auslandsbeziehungen der Olmützer Universität) und Aleš Brezina (Musiker). Die Gespräche werden im Wintersemester weiter fortgesetzt und danach für Rundfunksendungen verarbeitet.

Im April 2015 fand in Zusammenarbeit mir der Olmützer Studienbibliothek der 1. Jahrgang der 'tschechisch-deutschen/österreichischen Kulturtage' statt, die innerhalb einer Woche eine Reihe von Veranstaltungen (Film- und Theatervorstellungen, Stadtführungen, Vorträge und Diskussionen, Dichterlesungen, Ausstellungen usw.) angeboten haben. Weitere Jahrgänge werden folgen.

In Zusammenarbeit mit dem Rundfunk (Český rozhlas Olomouc, Český rozhlas Vltava) sind dreizehn neue Sendungen zur deutschmährischen Literatur entstanden.

Die Mitglieder der Arbeitsstelle hielten mehrere öffentliche Vorträge über die deutschmährische Literatur (so z.B. im Ringvorlesungszyklus der Professorenvereinigung 'Societas cognitorum') in diversen Bildungs- und Kulturinstitutionen der Stadt und Region.

Mehrere Autorenlesungen und 'Österreich-Events' fanden statt, Ankündigungen, Einladungen und Berichte waren der Webseite zu entnehmen:

- 11. März 2014 Radek Maly: Rilke
- 19. März 2014 Franzobel

- 14. April 2014 Elisabeth Buschmann
- 4. November 2014 Roman Karl Scholz + die Vissegrad-Nummer der Zeitschrift *Plav*
- 11. Dezember 2014 Weihnachtskonzert der Wiener Jazz-Sängerin Irena Nosková
- 24. März 2015 Milena Oda

Das Österreich-Zentrum ist Mitträger der 'Kampagne Deutsch als Sprache der Geisteswissenschaften', die sich an Studierende der ganzen Welt wendet und sie zum Studium – in dem Fall zur Abwechslung auf Deutsch – nach Olmütz einlädt. Am 1. Jänner 2015 wurde auf Initiative und unter Mitwirkung des Österreich-Zentrums an der Sprachschule der Philosophischen Fakultät der Palacký-Universität (UPLIFT) das 'ÖSD-Prüfungszentrum' errichtet. 'Österreichisches Sprachdiplom Deutsch' versteht sich als ein kommunikativ orientiertes Prüfungssystem mit dem Ziel, fremdsprachliche Kompetenz im Hinblick auf reale Verwendungssituationen zu überprüfen. Am Olmützer Prüfungszentrum kann man zweimal jährlich Prüfungen aller Sprachniveaustufen ablegen, wobei auch Vorbereitungskurse angeboten werden.

Insgesamt und abschließend ist festzustellen, dass das Olmützer Österreich-Zentrum 2014/2015 eine ansehnliche Reihe von Aktivitäten entwickelt hat. Die finanzielle Unterstützung des Österreichischen Bundesministeriums für Wissenschaft, Forschung und Wirtschaft ermöglichte uns nicht nur, die bereits seit Jahren funktionierende Arbeitsstelle für deutschmährische Literatur zu sponsern (v.a. Datenbank und studentische Mitarbeiterinnen und Mitarbeiter), sondern ermöglichte auch, über den Rahmen der Aufgaben und Ziele der Arbeitsstelle hinaus – viele weitere Aktivitäten. Das Österreich-Zentrum hat den Ehrgeiz, eine wichtige Kultur- und wissenschaftliche Institution zu werden, die sowohl im Rahmen der Palacký-Universität als auch in der Region und überregional wahrgenommen wird, wozu 2014/2015 erste erfolgreiche Schritte unternommen wurden.

Articles

I. Concepts, Discourses & Methods (Re-)visited

Giovanni Matteo Quer

Israel-Washing: The Radical Right in Europe, Anti-Semitism, and Israel

Hebrew University of Jerusalem

Introduction

The recent rise in popular support of the radical right has rekindled the alarming attention on anti-Semitism in Europe. The electoral success of radical right parties in national and in the European Parliaments has revived the debate on the incitement to hatred against ethnic minorities (*e.g.*, Roma) and migrants (*e.g.*, Muslims), alongside the increasing popular distrust in European institutions and anti-Semitism. Anti-Semitism in Europe follows changing patterns and comprises traditional hatred against Jews heir of the Nazi past and new forms of hatred that associate Jewish communities with Israel, Zionism, and the Arab-Israeli conflict.

Over the last 20 years, and specifically since the Second Intifada in the early 2000s, the new anti-Semitism is overtly connected with political advocacy against Israel, with particularly acute peaks during armed conflicts involving Israel and terrorist militias. In this sense, pro-Palestinian advocacy, which is increasingly successful in portraying Zionism as a colonialist enterprise and Israel as a murderous and racist state, has a significant component of anti-Semitism that comes from the left. Wistrich has extensively analyzed the remarkable similarities between anti-Zionism and anti-Semitism[1], exploring the importance of Marxist theories as well as Socialist and Trotskyist views in the hostile attitudes toward Israel and Zionism in the left.

Another element that is of alarmingly growing importance is the anti-Semitism that spreads among the Muslim communities of Europe, which nurtures itself of religious Islamic aversion against Jews and of militant Islamist hostility against Israel. Colombo has analyzed anti-Semitism in the Muslism world[2], while Gerstenfeld has described the growing incitement against Jews[3], Israel, and the West in Is-

1 Robert Wistrich, From Ambivalence to Betrayal. The Left, the Jews, and Israel, Lincoln 2012; Robert Wistrich, The Left Against Zion. Communism, Israel, and the Middle East, London 1979.

2 Manfred Gerstenfeld, Behind the Humanitarian Mask. The Nordic Countries, Israel and the Jews, Jerusalem Center for Public Affairs, Jerusalem 2011.

3 Valentina Colombo, La cultura degli stereotipi. Negazionismo nel mondo arabo-islamico [Culture of Stereotypes. Negationism in the Arab-Islamic World], in: Francesca Recchia Luciani – Luciano

lamic communities all over Europe, specifically through the political activism of militant Islamist organizations among Muslim youths, descendants of immigrants from Arab and Islamic states.

The interesting phenomenon is the convergence of traditional hatred against Jews with the new forms of hatred against Zionists and Israel, which was evident in the violent anti-Israeli demonstrations, nominally organized in solidarity with Gaza, in occasion of the Israel-Hamas armed conflict during the summer of 2014.[4]

As noted by several authors[5], the demonstrations that were organized around the European capitals in condemnation of Israel's attacks on Gaza in response to Hamas' firing of rockets over Israeli cities have been an occasion for inciting to violence against Jews, promoting anti-Semitism, and unshackling attacks against Jews and Jewish properties. Although a joint statement of France, Germany, and Italy condemned such manifestations of anti-Semitism, one major element has been largely overlooked, which regards the ethnic, ideological, and political identity of the participants. The participants in the anti-Israel demonstrations belonged predominantly to different leftist factions, Muslim communities, and extreme right organizations. As Gordon emphasizes, the new anti-Semitism is characterized by Muslim anti-Semitic mobilization and leftist moral indirect support for such manifestations rooted in one-sided pro-Palestinian support and anti-Israeli slander.[6]

While the most vocal were leftist demonstrators, the most violent were Muslim demonstrators, the extreme right participants were marginally active – in Rome, for instance, a list of Jewish-owned shop was distributed inviting citizenry to boycott them, an action attributed to extreme right movements.[7] However, these extreme right movements, which zealously participated in the anti-Israel manifesta-

---

Patruno (Eds.), Opporsi al negazionismo [Combatting Negationism], Genova 2013, 42–50.

4 Soon after the beginning of the Israeli military operation 'Protective Edge' aiming to stop the relentless firing of rockets by Hamas from the Gaza Strips onto Israeli civilian populations, violent manifestations took place in several European states, showing a converging hatred for Jews and Israelis stemming from different political and ideological camps. In The Hague, for instance, the crowd marching in protest against Israel's bombing of Gaza showed several flags of what is now known as Islamic State and chanted 'Death to Jews'. In the Belgian capital, a café showed a sign in Turkish and French allowing entrance to 'dogs,' but prohibiting it to 'Zionists'. The highest number of anti-Semitic incidents was registered in France, with several cases of physical attacks against Jews, the siege to the synagogue of Rue de la Roquette on 14 July 2014, and several attacks to Jewish-owned shops.

5 Ben Cohen, Jews Must Fight Back Against Anti-Semitism, *The Algemeiner*, New York 2014 July 21st, http://www.algemeiner.com/2014/07/21/jews-must-fight-back-against-anti-semitism/, 3 October 2014. Leslie Lebl, The Islamist Threat to European Security, in: Middle East Quarterly 21/3, Philadelphia, 1–13; Pilar Rahola, Que no lo lean …" [They should not read this, those who …], *La Vanguardia*, Barcelona 2014 July 7th, http://itongadol.com.ar/noticias/val/80223/que-no-lo-leanpor-pilar-rahola.html, 3 October 2014.

6 Murray Gordon, The New anti-Semitism in Western Europe, International Perspectives 50, Washington 2002, 1–17.

7 Joshua Levitt, Rome Blancketes with Posters Calling for Boycott of Jewish-Owned Shops, *The Algemeiner*, New York 2014 August 13th, http://www.algemeiner.com/2014/08/12/rome-blanketed-by-posters-calling-for-boycott-of-jewish-owned-shops/, 3 October 2014.

tions, are fringe organizations, which are often out of the common political map. On the contrary, extreme right parties have largely remained silent and refrained from backing or condemning the riots.

This summer's accidents show a new pattern, which indicates a major change in the extreme right in Europe with respect to Israel, Zionism, and the Jews. Overtly anti-Semitic manifestations have remained typical of fringe, marginal extreme right or neo-Nazi movements, while the parties belonging to the extreme right camp have increasingly become friendly toward Israel and less outspoken in anti-Semitic remarks. Yet, another major difference is evident between Western and Central Europe: While in Western Europe outspoken anti-Semitism has progressively been banned from the political discourse, in Central Europe, anti-Semitism echoes in public debate. Parties and movements belonging to the same extreme right-wing networks appear to hold radically different positions in terms of their relations with Israel, Zionism, and the Jews.

This article analyzes the extreme right parties in Western Europe, which have progressively come closer to Israel, by isolating openly anti-Semitic voices, and their counterparts in Central Europe, which have further consolidated their anti-Semitic sentiments as well as anti-Israeli policy. This difference is further reflected in the isolation of fringe extreme right, neo-Nazi groups in Western Europe, which, although belonging to the same ideological currents, are still manifestly anti-Semitic and anti-Zionist.

By analyzing the ideological development of such parties, it appears that, first, extreme right parties in Western Europe operate in a political and social space severely constrained by Holocaust remembrance, and, secondly, that their political agenda has progressively prioritized the opposition to immigration and multiculturalism over the Jewish question.

These factors, favored by the leadership change in the mid-2000s, have led to what may be defined as 'Israel-washing', which is the progressive development of an ideological proximity to Israel by extreme right parties, functional to their goal of establishing themselves in mainstream politics. In this respect, Central Europe has not yet endorsed social rebuttal of the anti-Semitic discourse, and therefore extreme right parties have not needed to 'Israel-wash' their policy.

This article argues that the 'Israel-washing' effect presupposes the necessity of these parties to distance themselves from anti-Semitic accusations, in order to gather general consensus for furthering their xenophobic agenda. Their proximity to Israel serves as an attempt to disassociate themselves from anti-Semitism, for furthering the xenophobic agenda against migrants, which also defines the extent to which these parties define this proximity, including the supposed common interest in a war against Islam and in a nationalistic policy. Regarding the former, while Israel is at war with Islamist forces, extreme right parties exploit the war on terror to pursue an internal xenophobic agenda, without a real discussion on the Islamist threat in terms of international policies. Regarding the latter, these parties believe that Israeli nationalism is akin to their vision of nation-state, which advances the ideal of a culturally homogenous country; on the contrary, Israeli nationalism does not aim to homogenize its society, but becomes a focal point in the conflict and against attempts to delegitimize Israel.

This article first analyzes the political identity of these parties, defining radical right parties in terms of Fascist or Nazi heritage, xenophobic advocacy, and aversion against the Jewish people.

Radical Right Wing Parties: Political Identity

This article builds upon the definition of radical right parties elaborated by Art[8], which includes parties whose policies are xenophobic and populist. Art draws from Betz's definition of xenophobic parties[9], which oppose cultural or ethnic mingling, and Mudde's definition of populism[10], which involves group of parties sharing nationalist, nativist and regionalist, xenophobic ideologies, although not necessarily rooted in Fascism or National Socialism. While Ignazi distinguishes between the Old Right, remnant of Fascism and Nazism and New Right, which does not have links to traditional radical right wing parties[11], Art refers to radical right as those political parties and groups that oppose immigration, including those which have a racial supremacist advocacy and those which have not.[12] Elaborating on Art's definition, this article refers to radical right-wing parties as groups endorsing ethnic pluralism in terms of separation, rejecting multiple identities, denying immigration, and exploiting popular resentment to supra-national institutions as well to immigrants.

Such parties include: the French Front National [FN, National Front], the Austrian Freiheitliche Partei Österreichs [FPÖ, Freedom Party of Austria], the Hungarian Jobbik – Magyarországért Mozgalom [Jobbik, Movement for a Better Hungary], and the Romanian Partidul România Mare [PRM, Greater Romania Party]. While this article will mainly focus on these parties, the former Italian Alleanza Nazionale [AN, National Alliance] and the Greek Chrysi Avgi [Golden Dawn] can also be cited as part of the same phenomenon, since the former has abandoned anti-Semitic speech and developed a friendly attitude toward Israel, while the latter shows overtly anti-Semitic, anti-Zionist sentiments, which can be ascribed to Greece's loops in democratization processes as in the case of Central European countries.

8 David Art, Inside the Radical Right – The Development of anti-Immigrant Parties in Western Europe, Cambridge 2011.

9 Hans-Georg Betz, Radical Right-Wing Populism in Western Europe, New York 1994.

10 Cas Mudde, Populist Radical Parties in Europe, New York 2007, 27–31.

11 Piero Ignazi, The Silent Counter-Revolution. Hypotheses on the Emergence of Extreme Right Parties in Europe, in: European Journal of Political Research 22/1, Oxford 1992, 3–34.

12 David Art, Inside the Radical Right – The Development of Anti-Immigrant Parties in Western Europe, Cambridge 2011, 10–12.

The common ideological ground of these parties includes the following features: Nazi or Fascist heritage, xenophobic advocacy, enmity toward international institutions, and anti-Semitic sentiments.

In this respect, this article excludes those populist regionalist political groups, which include, for instance, the Lega Nord [LN, Northern League] in Italy and the former Vlaamsblok, current Vlaams Belang [VB, Flemish Interest], in Belgium. While Mudde would define these parties as 'opportunist'[13] stressing their extreme right agenda in order to leverage people's fears and insecurity for gaining electoral success, this article excludes them in that they pursue a regionalist, often secessionist agenda, whereas the focus of the article is the extreme right with national and pan-European aspirations, rooted in Fascist political traditions. Moreover, these parties have never endorsed anti-Semitism as major political identity, although pursuing xenophobic and populist agendas.

Traditional anti-Semitism, based on irrational hatred against the Jewish people, and its new version, which focuses on opposing Zionism in connection to Israel, have long characterized extreme right parties, rooted in their Nazi, Fascist past. At times explicit, at times hidden under anti-Zionist declarations, anti-Semitism has been always a major element of the extreme rights public advocacy, coupled with the aversion for international organizations, and the disdain of ethnic minorities.

In this respect, a major difference comes forth between Western and Central Europe with respect to the anti-Semitic discourse[14]: while Western European extreme right parties disguise traditional and new anti-Semitism by limiting it to the fringe camps within their parties or by replacing it with other xenophobic statements, Central European parties blatantly use it in their political articulation.

The Radical Right in Western and Central Europe

Radical right parties in Western Europe are the heirs of Nazi and Fascist parties of 1930s, with elements of racism, anti-Semitism, and anti-Americanism. The necessity to convoy people's fears and anxieties brought these parties to construe an 'external enemy'[15], furthering conspiracy theories against the nation and the incitement toward the alien. While serving as harbor for former Nazi and Fascist officers, as well as nostalgic, the post-war policy of these parties has since been oriented to the 'inclusion in mainstream politics', for which they abandoned overtly supremacist statements in their ordinary political discourse, although tolerating anti-Semitic remarks within the party.

---

13 Mudde, Radical Parties, 69–73.

14 As Mudde emphasizes, xenophobia in Central Europe focuses on ethnic minorities, while the xenophobic agenda of Western European parties focuses on 'strangers', such as immigrants. By furthering this analysis, one can note that another major difference consists of the exploitation of the anti-Semitic discourse by these parties. See *ibid.*, 69–73.

15 *Ibid.*, 74–78.

The racial, *völkische* element was central in their precursors' political discourse, but in post-war Europe racist mobilization has become increasingly difficult both socially and legally. Legislation against incitement to hatred and hate speech, the consolidation of democratic principles against the Fascist past, as well as the increasing role of memory in society regarding the Holocaust and Nazi propaganda contributed to set aside racism from general political discourse. However, these tendencies have not been wiped out, while they have just been refashioned, by adapting to the modern social context. As Betz argues, 'in contemporary right-wing discourse, this means, above all, safeguarding and defending the achievements and gains of European culture and civilization against challengers ranging from American popular culture to Islam'.[16]

The originally Nazi, and later also Fascist, racial doctrine has progressively been abandoned in favor of a 'cultural separationist' doctrine, whereby extreme right parties do not officially reject ethnic and cultural pluralism, while instead they advocate for 'cultural purity' and separation of ethnic groups. Therefore, these parties often champion anti-American hatred, since America's multicultural model is considered a weakening danger[17], and latent anti-Semitism, because of ancient beliefs of Jewish corrupting capacities. By exploiting uncertainties and fears originating from postmodern radical changes in societies, economy, and culture, these parties 'market themselves as champions of a new politics of identity, aimed at defending Western culture and values, particularly against the growing presence and increasing assertiveness of Islam in Western Europe'.[18] In this sense, the enmity against international organizations and, in particular, against the European Union epitomizes the opposition to supranational powers that debilitate the nation coupled with the demurral of new multicultural projects.

Taking the example of the Italian extreme right party Movimento Sociale Italiano [MSI, Italian Social Movement], one can see this development occurred during 1980s. As Griffin describes, the party and its heir Alleanza Nazionale [AN, National Alliance], led by Gianfranco Fini, pursued a xenophobic agenda based on the protection of national identity, by developing a political narrative hostile to immigrants and multiculturalism.[19] Yet, given the growing consensus consolidating around Alleanza Nazionale, Fini decided to radically change the politics of its party, by refusing racism, condemning anti-Semitism, and rejecting Fascism.[20]

16 Betz, Populism, 394.

17 *Ibid.*, 411.

18 *Ibid.*, 417.

19 Roger Griffin, Ce n'est pas Le Pen [It's not Le Pen]. The MSI's Estrangement from the Politics of Over Xenophobia, in: Charles Westin (Ed.), Racism, Ideology and Political Organisation, Edsbruk 1998, 204–207. The author points out the different strategies of Rauti, first leader of MSI and Fini with regard to xenophobic narrative and discourse.

20 This 'turn' occured on 27 January 1995, during the annual party congress, in which Fini gave a speech that provoked the reaction of hardcore Fascists, who tried to found another party. See Alessandro Roveri, Gianfranco Fini. Una Storia Politica – Dal Movimento Sociale Italiano a Futuro e Libertà [Gianfranco Fini. A Political Story – From the Italian Social Movement to the Political

The real turn, however, occurred in November 2003, when Fini, then Deputy Prime Minister, visited Israel. Several pro-Israeli statements preceded this visit, concerning the growing anti-Israeli sentiments during the Second Intifada and the recurrent anti-Semitism in occasion of major armed conflict.[21]

This 'historical visit' was functional to Fini's goal of distancing himself from the Fascist past and the even more charged heritage of Fascist endorsement of Nazi anti-Semitic policies, including Fascist cooperation in the extermination project with the result of herding his party into a new stage of politics. To different extents, other extreme right parties in Western Europe have undergone the same process, in particular the Austrian FPÖ and the French Front National.

In Western Europe

With respect to the FPÖ, its political advocacy under the leadership of Jörg Haider[22], guiding the party from 1986 to 2000, included the elements that characterize the extreme right, including xenophobia, anti-Americanism, anti-Europeism, as well as anti-Semitism.

Xenophobia manifested through the *völkischen* discourse of racial superiority and purity throughout the 1980s, which was brought out in particular by former Nazis and nostalgics. The rhetoric of the party leader Haider was central in the elaboration of a modern version of Nazi ideology. As Hockenos holds,

> 'Beneath Haider's flexible rhetoric is a stable ideology, an illiberal political vision inherently at odds with the basic tenets of modern democracy. The central idea of the FPÖ, as with all of the New Right parties in Europe, is that of the Volksgemeinschaft, or ethnic community, a concept that was also at the heart of Nazi ideology.'[23]

While the constituency of former Nazis and nostalgics decreased, Haider refined its political language and adapted the old tenets of racial superiority to the new political language, by gradually introducing the concept of cultural and national distinctiveness. While hate speech was being criminalized, Haider redirected its racial focus toward cultural identity, by exploiting the fears stemming from societal

---

Movement 'Future and Freedom'], Padova 2011, 35–38. Unrepentant Fascists were reluctant to condemn Fascism and, instead, wanted to repurpose the Fascist alternative to capitalism and communism, by also developing a patronizing development narrative that advocated for the repatriation of immigrants in order to support Third World countries. See Griffin, Le Pen, 207.

21 Pierluigi Battista, Shalom Israele, *La Stampa*, Turin 2003 November 27th, 9.

22 As a student of political science and law, Haider was active in the nationalist students organization *Albia* (Burschenschaft). Later, he made a career for himself in the Freedom Party and became governor of Carinthia. After joining the coalition government in 2000, he resigned from party leadership in the same year after extensive reproval by European political leaders.

23 Paul Hockenos, Jörg Haider. Austria's Far Right Wunderkind, in: World Policy Journal 12/3, New York 1995, 75–80, here 77.

change in order to denounce cultural mixing. Consequently, ancient ideology of '*Volk* and *Rasse* are substituted by *Kultur*' against multiculturalism and 'racial mixture' with 'culture mixture' (*Kulturmischung*).[24]

In its populist advocacy, Haider's FPÖ developed antagonism to international organizations and the European Union, often connected to anti-Semitic discourse. To Haider and other FPÖ ideologues, such as Robert Duerr and Walter Ochensberger, international organizations and Brussels in particular represented the result of a plan elaborated by 'world Jewry' preordained to tyrannize Austria and the free peoples of Europe.[25] Their speeches and writings were replete of overtly anti-Semitic remarks, which warning about a 'Jewification' [*Judaisierung*] of the international community.[26]

Similarly, the Front National in France has developed in 1980s and 1990s a xenophobic and anti-European discourse largely based on anti-Semitic narrative. While the FN is not rooted in a traditional racial discourse, typical instead of those movements that are heir to a Nazi past, the French extreme right has immediately developed a xenophobic rhetoric slandering migrants and accusing international organizations, primarily the European Union, of menacing the cultural and social order of the *Republique*. In this sense, party leader Le Pen was able to mobilize fears and resentments of the masses, by exploiting racist feelings. As has been emphasized

> 'The National Front has risen to national prominence because it has succeeded in giving concrete political expression to a latent xenophobia, reinforced by the problem of immigration. It has succeeded in placing this latent xenophobic fear in the context of a general ideology of the extreme right [...]. Le Pen mobilizes opinion against the political elite [...]. By expressing it politically, the National Front has given both reinforcement and legitimacy to xenophobia.'[27]

Besides the debate on the nature of the Front National, which comprises authors arguing for an essentially Fascist ideology[28], opposed to those who believe that the FN is essentially populist and xenophobic[29], the FN appears to be a composite

24 Brigitte Bailer-Galanda – Wolfgang Neugebauer, Incorrigibly Right – Right Wing Extremists, 'Revisionists' and anti-Semites in Austrian Politics Today, Stiftung Dokumentationsarchiv des Österreichen Widerstandes, Anti Defamation League, Vienna/New York 1996, 17.

25 Documentation Centre of Austrian Resistance DOeW, Austria, in: Jean-Yves Camus (Ed.), Extremism in Europe – 1998 Survey. Editions de l'Aube – European Center for Research and Action on Racism and Antisemitism, Paris 1998, 28–38, here 34.

26 Bailer-Galanda – Neugebauer, Incorrigibly Right, 36–39.

27 Pierre Bréchon – Subrata Kumar Mitra, National Front in France. The Emergence of an Extreme Right Protest Movement, in: Comparative Politics 25/1, New York 1992, 63–82, here 80.

28 Jonathan Marcus, The National Front and French Politics. The Resistible Rise of Jean-Marie Le Pen, New York 1995.

29 Pierre Birnbaum, La France aux Français. Histoire des haines nationalistes [France to the French. History of Hatreds], Paris 1993.

camp entrenched in traditional revolutionary Fascism[30], whose use of anti-foreign rhetoric is functional to the defense of the nation, national cohesiveness, and national communality and fraternity.[31] In this xenophobic discourse, anti-Semitism played a major role.

The anti-Semitism elaborated by the Front National stems from the conception of Judaism as a foreign culture, which bears morally corruptive attributes.[32] Thanks to the ideologue Bruno Mégret[33] the traditional anti-Semitic postulation of a Jewish plot was also spread in the FN political discourse, also in connection to the vilification of international organizations and the European Union in specific.[34] In this sense, Le Pen's anti-Semitism was in line with Haider's hostility toward cultural mingling, envisioning a pan-European confederation of peoples, whose ethnical and national identities would not intermix.

While anti-Semitism cuts across all party policies, by using anti-Semitic tenets of Jewish conspiracy and Jewish capitalism in order to delegitimize international institutions and construing Jewish culture as a 'threat to the nation', in the 1990s, another element emerges, which both the FPÖ and the FN share: The anti-Israel connection. Anti-Jewish hatred in domestic politics was also expressed as anti-Israel venom, conceived as the essence of Jewish conspiracy in international politics. Anti-Israel attitudes manifested in the conception of Israel as a threat to international order and in the proximity cultivated with Israel's enemy in the Middle East, specifically with Iraq. Although 'it is not surprising that anti-Semites sympathize with those Arabic and Islamic forces who strive for the destruction of Israel and commit terrorist acts against Jewish institutions'[35], it is however stunning that both Haider and Le Pen sought the friendship of Saddam Hussein[36], whose views certainly reflected their vicious enmity toward America and Israel, but his identity represented all what they fought against in Europe.

Similar trends are recognizable in their extreme right kin in Central Europe, with a major difference in the 2000s. In the late 1990s, Western extreme parties

---

30 Pierre Milza, Le front national crée-t-il une culture politique? [Is the National Front Creating a Political Culture?] Vingtième Siècle, Revue d'Histoire 44, Paris 1994, 39–44.

31 Peter Davis, The National Front in France – Ideology, Discourse, and Power, London 1999.

32 This rhetoric was propagated by the extreme right daily publication *Présent*. *Cf.* Antony Lerman, Le Pen and La Rouche. Political Extremism in Democratic Societies, in: William Frankel (Ed.) Survey of Jewish Affairs. 1987, Cranbury 1988, 201–220, here 208.

33 Mégret started his political career in the Front National in 1980s, after a failed attempt to found a nationalist political movement of his own. Mégret was elected in the European Parliament in 1989 and remained until 1999. In the same years, he made his career in the National Front as a political ideologue, often criticizing Le Pen for his radicalism, which in his view prevented the party from gaining more consent among the public.

34 See René Monzat – Jean-Yives Camus, France, in: Jean-Yves Camus (Ed.), Extremism in Europe – 1998 Survey, Paris 1998, 130–149, here 132–134.

35 Bailer-Galanda – Neugebauer, Incorrigibly Right, 47.

36 See Anti-Defamation League, Jörg Haider and Saddam Hussein. Not-To-Strange Bedfollows, 13 December 2002, http://www.adl.org/combating-hate/domestic-extremism-terrorism/c/joerg-haider-saddam-hussein-bedfellows.html, 3 October 2014.

seek popular legitimacy, pursuing a fragmentary policy of disassociation from blatant anti-Semitic remarks and focusing more on the 'migrant threat', and on the 'European enemy'. On the contrary, Central European extreme right parties continue pursuing an anti-Semitic discourse, which is part of their racist ideology.

In Central Europe

In Central Europe, the process of democratization led by the EU under the Copenhagen criteria, is grounded on the promotion of human rights and pluralism.[37] However, the reforming 'rush' leads to neglect the alarming phenomenon of hate speech, which bears severe consequences today. After the fall of the communist regimes, extreme parties take power promoting a revanchist policy based on ethnic claims, which expressed old latent conflicts, such as Hungarian claims over Slovakia, or Romanian hostility toward Hungary. Moreover, as Kürti emphasizes, after the demise of Communist regimes in Central Europe, xenophobia, racism, and extremism have been legitimized by those parties that aimed to counter Communist repression of nationalist sentiment, while racism itself has often been sponsored by the state.[38]

Extreme right parties quickly gain popular sympathies by exploiting people's disillusion with the EU and capitalism, in which people reversed hopes for a better life. Besides their electoral success, largely based on populist exploitation of popular resentments, the extraordinary development of the racist and anti-Semitic rhetoric is also attributable to the continuous contacts with Western extreme right parties and anti-Semitic voices. While 'Post-Communist Europe is particularly vulnerable to racist demagoguery now because its populations have been unprepared for the inherent risks of capitalism', the process of democratization has been briskly concluded with these countries' accession to the EU, without a real endorsement of anti hate speech legislation, and, therefore 'notorious Western anti-Semites are busy exploiting the legal loophole'.[39] In this respect, Le Pen's efforts to build a pan-European network of extreme right parties were pivotal in the diffusion of anti-Semitic rhetoric.

In Hungary, the Justice and Life Party [MIEP, Magyar Igazság és Élet Pártja] was funded and directed by István Csurka[40] in the 1990s. This party explicitly endorsed Nazi propaganda together with Nazi symbolism. Csurka's speeches and

37 Tim Haughton, When Does the EU Make a Difference? Conditionality and the Accession Process in Central and Eastern Europe, in: Political Studies Review 5/2, London 2007, 233–246.

38 László Kürti, Racism, the Extreme Right and Anti-Gypsy Sentiments in East-Central Europe, in: Charles Westin (Ed.), Racism, Ideology and Political Organisation, Edsbruk 1998, 217–253, here 250–253.

39 Thomas Land, Disappointed Eastern Europe Confronts its Neo-Nazis, in: Contemporary Review 291/1694, London 2009, 280–288, here 280f.

40 Author and novelist, after the controversial past as informant during the Communist regime, Csurka became a right-wing politician in democratic Hungary. His political views incorporate Hungarian irredentism and overt anti-Zionism.

the party's press have had a pivotal role in consolidating anti-Roma and anti-Jew hatred in the general political debate.[41] The anti-Semitism developed by Csurka in his political rhetoric included conspiracy theories, anti-Americanism, and accusation of Judaism as a foreign culture responsible for Hungary's tribulations.[42] As happened in Austria and France, anti-Semitism also served the purpose to discredit international organizations, engaging in a campaign against Hungary's adhesion to NATO in 1998, by portraying it as a Jewish conspiracy to sell Hungary's interests.[43]

In Romania, the party Partidul România Mare has built upon the Communist regime's anti-minority campaigns, but presenting Romanian identity as a nationalist affair and also kindling popular resentment against Jews and Gypsies and revanchist sentiment against Hungarians mainly.[44] Corneliu Vladim Tudor is main party leader who made large use of anti-Semitic remarks to spread racist nationalism and anti-Israel hatred.[45]

In the absence of an appropriate legislation on hate speech, and the lack of implementation thereof, extreme right rhetoric can manifest freely in the press, in public, and in politics. Therefore, extremism is much more in the mainstream than in Western Europe.

In these countries, hate speech (against Jews and Roma in particular) is not only tolerated, but often promoted by the state, including the usual anti-Semitic accusations such as the 'influence of Jews in the media', the 'Jewish influence in international organizations', and the 'return of the Jews' from Israel, and the 'Jewish invasion in national markets'.[46] Moreover, as in France and Austria, the anti-Israeli connection is also part of these parties' propaganda. The Hungarian extreme right party established contacts with the Iraqi Embassy in the pursuit of anti-Israeli policies, translated in anti-Zionist propaganda diffused by extreme right press[47], accusing Israel of being the mastermind of regional and global instability, pursuing the goal of influencing and controlling international organizations and American politics.

While the anti-Semitic rhetoric and racist discourse is still diffused in Central Europe, in Western Europe a major change happened in the mid-2000s, when extreme right parties progressively disassociated themselves with openly anti-Semitic remarks, redirecting their priority toward anti-Muslim discourse and adopt-

---

41 Kürti, Racism, 230f.

42 Raphael Vago, Hungary, in: Jean-Yves Camus (Ed.), Extremism in Europe – 1998 Survey, Paris 1998, 183–192, here 186f.

43 *Ibid.*, 185.

44 See Kürti, Racism, 231f.

45 See Denise Rosenthal, 'The Mythical Jew'. Anti-Semitism, Intellectuals, and Democracy in Post-Communist Romania, in: Nationalities Papers. The Journal of Nationalism and Ethnicity 9/3, London 2001, 419–439.

46 Vago, Hungary, 186f.

47 *Ibid.*, 188f.

ing an increasingly friendly approach toward Israel. The next section will analyze the differences between Western and Central European parties, which still share the same views and stem from the same ideological matrix.

The Change After 9/11

The 2000s bring about a radical change that modifies these parties' relation with anti-Semitism. First, the Holocaust discourse has become part of Europe's collective memory and historical identity, and, secondly, the cultural clash with Islam. If the first element progressively expunged anti-Semitism from public discourse, the second element constitutes the main factor that has renewed the discourse on migration and Israel. Finally, in the 2000s, these parties underwent a major change in leadership, which brought about a reprioritization of the parties' policies and a new rhetorical fashion.

With respect to Holocaust remembrance, in the beginning of the 1990s, Holocaust education becomes part of school curricula in Western Europe, with major initiatives of the European Union Fundamental Rights Agency (FRA).[48] Holocaust remembrance ceremonies spread in late 1990s all over Western Europe, together with cultural initiatives that coalesced political and social refusal of anti-Semitic speech promoted by the European Parliament[49], and the establishment of the Holocaust Remembrance Day on 27th January by the United Nations.[50] The Holocaust memory discourse revived also for countering Holocaust deniers, whose freedom has been progressively restricted by legislation introduced in late 1990s and early 2000s.[51]

On the contrary, Central and Eastern European countries have been partly untouched, until recently, by the Holocaust remembrance process. Not only has the European FRA has implemented Holocaust education policies in Eastern Europe just in the mid-2000s, but the process of Holocaust remembrance itself is conducive to anti-Semitic manifestations.[52]

With respect to 9/11, the clash between the Islamic and Western worlds led to a radical change in the policies toward the US, the Islamic world, and the Islamic communities. However vocally anti-American and anti-Israeli, formulating populist accusations against the 'Zionist influence' in world politics and anti-Semitic

48 See The European Union Fundamental Rights Agency, Human Rights Education at Holocaust Memorial Sites Across the European Union. An Overview of Practices, Luxemburg October 2011.

49 See the European Parliament's resolutions on racism, hate speech, and anti-Semitism approved during 1990s and 2000s, including those of of 27 October 1994, 27 April 1995, 26 October 1995, 30 January 1997, and 16 March 2000.

50 UN General Assembly Resolution 60/7, adopted on 1 November 2005.

51 Michael Whine, Expanding Holocaust Denial and Legislation against It, in: Jewish Political Studies Review 20/1–2, Jerusalem 2008, 57–77.

52 Efraim Zuroff, Eastern Europe. Anti-Semitism in the Wake of Holocaust-Related Issues, in: Jewish Political Studies Review 17/1–2, Jerusalem 2005, http://jcpa.org/article/eastern-europe-anti-semitism-in-the-wake-of-holocaust-related-issues/, 3 October 2014.

remarks over the alleged inclination to war and conflict of Israelis, extreme right parties in Western Europe have increasingly focused on the Islamic terrorist threat and the cultural elements that cause it.

Although still maintaining ambiguous anti-American stances, such as alleged accusations of leading the West into war with the Middle East for uncertain national interests, extreme right parties have increasingly drawn their attention on the Islamic question, leaving aside their anti-Jewish obsession. In this respect, the anti-Islamic stance is functional to their xenophobic claims, whereby the anti-terrorist advocacy is mixed with the will to stop immigration. In this respect, a major difference distinguishes Western and Central right camps. Western Europe faces a major problem regarding its Muslim population, increasingly mobilized in the war against the Western enemy, whereas Central Europe has largely been untouched by Islamic migration and has not yet directed its racist rhetoric toward migrants.

Finally, the change of leadership has brought a significant reorganization of Western extreme right parties.

After FPÖ electoral success in 2000 and its short governmental experience in the coalition led by the Austrian People's Party (ÖVP), the party had a major backlash due to internal party disputes and also to EU sanctions against Austria and the social mobilization against the FPÖ.[53] The popular support gained by exploiting economic fears and xenophobic propaganda of Überfremdung [foreignization], for which Haider prioritized anti-migrant rhetoric over anti-Semitism[54], could not pay back any more in face of Austria's low international reputation. Heinz-Christian Strache took leadership of the FPÖ in 2005 and remained on the same ideological positions, but initiated major reforms of the party in order to lead it back to the mainstream politics. Unquestionably, one significant change in the FPÖ politics is the intensifying vicinity to Israel. The same trend, to a different extent, is also discernible in the French FN.

Since mid-2000s, Marine Le Pen, the FN leader's daughter, becomes more active in the party politics, assuming its leadership in 2011. Under her leadership, the party undergoes major reforms, such as the isolation of anti-Semitic voices, which led to frequent polemics with her father. Le Pen daughter's declarations on Jews and Israel reflect a notable veer in the party's attitude towards Israel and the Jews.

In pursuit of a renewed credibility, these reforms led to the marginalization and expulsion of certain extremists, who often founded fringe parties or pursued autonomous politics within the party – this is the case, for instance of Bruno Goll-

53 Ingmar von Homeyer, Participatory Governance in the European Union, in: Liana Giorgi – Ingmar von Homeyer – Wayne Parsons (Eds.), Democracy in the European Union. Towards the Emergence of a Public Sphere, London 2006, 43–78.

54 Lutz Musner, Memory and Globalization. Austria's Recycling of the Nazi Past and Its European Echoes, in: New German Critique 80, Special Issue on the Holocaust, Durham 2000, 77–91, here 84f.

nisch[55], who, after the defeat to the leadership of the FN, established contacts with the Hungarian Jobbik and continued to express his negationist positions.[56]

These changes paved the way to the 'Israel-washing', while Central European extreme right parties remain originally anti-Semitic. However, Western parties have never loosed the ties with Central European neo-Nazis, nor do they really break away from their past.

Israel-Washing

The 'Israel-washing' phenomenon consists of a substantial change in extreme right parties' politics, but their principal goal to become mainstream parties clashes with their traditional anti-Semitism and militant racism. Therefore, they have first isolated overtly anti-Semitic voices and inaugurated a new policy toward Israel.

The beginning of this change is traceable in the years during which the recrudescence of the Islam-West clashes echoes in Europe's capitals, with riots between the police and Muslim immigrants. The occasion of extreme right parties to increase popular consensus has come across with the anti-terrorist discourse, which they exploit for furthering their xenophobic agenda of ethnic, cultural purity, and halt of immigration.

Marine Le Pen, for instance, has given several speeches against uncontrolled immigration and on the need to control Muslim communities. A few days after the massacre in the Toulouse Jewish school by the Muslim radical Mohammed Merah[57], Marine Le Pen said that France needs to 'take back control over the whole territory' and to 'fight against Islamic radicalism'[58], without however condemning the specific act of anti-Semitism. In other cases, the episodes of anti-Semitism, which are increasingly connected to Leftist and Muslim militants, are an occasion to further the xenophobic agenda and the anti-leftist discourse. In

55 Academic and lawyer, Gollnisch, joined the National Front in 1990s, becoming an active member of the Catholic Faction. As European Parliament member since 1989, Gollnisch led the 'Alliance of European Nationalist Movements' from 2007 to 2013. Involved in a lawsuit in 2007 for controversial statement on the Holocaust, he was eventually found non guilty by the Court of Cassation in 2009.

56 Vincent Nouzille, Le Réseaux secrets du Front National, [The Secret Network of the National Front] *Le Figaro*, Paris 2013 November 8th, http://www.lefigaro.fr/politique/2013/11/08/01002-20131108ARTFIG00341-les-reseaux-secrets-du-front-national.php, 3 October 2014.

57 On 11, 15, and 19 March three different attacks were perpetrated: on a French soldier in Toulouse, on two French soldiers in Montauban, and on the Jewish school Ozar haTorah in Toulouse respectively. Mouhammed Merrah, a French citizen of Algerian descent carried out the attacks in 'revenge' of Muslims killed in Afghanistan and in Palestine. As part of a larger phenomenon, Merrah had a criminal past and was radicalized in prison, adopting radical Islamist views.

58 Abel Mestre, Marine Le Pen intend mettre l'Islam radical à genoux, [Marine Le Pen ants to curb down Radical Islam] *Le Monde*, Paris 2012 March 25th, http://www.lemonde.fr/election-presidentielle-2012/article/2012/03/25/marine-le-pen-entend-mettre-l-islam-radical-a-genoux_1675357_1471069.html, 3 October 2014.

the occasion of an anti-Israeli demonstration in Austria during the summer 2014, Strache criticized Islamic radicalism and leftist attitudes toward Israel.[59]

On the contrary, Central European extreme right parties endorse the old anti-Semitic tenets of a supposed Jewish conspiracy and Jewish disloyalty. The most evident example is the extraordinarily successful Hungarian party Jobbik, which

> 'rails against the establishment and has identified a host of scapegoats – anyone it deems harmful to Hungarian interests, ranging from multi-national corporations and foreign investors (with an obsessive focus on Israeli businesses) to neighboring states that abuse their large ethnic-Hungarian minorities'.[60]

Jobbik party member Márton Gyöngyösi proposed in 2012 to compile a list of Jews serving in the government and in the parliament, suggesting that they would pose a 'threat to Hungary' in relation to the Arab-Israeli conflict.[61] In its racist rhetoric, which also targets Roma people labeling them as 'criminals', Jobbik party exploits public malcontent for economic crisis, elaborating an anti-Zionist discourse which is essentially anti-Semitic.[62]

A similar process has been taking place in Romania, with Tudor's ambiguous revision of his past anti-Semitic remarks, which have not however impeded him from denying Romania's responsibility in the Holocaust and its troubled collaborationist past.[63] Even more openly anti-Semitic, the Romanian party Nouă Dreaptă [New Right] not only uses a virulent anti-Semitic rhetoric, but also mobilizes masses in anti-Semitic rallies and demonstrations.[64]

Central and Eastern Europe societies have not yet endorsed the social de-legitimization of anti-Semitism for the fallacious democratization process and the governmental approval of xenophobic discourse. Consequently, these parties have further developed their anti-Semitic stances into claims against Israel and Zionism. While the legal system is inadequate to combat anti-Semitism, the racist discourse is evidently not repugnant to societal eyes. On the contrary, extreme right parties in Western Europe have progressively silenced anti-Semitism and anti-Zi-

59 Reported in the party's website http://www.fpoe.at/aktuell/detail/news/gaza-konflikt-in-bischofshofe/, 3 October 2014

60 Michael J. Jordan, The Roots of Hate, in: World Policy Journal 27/3, Los Angeles 2010, 99–111, here 102.

61 Jeremy Sharon, Hunagrian Rightist. List Jews who Pose Security Risk, *The Jerusalem Post*, Jerusalem 2012 November 27th, http://www.jpost.com/International/Hungarian-rightist-List-Jews-who-pose-security-risk, 3 October 2014.

62 Jordan, Roots of Hate, 104.

63 Cnaan Lipshitz, European Parliament Member Denies Holocaust on Romanian TV, *Jewish Telegraphic Agency*, 24 October 2012, http://www.jta.org/2012/10/24/news-opinion/world/report-european-parliament-member-denies-holocaust-on-romanian-tv, 3 October 2014.

64 William Totok, Rumäniens neue Nationalisten [Romania's New Nationalists], *Deutsche Welle*, Berlin 2011 December 20th, http://www.dw.de/rum%C3%A4niens-neue-nationalisten/a-15600321, 3 October 2014.

onism while becoming closer to Israel. However, this proximity shows a certain dose of political opportunism, since its goal is to wash away their anti-Semitic past. This phenomenon of 'Israel-washing' consists of two aspects: the redressing of anti-Semitic discourse in anti-Islamic terms and the misconception of Israel's national identity.

While Strache and Marine Le Pen have become increasingly vocal in defending Israel against the 'Islamic threat', their focus is mainly 'Israel's right to defense' against what Le Pen calls the 'Islamic international'[65], thus building upon the anti-Semitic 'Jewish international'. Moreover, the FN party member Frédéric Chatillion, a fierce Hezbollah supporter and anti-Israeli, is still close to the party leadership. Strache's FPÖ has progressively embraces a pro-Israeli policy, with the adoption of the Jerusalem declaration in 2010, postulating a political entente between the party and Israel. However, this has not impeded him from being involved in episodes of anti-Semitism.[66]

More significantly, these parties' new proximity toward Israel seems to be founded on a misleading conception of Israel's national identity. The FPÖ's 'Jerusalem Declaration', in occasion of the party leader's visit to Israel in 2010, epitomizes the misconstrued connections. While the document celebrates a new era of political understanding of the party, it also frames entente on the common fight against radical Islam and the rejection of cultural relativism.[67]

In this respect, the ambiguous proximity to Israel serves the purpose of furthering the xenophobic and anti-immigration agenda. This is evident in Marine Le Pen's discourse on French identity, which postulates halting the immigration of non-Christian peoples[68], since non-Christians have always clashed with Europeans.[69] Moreover, in times of adversity such as the 2014 conflict between Israel and Hamas, the FN leader has not expressed a clear defense of Israel's right to self-defense not of condemnation of Hamas' attacks on the Israeli civilian population.

Thus, the misleading rapprochement between extreme right parties in Western Europe to Israel is a political strategic turn, which aims to bring these parties into the political mainstream, with a more acceptable political rhetoric.

---

65 See http://www.frontnational.com/2014/08/face-a-linternationale-islamiste-lurgence-dune-politique-dendiguement/, 3 October 2014.

66 Benjamin Weinthal, Austria. Anti-Semitic Cartoon Prompts Inquiry, *The Jerusalem Post*, Jerusalem 2010 August 22nd, http://www.jpost.com/International/Austria-Anti-Semitic-cartoon-prompts-inquiry, 3 October 2014.

67 See Patrick Moreau, The Victorious Parties. Unity in Diversity?, in: Uwe Backes – Patrick Moreau (Eds.), The Extreme Right in Europe. Current Trends and Perspectives, Göttingen 2012, 75–148, here 122.

68 See http://www.frontnational.com/le-projet-de-marine-le-pen/autorite-de-letat/immigration/, 3 October 2014.

69 See http://www.frontnational.com/2014/08/face-a-linternationale-islamiste-lurgence-dune-politique-dendiguement/, 3 October 2014.

Conclusion

'Israel-washing' is a phenomenon that explains the necessity of extreme right parties to wash away their anti-Semitic rhetoric, which has increasingly become intolerable in the public discourse, but is functional to further these parties' political agenda of xenophobia. Indeed, their fellow parties in Eastern Europe do not have the need to break away with anti-Semitism since it is still socially and politically acceptable as well as part of the mainstream.

In this respect, the proximity to Israel is in itself populist as it is formulated in xenophobic terms. It is built on enmity against Islam and supposedly shared views of nationalism. However, the Islamic policy of these parties is only internal, without a precise international policy toward the Islamic world and the jihadist threats, which remains ambiguously anti-American.

Finally, this proximity with Israel has not produced a real pro-Israeli policy, neither at the national nor at European levels. While these parties have not developed a real pro-Israeli agenda, their discourse on Israel remains functional to attack the left, showing a lack of genuinely pro-Israeli and pro-human rights policies.

Andra-Octavia Drăghiciu

The Dark Side of the Moon: Challenges of Oral History Interviewing in Post 1989 Romania

Andrássy University Budapest

Introduction

The Socialist regime of Romania has produced an unimaginable quantity of documents on all aspects of society. Despite the shortages in paper, which were invoked by the authorities in the 1980s as excuses to restrain certain publications, the official organizations consumed tons of it for their reports, protocols and dossiers. Along with the official press, the archives of the national television and radio station, these documents shed light mainly on the official discourse and ideology in the Romanian Socialist Republic. Some segments of Romanian society managed to express themselves through various channels, though, thereby producing sources of their own. This is mainly the case of intellectuals with connections to the 'West', who gave interviews for foreign newspapers and corresponded with Radio Free Europe, and of writers, who had their work published outside Romania.[1]

When researching the issue of youth in Romania before 1989, scholars quickly become aware of the fact that most of the available and accessible sources come from the authorities themselves. There are few documents produced by the youth itself, through which scholars could get an insight in the *Eigensinn*[2] of the youngsters and the way they perceived their lives under the Socialist regime. Such documents are diaries, letters, photos, and recordings, but also the testimonies of the people themselves. It is the latter category of sources that makes the object of this analysis. Oral History is the sociological method through which the testimonies referred to in this paper have been collected, evaluated, and interpreted in a pro-

1 See for example Paul Goma, Culoarea Curcubeului 77 [The Colour of the Rainbow], Oradea 1993, and the Swabian authors of the 'Aktionsgruppe Banat' in Sabina Kienlechner, Unter dem Einfluss der bürgerlichen Ideologie. Die 'Aktionsgruppe Banat' in den Akten der Securitate [Under the Influence of the Bourgeois Ideology. The Action Group Banat in the Documents of the Romanian Political Police], in: Sinn und Form 6, Berlin 2010, 746–769.

2 Mark Fenemore explains the concept of *Eigensinn* as 'one's own sense and own meaning', in: Sex, Thugs and Rock'n'Roll. Teenage Rebels in Cold-War East Germany, London 2007, 12.

cess which helps shed light on 'The Dark Side of the Moon'.[3] The metaphor was used by the band Pink Floyd in 1973, in order to describe the dark side each person has and keeps away from the world.[4] In this article, however, it stands for the unofficial side of youths' lives kept away (more or less) from the regime during the last 15 years of the Romanian Socialist Republic, which proved not to be dark, but more colorful and dynamic than expected.

This paper deals with the complexity of the Oral History process and the obstacles encountered by the author while conducting narrative interviews on the subject of youth culture in 1970s and 1980s Romania. As an introduction into the subject, some information about the official and unofficial parts of youths' lives will be given, followed by theoretical considerations on memory, remembering, and narrative interviews. The third part will depict the author's experience in the field while taking interviews for the dissertation project 'Youth culture in the Romanian Socialist Republic, 1974–1989', funded by the Austrian Federal Ministry of Science, Research and Economy. Finally, a conclusion will be drawn on how current Oral History-theory can or cannot be applied in the case of Eastern European societies.

The Moon

In order to assure an easy understanding of the historical context within which the lives of youngsters could unfold, the dichotomy official *vs.* unofficial can be illustrated by contrasting two representative persons on each side. On the one hand, Nicoale Ceaușescu[5], General Secretary of the Romanian Communist Party[6], stands as the embodiment of the Romanian Socialist regime, while the actor and singer Florian Pittiș[7], on the other hand, is portrayed as 'the other' who refused to obey the rules of this regime.[8] It is important to stress the fact that these spheres

3 Pink Floyd album 1973.

4 The Making of The Dark Side of the Moon, https://www.youtube.com/watch?v=ENU5dKJvVpY, 22 December 2014.

5 Nicolae Ceaușescu (1918–1989) was Secretary General of the Romanian Communist Party from 1969 to 1989 and the first Romanian president from 1974 to 1989. Surrounding himself with relatives and loyal party members, he promoted the ideology of 'Socialist patriotism' and his own cult of personality to its extremes until December 1989, when he was deposed, put to trial, and executed for crimes against humanity.

6 Ceaușescu introduced the name change of the Romanian Workers' Party to the Romanian Communist Party and that of the country from the Romanian People's Republic to the Romanian Socialist Republic in 1965. The office of the General Secretary of the Communist Party was created for him in 1969. He had been General Secretary of the Executive Committee of the Romanian Communist Party until then. Adam Burakowski, Dictatura lui Nicolae Ceaușescu 1965–1989. Geniul Carpaților [Nicolae Ceaușescu's Dictatorship 1965–1989. The Genious of the Carpathians], Iași 2011, 131.

7 Florian Pittiș (1943–2007) was a beloved Romanian singer and actor, who refused to cut his hair and was thus eventually banned from public television in the Romanian Socialist Republic.

8 *Cf.* Mihai Stamatescu – Raluca Grosescu – Dorin Dobrincu – Andrei Muraru – Liviu Pleșa – Sorin Andreescu (Eds.), O istorie a comunismului din România. Manual pentru liceu [A History of Romanian Communism. High-school Handbook], Iași 2014, 66.

were far from evolving independently from one another. Rather than unfolding as a parallel society, the unofficial side of life was intertwined with the official one on many levels. This phenomenon is very complex and will not be addressed here. Nevertheless, if we were to take the example at hand, Florian Pittiş became known among youngsters particularly because he was active in the official sphere in the second half of the 1960s. He had his own TV-show and performed in numerous plays, concerts, and films.[9]

Nicolae Ceauşescu followed Gheorghe Gheorgiu-Dej[10] as the head of the Communist Party in 1965. The latter introduced a political course of independence from the USSR after the Red Army withdrew its divisions from Romania in 1958. This process culminated in the rejection of the Valev plan, which proposed a division of labour within the Council for Mutual Economic Assistance (COMECON) in 1964. Romania was to become a supplier of agricultural products for the more industrialized socialist countries, which meant that its industrialization would not be a priority.[11] The new General Secretary, Ceauşescu, went even further and refused to participate in the Warsaw Pact invasion of Prague in 1968. He denounced the actions of the other socialist countries and sent messages of solidarity to Alexander Dubček[12] and the Czechoslovak people.[13]

The independent course in foreign policy depended on the support of the citizens. In order to achieve this, Ceauşescu and the nomenclature lowered the ideological pressure in art, science, and music. Thus, the international atmosphere of the 1960s could be felt by the youth in Romania as well. Bands such as 'Phoenix'[14] introduced the Romanian audience to Beat music and to international bands like 'The Beatles' and 'The Rolling Stones'. The music of Woodstock could be heard at the official radio station Radio Bucureşti as well.[15] This lasted until the beginning

9 BBC News, http://news.bbc.co.uk/2/hi/europe/6935438.stm, 21 December 2014.

10 Georghe Gheorghiu-Dej (1901–1965) was Secretary General of the Executive Committee of the Romanian Communist Party from 1945 until 1965 and presided over the processes of nationalization of private property and collectivization of agriculture. It was during his time in office that Stalinist methods were implemented, but after Stalins's death he distanced himself from Moscow and promoted a more nationalistic way towards Socialism, for example by rejecting the Valev Plan.

11 Comisia prezidenţială pentru analiza dictaturii comuniste din România. Raport Final [The Presidential Committe for the Analysis of the Communist Dictatorship of Romania. Final Report], Bucureşti 2006, 22.

12 Alexander Dubček (1921–1992) was First Secretary of the Slovak Communist Party from 1963 to 1968 when he became First Secretary of the Communist Party of Czechoslovakia and the lead figure of the Prague Spring. Dubček tried to reform the prevailing communist system, but was forced to resign as soon as the armed forces of the Warsaw Pact entered the country and supressed the movement.

13 *Cf.* Comisia prezidenţială, Raport, 105.

14 The official website of the band 'Phoenix', http://www.transsylvania-phoenix.net/, 21 December 2014; for the autobiographical testimony of the band leader Nicolae Covaci see Nicolae Covaci, Phoenix, însă eu ... [Phoenix, but Myself ...], Bucureşti 1994, available online at http://www.scribd.com/doc/15436286/Nicolae-Covaci-Phoenix-Insa-Eu#scribd, 21 December 2014.

15 Website about Cornel Chiriac, http://www.cornel-chiriac.org/cronologie.html, 21 December 2014.

of the 1970s. After a visit to North Korea and China in 1971, Ceaușescu presented his Small Cultural Revolution [Mica Revoluție Culturală] which reintroduced ideological control in all aspects of life. Education, art, and science were subdued to the control of party representatives and committees. All foreign influences were rejected as 'decadent'.[16]

The youths, as the most avid consumers of 'Western' mass culture, were affected deeply by these changes. Wearing jeans, listening to Beat and Rock music and foreign radio stations, as well as growing their hair and beard (in the case of boys and young men) became a risky enterprise. The afore-mentioned actor Florian Pittiș was no longer allowed to appear on TV because he refused to cut his hair[17], many members of the band 'Phoenix' emigrated or flew to the 'West'[18], as well as other personalities of the Romanian music industry like Cornel Chiriac, Andrei Voiculescu, and Radu Teodor.[19] The latter three continued their work in Federal Germany within the Romanian department of Radio Free Europe, where they hosted music programs for the youths in Romania.

The youngsters themselves were forced to develop a parallel lifestyle to the official one within the Socialist state. What the government asked from them was conformism and alignment in thought, clothing, and behavior in order to shape them into 'new men' (and women). The instrument of this transformation would have to be labour. Ceaușescu propagated the connection between labour, education, culture, and sports as the key to 'the happiness of our Socialist nation'.[20] Children and youths were incorporated into mass organizations with specific uniforms and codes of conduct. The organization for kindergarten children, The Falkons of the Fatherland [Șoimii Patriei], was created in 1976 and comprised all children between four and nine years of age.[21] Once children were enrolled in primary school, they became Pioneers [Pionieri] and switched to the Union of the Communist Youth [Uniunea Tineretului Comunist] during high-school and university or at the working place until they reached the age of 25.[22]

Being part of these organizations meant that one had to wear the imposed uniform in school, keep one's hair neatly and respect the elders. Even extracurricular

---

16 Ana-Maria Cătănuș, Sfârșitul perioadei liberale a regimului Ceaușescu. Minirevoluția culturală din 1971 [The End of the Liberal Period of the Ceaușescu Regime. The Small Cultural Revolution], București 2005, 31.

17 Stamatescu – Grosescu – Dobrincu – Muraru – Pleșa – Andreescu, Istorie, 67.

18 Covaci, Phoenix, 428.

19 Interview with AV, 26.07.2013, Bucharest, transcripts in the author's possession.

20 Nicolae Ceaușescu, Programul privind dezvoltarea activității de educație fizică și sport pe perioada 1976–1980 [Program regarding the Development of Physical Education and Sports during the Period between 1976 and 1980] quoted in Stamatescu – Grosescu – Dobrincu – Muraru – Pleșa – Andreescu, Istorie, 67.

21 Document of the Romanian National Archives, http://www.arhivelenationale.ro/images/custom/image/serban/Fond_CC_al_UTC_Sectia_Cadre_Alfabetic_Litera_A%5B1%5D.pdf, 21 December 2014.

22 Comisia prezidențială, Raport, 154.

14 year old girls in uniform 1978 (blue dress, white stockings and white headband). Photo from the private collection of the author.

activities like sports were under the auspice of the official sphere. The state aimed at organizing the spare times of youths as well, by involving them in 'voluntary' work and offering them camps to various subjects. The national festival 'Cântarea României' [Song to Romania] and the sports competition 'Daciada' [The competition of the Dacians] were the two most important fora for youngsters with artistic and athletic qualities, where they could achieve national recognition as long as they respected state politics.[23]

While the official part of their life gave youths the opportunity of social and professional recognition, it did not offer them the means they needed to enjoy their youth. The liberalization period of the 1960s and the beginning of the 1970s had allowed them a glimpse into 'Western' youth culture with its fashion, music, and lifestyle. There was no turning back now. Through various means, girls and boys remained connected to their peers in the 'West' and sought to imitate their lifestyles. They listened to Radio Free Europe's youth programs and wrote to the staff in order to ask for music or to participate in competitions, they sought for 'Western' items on the black market, especially for jeans and records, they organized unofficial discotheques and concerts and befriended foreign students who offered them various consumer goods.[24]

23 *Ibid.*, 603.

24 For more information about the relationship of Romanian youths with the foreign students studying in Romania before 1989 see Andra-Octavia Drăghiciu, Between 'Totalitarianism' and 'Terrorism'. An Introductory Study about the 'Arab' Students in the Romanian Socialist Republic (1974–1989), in: Caietele CNSAS [Notebooks of the National Council for Studying the Archive of the Political Police], VI, 1–2/11–12/2013, București 2014, 323–334.

19 year old student with 'Hendrix' hairstyle at a private party, listening to rock music, 1984. Photo from the private collection of the author.

This part of youths' lives, which is regarded in this paper as 'The Dark Side of the Moon', is particularly difficult to reconstruct from the available written sources. The documents in the archive of the political police [Securitate] reflect the youngsters' conflict with the state, a very important aspect nonetheless, while the press and the official documents only show how the authorities wanted youths to be. The fact that the people concerned are still alive is an advantage for the scholar dealing with this period and it would be an immense loss if one would not take the time to listen to their testimonies. These testimonies should, of course, be analyzed in comparison and connection to one another as well as to other sources. The process of Oral History in post 1989 Romania was a fascinating and sometimes frustrating endeavor for the author of this paper, the development of which will be narrated below.

Theoretical Considerations on Memory, Remembering, and Truth

If once we thought that memory was a safe place within our (un-)consciousness, where past experiences and impressions were kept intact, neuroscientists have long proven that this is not the case.[25] As Aleida Assmann argues, memory does not work as a camera, which captures and stores images, but rather as a mechanism which retouches memories and adapts them to the status quo.[26] Moreover, our memory records only fragments and pieces and not coherent plots. It is up to the remembering subject to make sense of these elements of memory and to piece them together into a story, *i.e.* to remember.[27]

The impulses which generate memories are twofold: On the one hand, the active, voluntary 'I-memory' (Ich-Gedächtnis, *mémoire volontaire*) is generated by interaction with other people, on the other hand, the passive, involuntary 'Me-memory' (Mich-Gedächtnis, *mémoire involontaire*), popularized by Marcel Proust[28] in his novel "Á la recherche du temps perdu" is generated by objects, places, and

25 Aleida Assmann, Der lange Schatten der Vergangenheit. Erinnerungskultur und Geschichtspolitik [The long Shadow of the Past. Cultures of Memory and the Politics of History], München 2006, 129.

26 *Ibid.*, 134.

27 *Ibid.*, 135.

28 Marcel Proust (1871–1922) was a French writer and literary critic, famous for his novel "À la recherche du temps perdu" [In Search of Lost Time], 1913–1927.

sensations.[29] The voluntary memory is based on active reconstruction. The subject retrieves memories consciously and shapes them into a story, thus conveying them meaning. In contrast, the involuntary memories cannot be activated by will. They are generated when external factors meet a certain inner disposition and thus make their way from the preconscious *mémoire involontaire* to the conscious *mémoire volontaire*.[30]

There is, however, a category of memories, which seems to be accurate and remains vivid for a long period of time. These memories, called 'flashbulb memories'[31], bring forth a singular experience recorded accurately by memory, which does not seem to fade. They occur with regard to very important moments. Thus, subjects remember in detail what they were doing, wearing *etc.* when they received news of great importance to them.[32] In the case of the interviews analyzed in this study, the 'flashbulb memories' occur regarding the revolutionary events in December 1989. Each interviewed person seemed to remember exactly what they did during those days. This comes to support Samuel Butlers thesis that one remembers best the extraordinary and the most ordinary things and activities. According to him, it is novelty and routine, which influence memory the most, but the way extraordinary experiences are remembered is different than the way routine is remembered.[33]

What most scholars of Oral History agree upon is the fact that the present plays the decisive part when it comes to the way we remember. The Romanian historian Neagu Djuvara defines history itself as 'the attempt to narrate and understand past human experiences from the perspective of the present'.[34] During the process of remembering, what one perceives to be the past is interpreted according to the present.[35] It is the social, cultural, and historical context of the present, *i.e.* the memory milieu[36], and the relation of present and past at the time of remem-

29 *Ibid.*, 120.

30 *Ibid.*, 123.

31 Assmann, Schatten der Vergangenheit, 129.

32 *Ibid.*, 127.

33 *Ibid.*, 128.

34 Neagu Djuvara, Există istorie adevărată? Despre 'relativitatea generală' a istoriei. Eseu de epistemologie [Does True History Exist? About the 'General Relativity' of History. An Epistemological Essay], București 2011, 16.

35 Karin Stögner, Lebensgeschichtliche Interviews und die 'Wahrheit der Erinnerung'. Einige Überlegungen zum Mauthausen Survivors Documentation Project [Life Story Interviews and the 'Accuracy of Memory'. Considerations on the Mauthausen Survivors Documentation Project], in: Eleonore Lappin – Albert Lichtblau (Eds.), Die 'Wahrheit' der Erinnerung. Jüdische Lebensgeschichten [The 'Accuracy' of Memory. Jewish Life Stories], Innsbruck/Wien/Bozen 2008, 169–179, here 170.

36 Maria Ecker, 'Ich habe erst viel später erfahren, dass es Mengele war …' Falsche Erinnerungen in mündlichen Zeugnissen von Holocaust-Überlebenden ['I found out only later that it had been Mengele …' Inaccurate Memories in Oral Testimonies of Holocaust Survivors], in: Eleonore Lappin – Albert Lichtblau (Eds.), Die 'Wahrheit' der Erinnerung. Jüdische Lebensgeschichten [The 'Accuracy' of Memory. Jewish Life Stories], Innsbruck/Wien/Bozen 2008, 35–45, here 40.

bering which influence what part of the past one is given access to.[37] This means that within a certain political and cultural context only a specific part of the past is accessible to us.

Nevertheless, it is not only this constellation that influences what and how we remember. The setting, within which remembering takes place is also of fundamental importance. Aleida Assman talks about two different settings: The therapeutic one, where the patient goes on his/her own will. This setting represents a safe environment where one can talk about traumatizing memories in order to heal. In contrast, the juridical setting is a public place one is called to in order to establish the truthfulness of the memory. It is within this setting that private memories take collective proportions and have social and political consequences.[38]

At this point, the issue of the accuracy of memories should be discussed. For Karin Stögner, memories are 'the expression of the past in the present', influenced by the changes that have occurred between the experience itself and the moment of remembering.[39] They are translations on two levels: From impression to verbalisation[40] and from the language of the past into the language of the present.[41] The consequence of this translation is, as in any other translation, the shift and alteration of meaning.[42] Moreover, in the case of memories which have been narrated often, one tends to remember the words one used in the narrative rather than the experience itself, a fact that also leads to the modification of 'the past'.[43]

Another external factor, which influences memories, is what Maria Ecker calls 'Quellenamnesie', an amnesia induced by external sources.[44] Her empirical research showed that media and other sources, which we interact with in everyday life, have a big impact on our memory. External information is unconsciously integrated into our autobiographical memory[45], making it impossible for us to distinguish between experienced and acquired memories.[46]

Nevertheless, the memory milieu, the external sources, and the setting are not the only factors which generate inaccurate memories. Mark Roseman identifies guilt as a major trigger of false memories when talking about survivors of the Holocaust. These people have the tendency to modify their memories in order to be able to live with the guilt of having survived, while others, especially their friends

37 Stögner, Lebensgeschichtliche Interviews, 177.

38 Aleida Assmann, Erinnerungsräume. Formen und Wandlungen des kulturellen Gedächtnisses [Spaces of Memory. Shapes and Transformations of Cultural Memory], München 2010, 267.

39 Stögner, Lebensgeschichtliche Interviews, 171.

40 Assmann, Schatten der Vergangenheit, 124.

41 Stögner, Lebensgeschichtliche Interviews, 171.

42 Assmann, Schatten der Vergangenheit, 124.

43 Stögner, Lebensgeschichtliche Interviews, 173.

44 Ecker, Falsche Erinnerung, 43.

45 *Ibid.*

46 Assmann, Schatten der Vergangenheit, 132.

and family, did not.[47] This view is shared by Freudian psychoanalysts who believed that the suppressed memories can be retrieved with the help of psychoanalysis. A contrasting argument is that of Nietzsche, who regards will and pride as the inner generators of false memories.[48]

To sum up, memories are not representations of the past, but constructs. They are interpretations of past experiences from a contemporary point of view, translations of the past into the present, influenced by external and internal factors. Depending on the memory milieu and the setting, only certain aspects of the past can be remembered at a certain point in time.[49] These thoughts can be extended to history as a broader subject following Danto's thesis of the difference among 'History as Actuality', 'History as Thought', and 'History as Record'.[50]

If memories, the object of Oral History, can hardly be relied upon, then what is the point in conducting narrative interviews? Scholars, who set their minds on finding 'historical truth' through the method of Oral History, will be utterly disappointed. Due to the constructive nature of evidence and the fact that 'all experience is discursively mediated'[51], 'historical facts' are not given, but ever changing actualizations of the past from the position of the present.[52] History is a never-ending process, anchored in the prevailing political, social, and economic premises of the present.[53] What Oral History can offer is an insight into the interpretations of the remembering subjects and their interaction with what they believe to be their own past.[54] Moreover, the product of this method is the written account of the historian, who 'deforms' the testimonies according to the interest of his/her own research and his/her own cultural background.[55]

The Oral History interview is an oral account about history (not of)[56], a temporary 'community of memory' between the interviewee and the interviewer, within which the latter stands as an intermediary between the memories and the outside world.[57] The testimonies are reconstructed in the moment of the interview accord-

47 Mark Roseman, Surviving Memory. Truth and Inaccuracy in Holocaust Testimony, in: Robert Perks – Alistair Thomson (Eds.), The Oral History Reader, London/New York 1998, 230–243, here 240.

48 Assmann, Erinnerungsräume, 270.

49 *Ibid.*

50 Quoted in Djuvara, Istorie adevărată, 19.

51 Roseanne Kennedy, Stolen Generations Testimony. Trauma, Historiography and the Question of 'Truth', in: Robert Perks – Alistair Thomson (Eds.), The Oral History Reader, London/New York 1998, 506–520, here 510.

52 Stögner, Lebensgeschichtliche Interviews, 170.

53 *Ibid.*

54 Kennedy, Stolen Generations, 512.

55 Djuvara, Istorie adevărată, 23.

56 Alessandro Portelli, Istoria Orală ca gen [Oral History as a Genre], translation by Sidonia Grama, in: Ioana Cosman (Ed.), Anuarul de Istorie Orală vol. X [The Oral History Annual], Cluj-Napoca 2008, 199–228, here 199.

57 Stögner, Lebensgeschichtliche Interviews, 172.

ing to the expectations, the questions and the position of the interviewer, they are reactions to the given interview situation.[58] This means that the recipient, in this case the interviewer, plays a very important part in what is remembered and how, thus being a possible generator of inaccurate memories.[59] Another element, which influences the demeanour of the interviewee, is the recording device used by the interviewer.[60]

According to Fritz Schütze, a qualitative narrative interview has to be organized in a certain way in order to produce viable results. In an environment of mutual trust and consent, the interviewer has to ask a broad question in order to generate the flux of memory. This question can regard the life story of the interviewed person or focus on a certain topic. The speaker must not be interrupted until he/she finishes the story, at which point complementary questions should be asked as to exhaust the narrative potential of the interviewee. It is only then that questions implying interpretation and discussion should be asked.[61]

Oral History in post 1989 Romania – A Case Study

Research based on the method of Oral History has been conducted in Romania since the end of the 1990s. The most representative academic institution in this respect is probably the Institute for Oral History at the University of Cluj-Napoca, which published its first Annual in 1999. When skimming the contents of the thirteen numbers of this journal until 2013[62], one will reach the conclusion that most studies published here revolve around the process of collectivization, nationalization, and religious or armed anti-communist resistance. In short, the majority of articles leave out the period between 1974 and 1989. Moreover, there is no study dedicated to the youth, although it represented a crucial segment of Socialist society and ideology.

The Romanian ethnologist Narcisa Ştiucă criticized her conational colleagues working on and with Oral History for the lack of scholarly analysis in their studies, which, according to her, only show part of the Oral History process, namely the transcription of the interview.[63] This is the case with various publications by the sociology and communication professor Zoltán Rostás in cooperation with other

58 *Ibid.*

59 Ecker, Falsche Erinnerung, 43.

60 Portelli, Istoria Orală, 214.

61 Harry Hermanns, Die Auswertung narrativer Interviews. Ein Beispiel für qualitative Verfahren [The Evaluation of Narrative Interviews. An Example for Qualitative Procedures], in: Jürgen H.P. Hoffmeyer-Zlotnik (Ed.), Analyse verbaler Daten. Über den Umgang mit qualitativen Daten [Analysis of Verbal Data. About Handling Qualitative Data], Opladen 1992, 111–137, here 120.

62 The Oral Histoy Institue Cluj-Napoca, http://institute.ubbcluj.ro/iio/publicatii/periodice.html, 21 December 2014.

63 Narcisa Ştiucă, Istorie Orală – note polemice [Oral History – Polemic Notes], in Anuarul IEF 'C. Brăiloiu' [The Annual of the Institute for Ethnography and Folcore 'C. Brăiloiu'], tom XVII/2006, Bucureşti 2006, 29–34, here 30.

scholars.[64] These volumes contain the transcripts of Oral History interviews made by students to afore-settled themes under the pretence of offering 'a different history', a point of view not reflected in written sources.[65] The scholars refrain from any commentary other than short introductions to each volume and the description of the project (who were the interviewers, what was their theme, how did they find the interviewees, under what circumstances did the interviews take place), a fact that enforces Narcisa Ştiucă's critique years after it has been voiced. Nevertheless, these publications can be used as sources for scholars interested in Oral History testimonies by supplementing their own interviews. They can be seen as compendia of historical sources like any other source book.

A further point raised by Ştiucă in the same paper, is the question of objectivity, in her opinion disregarded by Oral History. She talks about the difference between the 'subjective truth' and the 'unanimously accepted truth', proven by 'generally recognized documents' and argues that the first should be measured by the latter, in order to achieve 'total objectivity'.[66] This point of view shows either the lack of awareness about the discussions around 'historical truth' in the international scientific community or their total disregard.

The object of the subsequent analysis is the experience of the author of this paper during the process of Oral History. This project is different than the aforementioned ones (the Annual of the Oral History Institute and the publications edited by Zoltán Rostás) because it was not affiliated to any Romanian institution and did not benefit from the relations, which come with such affiliations. It was up to the author to find connections leading to suitable interview partners, to persuade them to give an interview and travel to their places of residence in Romania and abroad. This was also the case with the students involved in Zoltán Rostás' and Florentina Ţone's project regarding interviews with 'revolutionists' of the 1989 December revolution in Romania and their conclusions were similar, as will be discussed below.

On the subject of youth culture in the Romanian Socialist Republic, my target group included women and men born between 1954 and 1974 who had spent their youth (age 14 to 25) in Romania between 1974 and 1989. It was important to talk to representatives of the Romanian orthodox majority, but also to ethnic and religious minorities coming from all parts of the country and from the entire social spectrum. In the end 18 interviews were conducted by the author between the summer of 2012 and spring 2013 with 14 men and four women from various

64 Zoltán Rostás – Florentina Ţone (Eds.), Tânăr student caut revoluţionar [Young Student Looking for Revolutionist], vol. I, Bucureşti 2011, vol. II, Bucureşti 2012; Zoltán Rostás – Antonio Momoc (Eds.), Bişniţari, descurcăreţi, supravieţuitori [Dealers, People who Scratched along, Survivors], Bucureşti 2014; Zoltán Rostás – Theodora-Eliza Văcărescu (Eds.), Cealaltă jumătate a istoriei – Femei povestind [The Other Half of History – Women Narrating], Bucureşti 2008.

65 Rostás – Ţone, Tânăr student, 6.

66 Ştiucă, Istorie Orală, 31.

towns in Transylvania and Crişana as well as from Bucharest.[67] Six of them belong to the German-speaking minority in Romania and they all currently live in Germany, one of them belongs to the Hungarian minority and lives in Romania. The others are ethnic Romanians living in Romania. Two come from families of peasants who lived in the countryside, but were forced to seek labour in the nearest town because of the collectivization, eleven are sons and daughters of workers and the other five come from families of intellectuals.

Eight of the interviewed persons studied at university in Romania before 1989, one person studied only after 1990 and the others never pursued a higher education. The six representatives of the German speaking minority either left Romania legally before 1989 together with their families or fled the country before and immediately after December 1989. There are two former Radio Free Europe employees among the interview partners, who left Romania at the beginning of the 1970s and returned after the fall of the Socialist regime. The anonymity of the sources was guaranteed to all participants in the project.

The first and biggest issue was finding people willing to talk about their youth on camera, a problem which the students in the revolution project also had to face.[68] It was particularly difficult to persuade women to talk about their experiences. Those approached were reluctant to take part in this project because they were convinced they could not contribute in any way. Generally, men showed a much higher disposition to talk, explain, and discuss. This is certainly an effect of the gender roles, which prevail in Romanian society, where the man is portrayed as the 'spokesman' of the family. Moreover, from the 51 interviewees of the students in the revolution project volume I and II, only seven were female[69], a fact which shows that this experience is not singular. In addition to this, Zoltán Rostás dedicated a whole volume to testimonies of women, which he entitled 'The Other Half of History'.[70] The necessity of such a publication suggests that women represent a different sector of Romanian society which is not regarded as part of the 'whole picture', but has to be sought out and brought to light as a special entity.

After having talked to people and enquired about the *Zeitgeist*, the author soon realized that making an announcement in local papers would have been futile in the attempt to find interview partners. It was only through personal connections and recommendations that people accepted to give an interview. Most of them were surprised by the proposition because they felt they had nothing to say, that their life was not 'special' enough for an interview. It was hard for them to accept

67 Needless to say, it was impossible to find interview partners in all the 'historic' regions of the country. Transylvania and Bucharest were the most accessible for the interviewer due to the existing personal connections and the connections which resulted from them. It is important to stress that a great amount of time is needed in order to make the trips, arrange the meetings, and establish a relation of trust with the interview partners.

68 Rostás – Ţone, Tânăr student, 468.

69 *Ibid.*

70 See *supra* n. 64.

that the interest lay particularly in the lives of ordinary people and that nothing extraordinary was asked of them. The fact that a video camera was used for recording the interview had a clear impact on the speakers. Gestures like arranging ones hair and clothes were frequent in the first ten minutes of the interview, but they seemed to forget about the device as they got deeper into their story. The reason for choosing a video camera as a recording device was the desire to capture the whole interview experience, verbal, as well as visual. It proved to be a good decision in most cases, because it allowed the recording of picturesque gestures and dynamic behavior induced by the story at hand.

The fact that the interviewed persons were recommended by mutual acquaintances had ambivalent consequences. On the one hand, the interview partners knew the background of the interviewer and this made it visibly easier for them to express their thoughts and share their experiences, thus confirming Portellis thesis that the more the interviewee knows about the interviewer, the less artificially will he/she shape his/her testimony.[71] On the other hand, it rendered some topics taboo, like naming important people from state companies or talking about sexual experiences.

It must be said that the latter topic was of particular difficulty not only for the interviewees, but also for the author, the interviewer. Coming from the cultural background of 1990s Romania, where sexuality was not something to openly talk about, it was particularly hard for the interviewer to address this issue. Only one attempt was fruitful with the Hungarian female interview partner who talked about methods of contraception, but projected sexuality onto her friends, insisting that it was not the case for her. Another attempt with a Romanian female interview partner, who at first seemed likely to be receptive, failed. She immediately dismissed the issue with an odd handgesture by saying that sexuality was not something they talked about. Seeing that this topic upset and set off the female interview partners, it was never addressed again. The men did not even offer the opportunity for this subject to arise.

This attitude of the interviewees regarding the subject of sexual experience sheds light on the kind of sexual education they received (or did not receive) in the 1970s and 1980s. Relationships between men and women were discussed by the propaganda only in terms of family and within marriage, as has been established by the author from written sources. The prudishness of the representatives of the regime and of the parent generation of these youngsters transpires from their refusal to talk about sexuality even 25 years later. They, in turn, as parents of the author's generation, have chosen to perpetuate this attitude after 1989 and have educated their children accordingly. The result was the impasse reached by the author as a scholar when confronted with this subject. A lighter, more matter of fact approach of the interviewer might have lead to different results in this respect.

71 Portelli, Istoria Orală, 212.

This, however, was not the only problem regarding the person of the interviewer. The male interview partners, especially the older ones, found it hard to regard the author, a young woman, as a historian. It was particularly hard for them to acknowlegde that such a person could be familiar with Socialism and pre-1989 history, often better than they were. This led to remarks like: 'You couldn't understand' or 'You are too young to understand these things'. Some maintained an air of superiority and slight irony all through the interview, which made the 'temporary community of memory' uncomfortable for the interviewer.

In addition to this, some of the interview partners insisted there were things they could not say or persons they could not name because they were still in high positions and could hurt them one way or another, although it was never asked of them to disclose such information. This is one of the reasons listed by the editor Florentina Țone when talking about the excuses potential interview partners used in order to refuse their participation in the interview project about the revolution.[72] The belief that the Romanian political police, called Securitate, still operates in the present, transpired from many of my interviews. This is why some remarks were made only after the interview was over and the recording device turned off. Other types of information were also kept 'off the record'. After finishing the interview, an interviewee disclosed 'bad jokes' the youths made among themselves, saying that they were not appropriate for the interview.

Other obstacles in the way of shaping the interview according to Schütze's demands were on the one hand the inability of some of the interview partners, especially those with a poor education, to create a logical narrative, on the other hand for those with higher education to concentrate on the topic. Representatives of the first category stopped after a few sentences and demanded more questions, while the others talked for hours, discussing, interpreting, and going further and further away from the topic.

Beside these problems regarding the content of the interview, formal issues also arose. In order to talk to representatives of the German-speaking minority, trips to Germany were required. The majority of Saxons and Swabians emigrated to Federal Germany before or after 1989. Those who still live in Romania are mostly older people, the parent generation of those who make the object of this study. The interviews in Germany had to be taken during a week-end annual meeting of the Saxons, during which they try to recreate the atmosphere of their youth in Transylvania. It was very interesting to observe the effort they underwent in order to cook, sing, and dance like they 'used to'. Transylvanian-Hungarian food, Romanian folk music and Saxon dialect were the core elements of the reenactment. This environment created a certain merry disposition and state of mind for those interviewed, in which they tended to diminish the negative aspects and focus on the positive side of their youth in Romania.

72 Rostás – Țone, Tânăr student, 470.

It is important to note that these interviewees employed a different attitude towards giving an interview than their counterparts in Romania. Except for the female Saxon interview partner – a fact, which reinforces the remarks above, none of them were reluctant to talk about their youth in the Romanian Socialist Republic – on the contrary. They were influenced, of course, by the feast that they were having, but they seemed more relaxed and at ease while discussing their experiences. This is probably the effect of having lived in (West-)Germany for the past 25 years or more. There was no mentioning of the current political situation in Romania, nor did any fears regarding the 'still operating secret police' emerge from their testimonies.

Conclusion

The purpose of this short empirical study was to discuss to which extent scholars can apply the method of Oral History in Eastern European societies by analyzing the Romanian example. The cultural, social, and political context is often an obstacle in this regard. People are not familiar with sociological methods like this one and they often believe that interviews are only ment for public persons. Furthermore, a wave of suspicion arises towards anyone interested in the Socialist past. The most common discussion regarding pre 1989 Romanian society in the media revolves around the informers of the political police. What people dread the most is to be accused of having collaborated with this institution. This is why in order to be able to make interviews, even anonymous ones, scholars have to either know the persons they want to talk to or be recommended by someone, thus proving to be trustworthy.

As argued in the theories mentioned above, the interviewer plays a very important part in the shaping of memory and the act of remembering. In this case, being a young woman worked to the disadvantage of the interviewer, especially when confronted with elder male interview partners. Their story tended to focus less on narrating memories and more on explaining things to a person who they think is not able to understand what they mean. Moreover, the cultural and social background of the interviewer is of utmost importance as well, because it sets the limits on what one believes is common sense to ask and what not.

Despite all the difficulties encountered during the process of Oral History in contemporary Romania, valuable information could be obtained about the unofficial lives of youths in the 1970s and 1980s, but especially about the way people perceive and interpret their past in the light of a present obssesed with the notions of communism and secret police. Last but not least, the interaction within the 'temporary community of memory' gave way to a serious self-reflection of the scholar as her own object of study.

This being said, it is of utmost importance that the premises of Eastern European societies be taken into consideration in further developments of Oral History theory. The demands of this sociological methodology are nearly impossible to meet in most cases, but this does not mean, that it cannot prove fruitful for scientific purposes. An especially valuable scientific insight about post-1989 Romanian society is precisely the fact that this method cannot be applied here as it can be applied in 'Western' societies. Finally, listening to and analyzing the testimonies of people who spent their youth during the last 15 years of the Romanian Socialist regime is a neccessary enterprize for scholars who wish to present a complete picture of pre-1989 Romanian society as well as understand its developments after the collapse of the regime.

Adéla Rossípalová

Anthropology of *Neue Sachlichkeit* in Paul Kornfeld's "Blanche oder das Atelier im Garten"

Palacký University Olomouc

Introduction

In the early 1920s, resulting from the end of the First World War, the exuberant expressionistic movement, with its cosmic views, ecstatic feelings, and pathos, gradually lost its place in the modern world of the Roaring Twenties. The society of the new republic started to focus on the present moment and immediate surroundings, and took a sober, unsentimental look at the world around. Here and now, *e.g.*, the everyday life, became the center of all attention. The excess of feelings, sentiment, cosmic dreams, and apocalyptic pathos typical of the expressionistic movement were no longer demanded. 'Der Mensch ist gut' [The man is good], the main motto of literary expressionism, transformed into its exact opposite. As George Grosz[1] (1893–1959), the main representative of visual art of *neue Sachlichkeit*[2], declared at the beginning of the 1920s 'der Mensch ist ein Vieh'[3] and as such must be freed from his dependence on society and its class system. This rejection of expressionism can also be found in works by Dadaists, Futurists, or Cubists; however, only the movement of *neue Sachlichkeit* presented an absolute opposite to all expressionistic tendencies so it was also labelled as anti-expressionism. In 1925, Gustav Friedrich Hartlaub[4], director of the Kunsthalle Mannheim, called an exhibition of post-expressionist painters *neue Sachlichkeit* and soon this term was accepted and used for the whole culture of the Weimar Republic.[5]

---

1 George Grosz was a German painter known as a member of the Berlin Dada and New Objectivity group of artists during the Weimar Republic. In 1933, he emigrated to the USA.

2 The term *neue Sachlichkeit* is usually translated as new objectivity into English; however, this translation does not fully correspond to the German original and therefore the German term will be used in this article.

3 See Wieland Schmied, Neue Sachlichkeit und magischer Realismus 1918–1933 [New Objectivity and Magic Realism 1918–1933], Hannover 1969, 14. [The man is a beast].

4 Gustav Friedrich Hartlaub (1884–1963) was a modernist art historian who coined the term *Neue Sachlichkeit* (*i.e.* New Objectivity) to distinguish non-Expressionist art in the interwar Germany.

5 In 1923, however, Franz Roh also tried to find an appropriate term for a group of the same post-expressionist painters and chose the term magic realism. This caused, and still causes, difficulties when defining these two concepts. Sometimes these terms are used as synonyms, sometimes they

First, the central views regarding literary *neue Sachlichkeit* that have been widely discussed in the literary theory will be introduced (Sabina Becker, Helmut Lethen, Gregor Streim) in this article. In the second part, the life and literary work of Paul Kornfeld, a Prague born playwright and novelist, will be presented as an introduction to the analysis of his only novel "Blanche oder das Atelier im Garten" [Blanche or The Studio in the Garden]. Since *neue Sachlichkeit* is closely connected with the culture of the Weimar Republic (1918–1933), it will be interesting to see what *neu-sachliche* features can be found in a novel written by a Prague German author and whether these features differ from German *neue Sachlichkeit*.[6] In this article, the novel will be analyzed with regards to three main aspects: first, main characters will be examined using Lethen's anthropological approach of classifying figures as cool *personae* (see below), second, *neu-sachlich* motifs in the novel will be presented, and third, *neu-sachlich* setting (houses, means of transport) will be analyzed.

Literary *neue Sachlichkeit*

Neue Sachlichkeit was a cultural and literary movement of the 1920s and the early 1930s, the period of the newly founded Weimar Republic (1918–1933) in Germany and the Czechoslovak Republic (1918–1938), whose German-speaking inhabitants had to deal with the fall of the Austro-Hungarian Empire and the decay of the old system of the monarchy.[7] It replaced its predecessor expressionism in both visual art and literature. Expressionism, a movement that arose in around 1910 in Germany and continued till the early 1920s, was an extrovert, subjective, and abstract movement that played with words, made use of ciphers. Its language was dynamic, appellative, and symbolic. The program of expressionism was introduced in numerous manifestos and anthologies and the main genres of literary expressionism were poetry and drama. Paul Kornfeld, who was a playwright for most of his life, is also known mainly for his expressionistic tragedies and comedies. On the other hand, *neue Sachlichkeit*, as a movement following expressionism, is characterized as its very opposite.

---

are described as two different concepts from the same period and sometimes magic realism is seen as a part of *neue Sachlichkeit* (See, *e.g.*, Michael Scheffel, Magischer Realismus [Magic Realism], Tübingen 1990; Uwe Durst, Theorie der phantastischen Literatur, Tübingen/Basel 2001).

6 In this article new research results regarding a PhD dissertation with the working title 'Die neue Sachlichkeit in der Prager deutschen Literatur: Erzähltexte weniger bekannter Prager deutschen Autoren' [The *neue Sachlichkeit* in Prague German Literature: Novels written by lesser known Prague German Authors] will be presented. In the dissertation *neue Sachlichkeit* will be analyzed in three more Prague German novels: Hans Natonek's "Kinder einer Stadt" [Children of a City] (1932), Otto Roeld's "Malenski auf der Tour" [Malenski on the Road] (1930), and Hermann Grab's "Der Stadtpark" [The City Park] (1935).

7 See Sabina Becker, Die literarische Moderne der zwanziger Jahre [Literary Modernism of the 1920s], in: Internationales Archiv für Sozialgeschichte der deutschen Literatur 27, Tübingen 2002, 73–95.

The origin of the term *neue Sachlichkeit* is also closely connected with fine art; namely, with the exhibition organized by art historian Gustav Friedrich Hartlaub in 1925 in the Kunsthalle in Mannheim. *Neu-sachlich* painters (such as Otto Dix, George Grosz, Christian Schad, or Gustav Wunderwald[8]) were fascinated with reality and painted even the tiniest objects in every detail. They felt solidarity with everything existing in this world, even with the lowest cripples and creatures.[9] Schmied defines five crucial characteristics of *neu-sachlich* paintings. First, the view of the painter should be sober, sharp, and unsentimental. Second, the theme of a painting should be banal, every-day, and unimportant. The painter should also not be afraid of ugliness. Third, the painting is static (in contrast to expressionistic dynamics). Four, there should not be any traces of the painting process left. Five, the painters' focus on the material/physical world.[10] The first three points can be applied to literary *neue Sachlichkeit*.

Hartlaub's exhibition, which he called *Neue Sachlichkeit*, is believed to have given the literary *neue Sachlichkeit* its name. However, Sabina Becker, whose work deals with the aesthetics of *neu-sachlich* literature, rejects this connection as she points out that there had been many works written before 1925 which were associated with the concept of *neue Sachlichkeit* (for example, Georg Kaiser's "Nebeneinander" from 1923, which is considered to be the first drama influenced by *neue Sachlichkeit*, or Egon Erwin Kisch's "Der rasende Reporter" from 1924) and so the literary *neue Sachlichkeit* had existed before the *neu-sachlich* visual arts.[11] The term itself had been, according to Wieland Schmied, mentioned more than two decades before Hartlaub's exhibition for the first time. He points out that German architect Hermann Muthesius[12] was the first one to use the concept *neue Sachlichkeit* when describing new, functionalistic architecture from the beginning of the 20th century.[13]

As for the definition of literary *neue Sachlichkeit*, there is no clear way of defining this movement. Rather than defining what it is, it seems to be more reasonable to define it as what it is not: that is through opposites. *Neue Sachlichkeit* is therefore characterized as anti-expressionism, anti-sentimentalism, anti-psychologism, anti-aestheticism, or anti-individualism.[14] In the early 1920s, art historian Franz

8 Otto Dix (1891–1969) and Christian Schad (1894–1982) were first influenced by the Dada movement and later, in the 1920s, they were associated with the New Objectivity movement based in Berlin. During the Nazi regime, both painters were classified as degenerated artists. Gustav Wunderwald (1882–1945) was not only a *neu-sachlich* painter but also a theatrical set designer.

9 See Schmied, Sachlichkeit, 11.

10 See Schmied, Sachlichkeit, 26.

11 See Becker, Moderne, 74.

12 Hermann Muthesius (1861–1927) was a German architect, architectural historian, writer and diplomat. His publications dealt mainly with English formal arts which he promoted in Germany; he emphasized especially the practical and functional aspects in architecture. Therefore, he had a big influence on German architectural modernism such as Bauhaus.

13 See Schmied, Sachlichkeit, 9.

14 See Becker, Moderne, 76.

Roh spoke about a new movement that he labelled *Nachexpressionismus*, *e.g.*, post-expressionism. Even though the main features of the post-expressionistic movement he describes in his book "Probleme der neuesten deutschen Malerei. Nachexpressionismus. Magischer Realismus" [Problems of the newest German fine art. Post-expressionism. Magic Realism] (1925) were intended for fine art (compare Schmied's characteristics of *neue Sachlichkeit*), most of them can also be found in *neu-sachlich* literature and as such are worth mentioning. Similarly to Sabina Becker, who uses opposites to define *neue Sachlichkeit*, Roh created a table consisting of features of expressionism on the one hand, and antonymous features of post-expressionism on the other one.[15]

Expressionism	**Post-expressionism**
Ecstatic objects	Sober, unemotional objects
Many religious rebukes	Very little religious rebukes
Suppressing objects	Emphasizing objects
Eccentric	Rather strict, puristic
Dynamic	Static
Loud	Quiet
Foreground	Foreground + background
Monumental	Focus on miniatures
Warm	Cold
Thick layer of paint	Thin layer of paint
Rough effect	Smooth effect
Like rough-hewn stone	Like shining glazed metal
Expressive deformation of objects	Harmonic smoothing of objects
Primeval	Cultivated

Nevertheless, it was neither in fine art nor in literature where *neue Sachlichkeit* was introduced for the first time. As Schmied puts it, it developed first in architecture. As early as in 1900, sociologist Georg Simmel uses the term *Sachlichkeit* in his article "Die Großstädte und das Geistesleben" [The Metropolis and Mental Life] to describe urban models of behavior. According to Simmel, people living in big cities live in accordance with their reason and pure objectivity: 'Sachlichkeit im Sinne von Blasiertheit und Reserviertheit soll [sie] gegen die großstädtische Reizüberflutung schützen, da [sie] sich ansonsten völlig atomisieren [würden].'[16] Big cities with all modern inventions their inhabitants have to face became an important locale of *neu-sachlich* art. Around 1900, discussions were held against the style of Art Nouveau resulting in the need for new functionalistic aestheticism.

15 See Michael Scheffel, Magischer Realismus [Magic Realism], Tübingen 1990, 11f.

16 Sabina Becker, Neue Sachlichkeit. Die Ästhetik der neusachlichen Literatur (1920–1933) [Neue Sachlichkeit. The Aestheticism of New-Objective Literature (1920–1933)], 1, Köln/Weimar/Wien 2000, 74. [Objectivity in terms of blasé and reserved behavior should protect them from overstimulation of a big city since otherwise they would end up fully atomized.]

Ornaments hiding the actual function of a building or an object were no longer demanded. Once again, this feature is also typical of *neu-sachlich* literature since it became sober, objective and stripped of any 'decorative' descriptions.[17] According to sociologist Helmuth Plessner, Bauhaus architecture (founded by Walter Gropius in 1919 in Weimar) reflected social needs that were necessary for survival in the society of the Weimar Republic. In these buildings, people could come close without actually meeting each other and they could retreat without hurting each other.[18] Simple geometric lines, usage of tiles on walls, clear space without ornaments, industrial design and typography satisfied the need to escape from the oppressive coexistence and supported the behavioral code of distance of that time. We will see that in Kornfeld's "Blanche oder das Atelier im Garten", there is a clash of two architectural styles: the modern functionalistic one and the older architecture of Historicism.

The Golden Twenties and the period of *neue Sachlichkeit* ended with the fall of the Weimar Republic and Hitler's *Machtergreifung* [seizure of power] in 1933 in Germany. In Czechoslovakia, where Paul Kornfeld grew up, the milestone was the year 1938 when Germany annexed Sudetenland to Germany and when Czechoslovakia was occupied. However, Kornfeld had left Prague in 1914 and lived in Frankfurt am Main, Darmstadt, and Berlin until he returned in 1932, so he could experience the atmosphere of the Roaring Twenties in German big cities, especially Berlin, which Döblin describes as follows:

> 'Es ist wahrhaft eine moderne Stadt, eine großartige Stadt, eine Siedlung heutiger Menschen. Die Straßen sind mäßig beleuchtet, man fliegt von Bahnhof zu Bahnhof [...], da ein helles Licht, das muß ein Kino sein, plötzliche Lichtwirbel, aber wie belanglos in diesem Dunkel, auf den Bahnhöfen nüchterne eilige Menschen und wieder Straßenzüge, Mietskasernen, Schornsteine, Brücken.'[19]

Berlin was the capital of *neu-sachlich* writings such as Döblin's "Berlin Alexanderplatz" or Kästner's "Fabian. Geschichte eines Moralisten" [Fabian. The Story of a Moralist]; however, *neu-sachlich* forms can also be found in other big cities; namely

17 Two of the most important functionalist architects should be mentioned here. First, Viennese architect and writer Adolf Loos who developed ultimately functional architecture oriented purely on the object and its purpose without any subjectivist tendencies (for example the Looshaus near the Hofburg Palace in Vienna from 1910 or Villa Müller in Prague from 1928), and second, Walther Gropius, the founder of the Bauhaus school of architects.

18 See Helmut Lethen, Verhaltenslehre der Kälte: Lebensversuche zwischen den Kriegen [Cool Conduct: The Culture of Distance], Frankfurt am Main 1994, 163.

19 See Johannes G. Pankau, Einführung in die Literatur der Neuen Sachlichkeit [Introduction to the Literature of New Objectivity], Darmstadt 2010, 23. [It truly is a modern city, a magnificent city, a settlement of today's people. The streets are moderately lit, you fly from one station to another, then bright light, and it must be a cinema, sudden vortex of light, but how insignificant it is in this darkness, at the stations sober people are in a hurry and then again: trams, tenement houses, chimneys, bridges.]

in Munich, Hamburg, Stuttgart, Frankfurt am Main, Dresden, Leipzig, Vienna, or Prague. To see the big city and its inhabitants in the true aspect it is necessary to 'richten [den Blick] auf das Hier und Heute, darum ging es, den Blick aus dem Fenster und auf den Alltag und den Asphalt vor dem Haus, den Blick auf die Gasse und in die Gosse, in die Fabrikshalle und in die Schiffswerft, in den Operationssaal und ins Bordell [...]'.[20]

As opposed to expressionism, which is connected with many manifestos and collections defining expressionist art and ways of writing and painting, there was neither a unified group of *neu-sachlich* authors, nor were there any manifestos dealing with the program of *neue Sachlichkeit*. *Neu-sachlich* authors were a group of individuals whose novels, poems and drama were written in a new cold and documentary style and became known as *neu-sachlich* works in the history of literature. Nevertheless, a group of authors formed in 1925 and met in a Berlin pub to talk about modern aestheticism. They called themselves Gruppe 1925 [Group 1925] and their theories were published in new magazines such as *Querschnitt* [The Cross Section], *Tage-Buch* [Daily Journal], *Scheinwerfer* [Reflector], *Die literarische Welt* [Literary World] or *Weltbühne* [The World Stage]. Among the artists we can find personalities such as Bertolt Brecht, Alfred Döblin, Erwin Piscator, or Ernst Blass. Even though the authors shared views and felt as though they were part of one collective, they were not publicly engaged, did not organize any public readings and did not perform in public.[21] According to Becker, Kisch's preface to his book of reportage "Der rasende Reporter" [The Raging Reporter] from 1924 can be actually considered as the first theoretical manifesto of *neue Sachlichkeit*.[22] In his preface he describes the main characteristics of *neu-sachlich* literature:

> 'Die spärlichen Versuche [...] die Gegenwart festzustellen, die Zeit zu zeigen, die wir leben, leiden vielleicht daran, daß ihre Autoren eben nicht die "ganz gewöhnlichen Menschen" [...] sind. Ihre Memoiren sind Rechtfertigungen, ihre Artikel sind Tendenz, ihre Bücher sind von ihrem Standpunkt geschrieben – also von einem Standpunkt. Der Reporter hat keine Tendenz, hat nichts zu rechtfertigen und hat keinen Standpunkt. Er hat unbefangen Zeuge zu sein und unbefangene Zeugenschaft zu liefern [...]. Nichts ist verblüffender als die einfache Wahrheit, nichts ist exotischer als unsere Umwelt, nichts ist phantasievoller als die Sachlichkeit. Und nichts Sensationelleres gibt es in der Welt als die Zeit, in der man lebt!'[23]

20 Schmied, Sachlichkeit, 13. [Look at the Here and Today, this is the point, to look out of the window and at the everyday life and the asphalt in front of the house, to look at the street and the sewage system, into the factory and ship-yard, at the operating room and brothel.]

21 See Becker, Sachlichkeit, 47f.

22 See *ibid.*, 41.

23 Egon Erwin Kisch, Der rasende Reporter [The Raging Reporter], Berlin/Weimar 1978, 659f. [The scarce attempts [...] to determine the present, to show the period we live in, probably suffer from the fact that their authors are not "absolutely common people" [...]. Their memoires are justifications, their articles are tendencies, their books are written from their point of view – thus from a certain point of view. The reporter has no tendency. They have nothing to justify and they have

Hence, *neue Sachlichkeit* is connected with contents and techniques such as dominance of the tangible and literary objects, documentary style, montage, reportage, objectivity, clarity, neutrality, precision, observation, or sobriety. Becker considers *neue Sachlichkeit* to be either the last phase of modernism or new naturalism.[24] Alfred Döblin, one of the main representatives first of literary expressionism and later of literary *neue Sachlichkeit* ('Berlin Alexanderplatz' from 1929 is seen as a *neu-sachlich* novel par excellence), openly expressed his affinity towards new naturalism in the article "Bekenntnis zum Naturalismus" [Commitment to Naturalism] from 1920, where he opposes the last phase of expressionism and its utopian ideas, and celebrates *neue Sachlichkeit* as a revival of pragmatism, every-day realism, and socio-political themes, which were typical of the movement of naturalism.[25] Similar to E.E. Kisch, Joseph Roth presents his new *neu-sachlich* way of writing in the preface to his novel "Flucht ohne Ende" [Flight without End] from 1927 where he states: 'Ich habe nichts erfunden, nichts komponiert. Es handelt sich nicht mehr darum, zu "dichten". Das wichtigste ist das Beobachtete.'[26] These frequently cited lines have become another manifesto-like statement of literary *neue Sachlichkeit.*

The style of *neue Sachlichkeit* is connected with photographic and realistic descriptions of the outer world, montage of styles, style of reportage and documentaries, third person narratives, precise observation, and camera views. *Neu-sachlich* novels in general are *Zeitromane* insofar as they are strictly connected to the time, in which they were written. In *neu-sachlich* novels, there is no use of courageous metaphors, expressionistic pathos, or lyricism. The most important locale of *neu-sachlich* plot is the big city. Big cities provide their inhabitants with positive estrangement and anonymity. They are fully industrialized and technically perfect: an important role is played by means of transport (trams, underground, buses, trains *etc.*), which guarantee free mobility and a quick/hectic pace of life.[27] Further topics typical of *neu-sachlich* novels are cold and emotionless relationships, unemployment, suicide, and eroticism with vivid descriptions of homosexuality and prostitution. A new type of woman is depicted: a strong, androgynous woman, who is independent, emancipated, ambitious, who can drive a car, smokes ciga-

no point of view. They should be unbiased witnesses and provide with unbiased testimony [...]. Nothing is more astonishing than simple truth, nothing is more exotic than our surroundings, and nothing is more imaginative than objectivity. And there is nothing more sensational in the world than the time we live in!]

24 See Becker, Sachlichkeit, 108.

25 See *ibid.*, 111.

26 Joseph Roth, Flucht ohne Ende [Flight without End], Köln 1994, 7. [I have invented nothing, made up nothing. The question of "poetic invention" is no longer relevant. Observed fact is all that counts.]

27 See Jost Hermand, Neue Sachlichkeit. Stil, Wirtschaftsform oder Lebenspraxis? [New Objectivity. Style, Form of Economy or Life Style?], in: Leslie Bodi (Ed.), Weltbürger – Textwelten, Frankfurt am Main 1995, 325–342.

rettes, has short hair, and can also be divorced.[28] Another popular theme is the cult of sport, body, and Americanism.[29]

Neue Sachlichkeit is not only a matter of style and new motifs but *neu-sachlich* authors developed their own cultural anthropologies. Helmut Lethen deals with these anthropologies in his "Verhaltenslehre der Kälte: Lebensversuche zwischen den Kriegen" [Cool Conduct: The Culture of Distance in Weimar Germany] (1994) and according to him the culture of the period of *neue Sachlichkeit* can be seen as *Schamkultur*: a culture of shame.[30] He differentiates between the *Schuldkultur* [culture of guilt], which is associated with the 1910s and expressionism, and the culture of shame, which is typical of the 1920s and 1930s. Both cultures determine human behavior. They tell people how to live an appropriate life, and what either the inner voice or society want them to do. In the *Schuldkultur*, our behavior is controlled by the inner voice and inner inspection: we are supervised by introspection. When we misbehave, the sanction is reflected in the fear of our conscience. Norms that direct our behavior are given by individual consciousness – a good conscience is also the only aim of our action. An emphasis is put on impulses that are hidden from the public.

The *Schamkultur*, on the other hand, is controlled by the outer voice and external inspection. Our behavior is supervised by the eye of other people, not by introspection. The sanction for misbehaving would be social fear. All norms are given by convention and society. Our aim is not good conscience but appropriate behavior. We focus on openly revealed signs connected with the human body. To sum it up, living in the culture of shame is living according to the rules of the social environment and convention. People have to fulfil expectations of the society, in which self-respect and dignity play an important role and in which self-assessment and subjective motives give way to objectivity and assessment by others. Therefore, *neu-sachlich* characters act according to the rules of society since they fear public embarrassment and as such pay less attention to their inner voice.

Lethen also differentiates three types of behavior corresponding to *neue Sachlichkeit*: the behavior of a cool *persona* [die kalte *persona*], a radar type [der Radar-Typ], and the creature [die Kreatur]. Most of the *neu-sachlich* characters present themselves as somebody else and hide their characters to survive in the modern world. As Helmuth Plessner puts it: 'Alles Psychische, das sich nackt hervorwagt, trägt das Risiko der Lächerlichkeit.'[31] The concept of a mask also plays an impor-

28 The new type of women is described, for example, in Kerstin Barndt's "Sentiment und Sachlichkeit: der Roman der neuen Frau in der Weimarer Republik" [Sentiment and Objectivity: The Novel of the New Woman in the Weimar Republic] (2003), or in Kirsten Reinert's "Frauen und Sexualreform: 1897–1933" [Women and Sexual Reform: 1897–1933] (2000).

29 See for example Frank Becker's 'Amerikanismus in Weimar. Sportsymbole und politische Kultur 1918–1933' [Americanism in Weimar: Sport Symbols and Political Culture 1918–1933], Wiesbaden 1993.

30 See Lethen, Verhaltenslehre, 32.

31 Helmuth Plessner, Grenzen der Gemeinschaft. Eine Kritik des sozialen Radikalismus [The Limits of Community. A Critique of Social Radicalism], Bonn 1972, 66. [Everything of mental and psy-

tant role. Pretense and playing a role are allowed since they protect from exposure of the inner thoughts and prevent from sentiment. However, people must be aware of the fact that everything that happens around can be artificial. We will see that in "Blanche oder das Atelier im Garten" many characters are to be classified as cool *personae* since they wear a mask and pretend to be somebody else to hide their inner life.

Paul Kornfeld and his cultural context

Paul Kornfeld is known for his expressionist tragedies and comedies such as "Himmel und Hölle" [Heaven and Hell] (1919), "Der ewige Traum" [The Eternal Dream] (1922), "Palme oder der Gekränkte" [Palme or The Offended One] (1924), "Kilian oder die gelbe Rose" [Kilian or The Yellow Rose] (1926), or "Jud Süß" [Suss, the Jew] (1929). However, his huge novel (almost 800 pages) "Blanche oder das Atelier im Garten", which he wrote in the 1930s and which was not published until 1957, can be seen as a novel influenced by *Neue Sachlichkeit*. The novel was edited and abridged by Kurt Kusenberg and published by Kronfeld's friend Ernst Rowohlt. Rowohlt advised Kornfeld to write a novel since his dramas ceased to be staged and gave him a small salary every month.[32] Nevertheless, the novel was published first 25 years after Rowohlt's order and 15 years after Kornfeld's death. Regarding Paul Kornfeld's life and work, two main monographs have been published so far: Markus Weber's "Expressionismus und Neue Sachlichkeit. Paul Kornfeld's literarisches Werk" [Expressionism and New Objectivity. Paul Kornfeld's Literary Work] in 1997, and Wilhelm Haumann's "Paul Kornfeld Leben – Werk – Wirkung" [Paul Kornfeld: Life – Work – Impact] in 1995, which, unfortunately, did not include an analysis of the novel "Blanche oder das Atelier im Garten".

Paul Kornfeld was born on 11 December 1889 in Prague, where he spent his childhood until he left for Germany in 1914. His ancestors were Bohemian Rabbis and his great-grandfather Rabbi Aaron was the last practitioner of traditional Jewish religion in Bohemia. He was the head of the Yeshiva institution until 1843 when it was closed. Kornfeld attended Stephen's grammar school in Prague (known as Stephansgymnasium) – Franz Werfel, Willy Haas, and Hans Janowitz were his classmates. Later on, Kornfeld and his clique became regulars at café Arco where they met Franz Kafka, Oskar Baum, Egon Erwin Kisch, Johannes Urzidil *etc.* Kornfeld was also captivated by the fashionable spiritual and occultist séances, which often took place in the houses of bored aristocrats. Mysticism, occultism, and the Kabbalah can be found in his works, especially in his tragedy "Himmel

chical quality that unveils our personality bears the risk of being ridiculed.]

32 See Markus Weber, Expressionismus und Neue Sachlichkeit, Paul Kornfeld's literarisches Werk [Expressionism and New Objectivity. Paul Kornfeld's Literary Work], Frankfurt am Main 1997, 42.

und Hölle" [Heaven and Hell] (1919). In 1914, when he was 25, Kornfeld decided to move to Frankfurt am Main, where he finally became a literary success. In 1922, Kornfeld answered, with many others (in the *Prager Tagblatt*), the question why he had left Prague as follows:

> '[Ich verspürte den] Wunsch, eine Atmosphäre zu verlassen, die notwendig abgebraucht sein muß, wie die Luft im geschlossenen Raum nach langer Zeit, und in der die Menschen einander alles gesagt [...] haben, und das umsomehr, als manche Freundschaft, entstanden durch die Gemeinschaft der ersten Jugend, ein anderes Gesicht bekommen muß [...] Und um wieviel mehr gilt das alles für eine Stadt, die, wie Prag für einen Deutschen, eine Kleinstadt ist!'[33]

For his literary career, Prague became a small town and Germany seemed to offer new inspiration and work opportunities. In 1918, Kornfeld married Fritta Brod; however, they divorced in 1926. He moved to Berlin in 1925, where he worked as a dramaturge under Max Reinhardt. Between the years 1927–1928 he was a dramaturge in the Landestheater (today Darmstadt State Theatre) in Darmstadt. His stay in Darmstadt may have inspired him to create Blanche's studio in the deserted garden. The setting of the novel cannot be assigned to any particular city; however, even today we can find a small tea pavilion in the middle of a little park in Darmstadt that used to belong to the family Wolfskehl. Its position matches the descriptions in the novel.[34] After one season in the Landestheater Darmstadt, he returned to Berlin where he had a love affair with the actress Maria Czamska. He worked in Berlin until December 1932, when he moved back to Prague to his mother. Soon after that, when Prague became an important center for exile literature, he started to work on his only novel "Blanche". Even though Kornfeld had both visa and flight tickets during the dangerous Nazi occupation, he underestimated the situation and decided to stay in Prague. In 1941 he was arrested by the Gestapo and deported to the ghetto in Lodz in Poland, where he died (probably of typhus) on 25 April 1942.

Anthropology of *Neue Sachlichkeit* in "Blanche oder das Atelier im Garten"

Kornfeld's "Blanche" cannot be seen as a purely *neu-sachlich* novel. First, because its formal structure and literary techniques do not fully match *neue Sachlichkeit*. Kornfeld, being a playwright, divided his novel into three main parts, which evokes a typical three-act structure in drama. He uses a lot of dialogues and opens

33 Weber, Expressionismus, 23. [[I wished] to leave the atmosphere that has begun to be as stale as the air in a closed room after a longer time and where all the people have said everything to each other, all the more that the friendships, which arose in early youth, have obtained a different face [...]. And all of that applies to a city like Prague, which remains a mere small town for a German.]

34 See *ibid.*, 41f.

his novel with a static description of the scene resembling stage directions.[35] The reader is introduced to a 28-year-old lady, Blanche, standing in front of an old garden house, which should become her studio. Kornfeld does not use any montage technique or style of reportage. On the other hand, the narrator describes every single detail such as clothes, equipment of the houses and the studio, or weather and he depicts both characters and their environment in a sober and an objective way. That is why Kornfeld's camera view is often compared to Marcel Proust's novels.[36] Detailed and precise depictions are typical both of literary and visual *neue Sachlichkeit*. Second, because the main character Blanche is the exact opposite of a *neu-sachlich* woman. The stout and chaotic Blanche Riedinger is not an androgynous flapper like her female friends. She enjoys painting pictures loaded with powerful feelings and writes very emotional and passionate letters to her imaginary lover. She is a person full of desire, dreams, and love and cannot face reality. She lives her life in inner loneliness. The others perceive her as a naïve woman lost in dreams. When she loses her beloved studio, which was the only place where she could feel free and live without a mask, she commits suicide. She attempts to live a life by the rules of the culture of shame, yet she fails. Blanche's death proves that a life lived in the *neu-sachlich* society must be either lived according to its rules, or will be lost.

Blanche's unbalanced life, that is, the conflict between her inner self and reality, is also reflected in the room she lives in. Her room is described as a place of chaos and mess, in contrast to the rest of the parents' house and the neatness of her studio.

> 'Zu Hause legte Blanche eine horrende Schlamperei an den Tag. Frau Riedinger wußte, daß sie, wenn ihr Mann schreiend ein Buch suchte, es in Blanches Zimmer unter einem Kleiderbündel oder in der Schublade ihres Waschtischs finden würde. [...] Ein einziges Mal hatte Blanche genäht, am Abend jedoch fand ihre Mutter die Nadel von oben her in ein Stück Torte gesteckt.'[37]

According to Kornfeld, chaos is a typical feature of a lively spirit[38], which Blanche sharply contrasts with *neu-sachlich* characters. However, only the reader can see into Blanche's soul and knows what she is doing in her studio, that is, painting emotional pictures and writing passionate letters to a fictional lover. On the surface she tries to show her other self and behave according to the standards of the

---

35 See *ibid.*, 159.

36 See *ibid.*, 139.

37 Paul Kornfeld, Blanche oder das Atelier im Garten [Blanche or The Studio in the Garden], Berlin 2000, 38. [Blanche was incredibly messy at home. Mrs. Riedinger knew that when her screaming husband was looking for a book she would find it in Blanche's room under a bunch of clothes or in one of the drawers of her wash basin. [...] Only once had she sewn and in the evening her mother found a needle stuck into a piece of cake.]

38 See Weber, Expressionismus, 162.

new society. She is also presented as a non-professional artist and it is revealed that she started with impressionist paintings, continued with cubism and ended with the style of *neue Sachlichkeit*. However, neither of these styles suited her. Her last unfinished portrait has nothing to do with realistic *neu-sachlich* paintings since it is a portrayal of her inner reality and dreams. In her portrait we can see a lonely red boat in blue sea with a passionate couple: herself and an unknown man without a face. Love, as she understands it, is a passionate act of devotion and overwhelming feeling that cannot be controlled. For Blanche, love is a higher thing standing above pure physiological needs and sexual satisfaction. Her character represents the conception of the old generation as opposed to the society of the 1920s that tried to reduce love to a physical action. Alfons Stadel, a cocky and flamboyant member of Riedinger's soirées, comments on the new transformed woman:

> 'Ah, es gibt heute Frauen nur noch anatomisch und physiologisch! [...] Der einzige Unterschied zwischen den Geschlechtern ist nur noch der, daß die Frauen hie und da ein wenig mehr Zeit brauchen, um sich zu der so erfreulichen Aktion zu entschließen – psychische Rudimente aus alten Zeiten!'[39]

But Blanche is not one of these new women and that is why she devotes herself to the inner world of love and dreams. In her phantasies she knows that powerful feelings bring storms and 'der großen Liebe wahrhaftig würdig ist nur der Tod.'[40] Her love to an unknown man becomes ultimate at the moment Blanche lays down her life for it.

The novel is also considered to be timeless according to some critics since it deals with people, who try to find the meaning of their lives and fail to do so. On the other hand, the novel should be understood as a *Zeitroman* since it reflects the atmosphere of the 1920s: it depicts the decay of an era as well as the atmosphere of the Roaring Twenties with its nightlife, and a society of people who are hiding their inner souls and thoughts only to be able to survive in the *neu-sachlich* and economy-oriented world. Even though many literary critiques understood 'Blanche' as a timeless novel presenting general humanistic values and characters looking for the meaning of life, the novel is inseparably connected with the late 1920s. As Grözinger puts it:

> 'Der Roman, den Kornfeld in den Jahren des Exils schrieb, berührt heute wie eine Wiederkehr des Geistes der Zwanzigerjahre, wie ein von der Geschichte selbst geschriebener historischer Roman. Seine Menschen haben noch das Gehabe der Bürger der Wilhelminischen Ära, aber mit jener leichten Verzerrung der Züge, die

39 Kornfeld, Blanche, 103. [Ah, women exist only anatomically and physiologically today! [...] The only difference between both sexes lies in the fact that from time to time women need a little bit more time to resolve to this pleasant action – these are psychical remnants of the old times!]

40 *Ibid*, 142. [Only death is truly worth the great love].

> den kommenden Untergang hippokratisch spüren läßt. [...] Der im Grund kaum motivierte Selbstmord der beiden weiblichen Hauptfiguren ist das Zeichen des vollendeten Verfalls und steht für den Abschluß einer ganzen Epoche.'[41]

Hence, "Blanche" is a novel portraying human souls imbedded in the late 1920s. The concept of a soul is of big importance for Kornfeld. He depicts both souls of emotional characters such as Blanche Riedinger and souls of ruthless pragmatic characters who reflect the *neu-sachlich* society. Kornfeld shows in "Blanche" that passionate people even when they commit sins are not the most outraging thing in the world. On the contrary, it is the emotionless people who lack passion and act irreproachably only for pragmatic reasons (accordingly *neu-sachlich* characters) who represent the actual dreadful state of the world.[42] The turbulent night life of the 1920s can be seen in the descriptions of a night club called La Princesse where Blanche and her friends are regular visitors. Inebriated dancers move their bodies in rhythmical shimmy, rumba, or gavotte, and many dancing couples consist of two women, some of which are wearing men's clothes. Yet again, Blanche does not fit into this environment. She spends one night dancing with Riedinger's fleshy client Heinzfurth with his massive buttocks and both end up laughed at and ridiculed. This robust sweaty pair becomes an eyesore for the audience. Enjoying their furious dance, Blanche cares neither about her clothes nor her make-up: she lets her delight in dancing win over the appropriate dress code and a suitable dancing partner.

The reader encounters a circle of people from the 1920s, who wear masks that both define them and differentiate them from other members of the circle. There is no place for any closer inner contact among them since it could threaten their personalities. 'Identifikation mit einem anderen Menschen, die zu einer innerlichen Annäherung führen könnte, ist innerhalb dieses Kreises verunmöglicht.'[43] At the beginning of the novel, Blanche and Müller-Erfurt, a librarian and an author, are both introduced to the reader assessing Blanche's future studio. Blanche is wearing a hat hiding her forehead ('Über den Kopf hatte sie vom Nacken bis zur Stirn eine Mütze gezogen.'[44]), which is, according to Lethen, a typical feature of *neue Sachlichkeit* since it creates certain protection and distance from other people as well as it prevents her companion from reading her facial expressions. This *neu-sachlich*

41 Weber, Expressionismus, 138. [Today the novel, which Kornfeld wrote in the years of exile, has the effect of a return of the atmosphere of the Twenties, as if it was a historical novel written by the history itself. Its people still have the conduct of citizens living in the Wilhelmine Period, yet with a slight deformation of their features implying the impendent fall. [...] The suicide of both main female characters, which in principle lacked motivation, is a sign of the fulfilled downfall and represents the end of the whole period.]

42 See *ibid.*, 139.

43 See *ibid.*, 165. [Identification with another person which could lead to getting closer to each other is made impossible in this circle.]

44 Kornfeld, Blanche, 6. [She had a hat pulled over her head from the back of her neck to her forehead.])

way of conduct is also depicted in Brecht's poem "Verwisch die Spuren" where he gives advice to readers about appropriate behavior:

'Wenn du deinen Eltern begegnest in der Stadt Hamburg oder sonstwo,
Gehe an ihnen fremd vorbei, biege um die Ecke, erkenne sie nicht,
Ziehe den Hut ins Gesicht, den sie dir schenkten,
Zeige, oh, zeige dein Gesicht nicht,
Sondern,
Verwisch die Spuren!'[45]

Both Blanche and Müller-Erfurt are people who want to believe in dreams and love; however, they do not allow anybody else to see that. Later on, Müller-Erfurt almost confesses his feelings for Blanche but in the end he fails to do so because he cannot give up his social role and continues to present himself as a satisfied man who enjoys his life. He brings Blanche a bunch of daffodils [in German Narzisse] symbolizing his narcissism and self-love. Even when he loses, he wants the world to see his determination which is reflected even in his walk: 'jede Bewegung schien Kraft und Energie wiederzugeben, und es war, als riefe die ganze Gestalt: Seht, wie sicher ich dahinschreite! Es geht mir gut! Es geht mir gut! Ich fühle mich sicher auf der Welt!'[46] After Blanche's refusal, he decides to keep his mask of a superior intellectual and womanizer and ends up in a brothel. Another of Blanche's suitors, Heinzfurth, tells Blanche how to think properly in modern society:

'Auch der Verstand soll wie eine Maschine arbeiten, nüchtern, sachlich und hart! [...] Präzision im Denken, klare Erkenntnisse, Wahrheit, der Wirklichkeit ins Auge schauen! Jeder liebt nur sich selbst, niemals liebt man den anderen Menschen.'[47]

His opinions define him as a cool person (in Lethen's terms) and as such a typical *neu-sachlich* figure. Nevertheless, it is his excessive openness that makes Blanche refuse him because she wants men to remain courteous gentlemen who know how to flatter women.

45 Bertolt Brecht, Gedichte. 1. 1918–1929: Bertolt Brechts Hauspostille. Aus einem Lesebuch für Städtebewohner. Geschichten aus der Revolution [Poems 1. 1918–1919: Bertolt Brecht's Devotions for the Home. Reader for Those Who Live in Cities. Stories from a Revolution]. Berlin 1961, 43. [If you meet your parents in the city of Hamburg or somewhere else/Pass them like a stranger, turn a corner, don't acknowledge theme/Pull the hat they gave you down over your face/Don't show, O don't show your face/But/Erase the traces.]

46 Kornfeld, Blanche, 366. [Every single movement seemed to reflect power and energy, and it was as if his whole figure was exclaiming: Look how confidently I'm walking! I'm fine! I'm fine! I feel secure in the world!]

47 *Ibid*, 381. [Reason itself should work like a machine, sober, objective and hard! [...] Precision in thinking, clear cognition, truth, to look reality into its face! Everybody loves just themselves, never do people love the others.]

As mentioned above, wearing a mask is a recurrent pattern throughout the novel. In fact, almost all of the characters play social roles and do not want to reveal their real selves. Some characters pretend their indifference towards the opposite sex they are in love with to preserve their dignity.[48] Müller-Erfurt's landlady, the widow Schöttler, presents herself as a calm martyr even though she is constantly devoured by hatred towards the new society and her own fate (she is an impoverished Colonel's daughter). She cannot accept the fact 'daß man sie im Brei der anonymen Masse aufgehen lassen wollte, innerhalb derer? es weder Rang noch Titel [...] gibt.'[49] Her eyes are cold and distant since people are not allowed to find out her inner feelings. Being friends, Blanche and the melancholic and vampire-like Carola should not hide anything yet they cannot get close enough to each other to throw away their masks. 'So ergab sich [...] zwischen ihnen ein Spiel wie das zwischen einem nur leicht geschminkten und einem maskierten Menschen.'[50] Their friendship presents another pretense in the novel because Carola cannot open up to Blanche. Blanche, on the other hand, also wears a mask since she does not want people to know about her secret life in the studio. Her dreams of intense love and the lack of real feeling in her life should remain unrevealed. In an intimate conversation with Müller-Erfurt, during which neither of them dares to disclose their emotions, Blanche lies to save her phantasies only for herself and says: 'Mein Gott, ich bin ein phantasieloser Mensch und im ganzen zufrieden mit allem, was ich habe, und genügsam.'[51]

The only character, who is open to everybody and does not hide anything, is Feding, a childless lawyer and Riedinger's old friend. He analyzes every occurrence with a sober look and draws rational conclusions. At the same time he does not care about the psychological face of affairs and focuses only on facts. As such, Feding could be identified with the radar type as it is described by Lethen. He is oriented towards the outside, he is constantly ready to react, and he is sentimental towards people and cynical towards institutions.[52] The *neu-sachlich* radar type is often a hedonist; Feding enjoys drinking excessive amounts of wine and turned his cellar into a little private wine cellar. However, even though he can be seemingly indifferent to the inside of people when solving a problem, he is not a cool person. In a conversation with Riedinger, Feding characterizes his way of thinking: 'Das ist schon eine Frage der Psychologie! Ich weiß es nicht, ich will es auch nicht wissen, denn ich bin ein oberflächlicher Mensch und halte mich nur an die

---

48 See *ibid.*, 8.

49 *Ibid.*, 61. [That she should disappear in the mush of an anonymous mass where there are neither ranks nor titles anymore].

50 *Ibid.*, 282. [There was a game between them as if it was played by a person with mild make-up and a person with a mask.]

51 *Ibid.*, 600. [My God, I'm an unimaginative person and I'm absolutely satisfied with everything that I have, and humble.]

52 See Lethen, Verhaltenslehre, 236.

Tatsachen!'[53] Feding does not fulfil one condition of being identified with the radar type: he is not obsessed with modern media and does not care about the newest inventions, in comparison to Blanche's father who loves everything new and young Feding remains the reasonable and contemplating one. During the soirees, he sits in his armchair and functions as a distant observer. He accepts the role of Blanche's father (he brings her books and presents, and helps her when she is losing her studio) and becomes her advisor: he tries to warn her against the dangers of dreams and phantasy but he does not succeed.

Mr. Riedinger, an old lawyer, is a *neu-sachlich* character par excellence. He does not want to grow older and pretends to love everything new that the society of the 1920s brings, even though he does not actually know how to cope with it. In his bed after he had suffered a heart attack, he is not interested in anything else but a description of a party in a nightclub: who danced and with whom, what kind of alcohol was drunk and what kind of dance was danced. He is oriented towards now or tomorrow; the past does not matter.

> 'Selbst vor seinen Freunden wurde die Krankheit verleugnet oder geheimgehalten. [...] Er wollte nicht alt sein. Er wollte keine Glatze und beklebte sie mit den zur Seite gelegten Haarsträhnen, er wollte keinen grauen Schnurrbart und färbte ihn [...].'[54]

He desires to be a member of the young generation and tries to do everything to become one of them, hiding his age at all costs and keeping his weak heart a secret even from his closest friends. During one of his parties, he mocks love in his pretense and, indirectly, also undermines his relationship to Blanche.

> 'Sehen Sie doch auf unsere Welt der Äroplane und Maschinen, des Sports und der Rekorde, der sozialen Umwälzungen und des Umbaus der ganzen sozialen Struktur, der neuen Interessen und der neuen Ziele, der Hygiene und der Überwindung einer alten Moral, der Überwindung der alten Prüderie und der alten Vorurteile, der Gründung einer neuen Psychologie mit besserer Einsicht in die Triebwelt [...] Ach was! [...] Wer glaubt denn noch an die Liebe!'[55]

---

53 *Ibid.*, 340. [But that is a question of psychology! I don't know it and I don't want to know it because I'm a superficial person and I adhere purely to facts!].

54 Kornfeld, Blanche, 95. [Even his illness was denied or kept secret, even from his friends. [...] He did not want to be old. He did not want a bald spot and combed his hair over it, he did not want a grey moustache and dyed it.]

55 *Ibid.*, 108. [Have a look at our world of aeroplanes and machines, sport and records, social changes and transformation of the whole social structure, new interests and goals, hygiene and surpassing of old morals, surpassing of the old narrow-mindedness and old prejudice, the foundation of a new psychology with a better view into the world of instincts [...]! Ah what! [...] Who would still believe in love!?]

His obsession with the outer world and the surface of things makes him oblivious to the deep, important problems: even on the night after his party, when Blanche leaves her parents' house to commit suicide in the studio, he does not suspect anything and sleeps peacefully during the whole night. Feding, on the other hand, finds out what Blanche is going to do and runs after her to save her. Even though he fails to save her life, he manages to save her secret and burns all of her love letters without reading them.

Besides flappers and *femmes fatales*, there is also a male *neu-sachlich* character: the modern dandy. The most elegant one is a poet Ladislaus Joachim. He is a muscular sportsman, wears a modern long tie and a tuxedo with massive pearls on his shirt, enjoys fast driving and skiing, and often brags about his literary works, especially his novel "The Beast" symbolizing life itself. He 'must master all those elements of self and situation whose unmastered presence constitutes the condition of embarrassments. These include spaces, props, equipment, clothing and body [...]'.[56] As a modern dandy, he has to take control of his emotions and stay cool. The anthropology of the 1920s is driven by the aestheticism of the *Fin de siècle* in the terms of living life as artificially as possible. Next to the statements of the world-famous dandy Oscar Wilde such as 'Man is least himself when he talks in his own person. Give him a mask, and he will tell you the truth'[57], descriptions by German-Moravian author Richard von Schaukal depict dandies of early modernism (namely his fictional character Andreas von Balthesser). These characteristics can also be found in the modern figure of a *neu-sachlich* dandy. In comparison to the dandy of the turn of the centuries, the modern dandy is no aristocrat, even though he tries to behave like one. His conduct classifies him as a charlatan.

> 'Man nennt mich einen Dandy. Die Bezeichnung will ich gelten lassen. Aber die Meinung ist falsch. Die letzte, sichtbare Zwiebelschale meiner Persönlichkeit ist der Dandy: sie begreift nur die Oberfläche. [...] Der Dandy ist jederzeit bereit zu schwimmen. Aber er trifft niemals Anstalten dazu. Anstalten treffen heißt: der Beobachtung zugängliche Anstalten treffen, und der Dandy ist überhaupt nicht zugänglich, am allerwenigsten der Beobachtung. Was jedoch nicht heißen soll, daß sich der Dandy nicht exponiere. Im Gegenteil: er exponiert sich gern. [...] Der Dandy ist von allen Seiten gleich unverdächtig. Verdächtig ist er nur im Innern [...]'.[58]

---

56 Lethen, Verhaltenslehre, 153.

57 See *ibid.*, 88.

58 Richard von Schaukal, Leben und Meinungen des Herrn Andreas von Balthesser, München 1917, 29f. [People call me a dandy. I will accept the label. But their opinion is wrong. Only the last, visible layer of the onion of my personality is the dandy: it comprises only the surface. [...] Anytime, the dandy is prepared to swim. But he never prepares himself for it. To prepare oneself implies preparation open to observation, and the dandy is not accessible at all, least of all to observation. This doesn't mean of course that the dandy doesn't expose himself. On the contrary, he likes exposing himself. [...] The Dandy is unsuspicious from all sides. He is suspicious only in his inside [...].]

Neu-sachlich characters also only show the surface and hide the inside of their soul. The outer skin of their self, which is perceivable by other people, guarantees their safe and dignified survival in society. Ladislaus Joachim (even this name is a mask since his real name is Ferdinand Müller) enjoys exposing himself and showing his knowledge of the world. He tries to use foreign words and talk about exclusive things ('er sprach von eleganten Dingen, er badete in ihnen'[59]), praises excellent French restaurants and Italian car races, and depicts various kinds of love life which he has experienced during his travels. Joachim, loving himself more than anybody else, successfully tries to seduce his female opposite: Riedinger's old client Mrs Leonhardt. She represents a modern woman who sells her individuality for a comfortable life with a husband she does not love. Mrs Leonhardt developed into a cold person relying purely on her appearance. She is able to bear her luxurious yet boring life in a provincial town only thanks to her occasional visits of the big city connected with love affairs. Joachim falls in love with her surface since possessing her extraordinary beauty during their sexual relationship reflects his own uniqueness. At the beginning her inner life is for him of no importance.

> 'Frau Leonhardt [...] verhielt sich am stillsten und sprach am wenigsten. [...] Doch anders und freier als ihr Inneres, strahlte sich ihr Körper aus. Der Teint war fehlerlos, war vorbildlich, und man hätte glauben können, er sei ein Kunstprodukt und nicht den Zufälligkeiten des organischen Lebens ausgesetzt, ihre Haut war zart und sanft wie die einer köstlichen jungen Frucht aus dem Glashaus.'[60]

There is no need to communicate with words because Mrs. Leonhardt lets her outside talk and because her inner life is subdued by her surface. She does not need to say anything in this society because she is perceived as a rich beautiful woman and it is the only way she wants to present herself. Their affair was predestined to end up as a mere sexual experience since the only thing they have in common is their beautiful appearance and vanity.

Regarding *neu-sachlich* motifs, suicide is an important subject matter. Altogether, there are four suicide attempts in the novel. Only the final one, Blanche's, is successful. First, an unknown servant maid steals veronal tablets from her doctor and almost dies of an overdose. Then, Carola, a depressed modern woman, tries to kill herself with the very same tablets to escape the torments of life and to draw even more attention to her fragile beauty. Photographer Gisela, on the other hand, who is a typical flapper of the 1920s with her slender figure, curly bobbed hair, exclamations such as 'Es ist ohnedies alles zum Kotzen'[61], and outrageous opinions

59 Kornfeld, Blanche, 85. [He spoke about elegant things, he bathed in them.]

60 *Ibid.*, 83. [Mrs Leonhardt [...] was the calmest guest and she barely spoke. [...] But her body radiated differently and freer than her inside. Her complexion was flawless, it was exemplary, and one would believe it is a piece of art and not something exposed to the chances of the organic life. Her skin was soft and smooth like delicious fruit from a greenhouse.]

61 *Ibid.*, 68. [Anyway, everything makes me feel like vomiting.]

('Alles zum Speien, alles zum Speien! Ah, ihr Männer seid Schweine!'[62]), tries to kill herself because there is too much going on in her life. After taking too many pills, she starts to shout that she does not want to die and proves, in contrast to Carola, how much she loves her life. Blanche must die after the loss of her studio because she loses the only place where she can be herself. She fails to accept the real modern world. Gisela represents an emancipated modern woman fighting for equality of both sexes: she is 'gegen jede Differenzierung zwischen den Geschlechtern'[63], which should be manifested even in sexual life – Gisela suggests that there should also be male prostitutes so that women can satisfy their appetite.[64] This seems to be an allusion to Kästner's novel "Fabian" since its character Irene Moll opens a similar establishment in this novel where both men and women can enjoy their sexuality.

Kornfeld frequently describes transport and means of transport, which is, besides big cities, a new topos in *neu-sachlich* literature. Noisy trams and cars present a setting of a couple of scenes. Also, new media such as telegraph or telephone are commonly used. The telephone is often used (by Gisela, Carola, or Müller-Erfurt) as a device of non-communication: they unplug it only to show their importance; that is, when they know somebody could call them and they want to pretend they are engaged with somebody else, or simply to block communication with others to escape from social conventions and protect their privacy. Therefore, they assign a new meaning to the means of communication and use them as a mean of supporting their importance and social position.

The setting of the novel is divided between *neu-sachlich* modern buildings and Blanche's old garden house. Her cozy studio situated in an old park serves as a nice hideout from the tumult of a big city. Here she is far away from 'den Geräuschen der Stadt, [dem] Klingeln, [dem] Hupen, [den] Rufen, [dem] Stimmengewirr und [dem] Gleiten der Räder.'[65] The studio with old Biedermeier furniture, which she uses as a shelter for her inner life and a refuge from the materialistic world as well as an escape place from the big city life, is the exact opposite of modern functionalistic, *e.g.*, *neu-sachlich* architecture; for example, the so called Bauhaus architecture. Tiled bathrooms, open spaces preventing from oppressive symbiotic co-existence, functionality, transparency, and sterility are the main features of a *neu-sachlich* building that is to house cool *personae*. Carola, Blanche's depressed and sickly friend, and a typical femme fatal, lives with her husband in a house depicted as a functionalistic modern building. Their villa is described as a lifeless fortress:

62 *Ibid.*, 75. [Everything makes me feel like puke, everything! Ah, you men are all pigs!]

63 *Ibid.*, 127. [Against any differentiation between sexes]

64 See *ibid.*, 164.

65 *Ibid.*, 439. [The noise of the city, ringing, hooting, shouting, turmoil of voices, and skidding of wheels.]

'Den Garten umsäumten hohe Pfeifensträucher, die [...] eine zweite, dichtere Grenze gegen die Außenwelt bildeten. Über Gebäude und Garten war die Haube der Stille gestülpt, und man konnte das Gefühl haben, daß sich die ängstliche Stille des Krankenzimmers bis ins Freie erstreckte. [...] Die weiße Villa, die fünf Zimmer enthielt, bestand, außer dem Erdgeschoß, nur aus einem Stockwerk und hatte, mit ihrem flachen Dach, die Gestalt eines Würfels. Ihre Mauern waren kahl, von mehr breiten als hohen Fenstern und einer gradflächigen Tür unterbrochen.'[66]

After Blanche's death, even her dreamful studio becomes a *neu-sachlich* building in the sense of its pragmatic usage: it becomes a hideout of two bachelors who decided to use the house as a love nest for their numerous affairs.

Conclusion

As it was implied in the second chapter *neue Sachlichkeit* is not a literary style that can be characterized easily. We have seen that even though Kornfeld started his literary career as an expressionistic playwright he developed his style, as did many other authors of his time, and succeeded in writing a modern novel influenced by *neue Sachlichkeit*. His "Blanche oder das Atelier im Garten" was analyzed in three main levels in this article: figures, motifs, and setting. It was proven that it is a novel full of *neu-sachlich* characters and descriptions, yet it cannot be classified as a purely *neu-sachlich* work since its main character Blanche is a dreamful person imbedded in a different period. Nevertheless, she commits suicide in the end because she is not able to fulfil her phantasies in her real life and loses her studio – the only connection to her inner world. The setting, time frame and modern society consisting of people wearing a protective mask fully correspond with the genre of *neue Sachlichkeit*.

66 *Ibid.*, 257f. [The garden was surrounded by tall English dogwood hedges that [...] created another thicker border against the outer world. The building and the garden were covered with extraordinary stillness, and the whole scenery reminded one of the anxious stillness of a hospital. [...] The white villa with its five rooms consisted, with the exception of the ground floor, of only one floor and had (with its flat roof) the shape of a cube. Its walls were bare, with rather wider than higher windows and a rectangular door.]

Michał Wiącek

The Polish Émigré Press in Paris and London and Its Post-World War II Discourses on Austria's Role in Central European Federation Schemes

University of Alberta

> 'Every strictly Austrian problem has always three features: Soviet, American, and ... well, Austrian.'[1]

Since Poland's accession to the European Union (EU), the country has gained an important role in the organization. Poland has become both a politically and economically valuable asset for the organization. Simultaneously, the EU has taken a significant role in Polish daily life, not only as a gracious donor paying compensation for the post-World War II (WWII) Yalta agreement, leaving the country under Soviet domination for nearly half of the century. From the perspective of full membership status (after the end of the transitional provision of the accession treaty), Poland needs to develop a more coherent position for every single European policy, ranging from agriculture and fishing to development cooperation and space programs. The member states from Western Europe have developed their positions in the areas at the same time they had been discussed at the European level or finally had been introduced to the treaties. This process did not have a chance to take place in Poland after WWII, as the country was still under the Soviet umbrella, yet Poles participated in the European discussion before and after 1945.

The influences of Polish emigration authors are present in the current declarations and political actions. Nine years before the accession of Poland, the EU was enlarged by Sweden, Finland, and Austria, three neutral countries during the Cold War. From a Polish perspective, the status of Austria or Finland was considered as a possible first step for reprogramming the geopolitical situation. Austria, as a Central European country, was closer to the Polish souls, maneuvered between the West and the East. However, Austrians strong interdependence with the European Economic Community (ECC) forced plenty of interaction, as well as formal agreements and membership negotiations during the 1960s and 1990s. These processes were freely observed and commented on in the Polish émigré journals and periodi-

1 Juliusz Mieroszewski, Europa zneutralizowana? [Europe Neutraled?], *Kultura*, Paris 1955/5/91, 107 [translated by M.W.].

cals only outside of Poland. In the first decade after WWII, Austria was seen as an element of Central European Federation and after 1955 the country became a model on how to leave Soviet domination and how to establish its own position on the international scene.

The Polish émigré press after WWII can be divided by distribution, area, and influence. The most influential titles were a monthly review *Kultura* [The Culture], a weekly *Wiadomości* [The News] and a daily *Dziennik Polski i Dziennik Żołnierza* [The Polish Daily and Soldier's Daily]. In contrast with local titles, they provided news and analysis of the daily lives of migrants. They also often took part in intellectual debates. Most of the content of these journals focused on the emigrant community; however, *Kultura* and *Dziennik* tried to influence Western politicians as well by providing special editions in English, German, or Czech. In this context, *Kultura* was primarily oriented towards the readers in Poland. The overseas distribution guaranteed the financial existence of the project.

Polish emigration has a long tradition of publishing periodicals, starting with the initiative of Adam Mickiewicz (1798–1855), the principal Polish poet of the Romanticism, who was editor-in-chief of the *La Tribune des Peuples* in 1849 in Paris.[2] During WWII the army decided to financially support several journals for the soldiers. Within the Polish army, intellectuals as artists like Józef Czapski (1898–1993), Gustaw Herling-Grudziński (1919–2000); journalists like Jerzy Giedroyc (1906–2000) and Juliusz Mieroszewski (1906–1976), and scholars served as the cultural or educational officers. Moreover, they edited two main military newspapers *Orzeł Biały* [The White Eagle] and *Dziennik Żołnierza* [The Soldier's Daily].

Polish émigré periodicals created a network of influence and interdependence; there, the same names appeared in titles and political activities. When the war ended, the Commander of the Second Corps[3], General Władysław Anders (1892–1970), decided to stay in Western Europe; first in Italy, and afterward in England. However, the *Institute Littéraire* [Literary Institute], established in 1947 in Rome, was created by military decision. General Anders appointed Jerzy Giedroyc as the editor-in-chief. Józef Czapski, Zofia Hertz (1910–2003), and her husband Zbigniew Hertz (1908–1979) constituted the editorial team. The main activity of the Literary Institute was publishing the periodical *Kultura* and books.[4] One year after its foundation, the Institute moved to Paris.

---

2 Henryk Jabłonski (Ed.), La Tribune des peuples. Edition phototypique [Tribune of the People. Phototypographic Edition], Wrocław 1963.

3 The fighting force formed in 1942 in the Middle East from former Polish prisoners of the Soviet Gulag camps and Polish deportees to the Soviet Union; see Władysław Anders, An Army in Exile. The Story of the Second Polish Corps, London 1949; Keith Sword, Anders' Army, in: Ian Dear – Michael Foot (Eds.), The Oxford Companion to World War II, Oxford/New York 2001, 27f.

4 Janusz Korek, Paradoksy paryskiej 'Kultury'. Styl i tradycje myślenia politycznego [Paradoxes of Parisian 'Kultura'. The Style and Tradition of Political Thinking in the Polish Exile Monthly 'Kultura'], Katowice 2008, 25.

Even if the most well-known periodical was published in Paris, the center of Polish political and cultural activities was in London, the headquarters of Polish government-in-exile. *Dziennik Polski i Dziennik Żołnierza* was a daily newspaper edited and printed in England and distributed worldwide. Despite self-determination as an independent title governed by a sovereign Trust, *Dziennik* was close to the emigration establishment. The editors were closely related with General Władysław Anders who was president of the Trust from 1956 until his death in 1970.[5]

Weekly *Wiadomości* was the third incarnation of the editor-in-chef Mieczysław Grydzewski (1894–1970). In 1924, he created *Wiadomości Literackie* [The Literary News] as a weekly social and cultural title of the progressive intelligentsia.[6] During the war, Grydzewski edited *Wiadomości Polskie* [The Polish News], which became anti-establishment with its anti-Soviet rhetoric after the Sikorski-Mayski Agreement was signed in 1941 and diplomatic relations between Soviet Russia and the Polish Government in London were restored.[7] Eventually, the British government banned paper for the *Wiadomości Polskie* in February 1944. Two years later, *Wiadomości*, with no adjective, started new life for the next 37 years, while weekly press was published in London and in Brussels at the same time. During the first period most of the Polish authors wrote for the weekly periodical, including Józef and Maria Czapski (1894–1981), Wacław Zbyszewki (1903–1985), Jerzy Stempowski (1893–1969, usually under pseudonym Paweł Hostowiec), and Gustaw Herling-Grudziński. They were published in *Kultura* as well. Although authors published their articles in both journals, there was a clear distinction between the directions of the two major intelligentsia periodicals.[8] While the *Kultura* was oriented towards Polish readers in Poland and towards Poles in exile, *Wiadomości* become more radical. As Stefania Kossowska (1909–2003), an editor-in-chief of the *Wiadomości* from 1973–1981, stated in the preface of an anthology of articles from the journal that

> 'In the first years after the War, all Polish authors in exile published in the *Wiadomości*, sometimes with extremely differing views [...]. Afterwards, some of them stopped writing, discouraged by the persistence of the magazine that despite of the political climate never have resigned from the fight for true freedom in Poland and its culture'.[9]

---

5 Jolanta Chwastyk-Kowalczyk, Londynski 'Dziennik Polski i Dziennik Żołnierza' 1944–1989. Gazeta codzienna jako środek przekazu komunikatów kulturowych [Londonian Polish Daily and Soldier's Daily 1944–1989. The Daily Newspapers as the Cultural Communications Medium], Kielce 2008, 46.

6 Jerzy Giedroyc, Zwalczałem 'Wiadomości' [I fought against the News], in: Mirosław A. Supruniuk (Ed.), 'Wiadomości' i okolice. Szkice i wspomnienia ['The News' and its surroundings. Sketches and memories], Toruń 1995, 137–142, here 138.

7 The Polish-Soviet Agreement signed in London on 30 July 1941, see Stanislaw Mikolajczyk, The Pattern of Soviet Domination, London 1948, 289.

8 *Ibid.*, 140.

9 Stefania Kossowska (Ed.), 'Wiadomości' na emigracji. Antologia prozy 1940–1967 w wyborze i z przedmową Stefanii Kossowskiej [The News in exile. 1940–1967 Anthology of the prose. Selec-

Wiadomości was finally closed in 1981.

While *Dziennik Polski i Dziennik Żołnierza* had a traditional editorial board, *Kultura* was the original creation of Jerzy Giedroyc; therefore it closed in 2000 when Jerzy Giedroyc passed away. The Literary Institute headquarters, and home of Jerzy Giedroyc, Zofia and Zbigniew Hertz, and Józef and Maria Czapski, was Maisons-Laffitte, located in the Parisian suburbs. *Kultura* was a forum for discussion; and consequently, its pages were opened to all spectrums of political opinion. The editorial work was based on correspondence with Polish, European and American intellectuals. Thereby, through the decades *the circle of Kultura* was established, regrouping the main contributors, while the exchange of opinions was still encouraged and appreciated by Jerzy Giedroyc. Nevertheless, reconstructing the *Kultura* political agenda is challenging, and basing this challenge only on the content of the periodical – is even impossible. It is common, even for scholars, to use general expression to describe *Kultura* positions (*e.g.*, '*Kultura* saw', '*Kultura* wanted', '*Kultura* assigned', '*Kultura* advocated', '*Kultura* criticized'[10]). Notwithstanding, to express verified claims about *Kultura*, further research based on correspondence is essential.[11] The principal political author was Juliusz Mieroszewski, an unofficial *porte-parole* of the Parisian *Kultura* from 1952 to 1976.

Mieroszewski was born in 1906 in Kraków into a Silesian noble family[12], and raised in the post-Habsburg Central European environment. A journalist before the war, Mieroszewski became a blue-collar worker in London during the first years of emigration and started gaining popularity through his political analysis. From 1945 to 1953, Mieroszewski published in *Orzeł Biały*, *Wiadomości*, *Dziennik Polski i Dziennik Żołnierza*, and *Kultura*; however, progressively since 1950, his work was monopolized by Jerzy Giedroyc. They became the center of the *Kultura* circle for the next 25 years.[13] Leopold Unger (1922–2011, pseudonyms Pol Mathil and Brukselczyk [Bruxellois]), the journalist of the French-speaking Belgium newspaper *Le Soir*, tried to fill up the gap after Mieroszewski passed away in 1976.

---

tion and preface by Stefania Kossowska], London 1968, 6 [translated by M.W.].

10 See inter alia: Marek Suszko, 'Kultura' and European Unification, 1948–1953, in: The Polish Review, 45/2 Champaign 2000, 183–195.

11 Andrzej St. Kowalczyk, Od Bukaresztu do Laffitów. Jerzego Giedroycia rzeczpospolita epistolarna [From Bukareszt to Laffitte. Jerzy Giedroyc's Epistolary Republic], Sejny 2006.

12 Letter from Julusz Mieroszewski to Jerzy Giedroyc, 7 December 1962, Archive of the Institute Littéraire in Maisons-Laffitte (further: AIL); Piotr Wandycz, O Mieroszewskim i Mieroszewskich [Mieroszewski and Mieroszewskis], in: Jerzy Giedroyc – Juliusz Mieroszewski, Listy 1949–1956. Część Pierwsza, Warszawa 1999, 34–47, here 40; Arkadiusz Kuzio-Podrucki, Mieroszewscy. Między Śląskiem a Małopolską [The Mieroszewskis. Between Silesia and Little Poland], Tamowskie Góry 2010.

13 Rafał Habielski, Juliusz Mieroszewski i jego pisarstwo [Juliusz Mieroszewski and his Works], in: Juliusz Mieroszewski (Ed.), Listy z Wyspy. ABC polityki 'Kultury' [Letters from the Island. Political ABC of 'Kultura'], Paryż/Kraków 2012, 421–452. Perspective of social movement and circles was proposed by Paul F. Wheeler – Leopold Tyrmand (Ed.), Kultura Essays, New York 1970, VII–IX.

Although *Dziennik Polski and Dziennik Żołnierza* was close to the Polish émigré government, not only geographically but ideologically, *Kultura* gained its independence from the Polish Army and afterwards from the emigration establishment. *Kultura* took part in the intellectual debates at the end of the 1940s and in the first years of 1950s across the Western European countries and the United States. Even though research shows that the activities of James Burnham (1905–1987), Arthur Koestler (1905–1983) and Raymond Aron (1905–1983) were financed by the American Central Intelligence Agency[14], and some funds could be transferred via several foundations to the Literary Institute in Maisons-Laffitte, the work of the Institute was financed primarily by the subscriptions of its readers. While *Dziennik* advocated for pre-War values of the authoritarian military regime, *Kultura* progressively leaned towards the left-wing position.[15] A main reason was its cooperation with left wing ex-communist intellectuals through the Congress for Cultural Freedom, starting with the Berlin Congress in June 1950.[16]

Even though the topic of European integration was a subject of studies in *Kultura*[17], as well as the Polish political emigration groups, the comprehensive analysis of European debate through Polish émigré journals and periodicals has not been yet presented.

Central European Federation

Polish exiles were discussing the idea of Polish-Czechoslovak and Central European Federations for over a decade after WWII. The government Memorandum from December 1942 proposed the two-block federation: Northern including Czechoslovakia, Hungary, Lithuania, Poland, and Romania, and Southern including Albania, Bulgaria, Greece, Yugoslavia, and even Turkey. As Professor Marian Wolański, the expert of European Federal movement across Polish emigration, stated in his research that Poles expressed concern regarding Austrian participa-

14 Pierre Grémion, Intelligence de l'anticommunisme. Le Congrès pour la liberté de la culture à Paris (1950–1975) [Anticommunist Intelligence. The Congress for Cultural Freedom in Paris (1950–1975)], Paris 1995; Frances Stonor Saunders, Who Paid the Piper? The CIA and the Cultural Cold War, London 1999.

15 Habielski, Mieroszewski, 436.

16 Bernard Wiaderny, Der Kongress für kulturelle Freiheit und die polnische Exilzeitschrift Kultura [The Congress for Cultural Freedom and the Polish Exile Magazine Kultura], in: Zeitschrift für Ostmitteleuropa-Forschung 60/1, Marburg 2011, 50–77.

17 Marek Żebrowski, Dzieje Sporu. Kultura w emigracyjnej debacie publicznej lat 1947–1956 [The History of the Dispute. Kultura in the Public Debate in Exile 1947–1956], Warszawa 2007, 186–206; Janusz Korek, Ponętna utopia czy zimny realizm? (Federacja Europy Środkowo-wschodniej w myśli paryskiej Kultury) [Alluring Utopia or Cold Realism? (Federation of Central and Eastern Europe in the Thought of Parisian Kultura)], in: Jerzy Kłoczowski – Sławomir Łukasiewicz (Eds.), O nowy kształt Europy. XX-wieczne koncepcje federalistyczne w Europie Środkowo-Wschodniej i ich implikacje dla dyskusji o przyszłości Europy [The new shape of Europe. Twentieth Century Concepts of Federalism in Central and Eastern Europe and Their Implications for the Discussion on the European Future], Lublin 2003, 189–213; Iwona Hofman, Zjednoczona Europa w publicystyce paryskiej Kultury [A United Europe in Parisian Kultura], Lublin 2001.

tion in the Central European Federation as an outpost of German influence; moreover, they called any Danubian union excluding Poland as a Habsburg revisionism that '[...] might become the instrument of a revived German imperialism'.[18] The project was developed after the war by the Federal clubs in London, Paris, and Rome as 'the *Intermarium* Project' and promoted by its own *The Intermarium Bulletin* published in Polish, English, and French and in the Polish emigration periodicals.[19] In 1948 the Central and East European Federal Club based in Paris prepared the comprehensive vision of a Central and East European community of 16 countries: Albania, Belarus, Bulgaria, Croatia, the Czech Republic, Estonia, Greece, Hungary, Lithuania, Latvia, Poland, Romania, Serbia Slovakia, Slovenia, and Ukraine. Some clubs considered the possibility of Austria joining the *Intermarium* community, but the Federal Club of Central and Eastern Europe from Rome opposed this because '[...] there were barriers that were impossible to overcome, namely the nostalgia of Austrian society for the lost Habsburg monarchy, Austria's pro-German attitude'.[20] The position was popular as the cores of Federal clubs were constituted by former members of the Polish foreign ministry or Polish government war entities.

In addition to articles written by the members of the Federal Clubs, Polish periodicals contained commentaries written by their regular political analysts. Stanisław Mackiewicz (1896–1966) commented on the '*Intermarium* project' and advocated eliminating the Adriatic and Mediterranean Seas. 'We have to limit the number of water within the Intermarium swims'.[21] He claimed that influence in the Balkans should be divided between Italy and Turkey. Furthermore, the idea of small national units of federation would be against the Polish *raison d'État*, particularly regarding Belarus and Slovakia. Mackiewicz saw the Belarusian nation as an integrated part of the Polish state. An independent Slovakia meant the end of the Czechoslovak republic and, as such, promotion of this idea by the Polish émigré would intensify Polish-Czech antagonism. Moreover, Hungarians opposed independence from Slovakia. Finally, Mackiewicz argued that Poland must closely collaborate with two natural allies – Hungary and Romania; therefore, the emigrants from these three counties ought to work together in the spirit of a united whole Europe.

Dziennik and *Kultura* took vivid part in the European debates, both in favor of unification under the American superpower. Nevertheless, *Dziennik* mainly reported on the next steps of Western countries from the daily newspaper perspective, the readers could find the political analysis as well. The most influential were Aleksander Bregman (1906–1967), Leszek Kirken (1897–1978), and Władysław

18 Thomas Lane – Marian Wolański, Poland and European Integration. The Ideas and Movements of Polish Exiles in the West, 1939–1991, Houndmills/Basingstoke/Hampshire 2009, 30.

19 *Ibid.*, 59f.

20 *Ibid.*, 61.

21 Stanisław Mackiewicz, Międzymorze [Intermarium], *Wiadomości* 30 (278), London/Brussels 1951 July 22nd, 2 [translated by M.W.].

Besterman (1903–1974, pseudonym Vigil). As they all endorsed the federation movement, the emphasis was put on inclusion of Central European political immigrants in the Europeanization process. Moreover, the journalists from *Dziennik* assimilated the negative British narration against the integration of six western countries since 1951.[22] The European discourse in *Wiadomości* was present in the historical analysis of the 19th and 20th century, as well as in deconstruction of the political thought of Józef Piłsudski (1867–1935) and Roman Dmowski (1864–1939). The short commentaries can be found in the column called *Puszka* [the Vase], written by Adam Pragier (1886–1976) and Stefania Zahorska (1890–1961) or in the column called *Silva Rerum*, written by the editor-in-chief Grydzewski.

For Jan Zadeykański, who published several articles in *Kultura* and *Wiadmości* between 1949 and 1950, Austria was an old roommate or a well-known hostess. While recalling Habsburg history of the last decades of the empire, he put an emphasis on the role of Chancellor Heinrich Lammasch (1853–1920) and his idea of autonomy within 'some kind of united states'.[23] Finally, he called for a dream about a new, European, Austria. Officially, Austria started to play a role in European discourse in the most influential Polish émigré periodicals.

The two main discussions around the role of Austria from a geopolitical perspective were published in *Wiadomości* in 1949 and in *Kultura* between 1952 and 1955. While the Federal Republic of Germany was constituted, the dialogue regarding Austria and Germany was conducted between Jędrzej Giertych (1903–1992) and Stanisław Stroński (1882–1955).

Giertych, a politician and a journalist, argued in July 1949 that Germany must be divided into two parts, Northern with the capital in Berlin and Southern with the capital in Vienna. For him, the ideas for the future of Germany after WWII were the same as in the Treaty of Versailles – in the spirit of Otto von Bismarck (1815–1898). He claimed that the frontier at the Main and Rhine rivers guaranteed peace for Poland and all of Europe; thus '[...] Vienna would feel like a capital again, equal to Berlin, and would regain its political ambition and willingness to play a greater role'.[24] He did not mention a word about the Soviet Union's occupation of East Germany and East Austria. Afterwards Giertych developed his advocacy of the claim that Austria needed to be removed from the mid-Danube and confederate with Bavaria, Württemberg, Baden, the Rhineland and parts of Hessen. He presented a simple demographic and statistical analysis based on religious cleavage, and started a six month-long dispute with Stanisław Stroński.

22 F. Frankowski, Światła i cienie na drodze do Federacji Europejskiej [Lights and Shadows on the Road to the European Federation], *Dziennik Polski i Dziennik Żołnierza*, London 1953 January 6th, 2f.

23 Jan Zadeykański, Refleksje naddunajskie [Danube's Reflexions], *Wiadomości* 12/13 (155/156), London/Brussels 1949 March 27th, 2.

24 Jędrzej Giertych, Sprawa Niemiec [Germany's Question], *Wiadomości* 26 (166), London/Brussels 1949 June 5th, 1 [translated by M.W.].

Stroński, a politician and journalist as well, had a hypothesis that Austria could survive as an independent state within its post-World War I borders, and can manage after WWII. While he expressed a strong opinion regarding national unity between Germans and Austrians, he argued that the real problem for Europe was not Northern Germany, but Prussia.[25] Nevertheless, he claimed that the union between Austria and Bavaria is possible, but only as a democratic decision. 'Obviously, I would agree, when – applying "if I were German" hypothesis – Munich people would agree'.[26]

More comprehensive discussions regarding Central Europe were promoted in *Kultura*. The most interesting debate in the Polish press was started by an article[27] written by the Czech politician and philosopher Hubert Ripka (1895–1958). He promoted the Polish-Czech federation as a central pillar of the Central European Federation between Czechoslovakia, Poland, Hungary, Romania, Yugoslavia, Bulgaria, and Austria.[28] Ripka strongly supported involving Austria in the Central European project. He claimed that excluding Austria would give the impression of Polish and Czech Germanophobia. According to Ripka, the confederation must be against German imperialism and he advocated for both Austria's and Poland's participation in the project.[29] The Ripka article was completed by an editors' statement that they do not fully agree with the author. By that time, in 1952, Giedroyc and Mieroszewski supported unification of the entire continent.[30]

Ripka's ideas were not new for Polish scholars. In 1945, Feliks Gross (1906–2006) proposed a federation in Central Europe.[31] Based on 1937 statistics of the region, and the tradition of Karl Renner (1870–1950) and Otto Bauer (1881–1938) from early 20th century, and Tomáš Masaryk's (1850–1937) New Europe[32] from 1918, Gross believed that Austria must be part of a Central European Federation. Gross advocated for possible three versions; (1) the federation of nine countries – Austria, Poland, Czechoslovakia, Hungary, Romania, Yugoslavia, Albania, Bulgaria, and Greece, or (2) two-level federation with Austria, Poland, Czechoslovakia, Hungary, and Rumania, or, finally, (3) as a sub-Danube federation with Austria,

25 Stanisław Stroński, Gdybym był Niemcem … [If I were German …], *Wiadomości* 28 (171), London/Brussels 1949 July 10th, 1.

26 Stanisław Stroński, Gdybym był Niemcem … Do redaktora 'Wiadomości' [If I were German … Letter for the editor of The News], *Wiadomości* 45(188), London/Brussels 1949 November 6th, 4.

27 Hubert Ribka, O federację polsko-czeską [The Polish-Czech Federation], *Kultura*, Paris 1952/12/62, 3–14.

28 *Ibid.*, 11.

29 *Ibid.*, 13.

30 *Ibid.*, 14.

31 Feliks Gross, Crossroads of Two Continents. A Democratic Federation of Eastcentral Europe, New York 1945.

32 Tomáš Masaryk proposed that a federation in Central and East Europe (from Finland on the North, by Baltic stated up to Adriatic see) should be based on principle of freedom, as the federation of United Stated of America; Thomas Masaryk, The New Europe. The Slav Standpoint, Washington D.C 1918.

Hungary, and Romania.[33] As opposed to Ripka, who wants to convince 'an ordinary man', Feliks Gross was a scholar, and as such his work was recognized.[34]

In a positive review of Ripka's article, a Polish politician and member of the federation movement, Edward Raczyński (1891–1993), agreed that the participation of Austria in the Central European project is tempting; however, 'the details ought to be further discussed in the future'.[35] Ripka himself provided the chance for that.

Hubert Ripka developed his concept in a book titled "A Federation of Central Europe".[36] While he developed the arguments in favor of a Central European Federation of eight countries, he advocated two realistic alternatives in a post-Soviet scenario. Whereas the European Union would not to be established by that time, a Central European Federation was first needed to organize a common army and transportation systems in the region.

Whereas Juliusz Mieroszewski advocated for Ripka's works being popularized in *Kultura*[37], he did not agree with all of Ripka's ideas. The true intention of Mieroszewski was to '[...] keep Ripka warmly, as he is a liberal, cultured and educated gentleman, who however has many enemies'.[38] Mieroszewski, in his review, appreciated Ripka's criticism of any 'Habsburgian' federation project including only Czechoslovakia, Hungary, and Austria.[39] Nevertheless, for Mieroszewski it was highly unlikely to create such an entity, and it is more probable for him that independent Ukraine would join the Central Europe Federation instead. He put emphasis on the Austrian threat caused by Polish-German tensions.[40] A more positive review of Ripka's project was Raczyński's piece published in *Kultura* one month later.[41] In terms of admission of Central European countries to the European Union, Raczyński did not share Ripka's enthusiasm. He claimed that Ger-

---

33 *Ibid.*, 9–17.

34 Crossroads of Two Continents was highly reviewed between 1945–1946; see: Hannah Arendt, Power Politics Triumphs (review), in: *Commentary. A Jewish Review*, 2, December 1945, in: http://www.commentarymagazine.com/article/crossroads-of-two-continents-by-feliks-gross/, 11 December 2014.

35 Edward Raczyński, Czechosłowacja i Polska w organizacji przyszłego ustroju Europy środkowowschodniej [Czechoslovakia and Poland in the Proces of Organisation Future Central an East European regime], *Dziennik Polski i Dziennik Żołnierza*, London 1953 April 10th, 2.

36 Hubert Ripka, A Federation of Central Europe, New York 1953.

37 Mieroszewski advised to publish in *Kultura* two reviews, one written by Raczyński and second by himself. Letter from Juliusz Mieroszewski to Jerzy Giedroyc, 1954 February 3rd, in: Jerzy Giedroyc – Juliusz Mieroszewski, Listy 1949–1956. Cześć pierwsza [Letteres 1949–1956. Vol. 1], Waszawa 1999, 350.

38 Letter from Juliusz Mieroszewski to Jerzy Giedroyc, 1954 March 7th, in: *ibid.*, 358 [translated by M.W.].

39 Londyńczyk [pseudonim of Juliusz Mieroszewski], Federacja Ośmiu [Federation of Eight], *Kultura*, Paris 1954/4/78, 99.

40 *Ibid.*, 98–101.

41 Edward Raczyński, Europeizm czy regionalizm [Europeanism or Regionalism], *Kultura*, Paris 1954/5/79, pp. 98–108.

many would put pressure on the European Union preferring individual negotiation, rather than adhering to a Central European Federation *en block*.[42]

While the United States, Soviet Union, United Kingdom, and France negotiated an independent and neutral Austria, *Kultura* published a series of three articles devoted to the neutralization of Central Europe. 'We believe that in view of the forthcoming Conference of the Four Powers concepts to create 'a safety zone' by neutralizing the Central and Eastern Europe becomes the central problem of our peoples'[43], stated the editorial note preceding the article written by Hubert Ripka.[44] The Czech politician claimed that the Soviet agreement for Austria independency was the result of the North Atlantic Treaty Organization's (NATO) pressure; moreover, the transatlantic cooperation must have been strengthened by the Western European integration process, including France, Great Britain, and Germany. Ripka suggested how the Soviets could leave Central Europe and how the region could confederate itself. As a next step, Central Europe should join the Western European community to guarantee the balance of power between West Russia and China. 'Excluding war as a means of liberalization, we believe that it can be achieved by the well-organized three-factor action of the free world – the combination of military force, creative diplomacy, spiritual and moral power.'[45]

Mieroszewski cynically argued that in the era of nuclear warfare, neutral Austria was a 'capitulation in installments'.[46] While he advocated for the neutrality of Europe as a step towards global government, he underlined that Americans and Russians could accept the European draw, but Europeans must not. 'Nowadays Europe is a "bigger Austria", and as such neutral Austria is similar to the "Krakau Republic" [The Free, Independent, and Strictly Neutral City of Cracow with its Territory, created by the Congress of Vienna in 1815 – M.W.].'[47] Moreover, in his opinion, Austria is not a good example for Poland or any of the satellite states. 'For a Pole Austria is not a good illustration of liberation by neutralization – because this nice country was not a satellite'.[48] Nevertheless, the liberation of Austria from the Soviet army was important for Jerzy Giedroyc, as he decided to publish the coverage from Vienna and the Neusiedler See by Bohdan Brodzinski in the 1955s last volume.[49]

The conceptual debates on Central Europe and its limits were present in two major Polish émigré periodicals. The idea of *Intermarium* was directly related to

42 *Ibid.*, 99f.

43 Editorial note, *Kultura*, Paris, 1955/06/92, 81.

44 Hubert Ripka, Konferencja Czterech a Europa Wschodnia [The Four-Power Conference and Eastern Europe], *Kultura*, Paris 1955/06/92, 81–89.

45 *Ibid.*, 88f.

46 Mieroszewski, Europa, 113 [translated by M.W.].

47 *Ibid.*, 107f. [translated by M.W.].

48 Juliusz Mieroszewski, Dramat wyzwolenia [Drama of Liberation], *Kultura*, Paris 1955/7-8/93–94, 151.

49 Bohdan Brodzinski, Wiedeń w przeddzien uwolnienia [Liberation's Eve in Vienna], *Kultura*, Paris 1955/12/98, 63–66.

the negotiation between Poland and Czechoslovakia during WWII. Nonetheless, discussion of the project was limited to the members of the Federal Clubs. Stanisław Mackiewicz in *Wiadomości* critically argued for revision of the idea in light of Poland as the superpower in Eastern Europe. On the other hand, both Jędrzej Giertych and Stanisław Stroński were detached from the situation in Central Europe after WWII. Their debates were based on 19th century fundaments, completely out of date in 1949. Eventually, Stroński admitted that the possible federation of Southern Germany with Austria needed to be the result of a democratic decision of the people. *Kultura* was highly engaged to promote the Czech Hubert Ripka's vision of Central Europe. Although Juliusz Mieroszewski was not likely to fully agree with his ideas, the discussion raised a question of Central Europe and its boundaries, including the position of Austria. Juliusz Mieroszewski was the only one who questioned the idea of neutrality as a possible political tool. In the following years, Juliusz Mieroszewski developed a concept of a neutral zone and Atlantic community, where Austria played the role of Central European country without any particular specificity.[50]

Austrian Balderdash

Dziennik reports frequently discussed the situations in Austria from 1945 to 1955. The vast majority of attention concerned the West-Soviet negotiations under the Council of Foreign Ministers meetings in Moscow, London, Paris, and Berlin.[51] The discourse shifted between two proverbs: *bella gerant alii, tu felix Austria, nube* [let others wage war; you, happy Austria, marry] and 'Austrian balderdash', the Polish proverb describing debates in the Austrian parliament in 19th century, here as a critic of the strategy of the US, France, and the UK.[52] The main concerns were oil concessions for the Soviet Union and the industry police forces; the question of the full independence of future Austria was raised. Nevertheless, newspapers' releases from 1947 to 1953 reflected Austria as a *modus vivendi* for Germany and Berlin.[53]

Although *Kultura* advocated that the situation in Poland and other Central European countries would evolve after the 20th Congress of the Communist Party of the Soviet Union, which took place between 14–25 February 1956, due to internal evolution within the communist parties, the Polish community in London was

---

50 Michał Wiącek, Przesłanki zjednoczenia Europy według Juliusza Mieroszewskiego i Kultury [Conditions for European unification by Juliusz Mieroszewski and Kultura], in: Niemcoznawstwo 20, Niemcy we współczesnym świecie. Problemy społeczno-polityczne [Germany in the modern world. Socio-political issues], Acta Universitatis Wratislaviensis 3428, Wrocław 2012, 29–46.

51 Further about the negotiations, see: Günter Bischof, Austria in the First Cold War, 1945–55. The Leverage of the Weak, Basingstoke/New York 1999, 106–156.

52 R., Austriackie gadanie [Austrian balderdash], *Dziennik Polski i Dziennik Żołnierza*, London 1952 January 23rd, 2.

53 Konferencja czterech dobiega konca po czterech tygodniach bezpłodnych obrad [The Conference of Four is coming to the end after four weeks of unfruitful debates], *Dziennik Polski i Dziennik Żołnierza*, London 1949 June 20th, 1.

more likely to believe in 'the Austrian way'. *Dziennik Polski i Dziennik Żołniarza* described how the country played its policy in the extremely divided Europe. While the rivalry between the USA and the USSR divided the continent between capitalist and communist blocs, the European integration separated Western Europe between two economic integration organizations. Austria, which had strong economic ties with ECC, due to the geopolitical situation became the member of the European Free Trade Association (EFTA). *Dziennik* showed in several articles Austrian struggles in the new context: politically neutral within the EFTA and economically dependent from ECC.

Contrary to *Kultura*, *Dziennik* did not developed comments on Austrian neutrality policy by 1955. Press releases put Austria alongside Finland, Sweden, and Yugoslavia as a neutral country.[54] Nevertheless, Wiesław Patek distinguished the neutrality of Switzerland and Sweden from Austrian neutrality in the context of possible membership in the EEC and the role the organization as the economic foundation of the NATO. He advocated that Austrian neutrality was the price paid in 1955 for Soviet soldiers to leave the country; therefore, Austria should become an associate member of the EEC.[55]

Nevertheless, the European integration process and the position of Austria were discussed in the Polish Daily in the 1960s. While the Austrian economy was tied to the six countries of the EEC, no one thought about Austrian participation in the project in 1956. Five years after declaring neutrality, together with Denmark, Norway, Portugal, Sweden, Switzerland, and the United Kingdom, Austria created the Outer Seven – the EFTA. However, Austrian politicians knew that it was not enough to protect the domestic economy. The bilateral negotiation between Austria and the European Coal and Steel Community (ECSC)/EEC, the question of continued existence of EFTA without the UK, and, finally, the possibility of an Austrian association with the EEC in the 1960s[56] raised concerns of public perception. This was reflected in *Dziennik Polski i Dziennik Żołnierza* articles.

For the England-based editors, the primary questions of EFTA's future and ECC-UK negotiations were crucial. In the context of the Austrian-EEC agreement, *Dziennik* argued that the Austrian State Treaty was '[...] the only real and achieved step of the West in the process of liberation in Central Europe from Soviet domination'.[57] As emphasized, the wording of the agreement had precedential character, as it tested Soviet policy. For the author it was at the same time a question of

54 14-ka i konferencja europejska [The 14 and European Conference], *Tydzień Polski. Dziennik Polski i Dziennik Żołnierza*, London 1969 November 29th, 2.

55 Wiesław Patek, Szwecja i zjednoczona Europa [Sweden and United Europe], *Dziennik Polski i Dziennik Żołnierza*, London 1962 June 8th, 2.

56 Michael Gehler, A Newcomer Experienced in European Integration. Austria, in: Wolfram Kaiser – Jürgen Elvert (Eds.), European Union Enlargement: a Comparative History, London/New York 2004, 139–158, here 142.

57 Orion, Wspólny Rynek i Austria [The Common Market and Austria], *Dziennik Polski i Dziennik Żołnierza*, London 1965 March 30th, 2 [translated by M.W.].

the responsibility of the EEC towards Central Europe. 'In Austria, the whole Common Market will take a tough and important exam, and the results will be observed around the world, and particularly in trapped, hungry, poor satellite states'.[58]

The 1966 election was Austria's chance to join the EEC in the eyes of Wacław Zbyszewski (1903–1985). He advocated that the 'young and energized' Josef Klaus (1910–2001) should create a majority government of the Austrian People's Party (ÖVP, Österreichische Volkspartei), and finish 20 years of immobility in the Austrian political life. The real concern for him was a strategy of the EEC itself and France in particular. As Bruno Kreisky's sabotage was out-of-date due to the general election, Zbyszewski criticized the policy of France towards the Soviet Union. 'I am fully convinced that if Austria overcomes the pettiness and cowardice of Kreisky and says: "we will join the Six and we do not care about Soviet threats", the Soviet Union will do nothing, as the USSR did nothing when the Federal Republic of Germany joined the North Atlantic Treaty Organization in 1955'.[59] Wacław Zbyszewski used a right-wing narrative well known to his readers and so characteristic for the Polish emigration in London. Moreover, his criticism of the Austrian political system was repeated, always with an adjective 'immobile'.[60] Far-reaching criticism of Bruno Kreisky was emblematic for *Dziennik Polski i Dziennik Żołnierza*.[61] It also explains the journal's decline of interest in Austria after 21 April 1970, the day when Kreisky started his 13-years ruling as Chancellor of Austria.

The Polish Daily and Soldier's Daily reported regularly on Austrian-EEC negotiations and evaluated the chances for Austrian membership. Two main political journalists, Aleksander Bregman and Wacław Zbyszewski, used the example of Austria as a possible role model for the transition of Poland and other satellite countries. Neither the Hungarian Revolution in 1956 nor the Warsaw Pact invasion of Czechoslovakia during the Prague Spring in 1968[62] redefined the position of Austria in Europe and Austrian neutrality according to the perception of the Polish émigré newspaper.

Finally *Kultura* took part in the criticism of the Chancellor Bruno Kreisky (1911–1990) position during the Schoenau crisis. In 1973, Leopold Unger recalled that every time Austria decided to capitulate it always meant capitulation of Eu-

58 *Ibid.* [translated by M.W.].

59 Wacław Zbyszewski, Zwycięstwo chadecji w Austrii [Christian Democrats won in Austria], *Dziennik Polski i Dziennik Żołnierza*, London 1966 March 16th, 2 [translated by M.W.].

60 Aleksander Bregman, Decydujące trzy lata [Crucial three years], *Dziennik Polski i Dziennik Żołnierza*, London 1966 December 1st, 2.

61 Wacław Zbyszewski claimed that Bruno Kreisky is unipersonal responsible for Austria joing the EFTA and not EEC in 1956; Wacław Zbyszewski, Kreisky, *Dziennik Polski i Dziennik Żołnierza*, London 1970 March 25th, 2.

62 Karin Liebhart, Transformation and Semantic Change of Austrian Neutrality. Its Origins, Development and Demise, in: Günter Bischof – Anton Pelinka – Ruth Wodak (Eds.), Neutrality in Austria. Contemporary Austrian Studies 9, New Brunswick/London 2001, 7–36, here 17–20.

rope.[63] The journalist of the newspaper *Le Soir* described in *Kultura* the background story of his interview with Chancellor Bruno Kreisky taken just after the Schoenau Ultimatum.

The Schoenau castle served as a transit facility for the Jewish emigrants from the USSR. Unger summarized the history of the castle and briefed his readers on the events, when a Polish State Railways train was attacked by two Palestinian terrorists in Marchegg (Lower-Austria) on 28 September 1973.[64] The kidnappers took four hostages and requested, *inter alia*, that the Schoenau facilities would be closed. The Austrian chancellor accepted the request. The primary goal of the hostage-taking in Marchegg was to fool Israeli intelligence before the Yom Kippur War preparations; the war called by Unger 'the agony of Europe'.[65] Describing the interview with Kreisky, Unger claimed that he was received in better circumstances than Golda Meir (1898–1978) on 2 October 1973; however, 'the talk exclusively smelled like oil'[66], as Kreisky explained that the Schoenau incident was not the capitulation, just his political strategy. As Wistrich shows the Austrian people broadly approved Kreisky's decision and shared his neutral position in the conflict between Israel and the Arabs.[67]

The NATO's and the EEC's reactions to the Yom Kippur War and the following oil crisis inspired Unger to ask if the European integration, created from coal and steel (reference to the European Coal and Steel Community), would die in disgrace by oil. The reaction of the ECC countries was for Unger the same as Kreisky's answer to the Schoenau ultimatum. 'It is all very similar to Vienna. EEC, as Austria, wants to convince us that they have thought for a long time the Arabs were right'.[68] Unger closed his argumentation by the assumption that the oil is the weapon for Arabs' colonization of Europe.

Conclusions

It has been shown how *Kultura*, *Wiadomości* and *Dziennik Polski and Dziennik Żołnierza* included Austrian discourse in the debates about the future of Europe after WWII. The readers of the Literary Institute had the chance to compare how social and political relations in Austria changed from 1945 to 1960[69] thanks to

63 Brukselczyk, Widziane z Brukseli [Viewed from Brussels], *Kultura*, Paris 1973/12/315, 31–39, here 32.

64 APA Austria Press Agency: Die Geiselnahme in Marchegg [The hostage-taking in Marchegg], http://www.historisch.apa.at/cms/apa-historisch/dossier.html?dossierID=AHD_19730928_AHD0001, 16 March 2015.

65 Brukselczyk, Widziane z Brukseli, 33.

66 *Ibid.* [translated by M.W.].

67 Robert S. Wistrich, From Ambivalence to Betrayal. The Left, the Jews, and Israel, Lincoln 2012, 490.

68 Brukselczyk, Widziane z Brukseli, 39.

69 Paweł Hostowiec, Notatki niespiesznego przechodnia (z Dziennika Podróży). Wiedeń – Wiedeń Franciszka Józefa – Legalizm Austriacki – Na Stadionie – Imprezy Festowalowe [Notes of a

Jerzy Stempowski's reports. While *Wiadomości* presented Polish Superpower narration for Central Europe order after 1945, the struggle with the Soviet domination in Eastern Austria were being regularly reported by the *Dziennik Polski i Dziennik Żołnierza* press releases.

Austria's role as a member of *Intermarium* or as a key to the German question after WWII were discussed by the *Wiadomości* authors as Stanisław Mackiewicz, Jędrzej Giertych and Stanisław Stroński. The common characteristic of the authors' thoughts was the predominant idea of Poland as a regional superpower in the eastern borders as established in the Treaty of Riga in 1921 and Western borders as established in Potsdam in 1945.

Austria was a key element of Hubert Ripka's Central European Federation proposal. He developed and publicized the ideas of Danubian federations elaborated during WWII by Feliks Gross. Hubert Ripka's proposals were more detailed and more argumentative in terms of Austrian participation. Despite the fact that the principal political journalist of *Kultura* did not fully agree with Ripka's projects, Austria appeared in the conceptual debate about a future Central European order. Juliusz Mieroszewski argued that Austria is too small to maintain its neutrality in the Cold War environment. For the *Kultura* spokesmen, the key for a united Europe was lay in divided Germany.

Furthermore, Austria was a key to developing the scenarios for Central European countries for liberation from Soviet domination and joining Western European institutions. The Austrian State Treaty changed the discourse from theoretical deliberations to the possible role model of Austria or Poland and other satellite countries. This role was promoted in the *Dziennik Polski i Dziennik Żołnierza*, especially in the 1960s when the Austrian People's Party won the elections. The results of the 1966 General Election were particularly interesting, as they opened the door to ending the period of the Great Coalition in Austrian politics. *Dziennik* published a series of articles considering membership of Austria within the European Economic Community. Nevertheless, the domination of Bruno Kreisky in Austrian politics caused the loss of interest of the more and more conservative and right-wing emigration in London.

The analysis of the Austrian discourse across the main Polish émigré periodicals shows that further research needs to be conducted in the comparative perspective including two-three major titles, as the authors published their articles at times in the *Dziennik Polski i Dziennik Żołnierza*, and at other times in *Kultura*. Moreover, the journalists were often committed to one title, so to deconstruct the public perception of Polish intellectual emigration, a researcher must establish the intertextual dialogue.

Leisurely Passer-by (From Travelling Jurnal). Vienna – Vienna of Franz Joseph – Austrian Legalism – The Stadium – Events], *Kultura*, Paris 1960/1–2/147–148, 15–25.

Il est urgent d'attendre. Post-conclusion

In October 1954 *Kultura* published an extensive report[70] concerning 'Österreichisches College and Europäisches Forum Alpbach' (EFA, European Forum Alpbach) by Pawel Hostowiec (pseudonym of Jerzy Stempowski). The author of one of the first books published by the Literary Institute *Journal from Austria and Germany (November–December 1945)*[71], returned to Austria in summer 1954 with a refreshing social and political analysis. Stempowski took part in the Forum thanks to the Jerzy Giedroyc's initiative and support.[72]

Stempowski underlines the community of memory and experiences of Austrian and other Central European nations, in particular the memory of the instability of institutions and living conditions. Appreciating the program (the organization for the very first time of an Eastern European Session during the Forum[73]), Stempowski presented the social relations in Alpbach. The idyllic image of the Alpbach valley (Tyrol), where traditional roles were still important and where the commodity economy only arrived with Austria's Anschluss, created the '[...] historical basis of formation of Europe, especially in comparison with American and Soviet formations'[74], threatened by industrial society. In this context, Stempowski analyzed why the German-speaking states of Austria forgot the federalist traditions of the Habsburgs and lost interest in Cisleithania so quickly during the interwar period. Furthermore, by describing the College's organization and program of the tenth Forum, the author highlighted the interdisciplinary character and the primary goal – to restore the lost universality of science. Stempowski also provided the analysis on a more general issue – the role of universities in market-driven countries. He claimed that universities were and should have been the last areas of modern states where economics did not reign.[75]

70 Pawel Hostowiec, 'Forum' Europejskie w Alpbach [European Forum in Alpbach], *Kultura*, Paris 1954/10/84, 31–38.

71 Jerzy Stempowski, Dziennik podróży do Austrii i Niemiec (listopad–grudzień 1945) [Journal from Austria and Germany (November–December 1945)], Rzym 1946. It was the coverage from Western-occupied territories of Germany and Austria.

72 Letter from Jerzy Giedroyc to Jerzy Stempowski, 22 May 1954, in: Jerzy Giedroyc – Jerzy Stempowski, Listy 1946–1969. Część pierwsza [Letters 1949–1956. Vol. 1], Warszawa 1998, 233.

73 There were no direct outcomes from the works, however, Giedroyc appreciated the networking opportunities for *Kultura* as 'fruitful and important', Letter from Jerzy Giedroyc to Jerzy Stempowski, 15 September 1954, in: Giedroyc – Stempowski, Listy, 249.

74 Hostowiec, 'Forum', 34.

75 Inspired by Jerzy Stempowski, I would like to express acknowledgment for the Federal Ministry of Science, Research and Economy and to all eight Austrian Centers around the world for organizing the annual convention; the platform of interdisciplinary exchange for young scholars conducting research focusing on Central Europe.

Ricarda Rindlisbacher

Juvenile Crime and Urban Planning: How to Measure Crime Factors and Promote Prevention by Using Geospatial Technologies?

University of Graz

Introduction

Pete, a little-ten-year old boy, is sitting on a bench, staring at the grocery store, feeling nervous. So much is going through his mind right now. His dad, who obviously has an alcohol problem and his mom, who is suffering from terminal cancer – the combination of that, does not make it easy for him. Pete got another 'F' on his last Math exam. He had to care for his mom and he did not think about studying. But now he is really scared his dad will find out and beat him hard. This has happened several times already. Pete wants to bring back some beer for his dad and an orange juice for his mom – she loves orange juice and it would make her very happy, as well as his dad. The problem is Pete cannot afford it, so he is planning on stealing it. He is waiting for the perfect opportunity – he does not want to get caught – again. He wants his dad and his mom to be proud of him. He loves them. And he wants to stop the beating.

Pete got caught for the seventh time, when he tried to steal some beer and some orange juice and he was sent to juvenile court. The big question now is: what exactly should happen to Pete? Is he really a bad young boy who deserves to be charged for his crime, regardless of how old he is? Should he be made to seek professional help? Or something else? Does your opinion about this case change when one tell you that the family's citizenship and origin is not Austrian? Where do the lines have to be drawn? What is justice? Is there justice at all?

As you can see, this is a case with a common problem, slightly adaptable of course, but the core message will remain the same. It is difficult to say that this is the correct answer, even though there is a law that seemingly tells us exactly what to do. How fair would the judgment be? And is there only one answer to that?

This research tries to look at these kinds of problems and wants to find a way to work more on preventive measures by using a trans-disciplinary approach.

Crime Prevention and its Challenges: A Problem Assignment

Crime is a topic that confronts us in our everyday life. From watching a colleague taking some paper or pencils back home from the office, burglaries in our neighbor's house, or even murders across the street. The list of crimes is long and very individual. It should be noted that all these various crimes depend on individual's backgrounds and that one specific crime can be the subject of various disciplines. *E.g.*, a burglary in the neighborhood can happen due to the environmental design in a certain area (*e.g.*, many green areas around the block, no obviously installed alarm systems, not enough lighting, *etc.*), or its origin lies in social matters. Professional organized gangs are specialized in breaking into very expensive houses or apartments, very rich people own – so they will sell their stolen goods on the black market. Another cause for burglary could also be the bad economic situation in a country, which apparently forces *e.g.*, unemployed people to commit a crime. However, the latter could also be a social problem. Moreover, some studies have proved that criminal behavior may stem from individuals' genes.[1] These examples clearly demonstrate that a burglary cannot be seen from only one point of view. It involves much more, and most of the time a crime occurs because of a chain of events that involves many individual variables. Every single factor seems to be part of a specific system, however, this is part of a whole and the goal of this research is to look more closely at the big picture.

On the basis of the literature review it seems that the topic 'Spatial Crime Analysis and Prevention' has its origin in the USA, Great Britain, Australia and New Zealand and is a big issue in these regions. Of course, the crime rate or even the crime types of, *e.g.*, the United States cannot be compared with those of Austrian (due to cultural issues, different laws, different size of the country, *etc.*); nevertheless, Austria can respective should learn and adapt a lot from all these preventive approaches from other countries. Despite this, crime prevention is becoming more important in Austria, as the latest report of the Criminal Intelligence Service Austria (BK, Bundeskriminalamt) shows. Due to the development of new strategies (amongst others, educating and implementing special task forces for combating organized crime, human trafficking, drugs, cyber-crime, ATM crimes, *etc.*) over the past few years, the total crime rate in Austria has declined by ten percent and the level has remained constant until today (see Figure 1) – hence, a continuous downward trend can be noted. The period of 2004 to 2012 even shows a decrease of about 15 percent. In 2004, 643,648 crimes were registered, whereas in 2012 'only' 548,027 crimes were recorded. Nevertheless, 2012 (compared with 2011) saw an increase of 1.5 percent, which can be traced to new forms of crime, such as cyber-crime.[2]

1 Herschel Prins, Offenders, Deviants or Patients?, New York ³2005, 33.

2 BM.I/Polizei – Bundesministerium für Inneres (Ed.), Sicherheit in Österreich: Kriminalitätsentwicklung und Maßnahmenpakete 2013, Pressegespräch vom 5. Februar 2013, [Safety in Austria:

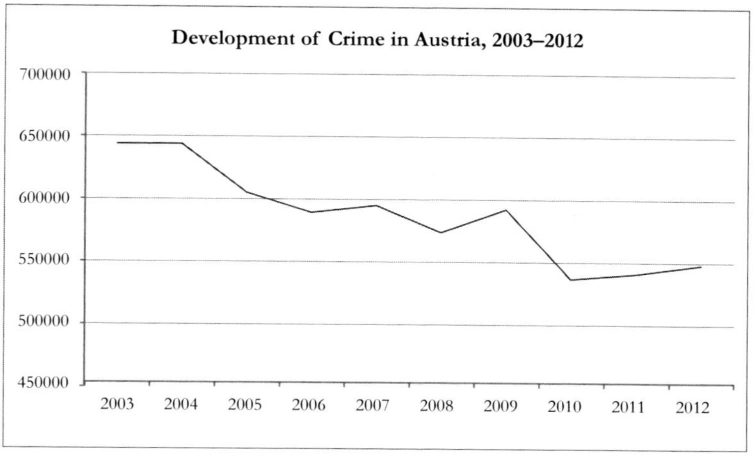

Figure 1: Development of Crime in Austria – 2003–2012 (illustrated by R.R.[2]).

Nevertheless, the above mentioned figures show that even if there a declining trend can clearly be observed, a lot more precautions have to be set – crimes are always getting more innovative and as long as people collide with each other or with other cultures, any form of crime will always exist. So, attempting to get rid of crime completely would be virtually impossible, everybody can comprehend that. The correct way of saying this would be to reduce crime as much as possible, or, rather, to reduce all the opportunities for criminals, because crimes usually happen because of such opportunities. The way to do this would be to use all the facts we have and combine them into a whole unit. Thereby, we can get an overall view and it would finally be possible to derive essential prevention measures. It is believed that prevention is the most crucial part in fighting crime, starting with children at an early stage.

However, looking at previous years and due to the slight decreases in the crime rate, one can argue that prevention is already effective. The consequence within strategic planning is to extend the traditional forms of crime prevention and social measures of integration with the help of urban planning and environmental design and to keep on working beyond this point.

Research Questions

Usually, when analyzing crime, one would only concentrate either on environmental, social, psychological, or economic factors on their own, but this research project combines all of these aspects. This holistic approach anticipates a fully new

Development of Crime and Measurement Packages 2013, Press Conference on 5 February 2013], 2013, 2. http://www.bmi.gv.at/cms/BK/presse/files/522013_KrimEntwicklung.pdf, 15 March 2013.

and innovative gaze at the topic of crime. This results into a trans-disciplinary research framework, because the crime factors affect the environmental, social, psychological, and economic disciplines, which are discussed and evaluated with experts from these fields. Moreover, interviews will be conducted with prisoners and these results will be contrasted with the experts' assessment of the causal factors of crime. Moreover, as a counter-point to these results, specific data analysis with Geographic Information Systems will be performed. Out of these different approaches, target oriented prevention measures can be diverted.

- What are the factors that influence crime and which are the most important ones?
- Why are exactly these factors the most influential ones?
- How does the environment influence factors and hot spots (remote sensing in combination with crime)?
- Where are hot spots of crime in the Styrian state capital Graz, and why are hot spots exactly where they are (various analysis methods by using all the information of the influencing factors with the help of Geographic Information Systems – GIS)?
- What is the point of view of the delinquent people, why did they choose exactly that specific location (interviews with delinquents)?

Result:

- Finding, testing, and evaluating new concepts for crime prevention (and to make it measurable) – an iterative model.

Crime and GIS

> 'Knowledge about how the world works is more valuable than knowledge about how it looks because it can be used to predict.'[3]

Crime in combination with GIS usually deals with analyzing, modeling, and mapping crime, which will be a major part of the empirical part of this research. However, GIS will play an important role when it comes to crime analysis. But GIS is much more than analyzing – according to Clarke[4], GIS is a powerful tool for establishing individual models representing social, environmental, or economic issues. Chainey and Ratcliffe[5] mention that before GIS was available, law enforce-

3 Paul Longley – Mike Goodchild – David Maguire – David Rhind, Geographic Information Systems and Science, Jefferson City ³2011, 14.

4 Keith Clarke, Geocomputation's Future at the Extremes. High Performance Computing and Nanoclients, in: Jeffrey Hollingsworth (Ed.), Parallel Computing – Systems and Applications 29/10, Maryland 2003, 1292.

5 Spencer Chainey – Jerry Ratcliffe, GIS and Crime Mapping, West Sussex 2005, 8.

ment agencies were working with pin maps. And it is wrong again to say that GIS only makes a digital version of pin maps. GIS is a powerful modeling and decision support tool, thus, a prevailing strategic analysis tool, which most law enforcement agencies are using nowadays. They know about its value, in the last couple of years there has been a significant rise in using GIS for crime analysis.

Crime analysis in combination with GIS is making significant progress and is getting more and more important and contributing more than in the past – GIS is substantial when having to make decisions – that is for sure.[6]

Over the past 30 years crime analysis/modeling has been an issue many scholars have dealt with and, actually, still are.[7] Depending on the disciplines, crime analysis has always got a different meaning; *e.g.*, a police department would do crime mapping and would be producing statistics; on the other hand, crime analysis could also mean tracking serial killers or other kinds of offenders, or analyzing police reports.[8] Over the course of time, many various definitions have been developed by scholars.[9] Even though most of the definitions are diverging, they would always share a common element.[10]

Boba[11] defines crime analysis as follows: 'Crime analysis is the systematic study of crime and disorder problems as well as other police-related issues – including socio-demographic, spatial, and temporal factors – to assist the police in criminal apprehension, crime and disorder reduction, crime prevention, and evaluation.'[12]

However, crime analysis means analyzing crime and moreover, filtering out information from the infinite expanse of data that is available and finally, passing it on to the officers and investigators in the field. Crime prevention plays a significant economic role within crime analysis, as prevention costs less than apprehending criminals after the crime has happened.[13]

Using GIS for Crime Mapping

Maps play a major role in crime analysis – they already have a long tradition, but since the 1990s innovations in technology, internet, databases, and software have been helping to establish the maps as an inherent part of every police department,

---

6 Fahui Wang (Ed.), Geographic Information Systems and Crime Analysis, Pennsylvania 2005, vi.

7 Rachel Boba Santos, Crime Analysis with Crime Mapping, California 2013, 2–6.

8 Deborah Osborne – Susan Wernicke, Introduction to Crime Analysis. Basic Resources for Criminal Justice Practice, New York 2003, 1.

9 *Cf. inter alia* Karim Vellani – Joel Nahoun, Applied Crime Analysis, Massachusetts 2001, 8; Steven Gottlieb – Sheldon Arenberg – Raj Singh, Crime Analysis. From First Report to Final Arrest, California 1994, 13; Margaret Emig – Robert Heck – Marjorie Kravitz (Ed.), Crime Analysis. A Selected Bibliography, National Criminal Justice Reference Service, US Department of Justice, National Institute of Justice, Michigan 1980, 5.

10 Boba Santos, Crime Analysis, 2f.

11 Rachel Boba Santos, Crime Analysis and Crime Mapping, California 2005, 6f.

12 *Ibid.*

13 Osborne – Wernicke, Introduction, 1f.

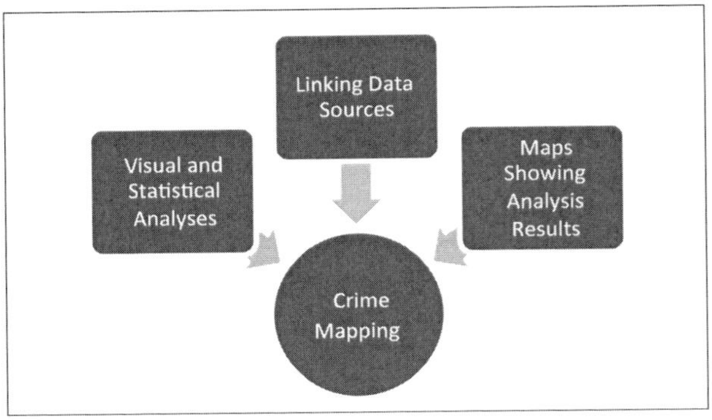

Figure 2: Three Main Functions of Crime Mapping within Crime Analysis (illustrated by R.R.).[16]

by not only using hand drawn wall maps with pins on it. Nowadays, the most common way of mapping is using GIS.[14] GIS does not only consist of many digital maps, it is more like a problem-solving tool, hence, a spatial decision support system, with the possibility of doing analyses and making things visible that one would not see on an ordinary map.[15] Boba Santos defines GIS as a tool for analyzing, querying, visualizing, and modifying spatial data. However, within the discipline of 'Crime Analysis' three main functions of crime mapping do exist, as Figure 2 shows.

Statistical data can be mapped by using various methods. The map can also be analyzed visually. Various data sources can be linked to each other, *e.g.*, suspects and properties to potential relationships, which support solving a case. Crime mapping also means to visualize analysis results.

In this information era, it is highly important to conduct numerical analysis (algorithms that usually use numerical approximation) and visualize analytical approaches, so that the large amount of spatial data, especially for crime, can finally be analyzed and visualized reasonably.[17] According to Eck[18] or Chainey and Ratcliffe[19], all these visualizing approaches can only be applied in a limited way, as most analysis tools only consider the spatial component, and not the time

14 Boba Santos, Crime Analysis, 2f.

15 Longley – Goodchild – Maguire – Rhind, Information Systems, 16.

16 Boba Santos, Crime Analysis, 2f.

17 Marco Helbich – Julian Hagenauer – Michael Leitner, Raum-Zeitliche Analyse von Verbrechens-Hotspots mittels Trajektorien und Kohonen-Karten [Spatio-Temporal Analysis of Crime-Hotspots using Trajectories and Kohonen-Maps], in: Mitteilungen der Österreichischen Geographischen Gesellschaft 153, 291–304, here 291–293.

18 John Eck, Crime Hot Spots: What They Are, Why We Have Them, and How To Map Them, in: John Eck – Spencer Chainey – James Cameron – Michael Leitner – Ronald Wilson (Eds.) 'Mapping Crime. Understanding Hot Spots', Washington 2005, 33.

19 Spencer Chainey – Jerry Ratcliffe, GIS and Crime Mapping, West Sussex 2005, 224.

or attribute component, as, *e.g.*, the Kernel Density method[20] would do. Helbich and Leitner[21] argue that data mining methods (such as cluster analysis, space-time approaches, regression analysis, *etc.*) contribute to decision-making processes and, thus, extend the tools that can be used for analyzing crime. However, the space-time approach[22] has yet not been debated that much in research. Those who have dealt with that method (*e.g.*, Roth[23] or Nakaya and Yano[24]), have not considered the missing link: 'context', or the socio-economical attributes of the areas. Environmental, economic, and social issues can influence crime hot spots. This hot spot approach combines space-time scan-statistics for the detection of crime hot spots, with a classification of the context on the basis of a Self-Organizing Map (SOM), coupled with the visualization of hot spots on SOMs with trajectories. Socio-economic attributes of an area inhibit or boost the appearance of crime – hence, it is crucial to combine the aspects of space, time, and context and, furthermore, analyze them simultaneously. Keeping that in mind will support the analysis of juvenile crime in Graz immensely and it is believed that the results will be much more accurate than when working with ordinary methods.

Juvenile Crime and Prevention: A Brief Historical Outline of Juvenile Crime in the US, in Europe, and in Austria

In the US, juvenile crime is a serious matter and dates back thousands of years or even longer.[25] America's history has, unfortunately, offered some incisive events; *e.g.*, in the Mid-Atlantic States two serial killers were arbitrarily shooting children and adults. One of the killers was only at the age of 17 and he initiated some of the shootings. In 1999, one of the deadliest mass shootings happened at Columbine High School in Colorado. And sadly, this list can be continued until the present.[26] The situation in Europe is not really different. In 1997 Christian Pfeiffer, a Ger-

---

20 Kernel smoothing or Kernel Density Estimation (KDE) basically deals with analyzing spatial point patterns and is a popular method for detecting clusters (Michael Leitner – Petra Staufer-Steinnocher, Kernel Density Estimation. An Innovative Exploratory Tool for Geomarketing, Salzburg 2001, 2; Trevor Bailey – Anthony Gatrell, Interactive Spatial Data Analysis, Essex 1995, 84f.).

21 Marco Helbich – Michael Leitner, Evaluation of Spatial Cluster Detection Algorithms for Crime Locations, in: Wolfgang Gaul – Andreas Geyer-Schulz – Lars Schmidt-Thieme – Jonas Kunze (Eds.), Challenges at the Interface of Data Analysis, Computer Science, and Optimization. Studies in Classification, Data Analysis, and Knowledge Organization, Berlin 2012, 193.

22 Helbich – Hagenauer – Leitner, Raum-Zeitliche Analyse, 291f.

23 Robert Roth – Kevin Ross – Benjamin Finch – Wei Luo – Alan MacEachren, A User-centered Approach for Designing and Developing Spatiotemporal Crime Analysis Tools, Geo VISTA Center, Department of Geography, Pennsylvania 2010.

24 Tomoki Nakaya – Keiji Yano, Visualising Crime Clusters in a Space-Time Cube. An Exploratory Data-Analysis Approach Using Space-Time Kernel Density Estimation and Scan Statistics, in: Transactions in GIS 14/3, New Jersey 2010, 223–239.

25 Donald Shoemaker – Timothy Wolfe, Juvenile Justice. A Reference Handbook, ABC-CLIO, Santa Barbara 2005, 1–3.

26 Shoemaker – Wolfe, Justice, 1f.

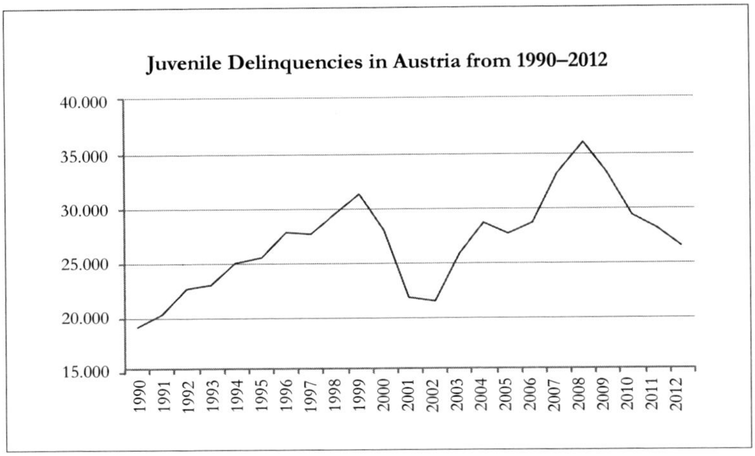

Figure 3: Juvenile Delinquencies in Austria from 1990–2012 (illustrated by R.R.).[29]

man criminologist, was assigned by the European Union (EU) to conduct a survey of juvenile crime showing its impacts and trends in Europe. He started collecting data from most of the European Countries and Switzerland, and he also integrated the Unites States into his studies, as the US usually has a significant influence on crimes and events that happen in Europe.[27] Pfeiffer recognized that patterns were similar in most of the countries; *e.g.*, since the mid 1980s, juvenile crime (group of under the age of 18), in particular robbery, violence, and severe forms of physical harm, amplified extremely. In contrast to that, only a slight increase, if at all, could be recorded within the age group of 18 to 20. Another conclusion of the survey demonstrated that juvenile offenders choose victims of the same age or younger – hence, for young people the likeliness of being a victim is much higher than it is for adults. All in all Pfeiffer tried to compare several countries in Europe (such as England and Wales, Sweden, Germany, Netherlands, Italy, Austria, France, Denmark, Belgium, Spain, Greece, Switzerland, Poland), and the US However, due to partial inconsistency in the data and that each country has its own regulations in defining policies, thefts, assault offenses or even the term 'juvenile', the trend of juvenile crime can only be concluded indirectly from all these studies. For Austria, Pfeiffer investigated the period from 1980 to 1995 as this was the only data available. Compared to the other countries, only a modest increase in crime could be noticed. The following image (Figure 3) shows, in addition to the study of Pfeiffer[28], the trend of juvenile delinquencies in Austria between 1990 and 2012. In 1990, 19,164 offenses were recorded and since then a continuous upward trend has been documented until it reached its highest value in 1999 with 31,357 incidents.

27 Christian Pfeiffer, Juvenile Crime and Violence in Europe, in: Crime and Justice 23, Chicago 1998, 255–328.

28 Pfeiffer, Juvenile Crime, 255f.

Then, until 2002, there was a rapid decrease of 9,796 offenses. However, since then it has been rising significantly again and in 2008 it reached its uppermost peak with 35,912 crimes. Between 2008 and 2012 there has been a steady downward trend. Please note, that Figure 3 shows all juvenile offenses, but from 1990 until 2001 juveniles at the ages of 14 to 18 were considered teenagers. Since July 2001, teenagers mean ages 14 to 17, as a new age group (18 to 20), called 'young adults', was implemented.

Risk Factors and Routine Activities of Juveniles

When a juvenile commits a crime, it cannot be tracked down to only one single reason that provoked the undertaking. It always involves additional causes, such as social or psychological matters.[30] A Study in Cambridge proved that 55 percent of 400 males who were convicted lived in families, in which their parents neglected their duties.[31] However, juveniles who have a lower class background usually tend to be more criminal than others, as these young people find it hard to succeed and find acknowledgment within the peer.[32] Referring to various studies, Cohen and Felson[33] found out that most of the crimes occur where the juveniles spend most of their time. Thus, most of the crimes committed by juveniles are around schools, around their home, or on the delinquent's way between school and home. Usually, the acts are a matter of prestige, peer pressure, and status, however, Thompson and Bynum[34] mention that there are three different types of response to these issues:

- College-Boy: In this case the so called Merton's Conformity mode of adaption comes into play, which basically means that lower-class juveniles are trying to adapt to the expectations and needs of middle-class groups. However, according to Cohen[35] this is not really common as the lower-class people are struggling with money and they usually cannot afford going to college and graduate:
- Corner-Boy: This type of response is the most likely one, Cohen argues. This theory mostly affects working-class juveniles who do not have to compete with middle-class peers and prove themselves. This type of group is not delinquent,

---

29 Statistik Austria, Polizeiliche Kriminalstatistik 1990 bis 2012, http://www.statistik.at/web_de/statistiken/soziales/kriminalitaet/anzeigen_polizeiliche_kriminalstatistik/020113.html, 05 January 2014.

30 WHO – World Health Organization, Youth Violence Factsheet, http://www.who.int/violence_injury_prevention/violence/world_report/factsheets/en/youthviolencefacts.pdf, 15 December 2014.

31 David Farrington – Brandon Welsh, Saving Children from a Life of Crime. Early Risk Factors and Effective Interventions, New York 2007, 17.

32 William Thompson – Jack Bynum, Juvenile Delinquency – A Sociological Approach, New York 2012, 96.

33 Lawrence Cohen – Marcus Felson, Social Change and Crime Rate Trends. A Routine Activity Approach, in: American Sociological Association 44/4, Washington 1979, 588–608, here 592.

34 Thompson – Bynum, Juvenile Delinquency, 96f.

35 Cohen – Felson, Social Change, 592f.

but is involved in delinquent activities, such as drinking alcohol, smoking, and/or playing truant skipping school[36];

- Delinquent-Boy: This type of group tries to get attention by acting against the norm. They are not accepted by society, but within their group they live together in harmony, at least according to their expectations.[37]

Contrary to the theories of Cohen and Merton, Cloward and Ohlin have extended these and say that delinquencies occur because of opportunity and the criminal traditions juveniles might find in their neighborhood.[38] As one can see, these theories are highly debated.

Even though all these various theories have been discussed over the centuries by scientists and experts, none of them have been fully accepted by any researcher, as only some of the aspects could be applied, but never all of them.[39] This statement shows how complex the definition of delinquency or the origin of crime is, as it does not only deal with social issues, but also with environmental, psychological, and economic issues.

The debated risk or influencing factors that primarily cause juvenile delinquency are undeniably unstable homes and social environments (*e.g.*, negative impact can result in antisocial behavior of children). Parents represent a role model for their kids, they show them how to interact with other people, how to behave in society, *etc.* which means, they pass on those norms to them, whether they are functional or dysfunctional. A healthy family base is crucial – according to the literature, it is even more likely that children, who suffer from their parents' divorce, become a delinquent. This does not mean that all the children within a single parent household will be delinquent – it is more the fact that divorce can have a massive effect on children.[40] However, their class, or social background plays a significant role in developing criminal streaks. Martin mentions that in the past people believed that becoming delinquent is more probable if the children were born into the so-called 'dangerous classes' (poor and working-class backgrounds), and until the early 1960s this approach was still regarded as a significant key factor in delinquency. However, with the help of statistical data this assumption could be falsified, as a steady trend of criminal activity within the juvenile middle-class could be noticed, which amongst others originated in peer and parental pressure, drug abuse, strong sub cultures, *etc.* The factor: 'school' or 'education' also plays a significant role in becoming delinquent or not. Not everybody can afford good education, and school can shape juveniles' attitude. There is also enormous pressure,

36 Farrington – Welsh, Saving Children, 17f.

37 *Ibid.*

38 Frank Hagan, Introduction to Criminology. Theories, Methods, and Criminal Behavior, California 2012, 164.

39 Gus Martin, Juvenile Justice. Process and Systems, California 2005, 64.

40 *Ibid.*, 65–67.

especially in the US to have a good education, and only with a good education will you have success. [41]

Prevention at an Early Age

In our everyday life, a lot can be read or is heard about prevention, and many researchers have already dealt with it. To wrap it up and referring to ICPC[42], one could say that prevention is more like endorsing the well-being of people by supporting social, economic, educational, and health-related needs – the emphasis lies on children, juveniles, and women, as well as on risk- and protective factors, which are related to crime and victimization. Prevention is also the initiative of building strong (neighborhood-) communities. Moreover, through environmental design and other measurements, like increasing the risk of getting caught, opportunities for criminal offenses have to be reduced. When talking about prevention, one must never forget that there should always be relief in the form of the resocialization-process of felons. Besides, actors, like the police and civil society, the courts of justice should permanently be involved in the development of crime prevention policies.[43] By considering all these essential guidelines, a good basis for prevention is given. But what does it mean, in the matter of juveniles? According to Schumacher and Kurz[44], it is three or four times more likely that a juvenile, who commits a crime at the age of 15 or younger, will both reoffend and participate in crime than an older person. As a matter of fact, the criminal justice system has a meaningful influence on that circumstance as young teenagers never get that much attention and the intervening support they would need at this age. However, the first perpetration of a crime at this age group would be shoplifting or stealing – gun shooting would more be an exception. Referring to Farrington and Welsh[45] it is has been proven that various prevention programs on family, school/communities, or individual levels are effective in preventing offenses. The US made it a number one top priority issue in government to conduct prevention at an early stage, as the results were so promising. All the children have to be saved from a life of crime, as far as it is possible.

Farrington and Welsh distinguish between the term 'delinquencies' and 'offenses'; juveniles commit 'delinquencies', whereas 'offenses' are committed by adults. Keeping that in mind, Farrington and Welsh also define three different

---

41 *Ibid.*, 65f.

42 ICPC – International Centre for the Prevention of Crime (Ed.), Zusammenfassung Kriminalprävention und Kommunaler Sicherheit, Internationaler Bericht 2012, [Summary of the 2012 International Report on Crime Prevention and Community Safety], International Centre for the Prevention of Crime], Montreal 2012, 3.

43 ICPC, Zusammenfassung, 3f.

44 Michael Schumacher – Gwen Kurz, The 8 % Solution. Preventing Serious, Repeat Juvenile Crime, California 2000, 13f.

45 Farrington – Welsh, Saving Children, 4–7.

types of features of prevention. One would be that prevention measures take place from the beginning of life (or sometimes even prior to that) until teenage years. The second approach is to undertake precautions to avoid young kids being confronted with crime at all. The last feature is to prevent the development of criminal potential within the individual or within communities, institutions, *etc.* Martin[46] states in his publication that most adult offenders have already been a delinquent when they were young, starting at an early age. However, it can also happen that some juvenile criminals stop engaging with offenses once they get older; they somehow 'outgrow' it, as they start becoming responsible and adapt to a mature behavior.

How to Measure Crime, Prevention, and its Impacts?

One goal of this research is that prevention should be made measurable. For this, crime or violent crime has to be measured first. Within this subsection, the challenging problem of 'How to Measure Prevention?' will be discussed.

One possible reason why the trend of juvenile crime is rising is the perception of the public and their pragmatic attitude toward crime.[47] But how can crime be measured? Krug[48] defined some guidelines of how to do so. It usually depends on which kind of data for which kind of purpose will be needed. The overall rule would be: describe, understand, and know, which actually means the following:[47]

- Describe the degree and impact of violence!
- Understand all the factors, which affect the increasing risk of violence and crime!
- Know how effective violence prevention programs are!

Keeping these rules in mind, a significant step for measuring crime or violence is set.

Most of the experts and scientists would argue that prevention cannot be measured.[49] It is more about defining long-term prevention measurement goals/outcomes rather than measuring prevention.[50] Some scientists further argue that crime prevention may work but does not necessarily have to work, as some policies are preventive, but for some these policies are criminogenic, thus causing more

46 Gus Martin, Juvenile Justice. Process and Systems, California 2005, 68.

47 Kathleen Maguire – Ann Pastore (Eds.), Sourcebook of Criminal Justice Statistics 1997, US Department of Justice/Bureau of Justice Statistics, Washington 1997, 99.

48 Etienne Krug – Linda Dahlberg – James Mercy – Anthony Zwi – Rafael Lozano (Eds.), World Report on Violence and Health, WHO – World Health Organization, Geneva 2002, 7f.

49 Timothy Crowe, Crime Prevention Through Environmental Design. Applications of Architectural Design and Space, Massachusetts 2000.

50 Australian Institute of Criminology (Ed.), Crime Reduction orPrevention: Is there a Difference?, Canberra 2003, 1.

crime. However, punishment would be one option to achieve that result, but the question is whether it is the right one.[51] Even though all this seems to be a logical explanation, there is still a way to measure crime somehow. Because, all the steps of how to reach the final goal can be measured.[52] *E.g.*, a fire department does not measure how many houses they have saved from fire or not, but they measure the response time to see the efficiency compared to the investment they make. Woodbury also gives another example in his paper. It is impossible to measure whether a lighthouse has prevented ships from getting wrecked or not. However, the design and the position of the lighthouses can be analyzed and evaluated.

Woodbury suggests establishing a model with sub-categories and measuring all the individual components within that system. Thus, this systematic model demonstrates its effectiveness within each measurable component. If the overall model is soundness and effective due to its individual elements, conclusions can be drawn concerning prevention. The pioneer Harry P. Hatry introduced some methods for how to measure efficiency and in his book "Performance Measurement"[53] he stresses that only results count, and not the way of getting there. The following brief story at the beginning of chapter one in his book demonstrates that clearly:

> 'In New York City, a priest and a taxicab driver died and went to heaven. Saint Peter showed the priest his eternal dwelling place – a shack. Saint Peter then showed the driver his eternal dwelling place – a mansion. The priest was angry and asked Saint Peter, 'Why the difference?' Saint Peter said, 'When you preach, people sleep. When riders get into his cab, they pray!'

One of the significant steps is to define the major components of the system and then think about the sub-categories within each component. Woodbury[54] sees this approach as an effective and promising method to finally make prevention measurable by looking at the individual parts of the whole.

On the basis of the previously mentioned approach, an iterative system model will be derived and implemented for Graz, which will be developed in the course of this research. This should lead to new perspectives in prevention measurements for Styrian task forces, and in succession, for task forces all over Austria, and hopefully further than that.

---

51 Lawrence Sherman – Denise Gottfredson – Doris MacKenzie – John Eck – Peter Reuter – Shawn Bushway, Preventing Crime. What Works, What Doesn't Work, What's Promising – A Report to the United States Congress, Maryland, https://www.ncjrs.gov/works/chapter2.htm, 17 May 2015.

52 Glen Woodbury, Measuring Prevention, in: Homeland Security Affairs 1/1, California 2005, 2–8.

53 Harry Hatry, Performance Measurement. Getting Results, Washington 2006, 3.

54 Woodbury, Measuring, 2f.

Research Area Graz: Data Availability and Data Quality

Data acquisition is always the hardest part within a research project, especially when working with highly sensitive data. The Criminal Intelligence Service Austria (.BK) courteously provided all the relevant crime data for the research area Graz, Austria's second largest city with about 250,000 inhabitants, which will be used for the research. A first basic analysis shows (Figure 4) that 32 percent of all crimes in Graz within the period 2005 and 2014 are committed by juveniles (Austrian law regards juveniles as juvenile delinquents up to the age of 20). When looking closely at the crimes committed by juveniles (Figure 5) it can be noted that there has been a continuous upward trend from 2005 up until 2010. In 2011, it plummeted about 21 percent, followed by a slight rise in the next year. The year 2013 shows another minor decrease; however, the trend in committed crimes by juveniles is rising. In contrast to that, the crimes by adults show an alarming trend, too – in 2012, crimes skyrocketed and show its highest value of 7,648 crimes within the period from 2005 to 2013. [55]

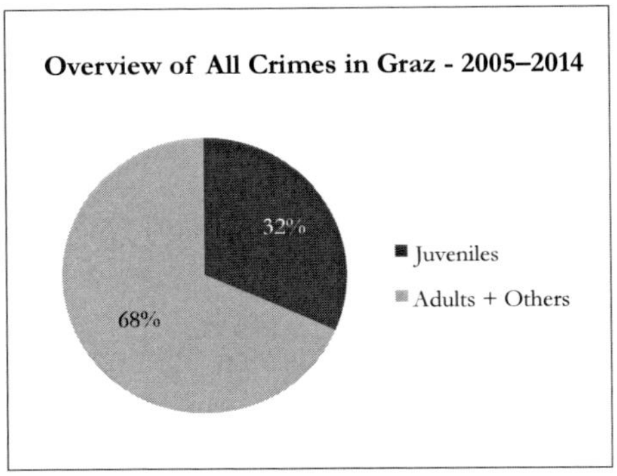

Figure 4: Overview of All Crimes in Graz – 2005–2014 (illustrated by R.R.).[55]

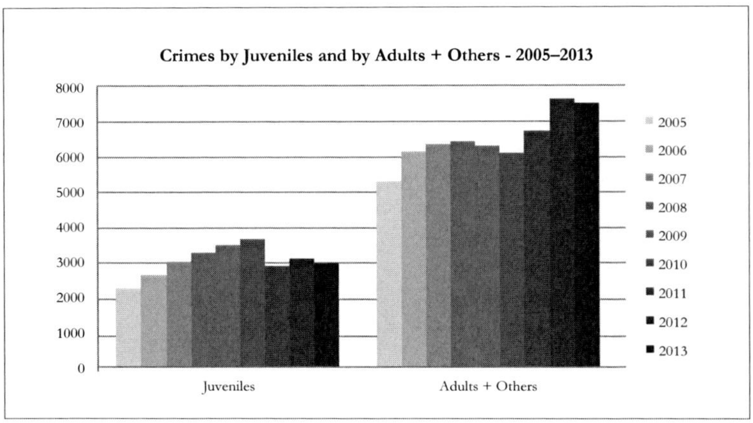

Figure 5: Crimes Committed by Juveniles and by Adults + Others from 2005–2013 (illustrated by R.R.[51]).

55 Data Source: Sicherheitsmonitor, Bundeskriminalamt Österreich/The Criminal Intelligence Service Austria (BK).

The DigitalGlobe Foundation[56] also gratefully supports this research with important satellite imagery of Graz. That way a probable change in the urban structure of the city can be investigated. Moreover, in combination with the data of the BK likely hotspots can be determined and can finally be traced back to the surroundings of the urban environment. The satellite imagery of the DigitalGlobe Foundation are not available for every year of the research period and the images vary in their satellite sensors, such as GeoEye-1, IKONOS-2, QuickBird-2, WorldView-1, or WorldView-2.[57] Due to the coverage problem, this analysis will concentrate on the years 2005, 2009, 2011, and then also on the years 2012 and 2013, as at this time many structural alterations have happened, such as the reconstruction of the main railway station Graz. It will be interesting to see whether these constructional changes have got an influence on the crime rate in these areas or not.

Due to an innovative project, called 'Open Government Data Graz' the City of Graz provides a platform with basic data from Graz that can be used for free, such as administrational, infrastructural, economic, and environmental data.[58] Beyond that the City of Graz also provided statistical data that can be combined with all the other data.

In the criminal code of Austria various categories and definitions of crime do exist. After some analysis of the data it was decided to concentrate on four crime types that juveniles commit most, such as burglary, assault, property damage, and drug abuse, as it can be seen in Figure 6.

These four categories of committed crimes form the basis for all the upcoming analyses. However, understanding WHY these four categories represent the most

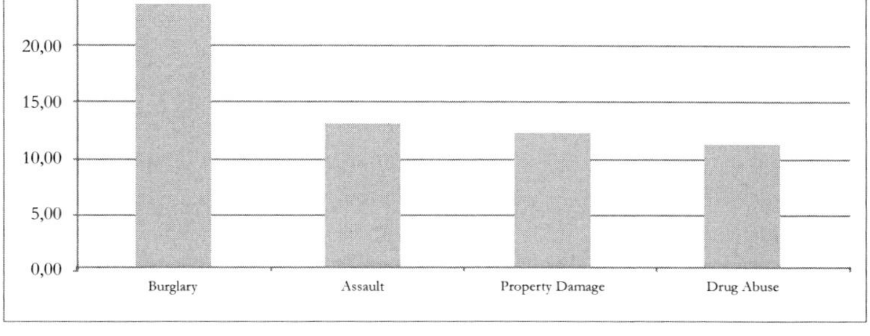

Figure 6: Most Committed Crimes by Juveniles in percent from 2005–2013 (illustrated by R.R.).[59]

56 Digital Globe Foundation, http://www.digitalglobefoundation.org/, 09 December 2014.

57 These names are satellites.

58 City of Graz, Open Government Data, Stadt Graz. – http://data.graz.gv.at/, 09 December 2014.

59 Data Source: Sicherheitsmonitor, Bundeskriminalamt Österreich/The Criminal Intelligence Service Austria (BK).

common crimes in Graz and knowing WHICH influencing factors are responsible for that is crucial – so selective measures can be undertaken. For that reason a special method can be used, which will be introduced in the next subchapter.

The Driving Factors for Crime: A Systems Approach

Within this research it was very important to know what the most committed crimes were and, as a second major step, what the actual driving factors for crime are. Therefore, all the potential factors were categorized into four main groups: environmental/spatial factors, economic factors, social factors, and psychological/physical factors. However, these four categories cannot be seen separately, as each of the groups would depend on each other. For example, an environmental factor, such as 'central places, hot spots' or 'densely populated areas' would influence 'demographic change'. However, the factor 'demographic change', on the other hand, which is part of the economic category, influences the other two factors at the same time. Seen from a social point of view, the 'demographic change' and the 'central places' again affect school and peer issues – *etc.* A similar example can be shown with the factor 'unemployment', which clearly is declared as an economic matter. 'Unemployment' (economic) can lead to 'poverty' (social) which will also affect 'schools and peers' (social) and the 'central places or hot spots' (environmental/spatial), as well as the 'densely populated areas'. These examples should demonstrate the complexity of the interaction between these four disciplines.

For that reason, a systems approach is implemented, based on that developed by Vester.[60] Vester's systems approach is a relatively simple approach that demonstrates the complex nature of interdependency and influence of variables within an effect matrix.[61] The overall aim of this method is to obtain decision support in the assessment of the effects of measures. A common understanding of complex relations between both active and passive interference can be achieved. At the beginning, factors indicators which are acting on a system have to be determined.[62] The indicator-based method should involve between 20 and 40 variables that describe the system.[63]

In this research 31 variables have been chosen for the system (45 variables were the result of the literature review, then they got diminished concerning the rel-

60 Frederic Vester, Die Kunst, Vernetzt zu Denken. Ideen und Werkzeuge für einen neuen Umgang mit Komplexität [The Art of Interconnected Thinking], München 1999.

61 Andreas Exner – Julian Matzenberger – Rosemarie Stangl, Operationalisierung der Regionalen Verwundbarkeit der Energiewende. Progress Report 3a: Konzeptionalisierung der Verwundbarkeit und Operationalisierung des flächendeckenden Resilienzkonzepts. Klima- und Energiefonds – Programm Neue Energien 2020 [Operationalization of the Regional Vulnerability of the Energy Transition – Progress Report 3a: Conceptualization of the Vulnerability and Operationalization of the area-wide concept of Resilience], Klagenfurt/Wien 2013, 230.

62 Günter Drews – Norbert Hillebrand, Lexikon der Projektmanagement-Methoden [Dictionary of Project-Management-Methods], München 2007, 153–157.

63 Exner – Matzenberger – Stangl, Operationalisierung, 230f.

EFFECT MATRIX – ASPECTS INFLUENCING CRIMES		Traffic infrastructure/road networks (Freeway exit & entry, Railway, Subway, Underground etc.	Lightning	Land utilization plan, Cadastral map (business district, urban residential district, industrial estate, green space)	Forest, Vegetation	Building shapes, height of construction, agglomeration, backyards	Densely Populated Areas
		1	2	3	4	5	6
Traffic infrastructure/road networks (Freeway exit & entry, Railway, Subway, Underground etc.)	1		0	2	2	2	2
Lightning	2	0		0	0	1	2
Land utilization plan, Cadastral map (business district, urban residential district, industrial estate, green space)	3	2	0		2	2	2
Forest, Vegetation	4	2	1	1		1	2
Building shapes, height of construction, agglomeration, backyards	5	1	1	2	1		2
Central places, Points of interest, Hotspots	6	0	1	0	1	2	
Densely Populated Areas	7	2	1	2	2	2	2
Ethnic Groups, Culture, Class, – Social Status	8	0	0	1	0	0	1
Gender	9	0	0	0	0	0	0
Age	10	0	0	1	0	0	0
Poverty	11	1	0	2	0	2	0
Ethics/Morality/Tolerance of Crime	12	0	0	0	0	0	0
Education	13	0	0	0	0	0	0
School, Community and Peers	14	1	0	0	0	0	2
Neighbourhood, Living Conditions, Domestic Circumstances	15	0	0	0	0	1	0
Alcohol and other Drugs	16	1	0	0	0	0	2
Educational System	17	0	0	0	0	0	0
Unemployment	18	0	0	0	0	1	0
Political Change	19	1	0	1	0	1	0
Demographic Change	20	2	0	2	1	2	1
Open Borders	21	2	0	1	0	0	0
Real Estate Market	22	2	0	2	1	2	1
Media Influence	23	0	0	0	0	0	1
Health System	24	0	0	1	0	0	0
Genes (Twin Studies)	25	0	0	0	0	0	0
Mental Disorder	26	0	0	0	0	0	0
Conduct Disorder	27	0	0	0	0	0	0
Family Environment/Parental Behaviours	28	0	0	0	0	0	0
Traumatic Childhood Experience	29	0	0	0	0	0	0
Alcohol and other Drugs	30	1	0	0	0	0	2
Emotions and Cognition	31	0	0	0	0	0	0

Figure 7: Effect Matrix including all the Influencing Crime Factors – this Figure demonstrates one example of how the Factors can be Assessed (illustrated by R.R.).

evance for the study area in Austria) in collaboration with experts from law enforcement and research institutions (*e.g.*, Portugal, Slovakia, Austria, Switzerland, USA). Collaboration with experts is essential within this process and should always be the basis for the implementation of an effect matrix.

After generating a matrix containing the 31 variables (see Figure 7), the direct effect of a variable on another will be assessed by using a grading scale from zero to two (zero means 'no influence/effect at all', one means 'average influence/effect', and two means 'strong influence/effect').[64]

64 *Ibid.*

										ACTIVITY SUM
2	1	2	0	0	0	1	0	2	0	**22**
	0	1	0	0	0	0	0	0	0	**15**
0		1	0	1	1	1	1	1	2	**18**
1	1		1	1	0	0	1	2	2	**16**
0	0	1		2	2	2	0	0	2	**13**
0	0	0	0		2	1	2	1	2	**13**
0	0	0	0	2		2	2	2	2	**16**
0	0	0	0	2	2		2	2	2	**21**
0	0	0	0	2	2	2		2	2	**16**
0	1	2	2	2	2	2	2		2	**31**
0	2	2	1	2	2	2	0	2		**28**
23	**12**	**28**	**7**	**22**	**24**	**31**	**16**	**36**	**43**	
PASSIVITY SUM										

Figure 8: Effect Matrix: An Extract of the Assessment, demonstrating the Activity and Passivity Sum (illustrated by R.R.).

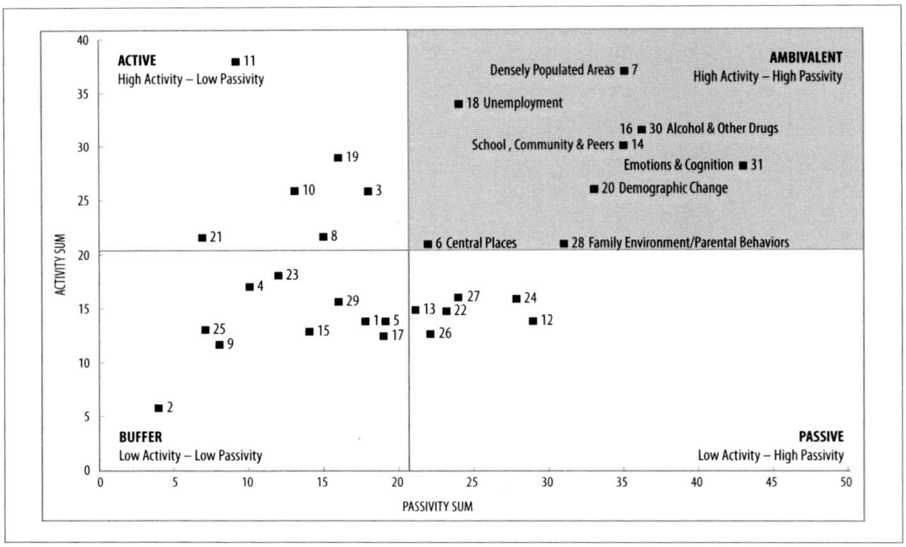

Figure 9: Scatter Plot divided into Quarters – Ambivalent, Active, Passive, and Buffer (illustrated by R.R.).

Having distributed all the influencing values in the matrix, the activity sum and the passivity sum for each indicator can be calculated, as Figure 8 shows.[65]

The values of both the activity and passivity sum will then be transferred into a scatter plot (Figure 9), where the mean of both x- and y-axis form four parts[66]:

65 Drews – Hillebrand, Lexikon, 153f.

66 Johanna Ehetreiber, Leitbilder in der Stadt- und Regionalentwicklung – "Zukunft Gestalten und Sichern" – Strategischer Planungsprozess für die Stadt Weiz; Stadtleitbildentwicklung 2008–2009, [Mission Statement for Urban and Regional Development – "Designing the Future and Protec-

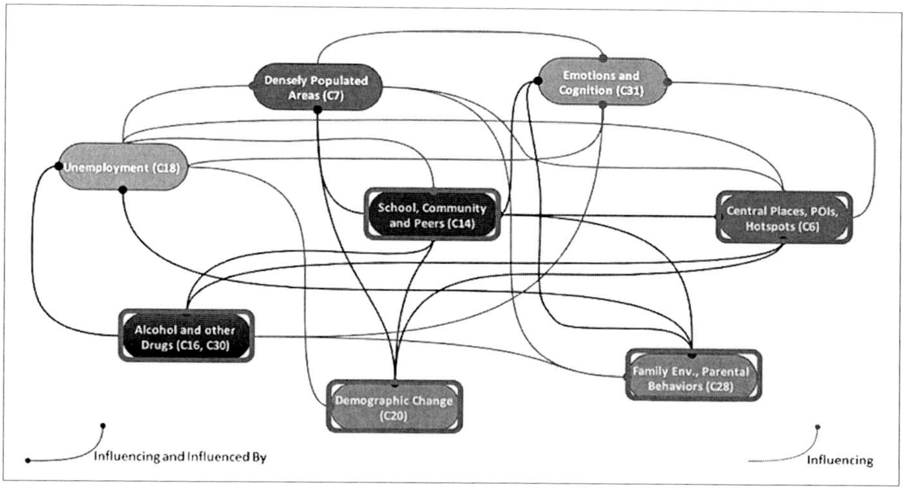

Figure 10: Effect Diagram: the Key Elements are 'School, Community, and Peers', 'Central Places, POIs, Hot Spots', 'Family Environment, Parental Behaviors', 'Demographic Change', and 'Alcohol and other Drugs' (illustrated by R.R.).

- Active – high activity, low passivity: the factors have a strong influence on the other factors within the system, but are hardly influenced by the other factors;
- Ambivalent – high activity, high passivity: the factors both strongly influence and are influenced within the system;
- Buffer – low activity, low passivity: the factors both hardly influence and are influenced within the system;
- Passive – high passivity, low activity: the factors are strongly influenced by other factors within the system, but hardly influence the other factors.

The ambivalent quarter of the scatter plot represents all the factors that are of great importance for the research area as the ambivalent factors have got a significant effect on it.

The system model will finally be represented as an effect diagram, where the relations within the system are demonstrated (Figure 10). Through the visualization of the system's interdependencies, some key elements become apparent. The key elements play a major role as they are both influenced significantly by other factors and still affect other indicators. It basically means that these key elements have a leverage effect within the system and if something has to be changed, it has to be started with the key elements.[67] The following effect diagram (Figure 10) represents all the ambivalent indicators. The key elements within this model are 'School, Community, and Peers', 'Central Places, Points of Interests, Hot Spots', 'Family

ting" – Strategic Planning Processes for the City of Weiz, Development of an Urban Mission Statement], Unpubl. Master's Thesis University of Graz, Graz 2010, 44–46.

67 *Ibid.*, 44f.

Environment, Parental Behaviors', 'Demographic Change', and 'Alcohol and other Drugs', as they are most influencing and act on the system at the same time (represented by the red lines).

The indicators mentioned above have a significant influence on other factors within the system and that is why this research focuses on juvenile crime in combination with social, economic, and environmental issues. As already mentioned previously, if crime starts at an early age, the probability that the juvenile remains a criminal is very high. However, in combination with the results of the systems approach, it is crucial to look into the social issue 'School, Community, and Peers', as this is the significant key to the major problem – a rising trend of juvenile delinquencies. That is why prevention should be conducted very early, starting at schools.

This is a basis upon which all other analyses that are essential to answering the research questions can be constructed. Additionally, with the inputs from delinquents through interviews, the side of offenders will be reflected so that new and effective sustainable concepts for crime prevention can finally be implemented.

Conclusion: The Challenge

This research approach deals with a comparably new research field in Europe: The concept of this project is trans-disciplinary, working closely with criminal investigation departments and urban planners to combine geospatial technologies with environmental and social aspects and applying it to (primarily juvenile) crime issues. Spatial analysis can support an urban planner, the police, *etc.*, and gives more visual information on crime hot spots. Referring to Bowers[68], the use of GIS is a big advantage for operational policing purposes, when analyzing and mapping crime data the results can easily be visualized with GIS maps. Moreover, factors, such as crime rate compared to crime prevention initiatives can be combined and monitored over a certain period of time.

Crime prevention plays a significant economic role within crime analysis, as prevention costs less than apprehending criminals after the crime has happened.[69] But why does this research primarily focus on juveniles? According to Schumacher and Kurz it is three or four times more likely that a juvenile, who commits a crime at the age of 15 or younger, will reoffend than an older person.[70] As a matter of fact, the criminal justice system has a meaningful influence on that circumstance as young teenagers never get that much attention and the intervening support that they would require at this age. However, it basically proves one more time that pre-

68 Kate Bowers – Shane Johnson – Ken Pease, Prospective Hot-Spotting. The Future of Crime Mapping?, in: The British Journal of Criminology 44, Oxford 2004, 643–646.

69 Deborah Osborne – Susan Wernicke, Introduction to Crime Analysis. Basic Resources for Criminal Justice Practice, New York 2003, 1.

70 Schumacher – Kurz, The 8 % Solution, 13f.

vention has to start at a very early stage. Violence and crime have to be stopped before they even start.[71]

The cooperation with the State Office of Criminal Investigation Styria (Landeskriminalamt Steiermark), the Federal Ministry for the Interior (Bundesministerium für Inneres, BMI), the DigitalGlobe Foundation, the State University of Louisiana, the Joanneum Research Graz, and the University of Graz, and all the other crime related organizations, as well as the GIS analysis approach, guarantee a trans-disciplinary approach with results that will not only concentrate on one aspect, but will deal with several perceptions.

All in all, this research project has potential in finding, testing, and evaluating new concepts for crime prevention in urban planning and to making valid statements and suggestions for a sustainable and a much more secure development of the urban space. Ecological, economic, and social variables can play a major role in enhancing the safety in urban regions.[72]

71 CDC – Centers for Disease Control and Prevention (Ed.), Youth Violence, Atlanta, http://www.cdc.gov/violenceprevention/youthviolence/index.html, 09 December 2014.

72 The results of this research will primarily be published as part of the author's dissertation. In addition, efforts will be made to present the research at conferences in Europe as well as the US.

II. Ethnicity (Re-)visited

Ferdinand Kühnel

The Silent Disappearance of Ethnic Minorities from Gravestones: Ethnic Homogenization in Carinthia's Bilingual Areas since 1918

University of Vienna

Introduction

The following article is based on the Dissertation, which the author is currently working on at the Institute of East European History/University of Vienna.[1] This paper will outline the concept of this doctoral thesis and provide preliminary findings. It will start out by focusing on the decreasing number of Slovenian-speaking Carinthians and present some data that was collected by the official population censuses and illustrate some existing critical interpretations of this data. The introductory paragraphs provide a rough overview on the topic's historical background and open up the field of inquiry. This will be followed by presenting some preliminary findings, illustrating the ways, in which this research will extend the existing literature. In a second step, the paper defines the scope of the thesis and narrows down the research questions. The methodological and theoretical approach of the dissertation is outlined in another separate chapter. The contribution will conclude with some remarks that demonstrate how the present approach may give new insights into the question of the decline of the Carinthian Slovenes in Austria.

> 'Kärnten ist ein europäischer Sonderfall – nicht, weil die Probleme und Herausforderungen in Kärnten so anders wären als anderswo in Europa, sondern, weil die Kärntner Antworten auf diese Herausforderungen so anders sind [...].'[2]

1 This article is based on a presentation held at the annual Conference of the Austrian and Central European Centers in Minneapolis in September 2014. The dissertation carries the title "DE DIFFUGIO. Vom lautlosen Verschwinden ethnischer Minderheiten von Grabsteinen. Ethnische Homogenisierung am Beispiel Kärntens seit 1918" and is supervised by Prof. Marija Wakounig.

2 Anton Pelinka, Kärnten – Ein europäischer Sonderfall? [Carinthia – An European Exception?], in: Martin Pandel – Mirjam Polzer-Srienz – Miroslav Polzer – Reginald Vospernik (Eds.), Ortstafelkonflikt in Kärnten – Krise oder Chance?, Wien 2004, 103–113, here 103. [Carinthia is a European exception – not because the problems and challenges in Carinthia were so different to those

The Austrian political scientist Anton Pelinka came to this conclusion in 2004, as he referred to the undignified spectacle around the installation of bilingual road signs in Carinthia that has shaped the political discussions over decades. The Carinthian government has failed and even openly refused to set up bilingual road signs in its numerous communities with Slovenian minorities. A compromise could only be achieved in 2011.[3]

The value of bilingualism has long been misunderstood and opposed. The number of Slovenian-speaking Carinthians has steadily declined since the first census in the former Duchy of Carinthia in 1880.[4] In 1910, around 222,000 people lived in Carinthia's bilingual areas. 135,000 (~60 percent) were German-speaking and 82,000 (~37 percent) were Slovenian-speaking.[5] The last census in Austria in 2001 reported a significant decline to around 13,000 people whose colloquial language is Slovenian, respectively 'Windisch'[6] in Carinthia; although the vast majority of

---

anywhere else in Europe, but because the Carinthian responses to these challenges are so different. Translation by the author]

3 For more information about the so-called *Ortstafelkonflikt* and the later achieved compromise, see, *inter alia*, Wolfgang Petritsch – Wilfried Graf – Gudrun Kramer (Eds.), Kärnten liegt am Meer. Konfliktgeschichte/n. Über Trauma, Macht und Identität [Carinthia Lies on the Sea. History/-ies of Conflict. About Trauma, Power and Identity], Klagenfurt 2012; Hellwig Valentin, Am Rande des Bürgerkrieges. Der Kärntner Ortstafelkonflikt 1972 und der Sturz Hans Simas [At the Brink of Civil War. The Carinthian Conflict about Bilingual Road Signs and Hans Sima's Overthrow], Klagenfurt/Ljubljana/Wien 2013; Jürgen Pirker, Kärntner Ortstafelstreit. Der Rechtskonflikt als Identitätskonflikt [The Carinthian Conflict about Bilingual Road Signs. The Legal Conflict as an Identity Conflict], Baden-Baden 2010; Martin Pandel – Mirjam Polzer-Srienz – Miroslav Polzer – Reginald Vospernik (Hgg.), Ortstafelkonflikt in Kärnten – Krise oder Chance? [The Carinthian Conflict about Bilingual Road Signs – Crisis or Chance], Wien 2004. Matjaž Klemenčič – Vladimir Klemenčič, Die Kärntner Slowenen und die Zweite Republik [The Carinthian Slovenes and the Second Republic], Klagenfurt/Wien 2010;

4 See, *inter alia*, Emil Brix, Die Umgangssprachen in Altösterreich zwischen Agitation und Assimilation. Die Sprachenstatistik in den zisleithanischen Volkszählungen 1880 bis 1910 [The Colloquial Languages in Cisleithania between Agitation and Assimilation. Language Statistics in the Cisleithanian Censuses from 1880 to 1910], Wien/Köln/Graz 1982; Albert F. Reiterer, Minderheiten Wegzählen? Methodische und inhaltliche Probleme amtlicher Sprachzählungen [Making Minorities Dissapear? Methodological and Contentual Problems of Official Language Censuses], in: Martin Pandel – Mirjam Polzer-Srienz – Miroslav Polzer – Reginald Vospernik (Eds.), Ortstafelkonflikt in Kärnten – Krise oder Chance?, Wien 2004, 25–38; Arnold Suppan, Zur Geschichte Südkärntens. Aus der Perspektive einer zweisprachigen Region [History of Southern Carinthia. From the Perspective of a Bilingual Region], in: Martin Pandel – Mirjam Polzer-Srienz – Miroslav Polzer – Reginald Vospernik (Eds.), Ortstafelkonflikt in Kärnten – Krise oder Chance?, Wien 2004, 128–199.

5 *Cf.* Suppan, Geschichte Südkärntens, 128.

6 The term 'Windisch' originally referred to Slavs respectively Slovenian-speaking people in Carinthia and Styria. The term became increasingly political, especially when the historian Martin Wutte introduced the so-called 'Windischentheorie' in 1927. He divided the Carinthian Slovenes into a German-friendly group and a group of national Slovenes. 'Windische' were henceforth *heimattreue* Slovenes who had voted for Austria in 1920 and were willing to leave their culture and language behind for the purpose of assimilation. In contrast national Slovenes insisted on adherence to the once guaranteed rights. They were denounced as Irredentists and defamed of disloyalty to the Austrian State. See, *inter alia*, Andreas Moritsch, Das Windische – Eine nationale Hilfsideologie [The Windische – A National Auxiliary Ideology], in: Andreas Moritsch (Ed.), Problemfelder der Geschichte und der Geschichtsschreibung der Kärntner Slovenen, Klagenfurt/Ljubljana/Wien 1995,

today's population can be considered descendants of the people who lived there at around 1900.[7] The already mentioned dramatic decrease, as evidenced by the censuses, stands in contradiction to other surveys and trends that were observed in recent years. For example, a micro-census, carried out in 1999, did not ask about language spoken colloquially but about language proficiency.[8] The results were astonishing, since a much higher number of Carinthians – precisely 60,000 –, stated that they would have at least some knowledge of Slovenian.[9] Beyond that, registrations for bilingual education have increased in primary schools that run bilingual programs: Since the 1990s, registrations for a bilingual education have more than doubled. From 4.5 percent in the school year 1990/1991 to 10.45 percent in the school year 2012/2013.[10]

The data collected by the micro-census as well as the number of registrations for bilingual education programs point to a significantly higher number of people with at least some knowledge of Slovenian and have repeatedly lead to a fundamental criticism of official censuses. When determining language affiliation, censuses tend to apply the criterion of group membership rather than asking for actual language use. Therefore, censuses should also be seen with respect to their political nature rather than in administrative terms alone. Censuses can be considered as instruments through which the majority derives fundamental rights for the minority. Moreover, they call for a commitment to a certain ethnic or national group that links ethnicity with language.

The political character of a census is illustrated by the example of the so-called 'Minderheitenfeststellung'[11], a large-scale count held among the minority popula-

---

15–29; Tom Priestly, On the Development of the 'Windischentheorie', in: International Journal of the Sociology of Language 124/1, Berlin 1997, 75–98. Judith Goetz, "Macht mir diese Land wieder deutsch!" Nationalsozialistische Verfolgung und die Deportation der Kärntner SlovenInnen ["Make me this Country German again!" Nazi Persecution and the Deportation of Carinthian Slovenes], in: Arbeitskreis gegen den Kärntner Konsens (Ed.), Friede, Freude, deutscher Eintopf. Rechte Mythen, NS-Verharmlosung und antifaschistischer Protest, Wien 2011, 206–219;

7 *Cf.* Suppan, Geschichte Südkärntens, 128. One must note, that the former Duchy of Carinthia included the areas Kanaltal (Val Canale, Kanalska dolina), the community/Gemeinde Seeland (Jezersko) and the Mießtal (Mežiška dolina). These areas had to be ceded to Italy and the Kingdom of Yugoslavia due to the Peace Treaty of Saint Germain.

8 *Cf.* Reiterer, Minderheiten, 29.

9 The micro-census was conducted by Albert F. Reiterer, an Austrian social scientist. 60,000 Carinthians at the age of 15 or above declared to have knowledge of Slovenian. *Cf. Ibid.* The Slovenian Government estimates that around 20 to 30 thousand people are living in Austria, whose colloquial language is Slovenian. *Cf.* France M. Dolinar *et al.*, Slovenski zgodovinski atlas [Slovenian Historical Atlas], Ljubljana 2011, 217.

10 *Cf.* Landesschulrat für Kärnten [Carinthian State Education Authority], Jahresbericht über das Schuljahr 2012/2013 [Annual Report on the School Year 2012/2013], 82, in: http://www.2sprachigebildung.at/jahresbericht2013.pdf, 01 August 2014; Enotna Lista/Einheitsliste, Zweisprachiger Unterricht boomt. Rekord bei Anmeldungen zum zweisprachigen Unterricht in Kärnten [Bilingual Education is Booming. Record in Registrations for Bilingual Education in Carinthia], http://www.elnet.at/dossier/zweisprachiger_unterricht/57/, 1 August 2014;

11 A secret 'Muttersprachenerhebung' [mother tongue Survey] or 'Minderheitenfeststellung' [minorities identification] should be the basis of the new 'National Minorities Act', which was boycotted

tions in Austria that followed the implementation of the so-called 'Volksgruppengesetz'[12] [National Minorities Act] in 1976. The meaning, or rather the non-sense of such a count was described very accurately by one of the responsible organizers with the following words: 'Die Minderheitenfeststellung war und ist objektiv unnötig, weil der Administration ganz genau bekannt ist, wo die Kärntner Slowenen siedeln und recht genau bekannt war und ist, wie viele es sind.'[13] The censuses carried out at the time of the Habsburg monarchy between 1880 and 1910 were already criticized by contemporaries: they referred to the censuses as a point of culmination of the national dispute and evaluated the results just as the outcome of the multifarious national confrontations.[14]

The Austrian philosopher Rudolf Burger delivered an even sharper critique. Burger knows how to combine the concept of the nation, understood as a socially constructed figure with a specific instrument of power, embodied by official statistics. For him, each empirical survey, asking for 'Nationalbewusstsein' [national consciousness] – or as in this case colloquial language – rather represents a test that is supposed to prove the state's propaganda impact.[15] Consequently he defines nation as 'Imagi-Nation' and 'Indoctri-Nation' as the nation 'is not created out of nothing but it is made out of the invented'.[16]

The starting point of this dissertation is the criticism of official statistics and surveys on colloquial language[17] as well as the officially registered demographic de-

---

by the Carinthian Slovenes. *Cf.* Hellwig Valentin, Der Sonderfall. Kärntner Zeitgeschichte 1918–2004 [The Exception. Carinthian Contemporary History 1918–2014], Klagenfurt/Laibach/Wien 2005, 211–213.

12 *Cf.* Bundesgesetz über die Rechtsstellung der Volksgruppen in Österreich (Volksgruppengesetz – VoGrG) [Federal Law Gazette No. 396/1976]. For a critique of the law, see Vladimir Wakounig, Der heimliche Lehrplan der Minderheitenbildung. Die zweisprachige Schule in Kärnten [The Hidden Curriculum of Minority Education. The Bilingual School in Carinthia], Klagenfurt 2008, 114–117.

13 Ralf Unkart – Glantschnig Gerold – Alfred Ogris, Zur Lage der Slowenen in Kärnten. Die Kärntner Slowenen und die Wahlkreiseinteilung 1979 – Eine Dokumentation [On the Situation of Slovenians in Carinthia. The Carinthian Slovenes and the Constituency Boundaries in 1979 – A Documentation], Klagenfurt 1984, 55; Reiterer, Minderheiten, 29. [The Minorities Identification was and is objectively unnecessary, since the administration knows very well, where the Carinthian Slovenes settle. Translation by the author]

14 Brix, Umgangssprachen, 432. ['"Kulminationspunkt" des nationalen Streits' deren 'Resultate als "Wirkungsergebnis" der vielgestaltigen nationalen Konfrontationen erscheinen']

15 *Cf.* Rudolf Burger, Patriotismus und Nation. Bemerkungen zu einem (nicht nur) österreichischen Problem [Patriotism and Nation. Comments to a (not only) Austrian Problem], in: Rudolf Burger – Hans-Dieter Klein – Wolfgang H. Schrader (Eds.), Gesellschaft, Staat, Nation, Wien 1996, 35–46, here 43.

16 Rudolf Burger, Die nachträgliche Nation. Gedanken zu einer unvollständigen Gegenwart [The Subsequent Nation. Thougts on an Incomplete Present], in: Andreas Khol – Reinhold Lopatka – Wilhelm Molterer (Eds.), Zukunft denken. Festschrift für Wolfgang Schüssel, Wien 2005, 21–38, hier 25. [Die Nation wird nicht] 'ex nihilo geschaffen [...], sondern aus Vorgefundenem gemacht']

17 The surveys on colloquial language from 1880 always demanded a national confession, as the manifold multilingualism of the population was not taken in consideration. In 1939 people were explicitly asked for their mother tongue and ethnicity. See Brix, Umgangssprachen, 102–115; Reiterer, Minderheiten, 28–30.

cline of the Carinthian Slovenes. On the one hand that brings up the question of the reliability and the relevance of such surveys. On the other hand, we need to ask why fewer and fewer people were willing to declare their Slovenian roots.

After World War I as well as after the Second World War, the concept of an ethnically homogenous nation-state was dominant, drawing its legitimacy from the postulated self-determination of peoples. Wherever this principle of self-determination was endangered – especially in border areas inhabited by a mixed-language population – one was confronted with the 'problem of an ethnic minority' that, from the point of view of an ethnically homogenous nation state, necessarily constituted a foreign body.[18]

The proclamation of the 'Republik Deutschösterreich' [Republic German-Austria] in November 1918 consequently declared the German-Austrian constitutive people as people of 'one tribe and one language'[19] and excluded, from this very moment, other ethnic groups from the nation state.[20]

> 'Die erste österreichische Republik verstand sich ganz und gar als deutscher Nationalstaat, in dem nur Deutsche echte Österreicher sein konnten. Da die Slovenen keine Deutschen waren, stellten sie einen völkischen Fremdkörper im deutsch-österreichischen Volkskörper dar.'[21]

Accordingly, ethnic homogenization appeared as an effective means of consolidating the nation state, which tied the assimilation of the Carinthian Slovenes to the German majority population. This policy of unification of the so-called *Volkskörper* was pursued both in the inter-war period and in the period of Nazism and can again be found in the agitation against the bilingual road signs in the recent past.[22] The term ethnic homogenization is defined as a policy that aims to consti-

18 National minorities appear almost as a paradox in history. In accordance with President Woodrow Wilson's doctrine of national self-determination within the meaning of the principle of nationalities, no minorities should exist at all. On the political and legal status of minorities and their origin see Philipp Ther, Die dunkle Seite der Nationalstaaten. "Ethnische Säuberungen" im modernen Europa [The Dark Side of Nation States. "Ethnic Cleansing" in Modern Europe], Göttingen 2011, 38–49; Wakounig, Lehrplan, 71–76.

19 Staatsgesetzblatt für den Staat Deutschösterreich, 18. November 1918, Zi 6, in: http://alex.onb.ac.at/cgi-content/alex?aid=sgb&datum=1918&page=27&size=45, 1 August 2014. [eines Stammes und einer Sprache]

20 *Cf.* Ernst Bruckmüller, Nation Österreich. Kulturelles Bewußtsein und gesellschaftlich-politische Prozesse [Nation Austria. Cultural Consciouness and Socio-Political Processes], Wien ²1996, 143

21 Andreas Moritsch, Nation Österreich und die Kärntner Slovenische Nationale Minderheit [Nation Austria and the Carinthian Slovenian National Minority], in: Andreas Moritsch (Ed), Austria Slovenica. Die Kärntner Slovenen und die Nation Österreich, Klagenfurt/Ljubljana/Wien 1996, 9–27, here 26. [The First Austrian Republic defined itself entirely as a German nation state, in which only Germans could be true Austrians. Since the Slovenes were not Germans, they were seen as a nationalist foreign body within the German-Austrian national body].

22 After the Carinthian Referendum of 1920, Landesverweser Arthur Lemisch (1868–1953) said that it would be a societal responsibilty to bring the Carinthian Slovenes again closer to German and Carinthian Culture. Hitler set the direction in 1941 with the slogan: 'Make me this country

tute an ethnic homogenous political entity. The means of achieving this aim range from voluntary assimilation and forced assimilation to expulsion and deportation. Hanns Haas[23] differentiates this concept into two types: forced assimilation and physical expulsion and extermination. The second type could be summarized under the term ethnic cleansing that can only be partially applied to the Carinthian case.

The dissertation concentrates on the supposedly demographic decline of the Slovenian-speaking population in Carinthia – as it seems to be proved by the censuses. It will analyze how the supposed disappearance that is caused by a policy understood as ethnic homogenization might best be explained by the political controversies and parameters since 1918. As an empirical approach, it investigates material artifacts that provide information about the effectiveness of this program of homogenization.

In the dissertation project, gravestones are considered exemplary artifacts. On gravestones, the dead's *memoria* is eternalized by means of engraving and inscribing them on an eternal material such as marble, iron or stone. This makes them an interesting object for the study of cultures of remembrance. Furthermore, a study of these artifacts promises culturally rich insights, as graves have a special meaning for the traditionally catholic Slovenes. However, I am not so much interested in the inscriptions *per se* – in the sense of an epigraphic approach. Rather, I want to focus on the change of ethnic attributions on gravestones, *i.e.* the change of identity through Germanization of the names on the gravestones. Preliminary research for this dissertation has shown that in the course of cemetery-relocations or cemetery-enlargements, the ethnic inscriptions – specifically also during the Nazi era – changed in favor of the majority language in Carinthia.[24]

German again!' Haider advertised the slogan 'Carinthia will become monolingual' in 2003. *Cf.* Wakounig, Lehrplan, 12, 80, 319; Helmut Rumpler, Die nationale Frage im Spannungsfeld von kärntnerischem Landespatriotismus, österreichischem Staatsbewußtsein und völkischem Nationalismus 1918–1938 [The National Question between the Poles of Carinthian Patriotism, Austrian National Consciousness and Ethnic Nationalism], in: Claudia Fräss-Ehrfeld – Helmut Rumpler (Eds.), Kärnten und Wien. Zwischen Staatsidee und Landesbewußtsein, Klagenfurt/Laibach/Wien 2005, 9–84.

23 See, *inter alia*, Hanns Haas, Ethnische Homogenisierung unter Zwang. Experimente im 20. Jahrhundert, in: Sylvia Hahn – Andrea Komlosy – Ilse Reiter (Eds.), Ausweisung – Abschiebung – Vertreibung in Europa. 16.–20. Jahrhundert, Innsbruck/Wien/Bozen 2006, 140–171; Hanns Haas, Typen und Verlaufsmodelle ethnischer Homogenisierung unter Zwang, in: Rudolf G. Ardelt – Christian Gerbel (Eds.), Österreichischer Zeitgeschichtetag 1995. Österreich – 50 Jahre Zweite Republik, Innsbruck/Wien 1996, 491–498; Alexander Moritsch, Formen "ethnischer Säuberung" in Kärnten, in: Moritsch, Austria Slovenica, 28–44.

24 According to interviews with contemporary witnesses this has happened at the cemeteries in the following parishes: St. Veit/Sankt Primus [Šentvid/Šentprimož] and Sittersdorf [Žitara vas] in the 1990s and in Sankt Kanzian [Škocjan] around the turn of the millenium. An entire register was requested at the archive of the diocese Gurk Klagenfurt.

Examples for the Change of Ethnic Attributions on Gravestones

Figure 1: Gravestone of family Klec/Kletz in Köstenberg/Kostanje, Municipality Velden am Wörther See/Vrba na Koroškem, 2015; in the author's archive.

In the following, some preliminary findings will be presented that stand as a *pars pro toto* for the whole research and may help to clarify the above stated change of ethnic attributions on gravestones. The first case arose because of discrepancies in the spelling of a family name on the grave of the recently deceased Mr. X.[25] On the death notice of Mr. X. and also on the erected wooden cross on his family's grave the name was written in accordance with its Slovenian origin. However, the grave of family X revealed an astonishing detail, as it now carries a Germanized family name.

The family initially grabbed the chance to Germanize the grave in the mid-1990s by changing the Slovenian grave inscription from 'Počivaj v miru' to 'Ruhet in Frieden' [Rest in Peace], when one cemetery (Waldfriedhof St. Veit im Jauntal/St. Vid v Podjuni) was transferred to a newly built cemetery (St. Primus/Šentprimož) nearby. The name, however, has been tacitly changed since the Second World War from Slovenian to German spelling; this only came to light on the occasion of the recent death that the family once Germanized the name but apparently failed to do so again. Perhaps they did not succeed a second time because of modern electronic data processing? Discrepancies such as this will be unveiled by the dissertation by means of archival research. The following picture (figure 1) shows a similar case and was taken from a cemetery in Köstenberg/Kostanje and demonstrates the intentional or unintentional commitment to minority or majority quite bluntly.

State of Research and Research Objectives

Hereafter, the scientific discourse respectively the existing literature will be examined, which deals with the Carinthian Slovenes in general and whose focus has been mainly the decades-long conflict between the German-speaking majority and the Slovenian-speaking minority. The divide that run between the Carin-

25 Unfortunately, the name of the family as well as the documented evidence could not be given, as this would jeopardize the progress of the investigation in the early phase of the research project.

thian Slovenes and the German Carinthians has already been addressed by a large number of scientific publications. Especially the following subjects occupied a prominent rank: the Carinthian referendum of 1920[26], the deportation and expulsion during the Nazi regime[27], the for a long time very restrictive minority politics of the Second Republic[28] and the 'nationale Frage' [national question][29] in Carinthia. In addition, several researchers dealt with the socio-economic situation[30] of the Carinthian Slovenes and their demographic decline.[31] The research was mainly conducted by Austrian and Slovenian historians and social scientists, who often had close ties to this region. In international research, the Slovenian minority played a minor role.[32] The embedding of the questions raised here in the in-

---

26 See, *inter alia*, Helmut Rumpler (Ed.), Kärntens Volksabstimmung 1920. Wissenschaftliche Kontroversen und historisch-politische Diskussionen anläßlich des internationalen Symposions Klagenfurt 1980 [Carinthian Referendum of 1920. Scientific Controversies and Historico-Political Discussions at the International Symposium Klagenfurt 1980], Klagenfurt 1981; Claudia Fräss-Ehrfeld, Geschichte Kärntens 1918–1920. Abwehrkampf – Volksabstimmung – Identitätssuche [Carinthia 1918–1920. Defensive Struggle – Referendum – Quest for Identity], Klagenfurt 2000.

27 See, *inter alia*, Valentin Sima, Kärntner Slowenen unter nationalsozialistischer Herrschaft. Verfolgung, Widerstand und Repression [Carinthian Slovenes under Nazi Rule. Persecution, Resistance, and Repression], in: Emmerich Tálos, *et al.* (Eds.), NS-Herrschaft in Österreich. Ein Handbuch, Wien 2000, 744–767; Stefan Karner – Janez Stergar (Eds.), Aussiedlung – Verschleppung – Nationaler Kampf [Deportation – Abduction – National Fight], in: Stefan Karner (Ed.), Kärnten und die nationale Frage, Vol. 1., Klagenfurt/Ljubljana/Wien 2005; Wilhelm Baum *et al.* (Eds.), Die Opfer des Nationalsozialismus in Kärnten [Victims of Nazism in Carinthia], Klagenfurt 2010; Brigitte Entner – Avguštin Malle – Valentin Sima (Eds.), Widerstand gegen Faschismus und Nationalsozialismus im Alpen-Adria-Raum. Internationale Tagung Klagenfurt 24.–25.2.2011 [Resistance to Fascism and Nazism in the Alps-Adriatic-Region], Klagenfurt/Wien 2011.

28 See *supra* n. 2 and Lisa Rettl, 60 Jahre Minderheitenpolitik in Kärnten/Koroška. Ein Streifzug [60 Years Minority Politics in Carinthia/Koroška. A Survey], in: Lisa Rettl – Werner Koroschitz (Eds.), Heiß umfehdet, wild umstritten. Geschichtsmythen in Rot-Weiß-Rot, Klagenfurt 2005, 95–140.

29 See, *inter alia*, Andreas Moritsch, Vom Ethnos zur Nationalität. Der nationale Differenzierungsprozeß am Beispiel ausgewählter Orte in Kärnten und im Burgenland [From Ethnos to Nationality. The National Process of Differentiation of Selected Places in Carinthia and Burgenland], München 1991; Andreas Moritsch (Ed.), Austria Slovenica. Die Kärntner Slovenen und die Nation Österreich [Austria Slovenica. The Carinthian Slovenes and the Austrian Nation], Klagenfurt/Ljubljana/Wien 1996; Stefan Karner (Ed.), Kärnten und die nationale Frage [Carinthia and the National Question], 5 Vols., Klagenfurt 2005.

30 *E.g.*, Andreas Moritsch (Ed.), Die Kärntner Slovenen 1900–2000. Bilanz des 20. Jahrhunderts [The Carinthian Slovenes 1900–2000. Balance oft he 20th Century], Klagenfurt/Ljubljana/Wien 2000; Mirko Bogataj, Die Kärntner Slowenen [The Carinthian Slovenes], Klagenfurt/Wien 2008; Hellwig Valentin, Kärnten. Vom Ersten Weltkrieg bis zur Gegenwart [Carinthia. From World War I to the Present], Klagenfurt/Ljubljana/Wien 2009.

31 See *supra* n. 3, 9, 12

32 See, *e.g.*, Tom Priestly, Denial of Ethnic Identity. The Political Manipulation of Beliefs about Language in Slovene Minority Areas of Austria and Hungary, in: Slavic Review 55/2, Champaign 1996, 364–398; Tom Priestly, Cultural Consciousness and Political Nationalism. Determinants of Language-Choice in Carinthia, in: Canadian Review of Studies in Nationalism 16, Charlottetown 1989, 59–77; James Gow – Cathie Carmichael, Slovenia and the Slovenes. A Small State in the New Europe, Bloomington/Indianapolis 2000; Tom Gullberg, State, Territory and Identity. The Principle of National Self-Determination, the Question of Territorial Sovereignty in Carinthia and other Post-Habsburg Territories after the First World War, Åbo 2000.

ternational research discourse is therefore necessary, and the theoretical and methodological approach of this dissertation is based on it. The approximation to the subject from the perspective of cultures of remembrance offers the opportunity to anchor in the postulated ethnic homogenization on historical artifacts. For this purpose the dissertation is based on Pierre Nora's concept of *lieux de mémoire*.[33] The study of *lieux de mémoire* can help to draw conclusions on the collective (national) memory[34] and its creation. Nora specifies *lieux de mémoire* as 'Orte – in allen Bedeutungen des Wortes – [...] in denen sich das Gedächtnis der Nation [...] in besonderem Maße kondensiert, verkörpert oder kristallisiert hat'.[35] Therefore, artifacts such as gravestones could be seen as *lieux de mémoire* and their analysis can uncover religious, political, or even national changes of identities.

The study of cultures of remembrance and *lieux de mémoire* has strongly influenced historiography in recent decades because it has succeded in relating the change of identity to concrete artifacts. The doctoral thesis wants to benefit from this by approaching the Slovenian's minority supposedly demographic decline in Carinthia from a new angle and to contextualize the official census results as a consequence of a specific policy aiming at an ethnic homogenization of Carinthia. The object of the dissertation will be, to examine the change of identity – which was previously only roughly conceived – from a bottom-up-perspective, which could show more comprehensively what social and local implications followed the policy of ethnic homogenization. Using this model, it is furthermore possible to better understand theories of ethnic homogenization by building on a more substantive understanding of their interactions.

Specification of the Research Question

The main research question of the dissertation project is:

> Is it possible to speak of a 'successful policy' of ethnic homogenization in Carinthia since 1918, as visibly indicated by changes of identity on gravestones?

The dissertation is based on the hypothesis that there is a discrepancy between the official census' results and the actual use of the Slovenian language. The Disappearance of the 'Slovenian' is mainly the result of a specific policy towards the

33 See, *e.g.*, Pierre Nora, Zwischen Geschichte und Gedächtnis [Between History and Memory], Berlin 1990, 17f.; Astrid Erll, Kollektives Gedächtnis und Erinnerungskulturen. Eine Einführung [Collective Memory and Cultures of Remembrance. An Introduction], Stuttgart 2005, 23f.

34 See Maurice Halbwachs, Das Gedächtnis und seine sozialen Bedingungen [The Memory and its Social Conditions], Berlin 1966; Maurice Halbwachs, Das kollektive Gedächtnis [The Collective Memory], Frankfurt am Main 1991; Jan Assman, Kollektives Gedächtnis und kulturelle Identität [Collective Memory and Cultural Identity], in: Jan Assmann – Tonio Hölscher (Eds.), Kultur und Gedächtnis, Frankfurt am Main 1988, 9–19.

35 Nora, Geschichte, 7. [Sites – in all common meanings of the word – in which the nation's memory has been specially embodied, crystallized or concentrated. Translation by the author]

Carinthian Slovenes, which can be summarized under the concept of ethnic homogenization. Furthermore, this policy at least pursues/pursued the objective to push back the 'Slovenian' or to create an ethnically homogeneous *Volkskörper* in the sense of the concept of ethnic nationalism. The artifacts will help to show how influential this homogenization might have been. It can therefore be assumed that variations in the level of penetration of the ethnically homogenous nation can be empirically traced with the artifacts.

The dissertation aims to analyze the changing of ethnic attributions on the basis of artifacts that are in this case understood as gravestones. This research attempts to show the effectiveness of such a policy and tries to locate the supposed change of identity on the seemingly indestructible and eternal artifact, namely the gravestones.

In addition to this main research question, another question should be examined, which is an empirical specification of the above-mentioned thesis and mainly affects the policy towards the Carinthian Slovenes. It will be important to relate the assumed change of identity, as evidenced by the gravestones to concrete historical events. A timeline on which the main divides in the relationship between the German-speaking majority and the Slovenian-speaking minority becomes visible, will be drawn in order to highlight possible coincidences. The main events and historical controversies are the so-called 'Kärntner Abwehrkampf' as a result of the First World War and the partisan warfare against the Nazi regime in Carinthia during the Second World War. The importance of both conflicts is highly controversial and primarily determined by the political standpoint. The ethnic policy towards the Carinthian Slovenes that is described in the present paper with the concept of ethnic homogenization means, above all, a political approach of various Carinthian governments that – to put it mildly – has not been marked by large concessions. The list of broken promises by the Carinthian authorities speaks volumes: bilingual primary education was assured after the Second World War, which has been not implemented sustainably after the signing of the State Treaty in 1955; the right to use of Slovenian as an official language has been thwarted; the lawful erection of bilingual road signs had been stalled for decades.

Against this background, a number of important issues can be raised: On how many gravestones can a change of identity be found and at what time has it frequently happened, which political occasions may have influenced the change, or what were the reasons for such a change? These questions can be summarized into the following sub-question:

> What coincidences might be determined between concrete historical events and the change of ethnic attributions on gravestones?

In this context, it will be of particular interest to examine at what times people have decided – or even had to decide – to abandon their ethnic and seemingly eternal identity on gravestones in favor of the majority population and whether it happened in response to the specific policy of ethnic homogenization. This will help determine variations in and drawing conclusions about the so-called 'success' of a policy of ethnic homogenization.

Theoretical and Methodological Considerations

The initial point of the doctoral thesis is the bilingual area in today's Carinthia that roughly covers the districts Hermagor, Villach-Land, Klagenfurt-Land, and Völkermarkt. The following figure (figure 2) shows a map that charts the results of the 2001 census and shows the communities with the highest rates of Slovenian-speaking Carinthians.

The evaluation period starts with the end of the First World War, as new borders were established according to the peace treaty of Saint Germain. The immediate post-bellum period was marked by border disputes with the newly constituted state and later Kingdom of Serbs, Croats, and Slovenes that came to an end after the national referendum in 1920. The territorial claims of both sides and the following military skirmishes entered the country's collective memory as the 'Kärntner Abwehrkampf'. It is certainly one of the starting points for the conflict between the German-speaking majority population of Carinthia and the Slovenian-speaking minority. Besides that, World War I and its end represent an important turning point in the history of Central Europe, as it helped to implement the idea of the nation state and constituted the overture of the ethnically defined nation state.

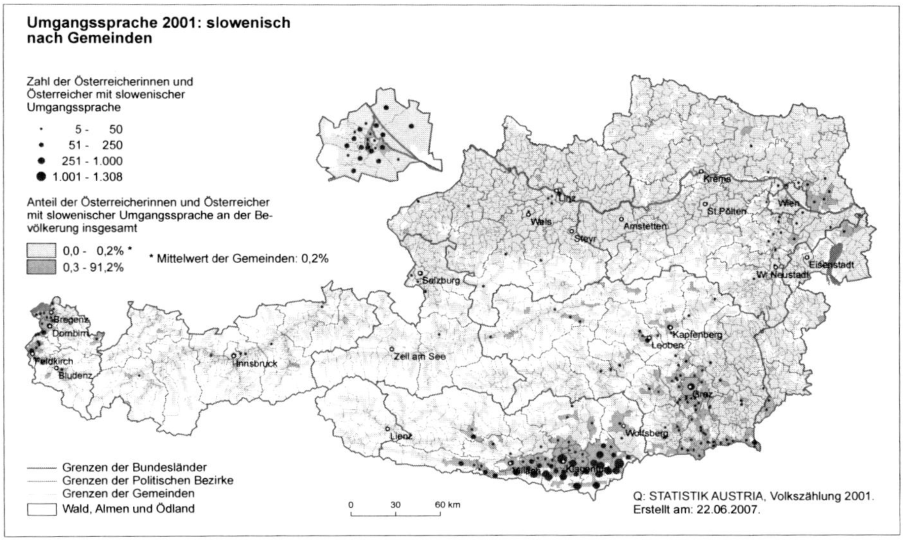

Figure 2: Colloquial Language: Slovenian by municipality.

Statistik Austria, Umgangssprache 2001: Slowenisch nach Gemeinde. Volkszählung 2001, in: http://www.statistik.at/wcm/idc/idcplg?IdcService=GET_NATIVE_FILE&RevisionSelectionMethod=LatestReleased&dDocName=026416, 10 September 2014.

The idea of the nation as well as the enforcement of the nation state and its impact on the people, living in the designated area is of particular importance for this dissertation. The doctoral thesis will be based on a concept of nation that does not classify nation as a timeless or natural category, but as a social construction.[36] The already mentioned Austrian Philosopher Rudolf Burger highlights the factor of construction, since the state is genuinely interested in selecting certain events and including them in a national history canon that enables to shape the aspired development of a political identity[37]:

> 'Gerade moderne Gesellschaften geben sich, um eine politische Identität herauszubilden, distinkte Nationalgeschichten. Dieses Narrativ ist immer auch Konstruktion. Bestimmte Ereignisse werden pathetisiert, andere werden lakonisiert, manche werden überhaupt nicht betont.'

Ernest Renan, Benedict Anderson, and Stuart Hall followed a similar approach. On the one hand, Renan emphasized the society's capacity to forget, on the other hand, he theorized the selection of historical landmarks and thus anticipated the social-constructivist position.[38] Anderson, however, focused on the imagination of Individuals within a political community and shaped the term 'imagined communities'.[39] Stuart Hall stressed the nation's process of construction by understanding the national culture as a discourse shaping identities by producing meanings about the nation.[40]

Following a concept of nation that stresses the social conditionality of national development, memory and remembrance play a crucial role in the nation-building process. The study of cultures of remembrance and *lieux de mémoire* can help to decipher the functional use of the past for present purposes in the formation of a

---

36 *Cf.* Emil Brix, Kontinuität und Wandel im öffentlichen Gedenken in den Staaten Mitteleuropas [Continuity and Change in the Public Remembrance in Central European Countries], in: Emil Brix – Hannes Stekl (Eds.), Der Kampf um das Gedächtnis. Öffentliche Gedenktage in Mitteleuropa, Wien/Köln/Graz 1997, 13–21, here 16.

37 *Cf.* Rudolf Burger, Hitler ist zum Pornostar geworden [Hitler Has Become a Pornstar], http://www.zeit.de/2012/36/A-Rudolf-Burger-Erinnern-Nationalsozialismus-Oesterreich/seite-2, 1 August 2014. [Especially modern societies give themselves distinct national histories, to help a political identity emerge. This narrative is always a construction. Certain events are overemphasized, others are concealed and some are not even given any significance, Translation by the author]

38 Ernest Renan, "Was ist eine Nation?" [What is a Nation], in: Michael Ritter – Henning Ritter (Eds.), Grenzfälle. Über neuen und alten Nationalismus, Leipzig 1993, 290–311, here 294f.

39 Benedict Anderson, Die Erfindung der Nation. Zur Karriere eines erfolgreichen Konzepts [Imagined Communities. Reflections on the Origin and Spread of Nationalism], Berlin1998, 14f.; Ruth Wodak – Rudolf de Cillia – Martin Reisigl – Karin Liebhart – Klaus Hofstätter – Maria Kragl, Zur diskursiven Konstruktion nationaler Identität [About the Discursive Construction of National Identity], Frankfurt am Main 1998, 32.

40 *Cf.* Stuart Hall, Rassismus und kulturelle Identität [Racism and Cultural Identity], Hamburg 1994, 201.

historically based identity.[41] The concept of cultures of remembrance more or less describes the system of collective memory maintained by a whole society or a certain social group.[42] In this context, system is defined as the way in which a society interlinks and organizes the various elements and modes of remembering – including *lieux de mémoire*.[43] Cultures of remembrance are always in tension between past and present and manifest themselves through monuments, museums, public rituals, memorials, or even a prevailing view of history.[44] Therefore *lieux de mémoire* occupy a specific significance when investigating cultures of remembrance. Gravestones are an exemplary source of empirical evidence for these theories.

The change of ethnic attributions on gravestones will be analyzed in Carinthia's bilingual area. The selection of cemeteries is based on a comparison of the registers of the Slovenian and bilingual parishes of the diocese of Gurk-Klagenfurt in 1918 and 2014.[45] Based on this data, the dissertation will focus on cemetery-relocations and cemetery-enlargements since 1918 and investigate the assumed change of ethnic attributions. This limitation of cemeteries that will be examined stems from a practical consideration: The Germanization could be carried out more easily, whenever a new gravestone had been commissioned. Moreover, the research of the supposed change of identity will also randomly include the birth-, marriage-, and death registers of the parishes and civil offices of the communities/ municipalities that are located in the bilingual areas to unveil a possible mismatch between the ethnic attributions in the registers and on the gravestones.[46] The comparison between the different registers and the gravestones will provide a first insight into the extent of the hypothesized changes of identity on gravestones. After the scope of the postulated change of identity has been detected, in a further step, both affected persons (especially relatives whose families changed their identity) and people who may have observed the change of ethnic attributions (for instance the parish clergy, the staff of the diocese Gurk-Klagenfurt, morticians or stonema-

41 Christoph Cornelißen, Erinnerungskulturen [Remebrance Cultures], in: http://docupedia.de/docupedia/images/b/b4/Erinnerungskulturen_Version_2.0_Christoph_Corneli%C3%9Fen.pdf, 1 August 2014.

42 Hans Hennig Hahn – Robert Traba, Zur Einführung [Introduction], in: *Idem* (Eds.), Deutsch-Polnische Erinnerungsorte, Band 3: Parallelen, Paderborn 2012, 11–19, here 12.

43 *Ibid.*

44 *Cf.* Bernd Faulenbach, Erinnerungskulturen in Mittel- und Osteuropa als wissenschaftliches und geschichtspolitisches Thema. Überlegungen zu Thema und Fragestellungen [Cultures of Remembrance in Central and Eastern Europe as a Topic for Science and Politics of Memory. Reflections on the Topic and Questions], in: Bernd Faulenbach – Franz-Josef Jelich (Eds.), Transformationen der Erinnerungskulturen in Europa nach 1989, Essen 2006, 11–21, here 11.

45 In 1917/1918 existed 131 Slovenian/bilingual parishes within the duchy of Carinthia. See List of bilingual parishes in Carinthia according to the register [Schematismus] of the diocese Gurk, in the author's archive. As of 2014, 69 parishes use Slovenian liturgy. See Catholic Church of Carinthia, http://www.kath-kirche-kaernten.at/krska_skofija#1, 1 August 2014.

46 The appropriate civil status data is both in the church archives and parishes as well as in civil registries of the municipalities. Attention is drawn to the legal retention periods, which are subject to both ecclesiastical and governmental authorities.

sons) will be interviewed using qualitative semi-structured interviews.[47] These interviews are based on an interview guide aiming to achieve the following: The anonymized interviewees should reveal their own subjective perspectives, connections, and interpretations about the change of ethnic attributions on gravestones that has been caused by 'ethnic homogenization' policies.

Concluding Remarks

This topic of the dissertation has been and is often interpreted as an 'explosive topic'. With this assessment was/is probably meant the joining of a hushed-up question with the disappearance of an ethnic minority from a *lieu de mémoire.* People may not want to be remembered of their origin as it has been considered for a long time as a stigma. Nevertheless, the author is of the opinion that this question should be dealt with and even be expanded, according to the famous saying of the Carinthian writer Ingeborg Bachmann (1926–1973) that the 'Wahrheit dem Menschen zumutbar sei'.[48] The author further believes that an individual will find it easier to accept the truth when she/he knows about its historical origins.

The doctoral thesis aims to analyze the changing of ethnic attributions on the basis of artifacts. The disappearance of the Carinthian Slovenes is mainly the result of a specific policy towards them that was/is driven by the concept of ethnic homogenization. This research attempts to show the effectiveness of such a policy and tries to locate the supposed change of identity on an eternal artifact, namely the gravestones.

The theoretical foundations of the concept of nation and of Nora's *lieux de mémoire*, coupled with empirical qualitative interviews, archive studies, and fieldwork, should help to unveil the structures and processes that caused the Carinthian Slovenes' steady decline, but will also help to grasp the true scope of this decline better. The long-term analysis in terms of a *longue durée*, ranging from 1918 to the present day will also assist to uncover complex relationships between the past and the present and to explore the historical significance of ethnic groups and nations. In addition, this research will be an incentive to pursue this subject further, as it seems to be applicable for all European countries that have or had an ethnically mixed population. In the future, this methodological approach could serve as a blueprint to investigate the success of 'ethnic homogenization' policies in former or present ethnically mixed areas. Cemeteries and gravestones – if they have not already been destroyed – are historical testimonies that must be just made to talk.

---

47 Interviews are based on methodological considerations of Andreas Diekmann, Empirische Sozialforschung. Grundlagen, Methoden, Anwendungen [Empirical Social Research. Basics, Methods, Applications], Hamburg [15]2006; Philipp Mayring, Einführung in die qualitative Sozialforschung. Eine Anleitung zum qualitativen Denken [Introduction to Qualitative Social Research. A Guide to Qualitative Thinking], Basel [5]2002.

48 Ingeborg Bachmann named her speech at the award ceremony of the radio drama prize of war-blinded man in Cologne with the words: 'The Truth shall be reasonable to man', http://www.ingeborg-bachmann-forum.de/ibpreis.htm, 01 August 2014.

Sebastian Sparwasser

Ethnic German Expellees from Hungary and Their 'Homecoming'

Andrássy University Budapest

Introduction

It is estimated that a total of twelve to thirteen million ethnic Germans were forced to move from Central and Eastern Europe to allied-occupied Germany and to Austria during the last months of World War II and in the years following the end of the war.[1] Hungary was one of the regions where these forced migrations took place. Recent research estimates that up to 180,000 people belonging to the German minority in Hungary had to leave their *Heimat,* their places of origin, in the post-war period.[2] The *svábok* [Schwaben/Swabians] – the term used in Hungary to describe the German-speaking minority – were expelled by the Hungarian administration between 1946 and 1948 at the behest of the Allied powers. The expulsion transports were sent to occupied Germany, mainly to the American zone of occupation in the Southwest of the country. Beginning in the summer of 1947, these transports were also sent to the Soviet zone of occupation. In the admitting areas, the evacuees were at first placed in temporary camps and were then quartered in the houses and homes of the resident population.

The displaced suffered material losses and experienced structural violence in the course of the expulsions, but it was the loss of what is referred to as *Heimat* that was the greatest burden for them. The personal relationships and social structures, which existed in the Hungarian homeland, were entirely broken as a result of the expulsions. In some towns and communities, more than half the population was displaced. The longing for *Heimat* became a central desire for many expellees, even though a return seemed almost impossible; the migration policies of both the allied powers and the Hungarian government did not support return. Efforts to remigrate[3] were penalized by both the Allied forces in Germany and the Hungar-

1 See Ray M. Douglas, Ordnungsgemäße Überführung. Die Vertreibung der Deutschen nach dem Zweiten Weltkrieg [Orderly and Humane. The Expulsion of the Germans after the Second World War], München 2012, 372.

2 See Mathias Beer, Flucht und Vertreibung der Deutschen. Voraussetzungen, Verlauf, Folgen [Flight and Expulsion. Preconditions, Courses, Consequences], München 2011, 114f.

3 In the following, the term 'remigration' is used to specify this specific migration movement. For theoretical approaches to remigration see Jean-Pierre Cassarino, Theorising Return Migration. The

ian government. Despite the obstacles, most of the expellees expressed a desire to return; ultimately, however, only a small proportion actually did. The Hungarian historian Ágnes Tóth estimates – based on extensive research in local and regional archives in Hungary – that up to 10,000 people moved back to their home towns in Hungary despite the penalties, prohibitions and other risks they had to face. Most of them returned to Hungary within months of their expulsion.[4] The *hazatértek* [those who actually came home] developed a variety of strategies for finding their way back into the now dramatically changed, Socialist Hungarian society.[5]

Return migration to Hungary can be regarded as an exceptional process within post-war migrations. There is no evidence that *Reichsdeutsche* or *Volksdeutsche* (these are contemporary terms used to define expellees with regard to their provenance) returned to areas other than Hungary in the post-war period. This raises questions about their motives, strategies, and incentives to return. In particular, their feelings of cultural, ethnic, and national belonging – their sense of *Heimat* – seem to be of special importance in this context. This paper aims to address these questions through reference to oral history interviews as well as to archival documents. The analysis proceeds through five sections:

- First, the research area and the methodology used will be presented.
- Second, the current state of research on the remigration of Hungarian German resettlers will be presented.

Conceptual Approach to Return Migrants Revisited, in: International Journal on Multicultural Societies 6, Paris 2004, 253–279; and Edda Currle, Theorieansätze zur Erklärung von Rückkehr und Remigration [Theoretical Approaches for Explaining Return and Remigration], in: Sozialwissenschaftlicher Fachinformationsdienst (soFid), Migration und ethnische Minderheiten 2, Bonn 2006, 7–23, http://nbn-resolving.de/urn:nbn:de:0168-ssoar-205927, 23 December 2014.

4 See Ágnes Tóth, Hazatértek. A németországi kitelepítésből visszatért magyarországi németek megpróbáltatásainak emlékezete [Homecomers. Memories of Hungarian Germans who Tried to Return after Their Expulsion to Germany], Budapest 2008, 16; Ágnes Tóth, Rückkehr nach Ungarn 1946–1950. Erlebnisberichte ungarndeutscher Vertriebener [Return to Hungary 1946–1950. Narrations of Hungarian-German Expellees], Schriften des Bundesinstituts für Kultur und Geschichte der Deutschen im östlichen Europa 43, München 2012, 20.

5 This paper is based on presentations held at the Annual Conference of the International Society for Ethnology and Folklore (SIEF) in Tartu/Estonia in July 2013 and the Austrian Centers Meeting in Minneapolis in September 2014. The paper discusses the main results of research for my ongoing dissertation project. Parts of this paper have been published in German in following conference proceedings: Sebastian Sparwasser, Ungarndeutsche 'Umsiedler' in der Sowjetisch besetzten Zone und die Heimkehr [Hungarian-German Resettlers in the Soviet Zone of Occupation and the Return], in: Enikő Dácz (Ed.), Minderheitenfragen in Ungarn und in den Nachbarländern im 20. und 21. Jahrhundert [Minority Questions in Hungary and the Neighboring Countries in the 20th and 21st Century], Andrássy Studien zur Europaforschung 8, Baden-Baden 2013, 181–196; Sebastian Sparwasser, Ungarndeutsche Vertriebene und die Heimkehr nach Ungarn [Hungarian-german Expellees and their Homecoming to Hungary], in: Andra Octavia Drăghiciu – Fabienne Gouverneur – Sebastian Sparwasser (Eds.), 'Bewegtes Mitteleuropa' [Central Europe on the Move], Tagungsband zur Zweiten Internationalen Tagung des Doktoratskollegs der Fakultät für Mitteleuropäische Studien an der Andrássy Universität Budapest, Mitteleuropäische Studien 8, Herne 2014, 103–130.

- Third, the historical circumstances surrounding the expulsion of Hungary's German population will be described. This section is divided into two sub-sections: (i) the politics surrounding the expulsion program; and (ii) the experience of expulsion as a central element in the narrated life stories of the expellees as well as in the decisions to return.
- Fourth, the paper discusses the political circumstances and the living and working conditions the expellees experienced in the admitting areas in occupied Germany. It is argued that the specific conditions surrounding admission played an important role in the decisions by individuals to remigrate.
- Fifth, since return must be regarded as a process that did not end with the moment of physical arrival – specific cases looked at in the study underline this point – the situation of the returnees in Hungary is also examined. This section is divided into two sub-sections: (i) the journey home; and (ii) life in Hungary.

Throughout the paper, examples will be taken from interviews with returnees to provide a sense of how these events appeared to the participants themselves. It is hoped that these oral histories will enrich our understanding of the motives, strategies, and individual perceptions that, taken together, led to a significant example of return-migration in the aftermath of World War II.

Research Area and Methodology

As part of a field research project conducted from 2010–2013, the author investigated the personal lives of the so-called *hazatértek,* a Hungarian term that translates as 'those who came home' or 'the homecomers'; it is used to specify those ethnic Germans from Hungary who were expelled in the aftermath of World War II and then returned permanently to their Hungarian places of origin. In the course of the research men, and women had been interviewed who witnessed this specific migration history.[6] Main regions of research were the southern Hungarian Counties of Baranya, Somogy and Bács Kiskun. This region, which is also called 'Schwäbische Türkei' [sváb törökország/Swabian Turkey], has included a large ethnic German population dating back to the Habsburg-supported colonization of the area by German settlers in the late 17th century and early 18th century.[7]

The interviews provide first-hand perceptions and personal experiences of expropriation and expulsion from Hungary, the living conditions of Hungarian German 'resettlers' in occupied Germany, the circumstances of their return migration and the process of reintegration of the *hazatértek* into the now-Socialist Hungar-

6 Most of the contacts were conveyed to me by Hungarian historian Ágnes Tóth (Hungarian Academy of Sciences), whom I want to thank for the generous help during the research.

7 Most of the research was conducted in the southern Hungarian towns Lippó, Feked, Nagynyárád, Véménd, Palkonya, Bája, Szigetbecse, Villány, Villánykövesd and Nemesnádudvar.

ian society. Twenty-one of these conversations have been recorded, transcribed, and – to facilitate deeper analysis – broken down into specific aspects: motivations for return, strategies for finding a way back in, and perceptions of home, identity, ethnicity, and belonging. All these research objectives required a comprehensive qualitative approach. Therefore, the interviews were conducted as open conversations where the conversational partners developed their own stories and chose for themselves which topics to highlight. In addition to the information gathered through the interviews, the study also relied on 'participant observation' [teilnehmende Beobachtungen] as well as archival documents.[8]

State of Research

There is little information about this specific case of post-war migrations in the existing historical literature. The first publication where the remigration of German expellees from Hungary appears to be mentioned was in German historian Theodor Schieder's (1908–1984)[9] oral history study "Schicksal der Deutschen in Ungarn", which was first published in 1957.[10] In "Schicksal der Deutschen in Ungarn", Schieder described the process of expulsion based primarily on personal written accounts and interviews. In a three-page chapter, Schieder also reports that there were displaced *svábok* who did not consider the expulsions as final and tried

8 The study is based on theoretical and methodological concepts developed by Gabriele Rosenthal, Albrecht Lehmann ('Lebensgeschichte'), and Philipp Mayring ('Qualitative Inhaltsanalyse', 'Narratives Interview', 'Teilnehmende Beobachtung'). See Gabriele Rosenthal, Erlebte und erzählte Lebensgeschichte. Gestalt und Struktur biographischer Selbstbeschreibung [Experienced and Narrated Life Story. Shape and Structure of Biographical Self-description], Frankfurt 1995; Albrecht Lehmann, Reden über Erfahrung. Kulturwissenschaftliche Bewusstseinsanalyse des Erzählens [Talking about Experience. Cultural Sciences and the Analysis of Narration], Berlin 2007; Philipp Mayring, Einführung in die qualitative Sozialforschung [Introduction to Qualitative Research], Basel 2002; Philipp Mayring, Qualitative Inhaltsanalyse. Grundlagen und Techniken [Qualitative Content Analysis. Basics and Techniques], Basel 2010.

9 Schieder's commitment during the Third Reich was subject to controversial debates after his death. See Götz Aly, Theodor Schieder, Werner Conze oder die Vorstufen der physischen Vernichtung [Theodor Schieder, Werner Conze or the Precursors of Physical Destruction], in: Winfried Schulze – Otto Gerhard Oexle (Eds.), Deutsche Historiker im Nationalsozialismus [German Historians in National Socialism], Frankfurt am Main 1999, 163–182; Michael Lausberg, Die 'Irrungen' eines 'Fehlgeleiteten'. Der Historiker Theodor Schieder und der Nationalsozialismus [‚Errors' of a ‚Misguided'. The Historian Theodor Schieder and National Socialism], in: DISS-Journal 19, Duisburg 2010, 10–13.

10 "Das Schicksal der Deutschen in Ungarn" was commissioned by the West German Federal Ministry for Displaced Persons, Refugees and War Victims [Bundesministerium für Vertriebene, Flüchtlinge und Kriegsgeschädigte] and was published within the multi-volumed edition "Dokumentation der Vertreibung der Deutschen aus Ostmitteleuropa" [Documentation of the Expulsions of the Germans from Easterncentral Europe]. Based on eyewitness accounts and autobiographies, a commission of historians documented the causes, courses and consequences of flight and expulsion from Central- and Eastern Europe. The documentation is considered one of the most extensive oral history projects in post-war Germany. See Bundesministerium für Vertriebene, Flüchtlinge und Kriegsgeschädigte (Ed.), Dokumentation der Vertreibung der Deutschen aus Ost-Mitteleuropa, München 2004.

to move back to their places of origin. He states that these attempts to return were beset by various problems, obstacles, and risks and usually were not successful. Many returnees were rejected or detained at the borders in allied-occupied Germany, Austria, or Hungary. Many of those wanting to return were caught and sent back to the admitting areas in occupied Germany. Schieder also mentioned that returnees, as well as Germans who had remained in the country, were regarded as political offenders by the Hungarian authorities and had to live as illegals with relatives and friends for years because houses had been given to ethnic Hungarian refugees after the expulsions. Due to the inadequate and incomplete sources, however, Schieder was not able to estimate the actual number of returnees who had permanently resettled in Hungary and he ended up concluding that it must have been a relatively small group.[11]

Schieder's documentation relied on oral and written sources that were collected in Western Germany. Documents from Hungarian archives were not accessible to his team because research on the causes and procedures of the expulsions were politically and ideologically suppressed in Hungary during the Socialist period until the mid-1980s. Hungarian governments suppressed the subject because this could have led to criticisms of Socialist involvement in the so-called *kitelepités* [the expulsion of Hungary's German population].[12] After the fall of the Iron Curtain in 1989/1990 and the democratization of Hungary, the country finally opened up to a discussion of these topics. The opening of the archives made it possible to work with sources that had not been accessible before, enabling source-based research, especially with official records and personal accounts, on both the expulsions and the phenomenon of return-migration of Hungarian-German expellees.

Hungarian historian Ágnes Tóth, in particular, has done extensive research on the return movement since then. In 2008, her study "Hazatértek: a németországi kitelepítésből visszatért magyarországi németek megpróbáltatásainak emlékezete" was published in Hungarian; in 2012, it was also published in German under the title "Rückkehr nach Ungarn 1946–1950. Erlebnisberichte Ungarndeutscher Vertriebener". The study breaks new ground in the study of Hungarian-German remigrants and is based on extensive research, including interviews and documents located in local and regional archives in Hungary. The study concludes that approximately 8,000 to 10,000 German expellees permanently resettled back in their Hungarian homeland. This is the first realistic estimation of the size of this par-

11 Theodor Schieder, Das Schicksal der Deutschen in Ungarn, in: Bundesministerium für Vertriebene, Flüchtlinge und Kriegsgeschädigte (Ed.), Dokumentation der Vertreibung der Deutschen aus Ost-Mitteleuropa II, München 2004, Introduction and 67E–69E.

12 Gerhard Seewann, Zur ungarischen Geschichtsschreibung über die Vertreibung der Ungarndeutschen 1980–1996 [Hungarian Historiography and the Expulsion of the Germans in Hungary 1980–1996], in: Ágnes Tóth (Ed.), Migrationen in Ungarn 1945–1948. Vertreibung der Ungarndeutschen, Binnenwanderungen und slowakisch-ungarischer Bevölkerungsaustausch [Migrations in Hungary from 1945 to 1948. Expulsion of Germans in Hungary, Internal Migrations and the Slovak-Hungarian Population Exchange], Schriften des Bundesinstituts für Ostdeutsche Kultur 12, München 2001, 7–16.

ticular migration movement. Her analysis of more than 50 oral history interviews showed that the reasons for return arose from several distinct motives. Homesickness [Honvágy, ragaszkodás a szülöföldhöz], the wish for family reunion [Családegyesítés] and the bad living and working conditions that were experienced in the admitting areas in occupied Germany [A rossz életkörülmények, különösen az élelemhiány] are retrospectively seen as the main reasons for having returned. Tóth's research also looks at the life-long struggle for identity that formed an important part of the returnees' stories, since expulsion and return put into question many of their established social and cultural assumptions.[13]

Historical Circumstances of the Expulsions

(i) Expropriation and Expulsion

The expulsion of Hungary's German population has to be looked at in the post-war European context of forced migrations and political developments in Hungary and occupied Germany. The 'ethnic paradigm' and efforts to reconstruct post war Europe along ethnic and national lines played an important role in these developments. Also, there was a wide variety of developments in local and regional contexts.[14]

In the last months of the war, many Germans were deported or fled from Hungary because of fear from the Soviet occupation and possible retribution for German acts during the war. In the winter of 1944–1945, as part of the work program *Malenki Robot* [a little work], approximately 50,000 Germans were deported from Hungary to work camps.[15] Also due to a land-reform program, many Germans in Hungary were resettled. This phase of 'wild expulsions' was later replaced by a program of systematic transfers. The regulatory framework, which underpinned the systematic transfer of much of Hungary's German population was negotiated by the allied powers in the Potsdam Agreement of August 1945. The provisional Hungarian government and its president, Zoltán Tildy[16], decided to implement the resettlement program two months later, in December 1945.[17] The actual trans-

13 Tóth, Hazatértek, 16–20.

14 Gábor Gonda, Ungarndeutsche Geschichte auf Mikroebene. Im Spannungsfeld von Bodenreform, Zwangsmigration und Ethnopolitik (1944–1948) [Hungarian-German History at the Micro-Level. Land Reform, Forced Migration and Ethnic Policies (1944–1948)], in: Enikő Dácz (Ed.), Minderheitenfragen in Ungarn und in den Nachbarländern im 20. und 21. Jahrhundert [Minority Questions in Hungary and the Neighboring Countries in the 20th and 21st Century], Andrássy Studien zur Europaforschung 8, Baden-Baden 2013, 165–180, here 165–169.

15 Tamás Stark, 'Malenki Robot'. Hungarian Forced Labourers in the Soviet Union (1944–1955), Minorities Research 7, Budapest 2005, 155–167, http://www.epa.hu/00400/00463/00007/pdf/155_stark.pdf, 30 May 2015.

16 Zoltán Tildy, 1889–1961, was a leading member of Hungary's Smallholder's Party. After 1945 he first served as Prime Minister and then as President of the provisonal Hungarian government. After the Socialist seizure in 1948 he had to resign and got arrested. During the upheavals of 1956 he became leading member of the anti-communist resistance movement.

17 Order 12330/1945 M.E. was ratified on December 22nd 1945. Article 1 states: 'Nach Deutschland umzusiedeln ist derjenige ungarische Staatsbürger verpflichtet, der sich bei der letzten Volks-

fers began in January 1946. The very first deportations took place in the county of Pest, a region close to Budapest. According to recent research, approximately 130,000 Swabians were expelled from their hometowns in the following months.[18] The whole expulsion process, carried out by Hungarian authorities, was hastily prepared and remained rather chaotic and disorganized, instead of 'orderly and humane' as it had been emphasized in the Potsdam Agreement.[19] During this first phase of the expulsion, the expellees were brought to the American Zone of Occupation in Germany, primarily to the region of Wuerttemberg in the Southwest. The houses and farms of the expelled families were confiscated by the Hungarian administration.

An evacuation of expellees to the Soviet Zone of Occupation was not planned at that time, but problems in the American Zone forced the allies to reconsider that position. The American military administration was simply not able to house the masses of refugees and Displaced Persons that arrived from all parts of Central- and Eastern Europe. Additionally, the provisional administration of the American zone of occupation accused the Hungarian authorities of not conducting the resettlement process in a 'humane manner' and refused to accept further transports.[20] The Hungarian Government then turned to the Allied Control Commission and demanded permission to continue the transfer of the country's German population. Their demand was supported by the Czechoslovak Government, which wanted to resettle its Hungarian population in Hungary while, at the same time, resettling Hungary's Slovak-speaking population in Czechoslovakia. The Hungarian and Czechoslovak demands were finally approved on the condition that the transports of Hungary's German population would now be sent to the Soviet Zone of Occupation in Germany.[21] In this second phase of the resettlement, which began in August 1947 and ended in June 1948, approximately 50,000 Germans from Hungary were expelled – mainly from the southern part of Hungary. One of

zählung zur deutschen Volkszugehörigkeit oder Muttersprache bekannt hat oder der seinen madjarisierten Namen wieder in einen deutsch klingenden ändern ließ, ferner derjenige, der Mitglied des Volksbundes oder einer bewaffneten deutschen Formation (SS) war.' [Hungarian citizens, who confessed German ethnicity or mother tongue in the last census or who changed their Magyarised name in a German-sounding name, also those who were a member of the People's League (Volksbund) or a armed German formation (SS), are obliged to be resettled.] See Schieder, Schicksal der Deutschen in Ungarn, Anlage 5, 91 E.

18 Beer, Flucht und Vertreibung der Deutschen, 96.

19 The Allied Powers had decided on the transfers on the condition that they would be carried out in an 'orderly and human' manner. Ray M. Douglas recently highlighted the euphemistic dimension of this subscription. See Douglas, 'Ordnungsgemässe Überführung'.

20 Miklós Füzes, Valami Magyarországon maradt. Etwas blieb daheim in Ungarn, Eingliederung der vertriebenen Ungarndeutschen in Deutschland [Something Remained in Hungary. The Integration of Hungarian-German Expellees in Germany], Pécs 1999, 90f.

21 Herefore see the chapter "Verbindungen zwischen ungarisch-slowakischem Bevölkerungsaustausch und Vertreibung" [Links between the Hungarian-Slovak Population Exchange and the Expulsion], in: Ágnes Tóth (Ed.), Migrationen in Ungarn 1945–1948. Vertreibung der Ungarndeutschen, Binnenwanderungen und slowakisch-ungarischer Bevölkerungsaustausch, Schriften des Bundesinstituts für Ostdeutsche Kultur 12, München 2001, 177–208

the main camps of admission in the soviet zone was the so-called *Graue Kaserne* [grey barracks] in the Saxon town of Pirna near Dresden.[22] It is worth noting that, in this second phase of the expulsions, the houses of the expelled families were signed over to Hungarian refugees from neighboring countries, primarily refugees who came to Hungary in the course of the Czechoslovak-Hungarian population transfers. There are case studies that show these Hungarian refugees often stood by waiting to move into their new houses while the Hungarian-German families were being removed from their homes. It is also worth mentioning in this context that not all Germans from Hungary were expelled; approximately 220,000–250,000 *svábok* actually remained in the country.[23]

(ii) The Expulsions as Biographical Turning Points

The narratives reveal the experiences of expropriation and expulsion as key moments in the life stories of the *hazatértek*. The expulsions were experienced as absolute breaks that put into question virtually all social values and assumptions. The memories of this historical and personal transformation are still very much alive. The specific details of the expulsions – the arrival of the resettlement committees, the transport, dates, times, and so on – were described in detail in all of the interviews. This can be illustrated with the narrative of Anna F., who was born in the southern Hungarian town Nagynyárád. The family was expelled in the summer of 1947, in one of the last transports to the Soviet Zone of Occupation. They returned to Hungary the following year. Anna F. now once lives again in her parents' house, in which Hungarian refugees from former Czechoslovakia had been quartered after Anna's family home was expropriated by the authorities. The arrival of the evacuation commission in Nagynyárad, the confiscation of their property and the expulsion of her family are experiences that are still present in her memory:

> 'I can clearly remember how we sat there as kids, out here in front of the house, and then the police came and the man said: "Here's the house". Then he came in and called us in order with names. Now we were supposed to pack, half an hour later the bus was there. Then we had to leave. Yes, this was difficult'[24]

---

22 The main camp for admission of the expellees from Hungary during this phase of the expulsions was the so-called *Graue Kaserne* in the town of Pirna in Saxony. See Nóra Rutsch, Die Vertreibung von Ungarndeutschen und ihre Integration in der sowjetisch besetzten Zone [The Expulsions of the Hungarian-Germans and Their Integration in the Soviet Zone of Occupation], in: Mariana Hausleitner (Ed.), Vom Faschismus zum Stalinismus. Deutsche und andere Minderheiten in Ostmittel- und Südosteuropa 1941–1953 [From Fascism to Stalinism. Germans and Other Minorities in Central and Southeastern Europe 1941–1953], München 2008, 121–135, here 122–126.

23 The specific conditions in the respective migration regime the expellees have been sent to after their expulsion had a great impact on the individual decision to return. It can be estimated that most of the *haztértek* returned to Hungary from the soviet zone of occupation. See Sparwasser, Ungarndeutsche 'Umsiedler', 182f.

24 'Ich kann mich noch gut daran erinnern, wie wir da als Kinder draußen gesessen sind hier vorm Haus, und dann ist die Polizei gekommen mit dem Mann und dann hat der Mann gesagt: "Hier ist das Haus". Dann ist er reingekommen und hat uns alle nach einer Liste der Reihe nach mit Namen

Of particular note is that all the narratives about evacuation and expulsion discuss issues of guilt and innocence, of acts of commission and victim(-ship) in a particular way. The thesis of 'collective guilt' of the German population, how it was argued in the resettlement provisions, is regarded as unjust by the interviewees. The question of guilt was formally transferred to the entire German population regardless of actual participation or involvement in the war or war crimes. Therefore, the measures carried out by the Hungarian authorities are seen as an act without any moral basis. The interviewees, for example, denied participating in the activities of the Volksbund [People's League of the Germans from Hungary] or the SS. Instead, it is argued that, although they always acknowledged their cultural 'Germanness', they also saw themselves as loyal to the Hungarian nation and state. A narrative taken from an interview with Elisabeth M. from Nemesnádudvar can illustrate this. She was 21 when she and her family were expelled to the Soviet Zone of Occupation in 1947. She later returned to her hometown: 'We just wanted to be in Hungary, although one has taken home and property from us. But anyway, we loved our country. They were bad to us, they've been cruel.'[25]

From the perspective of the interviewees, property was the main incentive for the expulsions; those *svábok* who had possessed houses and land were more likely to be affected by the evacuation efforts carried out by Hungarian officials than Svabian families who had not possessed land. The fact that a great number of Hungarian Germans were not affected by the resettlements and remained in the country would seem to support this view. The perceptions of the returnees, therefore, have their own internal logic. Return is seen by them as the legitimate response to the illegitimacy of the expulsions. This again was evident in the conversation with Elisabeth M.:

> 'When they took us and all we had, we said: "Well, we'll go there, but we'll come home again." [...] It all was wrong what they did to us. [...] Everyone thought that they are making fun with us. It wasn't justified. And it has not been justified. When they're talking about these things today, everyone says that should not have happened.'[26]

---

aufgerufen. Jetzt sollten wir packen in einer halben Stunde sei der Autobus da. Dann mussten wir fort. Ja, das war schon schwer.' Own translation of interview A.F., 2010. In the author's archive.

25 'Wir wollten halt in Ungarn sein, obwohl man uns schon Haus und Gut genommen hat. Aber trotzdem, wir liebten unser Land. Die waren schlecht zu uns, die haben uns Übel gemacht.' Own translation of interview E.M., 2010. In the author's archive.

26 'Na gut, wir gehen schon dorthin, aber wir kommen wieder heim. Das war gleich in unserem Sinn, dass wir wieder heimkommen. Wir wussten gleich, dass wir wieder zurückkommen. Das war ja alles falsch, was die mit uns gemacht haben. Jetzt hat man es ja schon bereut. Aber, na ja, es war geschehen. [...] Ein jeder hat den Gedanken getragen, die spielen uns eine Komödie vor, das ist nicht richtig. Und es ist auch nicht richtig gewesen. Wenn sie jetzt über diese Dinge reden, dann sagt ein jeder, das hätte nicht sein dürfen.' Own translation of interview E.M., 2010. In the author's archive.

In the receiving areas in Germany, the evacuated families were quartered in temporary camps where registrations and medical examinations were performed on arrival. Camp authorities would register each expellees name, date of birth, country of origin, and former profession. Work experience was important because the authorities tried to resettle families in areas where they could find jobs or where their skills were needed. In the camps of the Soviet Zone, men were also checked to see whether they were able to work in mining or the disassembly of heavy equipment; if they were found capable of such work, they were sent to the relevant locations. Regardless of their actual professions, a great number of men were sent to areas such as Annaberg, Aue, or Zwickau where they were required to work in mining. Though work in these assignments was described as voluntary, it was the only way for many to ensure survival, since opportunities for paid labour were rare. Those interviewees who were sent out to these assignments stated that the bad conditions and the lack of prospects for a better future were the main reasons for their decision to return to Hungary.[27]

The expellees were issued an 'Umsiedlerpass und Gesundheitsbescheinigung' [Resettlers passport and health certificate] by the authorities in the Soviet Zone camps; this document functioned as a form of identity card. Since the expellees had lost their Hungarian citizenship the moment they left Hungary, this was the only official paper they could use to identify themselves. The specification as *Umsiedler* [resettler] was regarded as euphemistic by the expellees. The term *Umsiedler* was used by the authorities of the Soviet Zone to underline the position that the evacuations were seen as a regular and – and this is relevant in this context of the decision by many to return – irreversible process. *Umsiedler* did not accurately describe the expellees' perceptions of the circumstances of their relocation to Germany; they saw the 'resettlements' as unjust and arbitrary, and many of the deported families wanted to return.[28] In fact many of the displaced tried to use every conceivable means to return home. They wrote letters to local authorities, diplomatic missions and church organizations to seek support for a return. They even expressed their desire to return to camp authorities. When German expellees from Hungary arrived in the transit camp Pirna in Saxony in January 1948, the camp authorities wrote in their 'political report': 'The desire of the Umsiedler would be to return to their homeland, namely to Hungary, within a short time, since they do not expect much for themselves in the Russian and American zones.'[29]

27 So far very little has been written about these developments. See Emil Magvas, Ungarndeutsche im Uranerzbergbau in der DDR [Hungarian Germans in Uranium Mining in the GDR], in: Deutscher Kalender [German Calender], Budapest 2015, 297–300.

28 See Michael Schwartz, Vom Umsiedler zum Staatsbürger. Totalitäres und Subversives in der Sprachpolitik der SBZ/DDR [From 'Umsiedler' to Nationals. Totalitarian and Subversive Elements in the Language Policy of the SOZ/GDR], in: Dierk Hoffmann – Marita Krauss – Michael Schwartz (Eds.), Vertriebene in Deutschland. Interdisziplinäre Ergebnisse und Forschungsperspektiven [Expellees in Germany. Interdisciplinary Results and Perspectives of Research], Schriftenreihe der Vierteljahrshefte für Zeitgeschichte, München 2000, 135–165, here 160 ff.

29 'Die Wunscherklärung der Umsiedler wäre, in Kürze nach ihrer Heimat, und zwar nach Ungarn, wieder zurückzukehren, da sie sich hier, sei es in der russischen sowie amerikanischen Zone, nicht

After several weeks in the camps, the expellees were housed in farms, houses, and apartments belonging to the local population. Since supplies were scarce, most of the infrastructure was destroyed and the overall economic situation was stagnant, the arrival of the expellees was seen as an additional burden by the resident population. It is reported that, in many cases, local residents tried to prevent families from moving into their homes because they feared this would worsen their own situation. In the host society, the expellees were seen as an 'unwanted' burden. Elisabeth M., who was expelled to Saxony in 1947 and had then returned to her hometown in Hungary the year after, stated: 'They regarded us as gypsies and were very angry because we came and they had to share food with us.'[30] In direct contacts between the expellees and the local population, conflicts arose and cultural differences became apparent. Although there are also many stories of friendships formed and genuine assistance offered, in general, the expellee narratives describe a feeling of social marginalization. Anna F., for instance, said that the contacts and social interactions in the new environment were often full of prejudices and hostility. Her family was sent to the transit camp Prossen in Bad Schandau and then was quartered in an apartment in a nearby village. She stated: 'They said we are "Hungarian gypsies". We said in response that we are *svábok*. Then they called us "dirty Swabians". There [in the occupation zones of Germany], we were "Hungarian gypsies".'[31]

The experience of social hostility and the inversion of social roles – among other examples, as Germans living in Hungary they shared the wide-spread prejudice against 'gypsies' and now in Germany they were called 'gypsies' – resulted in mental disorientation and emotional confusion. This not only strengthened their desire to return to Hungary, but also reinforced feelings of belonging to a unique group that was different than the people they encountered in Germany.

Despite the sense of loss, a return seemed almost impossible for the expellees. Expelled families did not have enough money or other assets to finance a return trip. Moreover, the occupation authorities had imposed a ban on return, in large measure to support the newly established borders in Central and Eastern Europe. Instead, the authorities focused on better integration and assimilation of the expellees. This included the adoption of several legal measures: the founding of expellee organizations was prohibited by the so-called coalition ban [Koalitionsverbot] in all occupation zones; incoming displaced groups were scattered to prevent the

---

viel versprechen.', "Politischer Bericht" [political report] concerning transport Nr. 4803, "Graue Kaserne" Pirna, January 27th 1947, in: Sächsisches Hauptstaatsarchiv (SächsHStA), Landesregierung Sachsen, Ministerium des Innern, Nr. 2286, edited in: Manfred Wille, Die Vertriebenen in der SBZ/DDR. Massentransfer, Wohnen, Arbeit, 1946–1949, Studien der Forschungsstelle Ostmitteleuropa an der Universität Dortmund 19/II, Wiesbaden 1999, 144.

30 'Die haben uns direkt als Zigeuner angeschaut und waren sehr böse, weil wir gekommen sind und auch noch mitessen.' Own translation of interview E.M., 2010. In the author's archive.

31 'Die haben gesagt, wir sind "ungarische Zigeuner". Wir haben gesagt, wir sind die *svábok*. Dann haben die uns "stinkende Schwaben" genannt. Wir waren halt die "ungarischen Zigeuner".' Own translation of interview A.F., 2011. In the author's archive.

formation of pressure groups[32]; flight, expulsion, and deportation were seen as irreversible, and persons caught attempting to cross borders could be sent to transit camps or prisons. The expelled families were considered to be stateless, since they had lost their Hungarian citizenship the moment they left Hungary.[33]

There were serious difficulties on the other side of the border as well. Those who wished to return could not expect to reestablish themselves easily back in Hungary. Houses and homes had been given to Hungarian refugees from other countries. Additionally, the massive post-war migrations had almost entirely broken the extensive networks of personal relationships and social structures that they had built up in their original homeland. But, despite all these obstacles, almost all expellees hoped to return. *Heimkehr*, a return to *Heimat*, surely was – as a recent publication called it – a 'central category' of thinking and desire in post-war Europe.[34]

The Return to Hungary

(i) The Journey Home

Most of the *hazetértek* returned only a few months after they had been expelled – even before the formation of the two German states in 1949. The illegality and irregularity of the return process did not deter those who had decided to return. For them, the desire to return was greater than the fear of being caught, imprisoned or led back by the occupation authorities or the Hungarian government. As the interviewed returnee Elisabeth M. put it: 'Most of them [the expellees] had the idea to

32 Mathias Beer, Deutsche aus Ungarn in West- und Ostdeutschland. Eingliederung der Flüchtlinge und Vertriebenen unter den Bedingungen unterschiedlicher Gesellschaftssysteme [Germans from Hungary in Western and Eastern Germany. The Integration of Refugees and Expellees under the Conditions of Different Social Systems], in: Gerhard Seewann (Ed.), Migrationen und ihre Auswirkungen. Das Beispiel Ungarn 1918–1995 [Migrations and Their Implications. The Example of Hungary 1918–1995], München 1997, 127–146, here 131.

33 Order 7970/1946 M.E. was ratified by Ferenc Nagy on July 12th 1946. Article 1 stated: 'Alle ungarischen Staatsbürger, die aufgrund des Beschlusses des Alliierten Kontrollrates vom 20. November 1945 zur Umsiedlung der deutschen Bevölkerung Ungarns nach Deutschland umgesiedelt werden, verlieren ihre ungarische Staatsbürgerschaft an dem Tag, an dem sie in Zusammenhang mit der Durchführung der Umsiedlung das Gebiet Ungarns verlassen.'[All Hungarian citizens who are resettled to Germany on behalf of the decision of the Allied Control Comission of November 20th 1945 for the resettlement of the German population of Hungary to Germany, lose their Hungarian citizenship the day they leave the territory of Hungary in connection with the execution of the resettlement. (own translation)] Printed in Ágnes Tóth, Rechtliche Regelungen zur Lage des Ungarndeutschtums 1938–1950 [Legal Regulations concerning the Situation of Germaness in Hungary 1938–1950], in: Manfred Kittel – Horst Möller – Jirí Pesek – Oldrich Tuma (Eds.), Deutschsprachige Minderheiten 1945. Ein europäischer Vergleich [German Speaking Minorities 1945. A European Comparison], Oldenbourg 2007, 253–296, here 292.

34 See Elena Agazzi – Erhard Schütz (Eds.), Heimkehr. Eine zentrale Kategorie der Nachkriegszeit. Geschichte, Literatur und Medien [Homecoming. A Central Category of the Post-War Periode. History, Literature and Media], Schriften des Italienisch-Deutschen Historischen Instituts Trient 23, Berlin 2010.

return at one point. They advocated return. But they did not have any luck or, how shall I put it, they did not dare to join the trip.'[35]

To minimize the risks of the journey, the actual preparations for return began weeks in advance. Maps and money had to be organized, as well as suitable and safe routes selected. One had to look for ways and means to circumvent the travel restrictions imposed by the authorities. The emigrants, therefore, relied on the assistance of their neighbors and the families that had housed them. As the interviews with returnees show, local residents supported the decision to return. András S., who was expelled in 1947 and returned alone to his hometown Vaskút in 1948, described these preparations as a weeklong process. In order to obtain information on border crossing options, friends and acquaintances provided him with maps and made recommendations for the safest routes and border crossings:

> 'I've thought ahead three or four weeks. You have to prepare well for something like this with maps – which road or railway you take, and where you cross the borders. All this. I've bought maps – old maps. I have looked at everything very well and I had it here [taps his forehead]. I've memorized everything. And in case there was a mistake, I asked for help.'[36]

It is worth noting that all of the returnees tried to avoid passing through Czechoslovakia even though this would have been the more direct route. There were two principal reasons: first, the Czech and Slovak language were not spoken by the returnees and they feared they would not be able to manage if they needed local help; and second, in the event they were arrested or detained, the returnees expected worse treatment at the hands of Czechoslovakian authorities than they would encounter anywhere else. Thus, the returnees choose routes leading through the American Zone of Occupation and the occupation zones in Austria. Paid smugglers, who were familiar with the area and knew safe crossing opportunities, often organized the actual crossings. Most of the distances were covered by train, hitchhiking, and on foot. As the interviews demonstrate, the memories of these specific events – the border crossings, the travel by night, and the encounters with police and other authorities – are still very much alive.[37]

---

35 'Die meisten waren auch auf dem Gedanken, zurückzukehren. Die haben das auch befürwortet. Aber die haben kein Glück gehabt oder wie soll man sagen, die haben sich nicht alle getraut, die Reise mitzumachen.' Own translation of Interview E.M., 2011. In the author's archive.

36 '[V]orausgedacht hab ich das drei oder vier Wochen. Da muss man sich gut vorbereiten auf so etwas mit Landkarten – welche Straße gehe ich, mit der Eisenbahn, und wo geht man über die Grenze. Das alles. Karten hab ich mir gekauft. Alte Landkarten hab ich angeschaut und hab alles hier gehabt [tippt auf die Stirn]. Das hab ich auswendig gelernt. Wenn da ein Irrtum war, da hab ich nachgefragt, das war nicht schlimm.' Own translation of interview, A.S., 2010. In the author's archive.

37 On their way back, some of the returnees were arrested or had been turned back. It is reported that returnees got captured in Hungary, were brought to collective points in Hungary and then got sent back again to Austria. *E.g.*, interview A.Sch., 2012. In the author's archive.

(ii) Life in Hungary

For those who did return, homecoming meant re-establishing the conditions they had experienced before the expulsion. The aim of return was to re-create *Heimat.* From the interviewees' point of few, the understanding of *Heimat* is closely linked to their actual places of origin. Most of the returnees tried to move back to their original towns, villages, houses, or homes – or at least as close as possible. Over the years, some of the returnees even managed to reacquire their original homes, which had been given to Hungarian refugees from neighboring countries after the expulsion of the *svábok*. In the years immediately after their arrival, however, the situation was difficult. Once the returnees made it back, they had to hide from the local authorities because – as expelled Germans – they did not have work permits or citizenship. They were considered to be stateless in both Hungary and Germany. To make a living, the *hazatértek* worked illegally on local farms and businesses as seasonal workers or as helping hands on construction sites. Since their original possessions had been given away, the returnees had to live with relatives, friends and acquaintances. Some of the returnees hid in wine cellars and vineyards to avoid being caught by the authorities. Nevertheless, since most of the returnees went back to environments where they were known, their illegal stay was generally tolerated by the local population and even by the local authorities as some cases show.

For the returnees, the years immediately following their return were dominated by efforts to regain a legal status in Hungary; in particular, Hungarian citizenship was critically important for them if they were to successfully participate in society. Passports were handed out beginning in 1950[38], but living conditions only began to really improve in the mid-1950s. Further, although the Socialist regime guaranteed minority rights in its 1949 Constitution and many of the returnees had managed to move back into their original homes in the 1950s, the practice of German culture and language was suppressed during this period and gradually disappeared from social and private life.[39] Many of the returnees married Hungarian partners. The *hazatértek* claimed they avoided speaking German in public because they feared social restrictions or even punishment; if the German language was spoken, it was within a familiar environment.[40] Even within families, use of

38 Order 84/1950 (III. 25) M.T., "Aufhebung der Anwendung der im Zusammenhang mit der Umsiedlung der deutschen Bevölkerung Ungarns erlassenen Einschränkungsverfügungen" ["Cancellation of the exertion of the restrictive regulations issued in connection with the resettlement of the German population of Hungary" (own tranlsation)]. See Schieder, Schicksal der Deutschen in Ungarn, 105E–106E.

39 See Gerhard Seewann, Geschichte der Deutschen in Ungarn (II) [History of the Germans in Hungary], Marburg 2012, 369–371.

40 'Na ja, wir konnten schon Deutsch sprechen. Nur in der Mittelschule nicht. In der Universität hab ich Volkswirtschaft studiert. Ich habe da nicht einmal geschrieben, dass ich deutsch war. Das hat man einfach nicht sagen können. [–] Damals war es nicht gut, Deutscher zu sein – lange nicht.' ['Well, we have been able to speak German, but not in middle school. In college I studied economics. I did never put down anywhere that I was German. It was just not possible to say (admit) that.

the German language fell sharply; today, the generation that grew up in Socialist Hungary and did not directly experience the expulsions rarely uses German as an everyday language.

All this was reinforced by the perceptions of the returnees that their efforts to re-establish *Heimat* depended on their meeting the expectations of the Socialist system. Most of the returnees eventually adapted to the regime and focused on professional and social advancement within the Socialist system. Career advancement became an important part of the returnees' strategies for social re-integration. Some achieved leading positions in Socialist cooperatives or public administration. Reintegration – the return to *Heimat* – meant gradually giving up their German identity and assimilating into Hungarian society. Although many of the perceived 'German' or 'Svabian' virtues such as industriousness, orderliness, and a sense of correctness have persisted, for most of the returnees still alive, German culture and language are more remembered than practiced.

Concluding Remarks

It has to be stated that only a comparatively small group of the Hungarian Germans expelled from their homeland returned to their places of origin. Hungarian historian Ágnes Tóth estimates in her study on the *hazatértek* that between three and five percent of all German expellees from Hungary actually remigrated.[41] The majority of the expellees settled well into Germany after a difficult start and gradually came to terms with their situation, while some others emigrated overseas. Although return migration can be seen as a somewhat exceptional response to the Hungarian expulsions, the desire for return should be understood as a central *topos* or theme of the post-war years. The longing to return to the homeland was widely shared. For those who actually did return, the reasons for doing so were complex and reflected individual and highly personal circumstances. Nevertheless, certain general typologies can be delineated. Due to the expulsions, which are seen as biographical turning points, the evacuees were unexpectedly pulled out of their familiar cultural and social environment. The evacuations and expulsions were perceived as absolutely unjust and arbitrary by the interviewees. From the moment of expulsion, their desire was to return back to the homeland. This feeling was strengthened by the many problems faced by the expellees in occupied Germany. The cramped and poor living conditions in the receiving areas were experienced as threatening. The admitting society was seen as hostile and the expellees were neither economically nor socially integrated. As the narratives also demonstrate, the evacuees were repeatedly exposed to discrimination because of their social status as refugees. The lack of social integration and the experience of for-

[–] At that time it was not good to be German – a long time.'] Own translation of interview A.St., 2010. In the author's archive.

41 See *supra* n. 4.

eignness ultimately reinforced their desire to return. Probably the most important motive for the resettlement, though, was homesickness. The expellees longed for the intact structures of *Heimat,* of life as they had experienced it before their relocation; as the life stories show, their understanding of *Heimat* was closely linked to their actual places of origin. At the same time, *Heimat* connected cultural 'Germaness' with a specific loyalty to the Hungarian nation, and that created a tension that could not be fully overcome. The returnees' efforts to re-establish themselves in Hungary – to recover *Heimat* – also meant coming to terms with the Socialist system and that, in consequence, meant gradually giving up their German culture, language, and identity.[42]

42 I want to thank the Austrian Agency for International Cooperation in Education and Research (OeAD) for the support, which allowed me to take part at the conferences and to work on this paper. I also want to thank Gary Soroka for his generous help in the completion of this article.

Noémi Nagy

Linguistic Legislation in Hungary during the Era of Dualism

University of Alberta

Introduction

This paper contains part of the results of the author's doctoral research project.[1] This project starts from the recognition that in today's world of globalization the functional decline of smaller or lesser-used languages, simultaneous with the expansion of English as a global *lingua franca*, is faster than ever. In this context, the issue of minority languages and linguistic rights is of utmost actuality and social importance. Although there have been significant developments and endeavors for standardization in the field of minority language protection at the European level, language policies, regulations, and practices related to the linguistic and minority issues of the individual states in Europe still vary considerably. This was perhaps even more so a few hundred years ago. Exploring these differences and raising awareness regarding their grounds (or groundlessness) among policy makers and legislators can serve as a major guide in shaping linguistic legislation.

To this end, the research project includes the analysis of the linguistic legislation and language policy of certain European states – namely, Spain, the United Kingdom, France, Hungary, and Austria – from the first appearance of language-related laws to the present. In addition to this historical approach, the above-mentioned states will be compared with each other, and will be evaluated in the broader context of international and European Union law on language rights. The ultimate goal of the research is to propose *de lege ferenda* recommendations on the standards of just and rightful linguistic legislation, which could contribute to the alleviation of majority-minority conflicts and the peaceful coexistence of different ethnic groups.

Such a complex research field as language rights is claimed by many disciplines: law, sociolinguistics, philosophy, political science, sociology, social psychology, *etc.* Although the research to a certain extent invokes the points of view of

1 This paper was presented at the Meeting of Austrian Centers in Minneapolis, Minnesota, 14–17 September 2014. The author owe thanks to Dr. Franz A.J. Szabo and Dr. Joseph Patrouch, Professors at the University of Alberta, for their helpful review of the manuscript, and for their useful comments.

each of these disciplines, it primarily falls in the scope of legal history. The research findings should always be interpreted in light of the chosen method – *i.e.* analyzing legislative documents related to 'the language issue' – and the purpose of the research (see above). Furthermore, although the subject-matter of language rights, due to the nature of legal regulation and also as a practical necessity, is bound in several ways to the protection of minorities, the research cannot take into consideration all the aspects of the minority question, instead it intends to focus on linguistic legislation.

This paper will discuss only a narrow part of the research project: Hungary's legislation on language use during the era of Dualism, *i.e.* the period of the Austro-Hungarian Monarchy (1867–1918). Nevertheless, presentation of the antecedents is necessary for the proper understanding of linguistic legislation in this period. Similarily, the conclusion will take advantage of the results of the comparative analysis of linguistic legislations of contemporary Western European states.[2]

Official Language Use in the Kingdom of Hungary before 1867: The Introduction of Hungarian as the State Language

The Kingdom of Hungary always consisted of various peoples, as was the case with other empires. However, in contrast to most Western European states, we find no legislation on the official status of the national (Hungarian) language – or on the issue of language use – from the establishment of the Kingdom of Hungary in the 11th century until the end of the 18th century.

In the Kingdom of Hungary, the language of public administration had been *de facto* Latin before the country became part of the Habsburg Empire (1000–1526)[3], and remained that way during 1526–1784 and 1790–1844. German was made the official language of public administration during 1784–1790 as a result of King Joseph II's language decree[4], and again during the period of neo-absolut-

---

2 For further information on the linguistic legislation of Spain, the United Kingdom and France, see the author's following papers (in English): Noémi Nagy, Linguistic Diversity and Language Rights in Spain, in: Studia Iuridica Auctoritate Universitatis Pécs Publicata 150, Essays of Faculty of Law University of Pécs Yearbook of 2012, Pécs 2012, 183–202; Noémi Nagy, Policies and Legislation on Autochthonous Languages in the United Kingdom, in: Studia Iuridica Auctoritate Universitatis Pécs Publicata, No. 151, Essays of Faculty of Law University of Pécs Yearbook of 2013, Pécs 2013, 129–150; Noémi Nagy, The History of Linguistic Legislation in France, in: Journal of European History of Law 4/2, London 2013, 137–143.

3 At least concerning written documents [*lingua diplomatica*]. However, Hungarian was widely used orally in every forum of public life [*lingua publica*], including the Diet (traditional name of the Hungarian Parliament), the royal council, judiciary, local administration, *etc.* *Cf.* István Berkeszi, Rendi országgyűléseink magyarsága [The Hungarianness of our Feudal Diets], Temesvár 1898; Mihály Herczeg, A magyar államnyelv jogai [Rights of the Hungarian State Language], Budapest 1904, 20–60; Orsolya Nádor, Nyelvpolitika. A magyar nyelv politikai státusváltozásai és oktatása a kezdetektől napjainkig [Language Policy. Changes in the political status of the Hungarian language and its education from the beginning until today], Budapest 2002, 43–56.

4 *Cf.* Ferenc Soós, II. József német nyelvrendelete és a hivatalos Magyarország [Joseph II's Order on the German Language and the Official Hungary], in: Ferenc Bíró (Ed.), Tanulmányok a magyar

ism[5], before the Austro-Hungarian Compromise (1849–1867). In the meantime, peoples of the kingdom were free to use their native languages in their daily business. As Baron József Eötvös, one of the most eminent Hungarian statesmen of the 19th century put it:

> 'As if the view that St. Stephen had expressed in his advising letters to his son – "a country where only one language and one custom prevails, is weak" – [...] had been accepted as a governing rule by his descendants: royal power did not work on the assimilation of the country's various peoples, on the contrary, it sought to preserve the special features of the individual parts of the dominion, so that their relationship with the crown do not change. [...] The residents of this homeland, although speaking different languages, considered themselves to be citizens of one country. In terms of their tongues, they remained Slavs, Vlachs, or Germans, but they never for one minute ceased to be Hungarians.'[6]

Ignác Romsics, a prominent contemporary Hungarian historian, shares the same view:

> 'As *nobilis Hungarus* referred to the whole nobility, the university of nobility, regardless of differences in language and origin, so did [...] *hungarus* apply to all inhabitants of the country. Hungarian feudal state law, which created such a deep gap between noble and non-noble, made no difference between Hungarian and non-Hungarian. The issue of nationalities in Hungary simply did not exist before the 18th century.'[7]

---

nyelv ügyének 18. századi történetéből [Studies on the History of the Cause of the Hungarian Language in the 18th Century], Budapest 2005, 261–301.

5 *Cf.* Ágnes Deák, "Nemzeti egyenjogúsítás" 1848–1860 ["National Emancipation" 1848–1860], Budapest 2000, 191–224.

6 ['Mintha a nézet, melyet szent István fiának adott tanácsaiban kimond, hogy «egy nyelvű s szokású ország gyenge! [...], utódai által kormányzási szabályúl fogadtatott volna el: a királyi hatalom nem az ország különböző népeinek assimilatioján dolgozott, sőt inkább abban kereste feladását, hogy a birodalom egyes részeinek sajátosságai feltartatván, a viszony, melyben azok a koronához állanak, ne változzék meg. [...] E hon külön ajkú lakói nyolcz századon át egy ország polgárainak érezték magokat, kik nyelvökre nézve slávok, oláhok, németek maradtak, de soha egy perczig nem szüntek meg magyarok lenni.'] József Eötvös, A nemzetiségi kérdés [The Nationality Question], Pest 1865, 17–23. Translated by the author.

7 ['Ahogy a *nobilis Hungarus* az egész nemességet, a nemesség egyetemét jelentette nyelvi és származási különbségekre való tekintet nélkül, úgy [...] a *hungarus* is az ország minden lakosára vonatkozott. A feudális magyar államjog, amely oly mély szakadékot vont nemes és nem nemes közé, magyar és nem magyar között semmiféle különbséget sem tett. A 18. század előtti Magyarországon nemzetiségi kérdés tehát egyszerűen nem létezett.'] Ignác Romsics, Nemzet és állam a modern magyar történelemben [Nation and State in Modern Hungarian History], in: Pál Pritz – Balázs Sipos – Miklós Zeidler (Eds.), Magyarország helye a 20. századi Európában [Hungary's Place in 20th Century Europe], Budapest 2002, 7–26, here 7f. Translated by the author.

In order to understand the above-mentioned, some terminological clarification is needed. 'Nationalities' is the preferred term in Hungarian legal tradition used instead of 'national minorities' or 'minority nations' to denote the different ethnic groups of the country. Similarily, the pre-modern term 'Hungarian nation' or '*natio Hungarica*' as articulated in Werbőczy's *Tripartitum* was made up only of the '*populus*' (nobles, clergy and free cities), which were not necessarily ethnically Magyar (Hungarian), while the '*plebs*' (serfs and others without political rights), many of whom were ethnically Magyar, were not members of the 'nation'.[8]

The radical change of this situation is due to the interplay of numerous social and political circumstances. József Eötvös's emphasizes five factors turning the issue of nationalities into a state of ferment at the end of the 18th century: (1.) the progress which the peoples of different languages living in Hungary made in civilization – this was manifested mainly in the cultivation of their own languages and literature; (2.) nationalist movements of the neighboring countries sharing a common ethnicity and language with part of Hungary's citizens; (3.) replacing Latin as the language of the legislature and public administration with Hungarian – this gave Hungarian-speakers an advantage they had not possessed before[9]; (4.) rapid progress in the field of politics – even though there was no legal difference between people belonging to different ethnic groups, the majority of the privileged classes *de facto* belonged to the Hungarian nationality, so antagonism between nobles and non-nobles intensified the conflict between nationalities; (5.) the influence, which the people of the country (regardless of language and ethnicity) have gained on public affairs since the democratic transformation.[10]

The introduction of Hungarian as the official language of the state was a gradual process that took place from the end of the 18th century, more significantly from 1830 onwards, by means of a series of smaller or greater concessions from the sovereign, being part of the dynamics of the emergence of modern nationalism.[11] It is important to note that these statutes only applied to Hungary proper (*intra fines regni Hungariae*), but not to the related territories such as the Kingdom of Croatia, the Grand Principality of Transylvania[12], and the Military Frontier.

8 *Cf.* Endre Arató, A magyar "nemzeti" ideológia jellemző vonásai a 18. században [Typical Features of Hungarian "National" Ideology in the 18th Century], in: György Spira – Jenő Szűcs (Eds.), Nemzetiség a feudalizmus korában. Tanulmányok [Nationality in the Age of Feudalism. Studies], Budapest 1972, 130–181.

9 But *cf. supra* n. 4.

10 Eötvös, A nemzetiségi kérdés, 24f.

11 On the construction of 'nation', see Benedict Anderson, Imagined Communities. Reflections on the Origin and Spread of Nationalism, London 1991. On the specific case of Hungary, see Endre Arató, A nemzetiségi kérdés története Magyarországon 1790–1849, I–II. kötet [The History of the Nationality Question in Hungary 1790–1849, Vol. I–II.], Budapest 1960. Oszkár Jászi, A nemzeti államok kialakulása és a nemzetiségi kérdés [The Formation of Nation States and the Nationality Issue], Budapest 1912. Imre Mikó, Nemzetiségi jog és nemzetiségi politika [Nationality Law and Nationality Policy], Budapest 1944.

12 On the official status of the Hungarian language in Transylvania, see Judit Pál, A hivatalos nyelv és a hivatali nyelvhasználat kérdése Erdélyben a 19. század közepén [The Question of Official Lan-

The first piece of the series of language laws was born as a response to Joseph II's language reform of 1784 replacing Latin with German as the empire's official language. In 'Act XVI of 1790/91' the king promised that henceforth no foreign language will be used in matters of any kind. This provision confirmed the official status of Latin in governmental affairs, if only temporarily. As a concession, the king also agreed to allow Hungarian to be taught at institutions of higher learning. For this purpose he pledged to appoint Hungarian-language teachers in high schools, academies and the university in Pest-Buda.[13] 'Act VII of 1792 on the teaching and using of Hungarian language' ordained the teaching of Hungarian as an ordinary subject within the borders of the country, and as an extraordinary subject in the related lands, so that after a certain period of time only those persons could hold public office who possessed a certificate to prove their knowledge of the national language. However, to the request that the Royal Council of Governors respond in Hungarian to all communications of the counties which it might receive in that language, only another promise was made: a committee will present a report on this issue at the next session of the Diet.[14] Under Emperor Francis I's absolutist system, official use of the Hungarian language disappeared from the political agenda.[15] In 'Act IV of 1805', the king permitted only that addresses to His Majesty and to the Hungarian Royal Chancellery should be drawn up in Hungarian and Latin with the text arranged in columns side by side; county municipalities might write to the Governor's Council in Hungarian; court proceedings might be started in Hungarian but had to be finished in Latin at the *Curia*.[16] Finally, the king promised to implement the provision of the 1792 law concerning the teaching of Hungarian as an ordinary subject.[17] According to 'Act VIII of 1830 on the use of the national language', the Governor's Council had to respond to county municipalities in Hungarian, and the *Curia* had to decide Hungarian-language appeals in the same language. Lawsuits pending before district, county, and city courts, as well as the tribunals of the Holy See might be conducted in the Hungarian language; but the above-mentioned tribunals, in which the Hungarian language had not been used so far, might decide lawsuits in either Hungarian or Latin. The Act also prescribed Hungarian language proficiency as a requirement for holding pub-

---

guage and Official Language Use in Transylvania in the Middle of the 19th Century], in: Regio 16/1, Budapest 2005, 3–26.

13 '1790/91. évi XVI. törvénycikk: hogy a nyilvános ügyek intézésére idegen nyelv ne használtassék, a magyar nyelv pedig megtartassék', in: *Corpus Juris Hungarici,* Digitalizált Törvényhozási Tudástár [Digitized Legislative Knowledge Base], Library of the Hungarian Parliament: http://dtt.ogyk.hu. The term 'act' refers to a legislative instrument formally adopted by the Hungarian Parliament and sanctioned by the king. Translated by the author.

14 '1792. évi VII. törvénycikk a magyar nyelv tanításáról és használatáról', *cf. supra* n. 14.

15 See Gyula Szekfű, Iratok a magyar államnyelv kérdésének történetéhez 1790–1848 [Documents Concerning the History of the Question of Hungarian State Language 1790–1848], Budapest 1926, 62–104.

16 Traditional name for the Supreme Court of Hungary.

17 '1805. évi IV. törvénycikk a magyar nyelv használatáról', *cf. supra* n. 14.

lic office (this did not apply to those already being in such a position), and – after 1834 – for passing the bar examination.[18]

From the second half of the 1830s, there was a marked acceleration in strengthening the official status of Hungarian. 'Act III of 1836 on the Hungarian language' ordered legislative acts to be published in Latin and Hungarian, where in case of doubt the Hungarian version was to prevail. Litigation before the Royal Court of Appeal (Royal Table) could henceforth be conducted in Hungarian, and in these cases the royal court of Vienna had to decide in the same language. The act also provided for the possibility of issuing official certificates and registering births in Hungarian, and for the establishment of a Hungarian-language department at the Romanian seminary and teacher-training institute in Arad.[19] Pursuant to 'Act VI of 1840 on the Hungarian language', addresses of the Diet and county municipalities were henceforth to be written only in Hungarian; rescripts and circular letters of the Royal Council of Governors were to be sent out in Hungarian; county municipalities were to write to each other as well as to the ecclesiastical authorities and the Hungarian regiments in Hungarian. The Royal Court Chamber, with those county municipalities which addressed it in Hungarian, were to correspond in the same language. After a lapse of three years, all parish registers had to be kept in Hungarian, even where the language of the religious service was not Hungarian; and from that point on only Hungarian-speakers would be admitted to church service (regardless of religion).[20] Finally, 'Act II of 1844 on the Hungarian language and nationality' made Hungarian the exclusive language of the Parliament, legislature, courts, documents issued by the Hungarian Royal Chancellery, as well as discussions and records of the Royal Council of Governors. Croats were allowed to speak Latin in the Hungarian Diet for six further years. Hungarian was also declared to be the language of public instruction, but this was left to be dealt with by a special law.[21]

These language laws contained no provisions for the official use of minority languages, which eventually led to ethnic conflicts. The situation further deteriorated during the 1848/1849 revolution and war of independence since Non-Hungarian nationalities were very disappointed that the recognition of their national existence and rights was missing from the revolutionary achievements.[22] From among the statutes of April 1848, two touched upon the issue of language use, both referring to the Hungarian language. 'Act V of 1848 on the election of parliamentary deputies on the basis of representation of the people' imposed the knowledge of the Hungarian language as a prerequisite for passive suffrage (the right to

18 '1830. évi VIII. törvénycikk a nemzeti nyelv használatáról', *cf. supra* n. 14.

19 '1836. évi III. törvénycikk a Magyar Nyelvről', *cf. supra* n. 14.

20 '1840. évi VI. törvénycikk a magyar nyelvről', *cf. supra* n. 14.

21 '1844. évi II. törvénycikk a magyar nyelvről és nemzetiségről', *cf. supra* n. 14.

22 *Cf.* László Katus, Nemzetiségi kérdés, nemzetiségi politika 1848–1849-ben [Nationality Question, Nationality Policy in 1848–1849], Kisebbségkutatás 11/1, Budapest 2002, 66–76.

run for office)[23], while 'Act XVI of 1848 on the temporary exercise of county authority' determined Hungarian as the only language of discussion at county committees and assemblies in the territory of Hungary.[24]

The 'Resolution of 28 July 1849 of the House of Representatives on the rights of nationalities' sought to find a solution for the nationality problem by securing linguistic rights for the free national development of every people living in the territory of the Hungarian kingdom. In matters of state, administration, justice, and the military, Hungarian as the language of diplomacy had to be used, but otherwise the freedom of language use was provided. Specifically, the act prescribed the following: during the deliberations of communities[25] and county municipalities, everyone could use either Hungarian or their mother tongue; records of communities could be drawn up in any language of their choice; records of county municipalities had to be drawn up in Hungarian and the language(s) of those ethnic groups which composed more than half of the population. The same rule applied to proceedings before juries and single-judge tribunals if oral proceedings took place. In elementary schools, the community or the ecclesiastical language was to be used. Petitions could be submitted in one's mother tongue anywhere. Unfortunately, the resolution on the rights of nationalities came too late, and it was never implemented because of the defeat of the war of independence.[26]

The 1868 Nationalities Act and its Heritage

Although the progressive provisions of the 1849 resolution were brushed aside by imperial autocracy, its spirit did not fade away. After 20 years of having German as the official language of Hungary, the 1868 Nationalities Act as well as several previous proposals contained the very same ideas. It is important to note that most of the provisions of these documents referred to the issue of language use. The reason was that the majority of Hungarian politicians considered almost exclusively the linguistic, and to a lesser degree, religious aspects of the nationality ques-

23 '1848. évi V. törvénycikk az országgyülési követeknek népképviselet alapján választásáról', *cf. supra* n. 14.

24 '1848. évi XVI. törvénycikk a megyei hatóság ideiglenes gyakorlatáról', *cf. supra* n. 14.

25 *I.e.* local municipalities/localities/settlements/villages not having a status of a city. In the traditional Hungarian meaning of the word, municipality [törvényhatóság] as the governing body of an administrative division having corporate status was used only for counties and cities. Therefore in this paper the term community [község] will be used when referring to the local level of administration. Note that in this sense community means something else than a group of people living in the same place or having a particular characteristic in common.

26 'A képviselőház határozata a nemzetiségek jogairól Szegeden', in: Sándor Balogh (Ed.), A magyar állam és a nemzetiségek. A magyarországi nemzetiségi kérdés történetének jogforrásai 1848–1993 [The Hungarian State and the Nationalities. Legal Sources of the History of the Nationality Question in Hungary 1848–1993], Budapest 2002, 43f. The resolution would have become Act VIII of 1849 if sanctioned by the king which never happened.

tion.[27] However, the representatives of the biggest nationality groups had already expressed the need for political or territorial autonomy as early as 1848/1849.[28]

The '1861 report of the House of Representative's committee on the nationalities question' identified two basic principles: on the one hand, that 'all citizens of Hungary regardless of the language they speak form politically one single nation, the indivisible and unitary Hungarian nation corresponding to the historic notion of the Hungarian state', on the other, that 'all the peoples living in the country [...] are considered as nationalities of equal rights'. According to the report, community and county assemblies were to decide on the language of administration but the local minority could also demand the use of its own language. The bill did not use the term 'state language', instead it referred to Hungarian as the administrative language of the Parliament and state authorities.[29]

The Parliament was unable to debate the bill due to its dissolution. Reopened in December 1865, the Parliament commissioned a 40-member committee to draft a nationalities bill in April 1866. The committee appointed a five-member sub-committee to draw up the text of the specific provisions. In February 1867, Romanian and Serb deputies presented their common draft to this sub-committee which recognized the six largest historic peoples of the country, namely Hungarians, Romanians, Serbs, Slovaks, Rusyns, and Germans as nations of equal rights (other ethnic groups, such as Slovenes, Croats, Greeks, *etc.* were disregarded). For the purposes of the representation of every nationality and to define the scope of languages, the minority proposal envisaged the rounding-off of counties and districts on the basis of the majority rule so that they would mainly be composed of one nationality. Deputies of nationalities were to be allowed to address the Parliament in their own language.[30]

'The Proposal of June 1867 of the sub-committee commissioned on the nationalities question', based on the compromissory principles of Eötvös, intended to ensure free language use in every forum of public life. In the lower and mid-levels of administration, the majority language was to be used along with the languages of nationalities above one-fifth of the population. The proposal did not contain any reference to the Hungarian political nation and continued to designate the Hungarian language as the administrative language of the government.[31] The proposal of the sub-committee stirred protest in radical Hungarian public opinion, especially among county assemblies and in the nationalist press, for being too liberal. More than a year passed before a new bill was prepared with considerable changes

27 There are counterexamples, as well: Eötvös, for instance, was a well-known advocate of self-government.

28 Katus, Nemzetiségi kérdés, 70f.

29 'Az 1861. évi képviselőházi nemzetiségi bizottmány jelentése', in: Balogh, A magyar állam, 47–49.

30 'A nemzetiségi képviselők törvényjavaslata a nemzetiségi jogokról', *ibid.*, 51–53.

31 'A nemzetiségi ügyben kiküldött albizottság 1867-es javaslata', *ibid.*, 54–58. There is only one allusion to 'the official language of the state', in Article 12, which must have remained in the text by accident.

to the text of June 1867.[32] The proposal of October 1868 of the 40-member nationalities committee put considerable emphasis on the official language of the state in mid-level administration as well. The official language of county municipalities was to be Hungarian, but records could also be kept in the languages of nationalities making up at least one-fifth of the population. The central drafting committee adopted the proposal of the nationalities committee almost unchanged.[33] The Nationalities Bill was discussed from 24 November to 4 December 1868 along with the minority proposal of February 1867. Ferenc Deák also presented his own alternative bill that, in addition to a few minor modifications in content and structure, differed in one significant point from the bill of the drafting committee: it returned to the concept of a single political nation used in the 1861 proposal. After a thunderous debate and despite nationalities' firm protest, the Nationalities Bill was passed on the basis of Deák's proposal.[34]

'Act XLIV of 1868 on the equal rights[35] of nationalities' declared in its preamble that 'all citizens of Hungary [...] form politically one nation, the indivisible unitary Hungarian nation, of which every citizen of this homeland is a member of equal rights, regardless to what nationality they belong [...]. [T]his legal equality may be subject to special rules concerning only the official use of the various languages of the country, and only in so far as is rendered necessary by the unity of the country, the practical possibility of government and administration, and the accurate administration of justice'.[36] Since the Nationalities Act clearly indicated that the regulations set out therein concerned the official use of the various languages, and since almost all of its provisions referred to the use of languages, it is obvious that it should be considered a language law.[37]

---

32 László Katus – József Eötvös – Ferenc Deák, Laws on Nationalities, in: Ignác Romsics – Béla K. Király (Eds.), Geopolitics in the Danube Region. Hungarian Reconciliation Efforts 1848–1998, Budapest 1999, 133–160, here 150.

33 Gábor G. Kemény (Ed.), Iratok a nemzetiségi kérdés történetéhez Magyarországon a dualizmus korában 1867–1918, I. kötet [Documents Concerning the History of the Nationality Question in Hungary during the era of Dualism 1867–1918], Budapest 1952, 106–111.

34 *Ibid.*, 125–162.

35 A loan-translation of the German word *Gleichberechtigung* [in Hungarian: *egyenjogúság*]. Other scholars prefer to translate the title of the law as 'the equality of nationalities' or 'the equality of nationality rights'.

36 '1868. évi XLIV. törvénycikk a nemzetiségek egyenjogúság tárgyában', *cf. supra* n. 14.

37 The Nationalities Act did not apply to Croatia since issues related to public law between Hungary and Croatia were arranged by a separate act on the enactment of the Croatian-Hungarian settlement (*i.e.* '1868. évi XXX. törvénycikk a Magyarország s Horvát-, Szlavon- és Dalmátországok közt fennforgott közjogi kérdések kiegyenlítése iránt létrejött egyezmény becikkelyezéséről'). Provisions concerning language use were the following: the coronation charter had to be issued in the Croatian language, as well (Art. 2); in the territory of Croatia, the language of legislature, administration, justice and the common government was Croatian (Art. 56–57); proposals and submissions in Croatian-Slavonic were to be accepted and replied to in the same language by the common government (Art. 58); in the common Parliament and its delegations, the Croatian language could also be used (Art. 59); statutes enacted for Croatia by the common legislature were to be issued in Croatian, as well (Art. 60). *Cf. supra* n. 14.

Although the Nationalities Act stipulated that the state language of Hungary is Hungarian, it ensured an extensive use of the languages of other nationalities in every forum of public life. One of the most important individual rights was that all citizens could address their respective community, county and church meetings and submit petitions to these authorities in their own language. Another significant provision referred to public employment: 'ability remains the only guiding principle for holding offices, and nationality status will not be considered an obstacle to rising to any office or position in the country. Moreover, the state government will make sure that in the national offices of judges and public administration, and especially the offices of Lord-Lieutenants, as much as possible, persons belonging to various nationalities will be employed who are perfectly proficient in the required languages and are otherwise suitable' (Art. 27).[38]

Detailed rules of the Nationalities Act can be grouped into five major areas: (1.) Legislature: The official language of the Parliament – including parliamentary debates and administration – was to be Hungarian. Laws were to be drawn up in Hungarian but also published in the languages of every nationality. (2.) Government: The official language of the government was to be Hungarian. All citizens could address the government in their mother tongue, and in response to these petitions, the government had to issue an authentic translation of the original Hungarian-version decision as well. (3.) County and city municipalities: The language of record and internal administration was to be Hungarian, plus any other language desired by one-fifth of the deputies. As much as possible, officials of municipal authorities were to use the language of their clients during official interactions with communities, individuals and associations. (4.) Communities were to have the right to choose the language of their records and internal administration (community language). In addition to this language, any other language had to be used if one-fifth of the deputies so desired. Officials of local authorities were obligated to use the language of their clients. (5.) Justice: Before community courts, everyone had the right to use their own language. Before district courts, (one of) the community language(s) could be used. Interrogation and any other judicial actions were to be conducted in the language of the parties/the interrogated person. Records of the trial and sentences were to be written in one of the languages of the respective county municipality. The official language of courts appointed by the state government (*i.e.* appellate and higher courts) was to be Hungarian. Church courts could decide about their own language of administration. (Church autonomy was secured in other areas as well.)[39]

Since education was to be regulated by a specific law, the Nationalities Act provided only a framework prescribing that it belonged to the duties of the Minister of Education to ensure that citizens of the same nationality living together in considerable numbers were to be able to obtain instruction in their mother tongue, be-

38 Translation of this provision is based on Katus, József Eötvös, 154.

39 *Cf. supra* n. 38.

low the level of higher (academic) education. As before, private individuals, associations, churches and communities of any nationality had the right to establish and run schools.

As we have seen, according to the Nationalities Act of 1868, the official use of the languages of non-Hungarian nationalities was legally ensured at all levels of the public sphere. This principle was reinforced by additional pieces of legislation, which touched upon areas regulated by the 1868 law.[40] Even if we do not go as far as stating that in light of these provisions Hungary actually had not only one but several state languages[41], we must certainly agree with Katus in that the Nationalities Act 'was an outstanding creation of Hungarian and East Central European liberalism'.[42]

Language Use in Education

According to the 'Act XXXVIII of 1868 on public education' (submitted by then Minister of Education Eötvös), 'every pupil shall receive instruction in their mother tongue as long as it is among the predominant languages of the community. For this reason, mixed communities shall employ teachers who are able to teach in the predominant languages. In populous communities, where a great number of speakers of various languages live together, so far as the community can afford, assistant teachers of different languages will also be employed.' Provision for mother-tongue education applied to elementary (6–12 years) and higher (12–15 years) public schools, and so-called civic schools alike. Furthermore, in non-Hungarian higher public schools, civic schools, and teacher training institutions, the Hungarian language became a compulsory subject.[43]

---

40 'Act IV of 1869 on the exercise of judicial power' (1869. évi IV. törvénycikk a bírói hatalom gyakorlásáról, *cf. supra* n. 14.) separated jurisdiction from public administration. It prescribed that when appointing judges to lower courts special attention should be given to the fair consideration of candidates of different nationalities living in the judicial district concerned (Article 4). One of the conditions of eligibility for judicial office was being able to meet the requirements of the Nationalities Act (Article 6). The same provision applied to prosecution officials and public notaries in accordance with 'Act XXXIII of 1871' (1871. évi XXXIII. törvénycikk a királyi ügyészségről, *cf. supra* n. 14.), Article 15, and 'Act XXXV of 1874' (1874. évi XXXV. törvénycikk a királyi közjegyzőkről, *cf. supra* n. 14.), Article 2, respectively. 'Act XLII of 1870' (1870. évi XLII. törvénycikk a köztörvényhatóságok rendezéséről, *cf. supra* n. 14.), Article 68, then 'Act XXI of 1886' (1886. évi XXI. törvénycikk a törvényhatóságokról, *cf. supra* n. 14.), Article 82, on municipalities, and 'Act XXII of 1886 on communities' (1886. évi XXII. törvénycikk a községekről, *cf. supra* n. 14.), Article 77, stated that the provisions of the Nationalities Act should also be considered when appointing municipal and community officials. Out of the above-mentioned public offices, only notaries were expressly required to be proficient in the official language of the state.

41 György Andrássy, Nyelvszabadság. Egy egyetemes elismerésre váró egyetemes emberi jog [Freedom of Language. A Universal Human Right to be Universally Recognized], Budapest/Pécs 2013, 176f.

42 Katus, József Eötvös, 157. Most scholars agree on that even if the elaborate provisions of the 1868 Nationalities Act 'were the most advanced such measures ever enacted in Europe', they were not properly implemented in practice. However, we lack detailed research on this issue. *Cf.* Robert John Weston Evans, Language and State Building. The Case of the Habsburg Monarchy, in: Austrian History Yearbook 35, Minneapolis 2004, 1–24, here 17.

43 '1869. évi IV. törvénycikk a bírói hatalom gyakorlásáról', *cf. supra* n. 14.

It was only a decade later – pursuant to 'Act XVIII of 1879 on the teaching of the Hungarian language in public educational institutions' – that Hungarian as a compulsory subject was prescribed in elementary schools as well. For this purpose, the law defined the required level of knowledge of the Hungarian language in the case of non-Hungarian teacher training, as well: in teacher training institutions, the Hungarian language should be taught in a number of lessons so that throughout the course every teacher candidate could acquire it in speech and writing. After 1882, only those could be appointed as schoolteachers who had a sufficient command of the Hungarian language both orally and in writing for being capable of teaching it. Provision for the education of the Hungarian language in elementary schools had to be put in place gradually: teaching of Hungarian had to be started in the year after the coming into force of the act in schools, in which there was a teacher capable of teaching the Hungarian language; in other places, only when a teacher capable of teaching Hungarian would be employed – that is, in 1882 the earliest.[44]

Teaching 'of (or rather in)' the state language was a common practice in contemporary Europe. In this respect, the education laws of 1868 and 1879 fit well into the liberal framework of linguistic legislation in Hungary in the middle of the 19th century. The image becomes more obscure when considering that the government did not give permission to open new secondary schools for the nationalities and closed a few of the existing ones. By dissolving three Slovak secondary schools in 1874–1875, mother-tongue secondary education for the Slovaks was eliminated completely.[45] This is reflected in the series of ministerial decrees[46], trying to enforce the implementation of the education law over 25 years. In the introduction to an 1885 decree by the Minister of Religion and Public Education Ágoston Trefort (1817–1888), 'Act XVIII of 1879 ordered the compulsory teaching of the Hungarian language in all public education institutions, and although [...] in my circulars I have repeatedly taken measures towards the correct implementation of the act, school owners quite often neglect the definite provisions of the law when it comes to employing teachers or including the Hungarian language in the curriculum'.[47]

Teaching of the Hungarian language was further extended to secondary (Act XXX of 1883) and pre-primary (Act XV of 1891) education, which met fierce resistance on the side of non-Hungarian nationalities. The act on secondary education prescribed the teaching of the Hungarian language as an ordinary subject in secondary schools (Articles 3–4). School completion certificates had to be issued

44 '1879. évi XVIII. törvénycikk a magyar nyelv tanitásáról a népoktatási tanintézetekben', *cf. supra* n. 14.

45 Balogh, A magyar állam, 11, 102.

46 These were issued in 1879, 1882, 1883, 1885, 1890, 1902 and 1905 (two in 1882 and 1905).

47 Trefort Ágoston vallás- és közoktatásügyi miniszter valamennyi kir. tanfelügyelőséghez, egyházi főhatósághoz és közigazgatási bizottsághoz intézett 20301/1885. sz. rendelete [Decree no. 20301/1885 of Ágoston Trefort, Minister of Religion and Public Education, to all royal school inspectorates, ecclesiastical authorities, and administrative committees], in: Balogh, A magyar állam, 122–124.

in Hungarian, accompanied by a translation upon request in the language of instruction of the given school or in Latin (Article 22). The language of examination for acquiring a secondary school teacher's certificate was Hungarian, but the Minister of Education could give exemptions for ten years (Article 70).[48] The Act on pre-primary education prescribed that children of three to six years having a non-Hungarian mother tongue had to be introduced to the knowledge of Hungarian as the state language (Article 8). It followed from this that kindergarten teachers and nurses were required to be proficient in Hungarian (Article 12).[49]

Although none of the educational statutes contained provisions for the 'language of instruction', in the second half of the 19th century, there was a perceptible shift in the proportion of Hungarian monolingual, nationality and mixed language (*i.e.* Hungarian and a nationality language in parallel classes) schools. Data concerning the distribution of elementary schools according to the language of instruction are as follows: in 1869, 42.2 percent Hungarian, 47.3 precent nationality language, and 10.5 percent mixed; in 1890, 53.5 percent Hungarian, 29.5 percent nationality language, and 17 percent mixed; in 1901/1902: 62 percent Hungarian, 19 percent nationality language, and 19 percent mixed.[50] The increase in the proportion of Hungarian monolingual schools can be explained by, among other things, socio-economic factors (not dealt with here) and school funding policy. Every attempt was made to avoid overt discrimination, but in certain cases the law permitted state intervention, which was especially prejudicial to the schools of non-Hungarian nationalities. For example, pursuant to 'Act XXVI of 1893 on the arrangement of the salaries of teachers working in community and denominational elementary schools', receiving state aid possibly entailed state intervention in the course of employing teachers or conducting disciplinary proceedings against them. Disciplinary proceedings could be conducted for example against teachers following an anti-state direction that meant, *inter alia*, misconduct against the use of the state language as specified by law (Article 13).[51]

As previously mentioned, provisions for the teaching of Hungarian were improperly executed in spite of repeated ministerial appeals. The Minister of Education Albert Berzeviczy (1853–1936) pointed out in his reasoning attached to a 1904 bill submitted by him that 'there are hardly any Hungarian-speakers among those pupils who attended denominational schools having a non-Hungarian language as the sole language of instruction', and 'we have 1340 public elementary schools where teaching of the Hungarian language did not take place' (data for the 1901/02

48 '1883. évi XXX. törvénycikk a a középiskolákról és azok tanárainak képesítéséről', *cf. supra* n. 14.

49 '1891. évi XV. törvénycikk a kisdedóvásról', *cf. supra* n. 14.

50 Balogh, A magyar állam, 173f. *Cf.* also László Marácz, Multilingualism in the Transleithanien Part of the Austro-Hungarian Empire (1867–1918). Policy and Practice, in: Jezikoslovje 13/2, Osijek 2002, 269–298, here especially 285–287.

51 '1893. évi XXVI. törvénycikk a községi, valamint a hitfelekezetek által fenntartott elemi iskolákban működő tanitók és tanitónők fizetésének rendezéséről', *cf. supra* n. 14.

Academic Year).[52] The government decided that it was time for firm action. The intelligentia of non-Hungarian nationalities greeted Berzeviczy's bill with strong aversion, and although it did not become law due to the fall of István Tisza's government, a substantial part of its content was included into the act named after the future Minister of Education Count Albert Apponyi (1846–1933).[53]

The infamous *Lex Apponyi* ('Act XXVII of 1907 on the legal relations of non-state elementary schools and on the salaries of teachers in communities and denominations') intended to improve the financial conditions of schoolteachers (and it actually did so), however, state aid entailed significant control and intervention. For example, teachers could get fired if they neglected the teaching of the Hungarian language, or followed a tendency considered hostile towards the State. The main linguistic rules of the act are included in Articles 18–19: in denominational schools, Hungarian-speaking pupils were to be instructed in Hungarian if they composed 20 percent of the class. If they composed more than 50 percent, Hungarian was prescribed as the language of instruction for all children. In non-Hungarian elementary schools, whether in receipt of state aid or not, pupils had to be taught the Hungarian language in the manner and for the time prescribed by the minister, so that children of non-Hungarian mother tongue on the completion of their fourth school year could express their thoughts comprehensibly in Hungarian both in speaking and writing. The act also ordered that wherever Hungarian had already been introduced as the language of instruction, the *status quo* could never be changed, and that in all continuation schools Hungarian had to be the language of instruction.[54]

The parliamentary debate of *Lex Apponyi* stimulated huge protests even outside the walls of Parliament. Yet, the implementation of the law began immediately after its passage, and further fueled the conflict between Hungarians and the other nationalities of the Kingdom.[55] In 1914, the new Minister of Education made some concessions to calm the turbulent atmosphere: He requested church authorities to use the pupils' mother tongue as the language of the cathecism[56]; furthermore, he provided for the use as an auxiliary language and the teaching as a subject of nationalities' languages in state (!) elementary schools, *i.e.* in those schools where the language of the instruction was obligatorily Hungarian.[57] Of course, non-Hun-

52 Out of the 17 299 elementary schools 3343 (19 percent) had a nationality language as the sole medium of instruction, and 97 percent of these (3249 schools) were maintained by church denominations. *Cf.* Balogh, A magyar állam, 173f.

53 *Ibid.*, 175.

54 '1907. évi XXVII. törvénycikk a nem állami elemi népiskolák jogviszonyairól és a községi és hitfelekezeti néptanitók járandóságairól', *cf. supra* n. 14.

55 *Ibid.*, 199f.

56 A m. kir. vallás- és közoktatásügyi miniszter 1914. évi 1797. eln. sz. megkeresése valamennyi főtisztelendő egyházi főhatósághoz a hitoktatás nyelvéről a népoktatási tanintézetekben [Request no. 1797/1914 of the Hun. Royal Minister of Religion and Public Education to all honorable ecclesiestical authorites on the language of religious instruction in public schools], in: *ibid.*, 205.

57 A m. kir. vallás- és közoktatásügyi miniszter 1914. évi 114 000. sz. rendelete (utasítása) az állami elemi népiskolákban a nem magyar anyanyelvnek kisegítő nyelvként való felhasználásáról, és mint

garian nationalities were also entitled to manage their own schools with their own language as the language of instruction. Although it was already too late to change the course of events, the intent and content of these regulations are commendable.

Further Legislation on Language Use

So far the most important pieces of legislation that determined most domains of language use have been discussed. These are the Nationalities Act of 1868, which remained in force during the whole period of Dualism, and a series of education laws. A few statutes remain to be examined which are less frequently mentioned in scholarship but are equally important in order to have a complete picture of linguistic legislation in Dualist Hungary. 'Act V of 1890' on the Hungarian army designated Hungarian (in Croatia, Croatian) as the language of military service and command (Article 18).[58] 'Act IV of 1898 on the names of communities and other localities' decreed that every locality was to have only one official name to be established by a special committee under the supervision of the Ministry of Interior.[59] Even though it was not set out that the official name must be Hungarian, in practice, in the case of bi- or multilingual communities, this rule prevailed.[60] 'Act XLIX of 1907 on the rules of the railway service' determined Hungarian as the official language of railway service. From then onwards only those people were to be employed by Hungarian railroad companies who had command of the Hungarian language.[61] Circular no. 152 635/1907 of the Minister of Interior required county officials who were 'in continuous and regular contact with the people [...] to have a command of the language of the population of the respective district, or at least to have such a level of language proficiency that they are able to freely communicate with the people'.[62] 'Act XXXVIII of 1908' on public health required the oral and written command of the Hungarian language from city, community, and district physicians, but also obligated them to acquire the language spoken by the majority of the population in the area of their activities, at least to the extent nec-

tantárgynak tervszerű tanításáról [Decree (order) no. 114 000/1914 of the Hun. Royal Minister of Religion and Public Education on the use as an auxiliary language and the systematic teaching as a subject of non-Hungarian mother tongues in state elementary schools], in: *ibid.*, 206–209.

58 '1890. évi V. törvénycikk a honvédségről', *cf. supra* n. 14.

59 '1898. évi IV. törvénycikk a község- és egyéb helynevekről', *cf. supra* n. 14.

60 Iván Kápolnai, A történeti Magyarország városainak és községeinek névváltozatai az Országos Községi Törzskönyvbizottság iratanyaga alapján (1898–1913) [Name Variations of Towns and Communities in Historic Hungary According to the Archives of the National Committee on Municipal Registers (1898–1913)], in: Statisztikai Szemle 75/8–9, Budapest 1997, 767–770.

61 '1907. évi XLIX. törvénycikk a a vasuti szolgálati rendtartásról', *cf. supra* n. 14.

62 A m. kir. belügyminiszter 1907. évi 152 635. sz. körrendelete valamennyi vármegyei törvényhatósághoz a vármegyék járási tisztviselőitől megkívánandó nyelvismeretről [Circular no. 152 635/1907 of the Hun. Royal Minister of Interior to all County Municipalities on the Language Knowledge Required from District Officials of the Counties], in: Balogh, A magyar állam, 201.

essary to comply with their medical profession (Article 7).[63] Pursuant to 'Act I of 1911 on the Code of Civil Procedure' the language of the judiciary uniformly became Hungarian; this was not expressly declared but clearly follows from the linguistic rules of the act. It was guaranteed that whenever a non-Hungarian speaking person was to be interrogated, an interpreter should be used (Article 229).[64] To summarize, part of the above-mentioned legislative instruments aimed at further establishing and securing the position of Hungarian as the state language, while others (including the educational decrees of 1914) ensured language rights for nationalities. This fact points to the ambivalent nature of Hungarian governments' nationalities policy at the end of Dualism.

Concluding Remarks

In Hungary, in contrast to some Western European countries, we do not find a single piece of legislation dealing with the official status or use of Hungarian (or any other language) from the establishment of the Kingdom to the end of the 18th century. The language of public administration was *de facto* Latin before the country became part of the Habsburg Empire in the 16th century, and after that Latin with two brief interludes of German. In the meantime, the peoples of Hungary were free to use their native languages in their daily lives. The first legislative instrument which can be considered as the embodiment of a proper language policy was probably Emperor Joseph II's order of 1784 making German the official language of public administration. Here began the struggle for the introduction of Hungarian as the official language of the state which happened step by step during the first half of the 19th century, encountering great resistance from the other ethnic groups within the Kingdom of Hungary.

Amid power struggles with the Austrian monarchy along with the rise of Hungarian nationalism, the devotion for securing the official status – and later on, the primacy – of the Hungarian language is understandable. However, the protest of other nationalities against Hungarian as the 'sole' official language of the country (enacted in 1844) is also justifiable considering that in the middle of the 19th century, out of 13 million inhabitants, only 5.4 million people, *i.e.* about 40 percent of the population were ethnic Hungarians. The remaining 60 percent consisted of 2.5 million Romanians, 1.8 million Slovakians, 1.5 million Germans, 1 million Serbs, 0.5 million Ruthenians, and 0.5 million other nationalities.[65]

There is no doubt that the Hungarian Nationalities Act 1868 was unique in contemporary Europe because, in addition to the state language, the languages of non-Hungarian nationalities were also permitted in the public space (and in pri-

63 'A közegészségügy rendezéséről szóló 1876:XIV. tc.II. rész I. fejezetének (Közegészségügyi szolgálat a községeknél) módositásáról', *cf. supra* n. 14.

64 '1911. évi I. törvénycikk a polgári perrendtartásról', *cf. supra* n. 14.

65 *Ibid*, 5.

vate life as well). To be precise, their official use was not only permitted, but legally ensured at all levels of public sphere. No wonder that Arthur May described the Nationalities Act as 'one of the most enlightened measures of its kind ever adopted'.[66] Positive values of the law were later recognized by originally protesting minority deputies as well. The problem was not with the law itself but with its improper execution[67] and that compared to such an exemplary regulation, everything else that followed could only be a step back. As Cieger pointed out, 'while the law of 1868 was intended by its creators (Eötvös, Deák) to be the starting point of a process, it was actually one of the last stages of the great liberal reform momentum preceding the [Austro-Hungarian] Compromise'.[68]

As for education law, other nationalities considered the introduction of the teaching of Hungarian as a serious violation of their equal rights. Thus, Hungarian education law from 1879 onwards might be a step back from the liberal regulations of 1868, nevertheless, it – including the controversial *Lex Apponyi* – still ensured significantly more language rights than education laws of contemporary Western European states.

66 Arthur May, The Habsburg Monarchy, 1867–1914, Cambridge 1965, 83. Cited by László Péter, Law XLIV of 1868 'On the Equality of Nationality Rights' and the Language of Local Administration, in: Miklós Lojkó (Ed.), Hungary's Long Nineteenth Century. Consitutional and Democratic Traditions in a European Perspective. Collected Studies of László Péter, Leiden/Boston 2012, 343–354, here 343.

67 Balogh, A magyar állam, 9f., 95. It is important to note however, that since implementation of the law mainly belonged to autonomous municipal, communal and parish bodies, the situation varied from county to county and from community to community. Katus, József Eötvös, 156f.

68 András Cieger, Liberalizmus és hatalmi érdek. A szabadságjogokra vonatkozó politikusi dilemmák a dualizmus kori Magyarországon [Liberalism and Power Interests. Politicians' Dilemmas on Rights and Freedoms in Hungary during the Era of Dualism], in: Magyar kisebbség 14/1–2, Kolozsvár 2009, 81–92, here 92.

III. Identity (Re-)visited

Nir Barak

Hundertwasser's Vienna: Architecture, Urban Identity, and Environmental Sentiments

Hebrew University of Jerusalem

This paper analyzes and interprets the Viennese works of Friedensreich Hundertwasser (1928–2000) and their possible contribution to theories of urban political identity and environmental theory. Hundertwasser was a prominent and influential figure in Austrian culture throughout the second half of the 20th century and his works are symbols of important trends in Austrian cultural heritage of post-World War II. His art was adored by the general public and is still inspirational for many people. His Vienna residential building is one of the most visited sites in Austria and his works still receive ongoing attention. His art and architecture are mostly appreciated due to their aesthetic beauty and their playfulness; however, it seems that the sociopolitical and ecological aspects are never fully realized.

The interpretive analysis offered in this paper is twofold and focuses mainly on the Hundertwasserhaus in Vienna.[1] The first analysis is synchronic which means assessing the relation of the building to other aspects at the same time and in the present. This analysis brings forward implicit ecological characteristics of this building. The main argument is that these implicit ecological features may provide a source of inspiration for environmental philosophy in urban areas. The second analysis is diachronic which means studying or establishing the relation of the building to previous historical expressions in the same branch of cultural activity. The analysis is in the light of contemporary theories of urban political identity and some historical perspectives on Vienna. The main argument is that this building is deeply Viennese in essence and constantly corresponds with – historically and symbolically. While focusing mainly on the Hundertwasserhaus, in both cases the analysis is not limited only to that building and refers to other works as well.

Many are familiar with Hundertwasser's art and professional biography, yet his level of absorption within Austrian-Viennese culture is not well known and the childhood experiences, which probably played a significant role in his cultural and political perspectives, are frequently overlooked. Thus, the first section introduces a short biography and concise thematic background. In addition, and be-

1 The inspiration for this twofold analysis is from the monumental work of Carl Emil Schorske, Fin-De-Siècle Vienna. Politics and Culture, New York 1980.

fore proceeding to the analysis, three short remarks on Hundertwasser's work are required. First, Hundertwasser wrote throughout his life in diaries, for art exhibitions, manifestos and letters; he edited, revisited, and translated the significant ones.[2] His works were published in various languages – though mostly in exhibition catalogues and art books (and sometimes different versions under the same title).[3] For our comfort and ease of access, all the references to Hundertwasser's texts are through the Hundertwasser Foundation website. The second remark regards Hundertwasser's style. He is at times prophetic, at times cynical and almost always critical and provocative. That provoking way of expression may come about in expressions like 'The architect acts like a criminal of war. He executes orders even against his conscience. He is building cancerous structures in concrete which are killing nature and man within.'[4] If this was to be written by a philosopher – it would be completely unacceptable since it imposes crude accusations in general statements that overlook social and political reality. However, the fact that it was written by an artist is a significant context for making such a text legitimate. Artists sometimes use provocative language and performance in order to draw attention that they would otherwise not receive. Also, major aesthetic manifests were written in provocative and prophetic tones. Lastly, Hundertwasser frequently symbolically replies to his predecessors. In the example above – the alleged 'crime' is a rejoinder to Adolph Loos' (renowned Austrian architect, 1870–1933) modernist manifest "Ornament and Crime" (1910 manifesto of modernist architecture calling for sterile facades and symmetrical shapes).[5] Determining the context was of some difficulty throughout the research, and the style may require some tolerance from the reader. The third remark is purely methodological. Some of the interpretive analysis is supported and based on archival work, interviews with friends, collaborators, and residents of his Viennese building.

Hundertwasser: Biography, Thematic Background, and Theoretical Introduction

Hundertwasser was born in Vienna in December 1928 as Friedrich Stowasser to a Catholic father and Jewish mother. His father died in 1929 and he was raised solely by his mother. Following the *Anschluss* of Austria into Nazi Germany in

2 He himself wrote in German, French, and English. Almost all of the English versions were either translated or approved by him – so that 'author intention' remains intact. The archived original versions of his writing were reread throughout the research.

3 The book "Schöne Wege" is an exception as it binds all his significant writings in one book. Friedensreich Hundertwasser, Schöne Wege. Gedanken über Kunst und Leben [Beautiful Paths. Thoughts on Art and Life], in: Walter Schurian (Ed.), Schöne Wege. Gedanken über Kunst und Leben, München 1983. An enlarged edition was published with the same title in 2004.

4 Friedensreich Hundertwasser, The Turn. 1980, http://www.hundertwasser.com/text/view-1.5.1.3?subtype=hw, 11 September 2014.

5 Adolf Loos, Ornament and Crime, in: Adolf Opel (Ed.), Ornament ad Crime. Selected Essays, Riverside 1998.

1938, he and his mother were forced to move to a different apartment with his aunt and grandmother. In order to cope with the anti-Semitic atmosphere, he was baptized as a Catholic in 1935 and even joined the Hitler Jugend (Nazi youth movement). These acts saved his and his mother's life, though he was unable to save his grandmother and aunt and witnessed their imprisonment. Most of his Jewish relatives were deported and killed in 1943. These childhood experiences gave rise to moral sentiments that are embedded in his works; his views and his ecological awareness are deeply associated with them.[6]

Hundertwasser commenced his artistic path in the Viennese Academy of Fine Arts in 1948 though he resigned after three months feeling uninfluenced.[7] In the same year, while still being completely anonymous, he delivered a speech titled 'everyone must be creative'. It reads: 'Art must fight with us; art must be an ally of mankind [...]. The world was never so turbulent as just now and art should not escape or flee this world [...] every great modern artist is a prophet who precedes great new things that has to come soon.'[8] Hundertwasser's decision to resign from the Academy and this text could be understood as a young artist setting out his artistic mission. Throughout the rest of his life, his art addressed everyday life and through it he tried to show alternative and creative ways of living and later to promote ecological goals.

In the late 1940s, he started traveling in Europe and to Africa. During those travels, he constantly wrote in his diaries about his strong attachment to the art of Egon Schiele and the extent of his influence upon him.[9] In those years, he developed his own unique style, which is characterized by colorful, spontaneous and even wild texture. The only regularity found in his works is the intentional objec-

---

6 This biographical note is often neglected in the interpretation of Hundertwasser's art and thought, though it is highly significant for a comprehensive analysis. During those years he made his first intentional nature paintings. Since he had to live a 'secret life', it is reasonable to assume that it was easier for him to resort to the 'Wienerwald' (Vienna forest) instead of the city. The only public documentations of these experiences are brought in one text and one archived interview with Maria Fialik, though he constantly corresponds with these experiences in implicit manners in his paintings and some of his written manifests. *Cf.* Friedensreich Hundertwasser, Zwischen "HJ" und Judenstern. [Between Hitler Youth and the Star of David], in: Andrea C. Fürst – Doris Truppe (Eds.), Der Unbekannte Hundertwasser [The Yet Unknown], München 2008, 253–256. In addition, he discusses these issues in his private diary entries between 1943–1946 and in private letters that he wrote to his mother (Elsa Stowasser). These letters were just recently discovered. At the moment, they are still in the archive and unpublished. Preliminary references to these sources are documented in: Pamela Kort, Friedensreich Hundertwasser. The Holistic Power of Art, forthcoming in 2015/2016. Finally, the assertion that Hundertwasser's childhood experiences played a significant role in his art, affection to nature and cultural views are also based on interviews with Hundertwasser's chief archivist (Andrea C. Fürst) and close friend and manager (Joram Harel).

7 Harry Rand, Hundertwasser, Köln/London [25]2007, 11.

8 Friedensreich Hundertwasser, Everyone Must be Creative, in: Pierre Restany – Friedensreich Hundertwasser (Eds.), Hundertwasser, New York 2007, 55f.

9 Friedensreich Hundertwasser, I Love Schiele. 1951, http://hundertwasser.com/text/view-1.4.0.1?subtype=hw, 11. September 2014. In his private letters to his mother he asks her to 'buy the most elaborate and modern and complete book about Schiele's paintings', and to send it to his residence in Paris.

tion to straight lines and right angles, which he perceived as inorganic and even pathogenic.[10] In his view, these, and geometric rationality in general, are all associated with instrumental and functional approaches to humans and non-humans alike. His oeuvre gradually developed from painting to tapestry, applied art, many written manifests and architecture and he started incorporating nature and reflections on the relationship with nature into his work.[11] As will later be discussed, his vernacular and organic architectural projects and models exhibit humbleness and deep understanding of human dwelling on Earth.

In the early 1950s, he gained fame and prominence. At first, he was involved in establishing different artistic and aesthetic projects and later used his international recognition to promote ecological awareness through his art. In 1980, together with the *Neue Kronen Zeitung* daily newspaper, he initiated the 'Mehr Grün für Wien' [More Green for Vienna] campaign, which urged the citizens of Vienna to plant Boston ivy on building walls and included an appeal to provide more green spaces in the city.[12] He donated his paintings and posters to conservation and anti-nuclear campaigns. For example: in 1980, he donated a poster titled 'Plant Trees – Avert Nuclear Peril' to Nader's Critical Mass Energy Project in Washington.[13] In 1981 he donated a poster titled 'Arche Noah 2000' to a European conservation campaign; his phrase 'you are a guest of nature – Behave!' became its icon.[14] In 1982 he donated his posters 'Save the Seas' and 'Save the Whales' to the Jacques Cousteau Society and Greenpeace respectively.[15] In these cases, and various others, the highly admired posters were utilized for the campaigns and the profits from

Friedensreich Hundertwasser, Brief an Elsa Stowasser, 14 November 1950. Quoted in Kort, Friedensreich Hundertwasser, 12. For elaboration on Hundertwasser's obsession with Schiele during the early 1950s see: Kort, Friedensreich Hundertwasser.

10 See, for example, Hundertwasser's texts on the 'Straight Line' and 'Spiral': Friedensreich Hundertwasser, The Straight Line Leads to the Downfall of our Civilization, 1953, http://www.hundertwasser.com/text/view-1.1.6.2?subtype=hw, 11. September 2014; Friedensreich Hundertwasser, The Spiral. 1974, http://www.hundertwasser.com/text/view-1.1.3.1?subtype=hw, 11 September 2014.

11 For some examples of his work please see: http://hundertwasser.com/oeuvre, 11 September 2014.

12 Friedensreich Hundertwasser, Mehr Grün. 1980, http://hundertwasser.com/item/object-list/?quick_search_work=181&type%5B%5D=apa&title, 11. September 2014. This campaign correlates to Hundertwasser's vision of 'forest-cities' see for example: Friedensreich Hundertwasser, Forestation of the City, 1971, http://www.hundertwasser.com/text/view-1.5.1.2?subtype=hw, 11. September 2014. It is said that in addition to this campaign he also provided teenagers with hammers and chisels to crack the pavements so that spontaneous vegetation will grow in the middle of the city.

13 Friedensreich Hundertwasser, Plant Trees – Avert Nuclear Peril, 1980, http://hundertwasser.com/item/object-list/?quick_search_work=109&type%5B%5D=apa&title, 11 September 2014.

14 Friedensreich Hundertwasser, Arche Noah 2000. You Are A Guest of Nature – Behave, 1981, http://hundertwasser.com/item/object-list/?quick_search_work=150&type%5B%5D=apa&title, 11 September 2014.

15 Friedensreich Hundertwasser, Save the Seas, 1981, http://hundertwasser.com/item/object-list/?quick_search_work=153&type%5B%5D=apa&title, 11. September 2014.
Friedensreich Hundertwasser, Save the Whales, 1982. http://hundertwasser.com/item/object-list/?quick_search_work=152&type%5B%5D=apa&title, 11 September 2014.

their sales supported them financially. In other occasions copyrights to his works were given under the condition that X trees will be planted.

His most significant efforts in promoting ecological awareness were through his architectural projects. In them, he wanted to set an example of an alternative type of constructed environment. One of his greatest successes was in his ability to recruit political officials to these efforts. The support of Bruno Kreisky (1911–1990, Austria's Federal Chancellor between 1970–1983) and Leopold Gratz (1929–2006, Mayor of Vienna between 1973–1984) gave Hundertwasser the opportunity to realize his architectural-ecological ideas in the building of a residential building in Vienna (Hundertwasserhaus).[16] In this project, he manifested his vision of an urban environment that is friendlier to its residents and more responsive to nature. Helmult Zilk (1927–2008, Mayor of Vienna between 1984–1994) commissioned Hundertwasser to redesign the Spittelau waste incinerator and he turned it from an industrial-functional building to a monumental work of art that is visible from all the corners of Vienna. It is probable that Zilk introduced waste separation in the city as this was a condition set by Hundertwasser to take over the work for Spittelau.

In addition to his support from high political officials, Hundertwasser was also deeply absorbed in Austrian culture. He had close friendships and collaborations with other prominent Austrian artists such as Ernst Fuchs, Arik Brauer, Arnulf Rainer, and more. His connection to Austrian culture was made most apparent from the mid-1980s when he spoke up against the EU arguing that it will dominate Austria's (and other European countries') particular culture, values, and lifestyle.[17] Besides his influential public manifests, he was repeatedly interviewed in Austrian newspapers, radio, and television.[18]

These are only a few examples of a lifetime effort that Hundertwasser took upon himself – to 'beautify' quotidian life and to promote environmental literacy (as he understood it). His works were exhibited in the most important museums worldwide and he built in many locations throughout Europe, the US, Australia, New-Zealand, Japan and others. At the peak of his career his work was admired for its authenticity, childish playfulness and environmental awareness. He died of heart failure on board of a ship on 19 February 2000. He was given an 'ecological burial' according to his specific instructions – in the 'Garden of the Happy Dead' in his property in New Zealand under a tulip tree.

---

16 Kreisky supported Hundertwasser in different occasions. For example, his 'world-traveling-exhibition' (1975–1987) was under the official auspices of Federal Chancellor Kreisky and was titled "Austria Presents Hundertwasser to the Continents", so he was in fact formally designated to be the country's cultural representative. In each country, the event was under a co-patronage with Kreisky's equivalent.

17 Friedensreich Hundertwasser, To Join the E.U. is to Betray Austria and Betray Europe. Why?, 1988–1994/1997, http://www.hundertwasser.com/text/view-1.4.5.1?subtype=hw, 11 September 2014.

18 This is supported by dozens of archive documents found in the 'Hundertwasser Archiv, Wien'.

This rather thin biographical sketch was brought only to introduce parts of Hundertwasser that are usually less accessible. Hundertwasser's biography is fascinating and much richer than described above. This study, however, is neither biographical nor historical, but rather aims to analyze Hundertwasser's contribution to theories of urban political identity and environmental theory.

Thematic Background and Theoretic Introduction

The starting point for analyzing the connections between Hundertwasser the artist and these theoretical issues is by assessing his model of 'the 5 skins'. This model depicts the self as having five skins, or five layers that compound to form the person-self. The first skin is the epidermis; the second skin is clothing (and by abstraction many personal commodities); the third skin is the house, building, and architecture in general; the fourth skin is the social and political environment of the self and includes family and friends, but also city, nation, and region; the fifth skin is the natural world.[19]

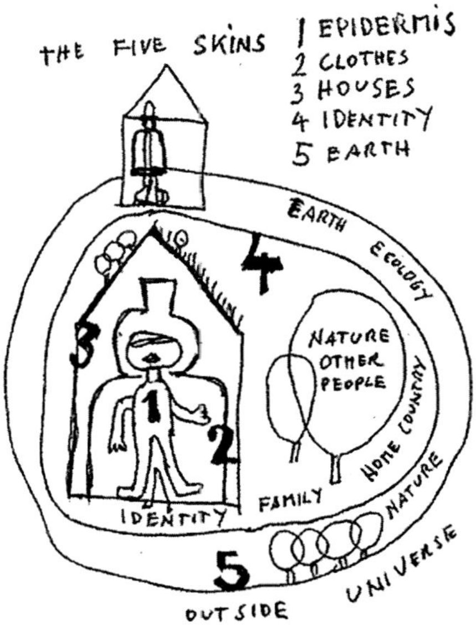

Image 1: Hundertwasser's Five Skins.[20]

This conception of the self is that of an essentially embedded self – embedded in its artificial environment (architecture), social and political environment, and natural environment. These all are inseparable of what or who a person is. It challenges the liberal-individualistic conception of the self and thereby corresponds with existing communitarian and ecological critiques on that individualistic conception.

The ecological critique is manifested in the concept of the 'ecological self'; it has different variants and nuances[21] though at large the critique goes along these lines:

19 This section is based on other work in the field of environmental ethics. For elaboration on the model of five skins and the challenges it poses on other conceptions of the self, see: Nir Barak, Hundertwasser as an Inspiration for Environmental Ethics. Reformulating the Ecological Self, forthcoming in 2015.

20 Published with permission. Image copyrights: © 2015 NAMIDA AG, Glarus, Schweiz. For an elaboration please see http://www.hundertwasser.com/skin; Pierre Restany – Friedensreich Hundertwasser, Hundertwasser. The Painter-King with the 5 Skins, The Power of Art, Köln 2001.

21 For different models of the 'ecological self' see: Arne Naess, Self-Realization. An Ecological Approach to Being in the World, in: Dregson Alan-Devall Bill (Eds.), The Ecology of Wisdon. Writings by Arne Naess, Berkley 1995, 3–10; Freya Mathews, The Ecological Self, London 1991; Bill

> 'Ecological thinking [...] requires a kind of vision across boundaries. The epidermis of the skin is ecologically like a pond surface or a forest soil, not a shell so much as a delicate interpenetration. It reveals the self ennobled and extended rather than threatened as part of the landscape and the ecosystem [...].'[22]

This critique depicts the self as deeply embedded in the natural world. The common thread that runs through the different depictions of the 'ecological self' is the critical approach towards ontological and epistemic segregation between humans and nature – a segregation that is considered as misconception.

This ecological critique shares a common thread with communitarian critiques of the 'liberal self'- *i.e.* that humans are defined by their communal bonds and are not self-sufficient as of themselves.[23] The alternative, communitarian conception of the self, argues that individuals are embodied agents in a community (or various communities) – and that has a high level of influence on their culture, values, and conceptions of the 'good'.

Interpretation of Hundertwasser's depiction of the 'five skins' challenges both models of the 'ecological self' and the 'communitarian self'. Unlike the model of the ecological self, the alternative five-skinned model does not leap from the first skin (epidermis) directly to the fifth (nature). It acknowledges all the other mediating skins or layers – including the artificial environment (the city) and the social and political environments. The challenge to the communitarian self is that although it does recognize the first and fourth skins (and possibly the second and third), this model fails to extend itself onward to the fifth skin (nature).

Having this challenge in mind, the twofold analysis in the following focuses mainly on the dynamics of the third skin by analyzing the Hundertwasserhaus. The synchronic analysis will indicate how architecture (third skin) mediates the relationship between the self and nature (fifth skin) in the context of environmental theory. The diachronic analysis will indicate how architecture corresponds with the social and political environment in the context of urban political identity.

Devall, The Ecological Self, in: Alan Drengson-Yuichi Inoue (Eds.), The Deep Ecology Movement. An Introductory Anthology, Berkeley 1995, 101–123; Warwick Fox, Toward a Transpersonal Ecology. Developing new Foundations for Environmentalism, Albany 1995.

22 Devall, The Ecological Self, 121.

23 For elaboration on the communitarian self see: Charles Taylor, Atomism, in: Philosophy and the Human Sciences, Cambridge 1985, 187–210; Charles Taylor, Sources of the Self. The Making of the Modern Identity, Cambridge 1992; Michael J. Sandel, The Procedural Republic and the Unencumbered Self, in: Political Theory 12/1, Thousand Oaks 1984, 81–96. For an overview of the debate between liberals and communitarians (or more precise – individualism and communitarianism) please see: Shlomo Avineri – Avner de Shalit, Communitarianism and Individualism, Oxford 1992; Daniel A. Bell, Communitarianism and Its Critics, Oxford 1993.

Synchronic Analysis: Urban Environmental Sentiments

Different notions of holism, interconnectedness with nature and interdependence between humans and the non-human world are intertwined in the history of environmental philosophy and ethics. Naming just a few – Leopold's "Sand Country Almanac" integrates 'the land' into ethical considerations[24]; in "Silent Spring", Carson recognizes the mutual effect of pesticides of humans and nature[25]; Commoner's first law of ecology argues that 'everything is connected to everything else'[26]; politically and socially oriented, Bookchin's social ecology analyzes correlating patterns of domination and exploitations of humans and nature[27]; and likewise in many other classical texts of environmental thought. Although these perspectives are different, they all bring forward a holistic understanding regarding the relationship between humans and nature. Humans are essentially embedded in nature and society and nature are interconnected and interdependent.

At a first glance however, it might be argued that the constructed urban environment is not the 'natural' locus for these environmental sentiments and concepts. This gap was recognized by several authors as a 'blind spot' in environmental ethics and it seems that it correlates to a strong anti-urban bias that dominates environmental philosophy.[28] In short, urban life is perceived as morally inferior to life closer to nature. However, as a growing number of people live in cities (now over a half of the world's population), this issue should gain more attention.

Integrating the concepts of holism, interconnectedness, and interdependence into environmental thought about urban landscapes may take one of two paths. The first one is eliminating or hybridizing the conceptual borders between nature and society. In the field of urban studies, Jacobs argued that urban environments 'are as natural as colonies of prairie dogs or the beds of oysters'.[29] In critical geography, David Harvey asserts that 'It is in practice, hard to see where 'society' begins and 'nature' end. [I]n a fundamental sense, there is in the final analysis nothing unnatural about New York City'.[30] Environmental ethicist J. Baird Callicott ar-

24 Aldo Leopold, A Sand County Almanac. With Other Essays on Conservation from Round River, Oxford 1966.

25 Rachel Carson, Silent Spring, Boston 1962.

26 Barry Commoner, The Closing Circle. Nature, Man, and Technology, New York 1971.

27 Murray Bookchin, The Ecology of Freedom. The Emergence and Dissolution of Hierarchy, Oakland 2005; Murray Bookchin, Post-Scarcity Anarchism, Oakland 2004.

28 Dale Jamieson, The City Around Us, in: Tom Regan (Ed.), Earthbound. New Introductory Essays in Environmental Ethics, Philadelphia 1984, 38–73; Alastair S. Gunn, Rethinking Communities. Environmental Ethics in an Urbanized World, in: Environmental Ethics 20/4, Charlottesville 1998, 341–360; Avner de-Shalit, Ruralism or Environmentalism? in: Environmental Values 5/1, Isle Of Harris 1996, 47–58; Avner de Shalit, Philosophy Gone Urban. Reflections on Urban Restoration, in: Journal of Social Philosophy 34/1, New Jersey 2003, 6–27; Andrew Light, The Urban Blind Spot in Environmental Ethics, in: Environmental Politics 10/, Charlottesville 2000, 115–131.

29 Jane Jacobs, The Death and Life of Great American Cities, New York 1992, 443.

30 Quoted by Nik Heynen – Maria Kaika – Eric Swyngedouw (Eds.), In the Nature of Cities. Urban Political Ecology and the Politics of Urban Metabolism, London/New York 2006, 1.

gued that that the notion of the wilderness needs to be abandoned since it conveys a nature-culture dualism that should be deserted.[31] Elsewhere, he maintains that 'Chicago is no less a phenomenon of nature than is the Great Barrier Reef'[32]; and more recently – that value found in the city 'is the way they integrate or incorporate nature into themselves.'[33] This line of reasoning seems somewhat questionable. It overlooks the fact that natural processes occur naturally, and that social and political processes like city planning are artificial.[34] Cities are characterized, among other things, by planning, deliberation, premeditation and politics – which are not natural processes. Although of course one could argue that there is some kind of rationality in ecosystems in the sense of planning, however the spontaneous and natural processes do not involve deliberation and politics. It is not done by a group or a collective and, therefore, it is a natural processes, as distinct from the planning which takes place in the city. The holistic recognition that economic, political, social, and environmental issues are interrelated does not eliminate the conceptual borders and the ability to discern between natural phenomena (reef formation, for example) and social processes. Moreover, failing to do so gives ground for justifying ruralist notions and it neutralizes political action and politics in general. Thus, eliminating the conceptual borders between cities and nature seems to be an unfounded direction.

The second path for integrating the concepts of holism, interconnectedness, and interdependence into environmental thought in urban landscapes is by recognizing the conceptual borders between nature and society and awarding nature a constitutive role in social processes. This implies the realization that humans and social affairs are essentially embedded in the natural world, though they are not the same in principal. Awarding nature a constitutive role in social processes means that nature ought to be taken under consideration in any social or political arrangement. On the one hand, this recognition imposes ecological, moral and political constraints; on the other hand, it imposes opportunities for human interaction and engagement.[35] The realization of the essential embedment and the con-

31 John Baird Callicott, The Wilderness Idea Revisited. The Sustainable Development Alternative, in: The Environmental Professional 13, 1991, 255–247.

32 John Baird Callicott, La Nature est morte, vive la nature!, in: Hastings Center Report 22/5, Garrison 1992, 16–23, here 18.

33 John Baird Callicott, The Role of Intrinsic Values for the Naturalization of the City, in: Girard Luigi Fusco (Ed.), The Human Sustainable City. Challenges and Perspectives from the Habitat Agenda, Burlington 2004, 107–120.

34 This argument does not oppose or counter the significant work being done in the field of urban political ecology. Their inquiry analyzes urban metabolism from the perspective of political economy. Gene Desfor – Roger Keil, Nature and the City. Making Environmental Policy in Toronto and Los Angeles, Tucson 2004; Eric Swyngedouw, Social Power and the Urbanization of Water Flows of Power, Oxford 2004; Heynen – Kaika – Swyngedouw, Nature of Cities. There, the critique on the segregation of society and nature is from the perspective of material flow analysis, and not a philosophical objection.

35 John M Meyer, Political Nature. Environmentalism and the Interpretation of Western Thought, Cambridge 2001; Peter F. Cannavò, Book Review: Return to Nature? An Ecological Counterhis-

Image 2: Hundertwasserhaus, Vienna, 1977–1986.[37]

straints and opportunities that it brings with it is brought about in symbolic manifestations of the concepts of holism, interconnectedness, and interdependence. The following interpretive analysis of the Hundertwasserhaus exemplifies this notion.

> 'The time has come for people to rebel against their confinement in cubical constructions like chickens or rabbits in cages, a confinement which is alien to human nature […]. The architect has no relationship to the building […]. The bricklayer has no relationship to the building […]. The tenant has no relationship to the structure […]. Only when architect, bricklayer and tenant are a unity, or one and the same person, can we speak of architecture. Everything else is not architecture, but a criminal act which has taken on form […]'[36]

The Hundertwasserhaus in Vienna and other Hundertwasser urban dwellings may be interpreted as 'three dimensional manifests' of environmental sentiments in urban areas; it engenders ongoing interaction between the resident to the building itself and the surrounding urban environment. A house is a unique creation – it has to be functional but also expressive and relational to its (inner) habitants and

tory by Fred Dallmayr and Plato's Revenge. Politics in the Age of Ecology by William Ophuls, in: Political Theory 41/3, Thousand Oaks 2013, 492–498.

36 Friedensreich Hundertwasser, Mouldiness Manifesto Against Rationalism in Architecture, 1958, http://www.hundertwasser.com/text/view-1.3.2.1?subtype=hw, 11 September 2014.

37 Photographer: Kurt Pultar. Published with permission. Copyrights: © 2015 Hundertwasser Archive, Vienna. Hundertwasser's first significant architectural project, located in the center of a 'standard' residential neighborhood in Vienna.

(outer-urban) surroundings. Besides its aesthetic qualities, this building also manifests symbols of holism, interconnectedness and interdependence with nature from an urban perspective and these will be elaborated in the following.

Holism Through the Practice of 'Window Rights'

Regarding houses and buildings, Hundertwasser asserts that 'some people say houses consist of walls. I say houses consist of windows.'[38] This sentence is very revealing. Walls segregate and windows are paths through those separations; walls impose oppositions, while windows break them. He criticizes what he understands as 'window dictatorship', which is basically his oppositions to uniformity and physical symmetry of windows. 'The apartheid of window races must cease. For the repetition of identical windows next to each other and above each other as in a grid system is a characteristic of concentration camps. In the new architecture of satellite towns and in new administration buildings, banks, hospitals, and schools, the levelling of windows is unbearable.'[39] Interpreting this quotation reveals two symbolical capacities of windows. The first is that they break dualistic oppositions between inner and outer realities. The second is that resistance to their uniformity yields aesthetic pluralism. These two symbolic capacities are manifested through the practice of 'window rights'.

Image 3: Window-right demonstration; left image: Vienna, 1972; right image: Bülach, Switzerland, 1972.[40]

> 'You must yourself become the author of your [urban N.B.] environment. You cannot wait for a permit or an authority. Not only your clothes and your rooms, but the face of the building in which you live belongs to you. Any kind of individual creation is better than this sterile death.'[41]

38 Friedensreich Hundertwasser, The Window Dictatorship, 1990, http://www.hundertwasser.com/text/view-1.3.2.11?subtype=hw, 11 September 2014.

39 *Ibid.*

40 Published with permission. Copyrights: © 2015 Hundertwasser Archive, Vienna.

41 Friedensreich Hundertwasser, Your Window Right, Your Tree Duty, http://www.hundertwasser.com/text/view-1.3.3.3?subtype=hw, 11 September 2014.

> 'The apartment-house tenant must have the freedom to lean out of his window and as far as his arms can reach transform the exterior of his dwelling space. And he must be allowed to take a long brush and – as far as his arms can reach – paint everything pink, so that from far away, from the street, everyone can see: there lives a man who distinguishes himself from his neighbours, the pent-up livestock! He must also be allowed to cut up the walls and make all kinds of changes, even if this disturbs the architectural harmony of a so-called masterwork [...]'.[42]

The practice of window rights is a symbolical act of engagement that represents embedment. When the observer leans out of the window and creatively expresses herself, she is interacting with the street, other buildings and all the neighboring residents. She shows herself as she is – inviting further interaction. In doing so, she 'leaves' part of herself outside, and while at it – lets some of the outside in. This is a meaningful, holistic, interaction. The barriers that were very clear before exercising her window-right are now a bit faded and more flexible. In the process, she is appropriating her third skin and extending to the fourth (social and political skin). The house is not confined to itself, it interacts with the world. The window becomes more than a hole in the window, it becomes a gate through which messages are sent out – and enter back in. It implies openness to the world and symbolizes constant interaction and engagement with it.

Interconnectedness, Modesty, and Interdependence by Redefining the Urban Space

Green roofs, roof gardening, and urban agriculture are a growing practice in recent years. This practice may be dated back to the hanging gardens of Babylon, traditional farmhouses in Europe or various kinds of vernacular architecture; however, the size and scale of this contemporary phenomenon is much wider than before. It is currently sponsored and promoted by municipalities in big cities like Chicago, Toronto, Copenhagen, Munich, Portland, Singapore, and more. Looking at the way in which this policy is promoted – there is a great emphasis on the utility value of it. The benefits of the policy are: more effective storm-water management[43], reduction of urban 'heat island effect', better insulation- which leads to a significant reduction of air-conditioning fees, improvement of air quality, extends the life of roofs by two to three times and adds beauty to the city landscape.[44] These are all utilitarian and instrumental justifications. This point is not being stressed as a critique, since there is nothing glamorous about a policy that is inef-

42 Hundertwasser, Mouldiness Manifesto Against Rationalism in Architecture.

43 Storm water runoffs is a major cause for overflowing drainage systems (sewers), flooding, pollution and land erosion.

44 These benefits are taken from the 'Chicago Green Roof Initiative' website, and they are repeated in most municipal projects. Green Roofs, Best Management Practices, N.D. http://www.cityofchicago.org/city/en/depts/water/supp_info/conservation/green_design/green_roofs_bestmanagementpractices.html, 19 July 2014.

fective or a practice that leads to undesired results. However, in order to make the argument for environmental sentiments and interconnectedness in urban spaces, these projects need to be justified in a non-instrumental manner. An example of a more essential justification may be found in the following:

> 'THE HORIZONTAL BELONGS TO NATURE, THE VERTICAL TO MAN. So, everything that is horizontal under the sky belongs to vegetation, and man can only claim for himself what is vertical. In other words, this means: FREE NATURE MUST GROW WHEREVER SNOW FALLS IN WINTER.'[45]

> 'All that is white in winter must be green in summer. All that gets wet with rain, all horizontal surfaces under the sky, belong to the realm of plant life. Woods shall grow on streets and roofs. One must again be able to breathe woodland air in the cities.'[46]

While acknowledging the utilitarian and instrumental benefits of green roofs, this practice is justified by determining a normative principle of how 'the land' ought to be shared from an urban perspective. To put it clear, density of population, high-rise buildings, cities, urban-infrastructure are all respectful of nature when they restore it horizontally.[47] Building vertically is a recognition of humanity's place in the world – which may seem a factor that needs no justification; however, it is posed as a counterargument to misanthropic and self-effacing trends that are sometimes mistakenly identified with non-anthropocentrism. Restoring nature horizontally, opens the vast realm of the vertical for human creativity and self-expression (window rights).

Like green roofs, 'vertical green' is also a traditional practice in different parts of the world. Boston ivy and other climbing plants are frequently used to cover the façade of a house or building, and like green roofs- 'green walls' are also gaining attention in current urban practices – mostly for decoration, but also for their effectiveness against pollution and insulation. Similar to the case of green roofs, along with the instrumental benefits of vertical green, these projects need to be justified in different terms. The example of it is brought about in the Hundertwasserhaus in 'tree tenants'.[48] A 'tree tenant' is not any tree planted in an urban area; it is a tree planted as an integral part of the apartments and the façade. Now, tradition flower planting along the vertical façade is one thing, though planting trees along the façade is somewhat different mostly since it physically demands more space. According to the horizontal-vertical principle introduced above, the vertical was declared

45 Hundertwasser, Forestation of the City. (Emphasis in original).

46 Hundertwasser, Your Window Rights, Your Tree Duty.

47 This assertion should not be taken at face value and does not refer to physical-environmental aspects, although various researches indicate that vegetation in cities yield encouraging results. This assertion refers only to philosophical and ethical notions.

48 See image 6.

as 'belonging to man'; the symbolic and practical act of 'opening up space' for tree tenants implies care, concern and solicitude. Most frequently, flowers are planted for aesthetic purposes, climbing plants are planted either for aesthetic or instrumental purposes, though planting trees along the façade symbolize something else. Hundertwasser writes: 'A tree tenant is an ambassador of the forest.'[49] Continuing and interpreting this reasoning, it could be asserted that a tree tenant functions as a silent reminder of the interdependent relationship between man and nature.

These examples above indicate essential human embedment in nature through symbolic manifestations. In each of them, the conceptual differences between nature and society are maintained in accordance with the concepts of holism, interconnectedness, and interdependence. The interpretations were focused on the constitutive role of nature in the social processes of building dwellings. This is not an obvious locus for that type of realization. Most frequently, the integration of nature into urban areas is brought about in open spaces, parks, and recreational facilities, however, dense building is probably the most significant characteristic of urban areas and it is the most quotidian aspect of city life. All this leads to the assertion that the implicit ecological aspects of this building may provide a source of inspiration for environmental thought in urban areas. In reference to the five-skinned self, most of the analysis so far was focused on the third skin. It was already suggested that by the engagement that the third skin engenders, a person who also starts interacting with the fourth, social and political skin. This aspect is analyzed in the subsequent section.

Diachronic Analysis: Spirit of Vienna

The "Spirit of Cities" novel is a theoretical framework in contemporary political theory and is most relevant for the diachronic analysis of the fourth skin.[50] It analyzes the different roles that cities play or may possibly play in a period in which globalization, with all it benefits, is also generating political, social and cultural homogenization. It is often suggested that in the face of these global pressure the nation state is becoming somewhat less potent, some even argue totally dysfunctional political institution[51], and that states are becoming more uniform in character.[52] In the face of these concerns, the "Spirit of Cities"-framework introduces two main arguments. The first argument is descriptive – that some cities have a unique ethos, source of identity and a sense of urban pride (civicism) that is fully distin-

49 Friedensreich Hundertwasser, Tree Tenant Letter. 1973, http://www.hundertwasser.com/text/view-1.3.3.4.1?subtype=hw, 11 September 2014.

50 Daniel A. Bell – Avner de Shalit, The Spirit of Cities. Why the Identity of a City Matters in a Global Age, Princeton 2011.

51 Benjamin R. Barber, If Mayors Ruled the World. Dysfunctional Nations, Rising Cities, Cambridge 2013.

52 Bell – de Shalit, Spirit, 1–17.

guishable from national identity or national patriotism. The second argument is normative – not only does civicism exist, but it ought to be fostered.

Architecture is one manner in which the spirit of a city is manifested and engendered. Frequently, spatial analysis of urbanism emphasizes city planning. For example, changes in the spirit of Paris are analyzed in relationship to the major changes in city planning undergone by Georges-Eugène Haussmann (1809–1891) during the 1850s–1870s.[53] The forthcoming analysis complements this perspective and scrutinizes the manners in which architecture of a specific building, the Hundertwasserhaus, corresponds with the spirit of Vienna. As stated above, this paper takes the Hundertwasserhaus as a three dimensional manifest; in it civicism is manifested in it by incorporation of various elements in the 'spirit' of Vienna as Hundertwasser understood it. Some examples may clarify this:

First, and probably most meaningful, the function of this building is public housing. It is owned by the city of Vienna and it houses 50 families according to the city's very progressive social housing program. This function (public housing) highly corresponds with Hundertwasser's Vienna. Hundertwasser was born in the post Austro-Hungarian Empire and by then Vienna was in a transitional period from being an imperial city to 'Red Vienna'.[54] In the late 19th century and early 20th century, and after the city walls were torn down and the Ringstraße was built, the inhabitants of the 'Innere Stadt' [Vienna's city center] – the aristocracy and high bourgeoisie elite, enjoyed a comfortable and abundant lifestyle. However, the massive expansion of Vienna during those years and the construction that complemented those efforts or rapid growth implied massive growth in urban poverty and socioeconomic inequality. The vast majority of people who lived in the outskirts or even just the bordering districts suffered from terrible living conditions.

The social-democratic party gained an absolute majority in Vienna after the collapse of the Habsburg dual monarchy and the proclamation of the Republik Deutschösterreich [Republic of German-Austria, 1918] and later I. Republik Österreich [I. Republic of Austria, 1919–1933/1934]. Backed by Viennese intellectual elite, the municipal government carried various social and economic reforms in employment, social and health services, financial policies, and public housing. The latter had some foundations in the last years of Imperial-Royal Government, though it gained prominence in 1925 with the 'Gemeindebauten'– buildings commissioned, built and owned by the municipality in order to provide low-cost public housing.[55]

53 *Ibid.*, 222–248.

54 'Red Vienna' became the term coined to describe Vienna between 1918–1934 when the city was democratically governed by social-democrat majority for the first time. See *inter alia* Peter Csendes – Ferdinand Opll (Eds.), Wien. Geschichte einer Stadt. Von 1790 bis zur Gegenwart [Vienna. A History of a City. From 1790 to the Present], vol.3, Wien/Köln/Weimar 2006.

55 See Helmut Gruber, Red Vienna. Experiment in Working-Class Culture, 1919–1934, New York 1991; Schorske, Fin-De-Siècle Vienna.

Of course, Vienna had undergone many significant and groundbreaking changes in the coming years: The 'Anschluss' and Nazi period, the massive damage of the Second World War, occupation by the Allied Commission (1945–1955), the Cold War which had a lot of influence due to Vienna's strategic location and the reestablishment of its central role in world politics by the creation of the UNO-City. However, the change of 'spirit' in its housing policy – from absolute neglect of poverty during the Habsburgs to the 'Gemeindebauten' lasted and even intensified through these changes. This change of spirit is a significant characteristic of Hundertwasser's Vienna. Throughout the research, it could not be verified whether Hundertwasser intentionally sought to participate in the construction of a public housing building – but this gap is insignificant. The fact that the Hundertwasserhaus belongs to the policy and culture of 'Gemeindebauten' is the significant part for the interpretation. Building in Vienna, the city of Freud and Psychoanalysis, the unconscious and implicit layers are as significant (if not even more) as the conscious intentionality of the artist-architect. Nevertheless, Hundertwasser was a proud citizen of his Vienna. As documented in a letter (1977) from Bruno Kreisky to Leopold Gratz, when Hundertwasser expressed his will to manifest his architectonic notion in Vienna, Kreisky writes:

> 'Hundertwasser's name is closely associated with Vienna. He feels his share of responsibility for what happens in Austria and that nation's capital in the field of architecture and what does not happen in the field of environmental protection [his] ideas on architecture and the environment have found worldwide recognition [and he] wants nothing more than to be heard in Austria, too.'[56]

Beyond the building's function, it also incorporates symbolic elements in order to correspond with the spirit of Vienna as Hundertwasser understood it. Besides Vienna's progressive social policies, it was also a melancholic city found in confusion with a type of longing for the monumental days of the empire. When Hundertwasser drew the 'gateway of the Heiligenkreuzerhof' in 1943 (image 5), it was already during the traumatic events of the Nazi period. To a large extent – this is his depiction of Vienna before the trauma and before all his life shuddered. That Vienna was progressive in its social reforms, yet still somewhat longing for the monumental days of the empire and emperor Franz Joseph.

Those recollections are manifested in architectonic symbols and features. Each of the windows in the façade has a decorative stone on top of it (image 4). Looking at Hundertwasser's youth drawing (image 5), these stones are recollections of Vienna's cultural heritage. Although Hundertwasser seriously objected his contemporary way of building and architecture, he reconstructed part of the old façade of the building (image 4). That was so that 'the spirits of the old house could live

56 Friedensreich Hundertwasser, in: Angelica Taschen (Ed.), Hundertwasser Architecture. For a More Human Architecture in Harmony with Nature, Cologne 1997, 180.

Image 4: Tree tenant, windows stones & old façade.[58]

Image 5: Gateway of the Heiligenkreuzerhof, (Vienna), 1943.[59]

in the new one'.[57] The onion domes on top of the building are a cultural emblem of Vienna and the region. When explaining this notion, Hundertwasser writes: 'From the time the Turks laid siege to Vienna, the realm of onion towers stretched from Bavaria to Russia, Byzantium, as far as India [...]. Vienna belongs to the great realm of the onion towers.'[60] Lastly, some of the bricks used in the construction were recycled material, but of a special kind. They were bricks with the imperial coat-of-arms, salvaged from torn-down buildings in Vienna.[61] Those bricks are also unique for reasons that Hundertwasser was probably not aware of. The coat-of-arms implies that these bricks were manufactured before 1918 and possibly in the late 19th century. At those times, bricks were produced locally, not imported, in factories between the 'Wienerberg' [Vienna Mountain] and the 'Wienfluss' [Vienna River]. Producing bricks in this area dates back to Roman times and during the massive reconstruction under the reign of Emperor Franz-Joseph the bricks were produced there by so-called 'Ziegelböhmen' [Bohemian and Moravian brick workers]. This fact and location implies that these bricks are produced of Vienna's

57 *Ibid.*, 197.

58 Photographer: Hubert Kluger. Published with permission. Copyrights: © 2015 Hundertwasser Archive, Vienna.

59 Published with permission. Image copyrights: © 2015 NAMIDA AG, Glarus, Schweiz.

60 Friedensreich Hundertwasser, The Onion Towers, 1985, http://www.hundertwasser.com/text/view-1.3.2.13?subtype=hw, 11 September 2014.

61 *Ibid.*, 190.

soil. It means that since the building was built with these bricks, it symbolically and materially engulfs, absorbs and internalizes Vienna in a deep sense.

Through these symbols, the spirit of Vienna is addressed and corresponded with. The extent to which it is indeed a successful framing of Vienna's spirit is, of course, debatable; but the significant factor is the idea of civicism as an integral part of the architecture of the Hundertwasserhaus.[62] All this leads to the assertion that this building is deeply Viennese in essence and constantly corresponds with – historically and symbolically.

Concluding Remarks

This paper took upon itself the analysis and interpretation of some of Hundertwasser's works and their possible contribution to theories of urban political identity and environmental theory. The biographic and thematic introduction set the ground for interpreting and understanding Hundertwasser and his motivations. The personal details, especially his childhood experiences, are often unacknowledged, although they were crucial for the development of his artistic conceptions and architectonic notions. The interpretation of Hundertwasser's model of the five skins enabled the comprehensiveness of the other analyses. The environmental and social aspects of the Hundertwasserhaus are interrelated in that they are different skins of the same thing – the individual creative and open person.

The synchronic analysis, studying the Hundertwasserhaus regardless of its historic context, brought to light the environmental concepts and sentiments that are embedded in the building. The building is known to be a manifest of environmentalism, though most frequently it seems that its appreciation rests on the incorporation of trees into the design. The analysis pointed to more essential themes. It indicated that it is possible to symbolize and conceive concepts like holism, interconnectedness, and interdependence with nature in the urban experience via architecture. In so, this analysis contributes and invites further development to urban environmental theories.

The diachronic analysis, within the historic context and historic references the building makes, indicated the extent to which the Hundertwasserhaus belongs in and to Vienna. The building is known as tourist attraction in Vienna or as another Viennese icon. The analysis pointed out that it is much more than an icon; the Hundertwasserhaus is deeply Viennese in its symbols, historical references, and materials. Thereby, the analysis shed light on the relationship between civicism and architecture through symbolism. This opens space for further research on architecture and urban political identity.

62 It is important to emphasize that the spirit of a city consists not only of its cultural symbols, but also its ability to foster a sense of community, values, and conceptions of the 'good'. This brings into consideration a wide range of political and distributional issues and this political aspect that need to be further developed. However, these aspects will not be discussed here due to the scope and goals of this paper.

This paper is concluded with a personal note. At present Hundertwasser's artistic, environmental and philosophic legacy is preserved in the 'Kunst Haus Wien' – a factory which he renovated or 'healed' as an 'architectural doctor' in 1991.[63] Besides many ongoing international exhibitions, the 'Kunst Haus Wien' functions as the permanent house for Hundertwasser paintings, architectural models, applied art tapestry. It exemplifies his ecological-architectonic ideas including a wide variety of indoor plants, green roof, and various tree-tenants. The museum was managed by Joram Harel (Hundertwasser's close friend and artistic manager) until 2007, when it was taken over by the 'Wien Holding' (Vienna's city-owned firm).[64]

While concluding this research, the author's last visit to the museum in January 2015 was rather random. He went to the museum shop to buy some postcards for his son. Knowing this building and its concepts very well, he noticed that something is significantly different. The plants at the ground level were missing. He decided to visit the rest of the museum to see if some other changes had taken place and noticed that all the plants in the staircase are also gone – and most disturbing – that some of the 'tree tenants' were sealed off in order to provide more space for the temporary exhibitions. He asked some of the employees and got the impression that they are not too pleased with these changes and that it was done intentionally. One of them told him that the decision to do so 'wounded the spirit and essence of the building'.

In an archived letter from 1976, Hundertwasser once wrote to a curator of an exhibition that 'the tree is part of my exhibition' when the subjected was raised.[65] Whether a person approves or rejects this line of reasoning is a question of taste; however, the fact that this is what Hundertwasser art and architecture are about is unquestionable. He continues in his letter:

'Since I am myself I always confronted society with art and art with ecological means. This is part of my self [(in original)] as artist, citizen of this world and human being [...]. Art is art only when it does not despise the comparison with nature. Art without tree is a road without exit.'

The author believes that this is a significant part of the cultural legacy of this unique building and that it ought to be preserved as it is – not due to conservative attitudes but rather out of appreciation of cultural pluralism. He could not understand the nature of this unwarranted change especially since at present the 'Kunst Haus Wien' is now being marketed as the first 'green museum'.[66] Overriding Hundertwasser's ecological philosophy and then branding the museum as 'green' seems more as greenwashing rather than further scrutiny of Hundertwasser's legacy.

63 Kunst Haus Wien. Museum Hundertwasser. https://www.kunsthauswien.com/en/home, 10 February 2015.

64 Wien Holding GmbH. http://www.wienholding.at/, 10 February 2015.

65 Friedensreich Hundertwasser, Letter to an Exhibition Curator, Vienna, 1974 June 24th, Hundertwasser Archive in the Hundertwasser Non-Profit Foundation, Folder IV, Archived Document #1174.

66 Neues Konzept für Kunsthaus Wien. 2015, http://oe1.orf.at/artikel/398764, 7 February 2015.

Maybe it is something deeper in the spirit of Vienna. Many Viennese artists were disregarded, criticized, disapproved, and had the backs turned on them by the cultural elite during their lives and are now cherished throughout the streets of the city (and profit its thriving tourism nevertheless). It is possible that this internal logic reversed for Hundertwasser. He was a proud citizen of Vienna and was admired and supported by the Viennese elite throughout his life and only now can his artistic and philosophic legacy be destroyed.[67]

67 The author is thankful for a research grant provided by the City of Vienna and the Center for Austrian Studies at the Hebrew University of Jerusalem that made this project possible. An early version of this paper was presented in the Annual Meeting of the Austrian Centers in Minneapolis in September 2014. A visit to the Hundertwasserhaus was generously hosted by Ms. Regina Pamperl. The author is thankful for the helpful remarks and comments of Or Alecksandrowicz, Dan Avnon, Piki Ish Shalom, Liron Lavi and for the ongoing support and encouragement by Avner de Shalit. This project would not have been possible without the full cooperation and support of the Hundertwasser foundation: Joram Harel, Doris Truppe, and mostly Hundertwasser's chief Archivist Andrea C. Fürst, who spent hours and days discussing my arguments and helping access the beautiful world of Hundertwasser.

Colleen Bertsch

Negotiating Identities and Cultural Representations: The Practice and Patronage of Roma-Transylvanian Folk Violinist Florin Codoba

University of Minnesota

Introduction

This paper is a case study of the musical and public life of Florin Codoba, a highly regarded, tradition-bearing violinist from multi-ethnic Transylvania. As early as his first Transylvanian fieldwork outing in 1904, composer, pianist, and comparative folklorist Béla Bartók attempted to draw distinct lines between Romanian and Hungarian melodic types by creating melodic categories based on sequences of disembodied notes.[1] Although he was famously meticulous with his data, he nonetheless admitted the endless trail of 'crossing and recrossing' influences found in Transylvanian musical practices.[2] Transylvanian string band music continues to be the subject of intense debate among Romanian and Hungarian politicians, scholars, and promoters. As a result, many Transylvanian musicians must often embody multiple, shifting identities in order to find enough employment to financially make ends meet. Florin Codoba is no exception. Like his father, uncle, and grandfather before him, Florin variously represents himself as a Hungarian tradition bearer or Romanian tradition bearer, depending on the sponsor who hires him. It is also telling that although he comes from a Roma family, he rarely represents himself as a Roma tradition bearer.

Although folk music is often described in ethnic or national terms, social scientists have largely recognized that ethnic and national identities are choices that are constructed, maintained, and performed. The move away from a purely biological understanding of ethnicity began in the early 20th century when Fredrik Barth recognized that ethnicity is a form of social organization based on the drawing and maintenance of boundaries, and not a result of some pre-existing state.[3]

1 Béla Bartók, Rumanian Folk Music, vol. I: Instrumental Melodies, The Hague 1967.

2 Béla Bartók, Race Purity in Music, in: Benjamin Suchoff (Ed.), Béla Bartók Essays, Lincoln 1992, 30f.

3 Fredrik Barth, Ethnic Groups and Boundaries. The Social Organization of Culture Difference, Waveland 1998, 9–38.

The genius of Barth's work was his focus on the social processes of creating ethnicity, which allowed for a discussion on human agency's role in ethnicity and group belonging. Telling stories about family and home is one such process. But stories about our own identity can also be framed by others. Because music is a human endeavor, and human identities are ascribed and mutable, ethnic and national labels of music are contingent and political acts.

Christian Karner expands Barth's take on ethnicity by defining three dimensions that help explain ethnicity's characterization as a process.[4] First, he says, ethnicity is a structure of action.[5] This view of ethnicity helps to reconcile social structure with individual agency and also allows ethnicity dialogue move toward a theory of power relations. Second, ethnicity is a way of seeing.[6] Third, ethnicity is a way of feeling, which allows for the emotional ties many members of ethnic groups feel about their experience identifying as a group member.[7] This last characteristic implies reflexivity on the part of group members, which for Karner is the single action that turns culture into ethnicity. When 'social actors begin to reflect on what they used to think and do in a largely taken-for-granted way prior to the onset of a crisis', ethnic identities take shape.[8] Reflexivity, in turn, requires explicit knowledge, a powerful tool that frames and defines the world.

Florin Codoba works within a constellation of institutions and organizations, situated in various countries that patronize Transylvanian folk musicians. The autor of this paper engages with Transylvanian music politics and patronage in Hungary, Romania, and the United States, in combination with interviews with Florin, the author attempts to produce a thoroughly contextualized ethnography that focuses on his processes of ethnic identity formation. The author looks at how state and social institutions have influenced the ethnic labels ascribed to Transylvanian folk music in general, and demonstrates how these social and political contexts influence how Florin performs, the words he uses about his music, and how he comes to understand his own music through foreign points of view. Institutions or individuals who have the funds to sponsor concerts, festivals, and recordings succeed in defining the ethnicities of Transylvanian folk music repertoires and thus frame the region's historical narrative. They are powerful community leaders in that the repertoires they support become common-goods that strengthen the common-identities of target ethnic or national communities.

The data on Transylvanian folk music patronage was collected with support from the Center for Austrian Studies at the University of Minnesota. The author

---

4 Christian Karner, Ethnicity and Everyday Life, London/New York 2007.

5 *Ibid.*, 27f.

6 *Ibid.* Note: Harris Berger's recently published book "Stance" demonstrates ways in which 'seeing' can be a rich source of information on how ethnicity works as a process rather than an *a priori* fact of human experience. See Harris M. Berger, Stance. Ideas about Emotion, Style, and Meaning for the Study of Expressive Culture, Middletown 2009.

7 *Ibid.*

8 *Ibid.*, 26.

conducted online research to gather data on current institutions and organizations that patronize Transylvanian folk musicians, including where their headquarters and events are located, mission statements, how they are funded, a list of musician beneficiaries, and ways in which the organization frames Transylvanian music. This research helped to contextualize the various sites of culture production as they pertain to Transylvanian folk music. The stipend also supported the trip to Csipke Tábor, a Hungarian music and dance camp in Michigan, in order to study with and interview Florin who was a special guest teacher at the camp. The author's activities at the camp included participation in the group fiddle lessons. Lessons were typically two hours long, three or four times each day and were informal, which allowed ample time for questions and story telling.

The most important sources of information regarding Transylvanian musician identity processes for this project stemmed from Florin's responses to the questions regarding violin technique, the stories that he told regarding past and present Transylvanian musicians, and the stories that were negotiated between him and other musicians. Although the 'facts' of his answers to the questions and the content of his stories are important pieces of data, the author is more interested in looking at 'how' Florin shared this information because it demonstrates identity formation processes in action. Florin learned how to become a tradition-bearing music from Pălatca through apprenticeship with his father and uncle. His knowledge is deep and embodied, and also tacit and thus far indefinable. Leaning most heavily on the processual information that one observed at the camp, and interpreting it along with the data collected on patronage systems, the author explored the nature of Florin's social and political roles in various Hungarian and Romanian communities. By focusing on examples where his personal identity is alternately pliable and subsumed under the stories of past hereditary musicians in Transylvania, the author examines how Florin, camp and festival organizers, and non-Roma musicians frame and define Florin's ethnicity, musical authority, and musical contributions.

Romanian-Hungarian Politics and Identity

While language is often considered a determining factor for ethnicity, this argument quickly looses clout in borderland regions. Transylvania was the eastern frontier of the Hungarian Kingdom and Austro-Hungary from roughly 1000 CE until 1918. During the majority of this time, the language of the land-owning ruling elite, and therefore the official national language, was Hungarian. Because of this, the Hungarian language was an important vehicle in the region for both Hungarians and non-Hungarians who lived there, regardless of biological heritage. Such was the case for the Kodoba family from the Transylvanian village Magyarpalatka (Pălatca). Florin Codoba's grandfather Ludovic (1907–1973), his father Márton (1941–2003), and his uncle Béla (1944–1999) are all known by the surname Kodoba, the 'K' indexing their Hungarian background.[9]

Until 1989, Transylvania was governed by the Romanian communist regime. Devoted to the projection of the country's singular ethnic Romanian identity, various laws affecting a person's perceived or official identity were enforced throughout this time.[10] The most personalized tactic was a name change requirement on ID-cards and other official documents. A Hungarian recalls the practice in the mid-1960s and 1970s, when people of all ages living in Romania with given names of Hungarian origin, like István, were officially changed to the Romanianized version, Ștefan.[11] Another tactic was to isolate Hungarian-majority villages with the goal of veiling their existence. One way they accomplished this was by building Orthodox churches in villages that had no Orthodox community, therefore symbolizing a Romanian presence in a predominately Hungarian community.[12] These strategies were used by the Romanian government to assimilate minorities into a Romanian ideal-type population and create the facade of a mono-ethnic state. These goals, of course, were not limited to Romania's government. By the 20th century, nation-building projects based on 'one-people, one-state' had become the primary political ideology for many European countries. A critical mass of people with a singular ethnic identity was the legitamizing force for the existence of a country with distinct borders.

There were, however, some examples where the Ceaușescu regime allowed Hungarian identities to be maintained, albeit under strict direction from the government. While given names were required to be Romanianized, surnames were impossible to translate, and therefore minoritites were allowed keep them as they were. Hungarian schools were also available in the Transylvanian city of Cluj up until the late 1980s. At that point, however, a majority of those schools became Romanian schools (that is, taught in the Romanian language), and subjects like the history and geography of Romania were taught in Romanian at the remaining Hungarian schools as well.[13]

The Romanian government's attempts at differentiating between who was and was not an ideal Romanian citizen set the stage for underground minority activities. Surreptitious excursions to isolated Hungarian villages to record and study

9 Pávai István, Az erdélyi magyar népi tánczene [The Folk Dance Music of the Transylvanian Hungarians], Cluj-Napoca 2012, 238f.

10 For an in-depth and thorough study of Romanian Socialist identity politics and culture, see: Katherine Verdery, National Ideology under Socialism. Identity and Cultural Politics in Ceaușescu's Romania, Berkeley/Los Angeles/London 1991.

11 István Lengyel, personal interview, 29 March 2014.

12 Csongor Könczei, De la Kodoba la Codoba. Despre schimbarea identității etnice secundare într-o familie de muzicanți romi dintr-un sat din Câmpia Transilvaniei [From Kodoba to Codoba. Concerning the Change of Secondary Ethnic Identity within a Family of Romani Musicians from Transylvania's Câmpia Region], in: Working Papers in Romanian Minority Studies 25, Cluj-Napoca 2009, 3–19.

13 Lengyel, interview.

folk traditions, speak Hungarian, and interview village natives were defiant acts of dissent against the oppressive system in which they lived.[14] Although Transylvanians were now officially incorporated into the Romanian nation, these isolated groups of people were designated, officially via actions taken against them, to not be 'true' Romanian when they spoke Hungarian or had a Hungarian name. This Romanian versus Hungarian dichotomy poses different problems for the Roma. For them, identifying as either Romanian or Hungarian is not only a posiblility, but an unspoken requirement for social acceptance and upward mobility. A Roma's secondary identity is fragile and mutable so that it can fit the predominant culture in which they live and work.

Figure 1: Excerpt from Codoba's Facebook Account.

The stories about the physical attributes of parents and grandparents, their homeland, what languages they spoke, and what foods they ate, are all performances of ethnic belonging. Florin Codoba describes his grandfather Ludovic (referred to as Lajos Kodoba in Hungarian scholarship), his father Márton, and his uncle Béla as Pălatca violinists, as his teachers, as Hungarian and not Romanian, and finally as cigany-ungarești [Hungarian gypsy]. He attributed their Hungarian identity to two facts: that they were from Pălatca, and that they spoke Hungarian.[15] Florin also considers himself Hungarian, but unlike the elder Kodoba family members, he does not speak Hungarian. Moreover, Florin spells his name with a 'C' instead of a 'K,' adopting the Romanian spelling.[16] His recent Facebook posts further demonstrate the confusion over ethno-linguistic cues in regards to both the Kodoba/Codoba family name and Transylvanian folk music (see figure 1).[17]

14 Wayne B. Kraft, Transylvanian Dancing in the Final Hour, in: The Anthropology of East Europe Review 22/1, Washington 2004, 51–59, here 54.

15 Florin Codoba, interview with the author, 3 July 2014.

16 Csongor Könczei develops a theory for the change in spelling in his article De la Kodoba la Codoba, in which he compares Pălatca censuses from 1948 and 2002 to show how Roma families moved away from the Hungarian Reformed church to the Romanian Orthodox church. The Romanian Orthodox church, therefore, is considered a tool in the Romanian nation-building project. See Könczei, De la Kodoba la Codoba, 3–19.

17 Martin Florin Codoba, http://facebook.com/martinflorin.codoba.?fref=ts.htm, 3 September 2014.

In this post, Florin shared a YouTube video of his late father playing Romanian dance music called *De-a lungul*. Because it is a Romanian-specific dance, he used the term *De-a lungul* throughout the post. The dance called *batuta*, however, is called *szökös* in Hungarian and so both words appear. Florin wrote his status update in Hungarian, even though he is only fluent in Romanian and Romanes. And even though his father and uncle used the Hungarian spelling of the family name as recently as the 1990s, today Florin uses the Romanian spelling. Florin's father Márton, his uncle Béla, and his grandfather Ludovic were Roma musicians who spoke fluent Hungarian, and the Hungarian *táncház* [dance house] community regarded them as masters of Hungarian folk music.[18] After Márton and Béla passed away, Florin's participation as a Hungarian folk music ambassador increased substantially. Although his Hungarian is limited, and although he subscribes to the Romania spelling of his name, Hungarians in the *táncház* movement actively support him as a Hungarian tradition bearer by hiring him for Hungarian-specific events.

Transylvanian Folk Music Patronage

Transylvanian string musicians, like Florin Codoba, have been supported in a number of ways by individuals and organizations around the world. This section documents the broad spectrum of patronage that some Transylvanian string musicians have received over the past forty years. The point here is to develop an understanding of the global network and various angles of interest concerning Transylvanian string band music in one article, rather than delve deeply into any one patron or organization.[19]

The most active, and arguably the most influential, support for Transylvanian string musicians over the past forty years has been the Hungarian *táncház* movement. The movement, also known by its Hungarian name, *táncházmozgalom*, has been been chronicled and analyzed extensively by scholars, journalists, and the movement's leaders.[20] In the late 1960s, a folk music and dance revival emerged in Hungary that began to replace the staged folk performances that were especially popular during the communist era. According to Colin Quigley, the *táncház* approach originated with one or two of these folk dance performance ensembles, most notably 'The Barók Ensemble'.[21] The ensemble's director Sándor Timár and

18 The *táncház* movement is a folk music revival that began in Budapest in the late 1960s. Hungarian-Transylvanian folk repertoire is especially favorited among its performers, teachers, and participants. See Colin Quigley, The Hungarian Dance House Movement and Revival of Transylvanian String Band Music, Oxford 2013.

19 Colin Quigley, ethnomusicologist at the University of Limerick, has written a detailed historical account of the activities of the pioneering individuals and organizations who established the *táncház* movement and its extensive network. See Quigley, Dance House.

20 Hagyományok Háza, Essays, http://www.heritagehouse.hu/page/22/, 12 January 2015. More essays and books in Hungarian are also available on this website.

21 Quigley, Dance House, 5–8.

musicians Béla Halmos and Ferenc Sebő were particularly interested in moving away from the Russian Moiseyev folkballet model of folkdance performance, and instead, began to develop a way of playing music for dance in a social-dance functional manner. Timár's legacy was his innovative approach to teaching folk dance in a way so that individuals could master the dance steps and techniques, and at the same time, master the art of improvisatory movement. This style of pedagogy became synonomous with the *táncház*, movement.[22]

A network of unassociated or loosely associated organizations began to provide various platforms for the *táncház* movement to flourish and it spread among the urban middle class in Hungary. Integral to the *táncház* movement's development was the Hungarian Academy of Science's Musicology Institute (MTA, Zenetudomány Intézet) in Budapest where they house Bartók's and Kodaly's folk music collections, as well as newer field recordings.[23] These archives are open and available to the public. The music department at the Nyíregyháza Főskola (College of Nyíregyháza) and the more recently established folk music department at the Liszt Academy (Budapest), train musicians in folk performance and pedagogy in the social-dance functional manner. The state-funded Hungarian Heritage House (Hagyományok Háza) funds music transcription projects of Transylvanian music. Their well-organized series of books and recordings can be purchased by the public at their bookstore.[24] However, these organizations have patronized Transylvanian folk musicians only sporodically during music collecting field trips or by producing and promoting new recordings of their music to a wider urban audience. The Hungarian Heritage House also sponsors the Hungarian State Ensemble, which has hired Transylvanian folk musicians for live concert performances and recordings. The fact that the Hungarian organizations credit Transylvanian musicians by name demonstates their dedication as patrons, rather than merely appropriators of Transylvanian folk music. This is only a small sample of Hungarian public organizations that fund projects that utalize Transylvanian musicians.

There are also Hungarian dance groups and individuals who support Transylvanian musicians by organizing summer music and dance training camps, for which the musicians are hired to teach or perform. Some of these camps are geared toward professional and semi-professional dance groups and experienced individuals who want to workshop dances from a specific village or region. For example, the 'Zala Dance Association organizes annual camps in the villages Vajdaszentivány, Nyárádselye, and Szászcsávás.[25] The 'László Lajtha Foundation' & 'Háromszék Dance Ensemble' organizes the annual 'Kommandói Gypsy Folklore

22 *Ibid.*

23 Magyar Tudományos Akadémia, Zenetudomány Intézet, Bartók Archívum, http://www.zti.hu/zti_uj/index_hu.htm?07, 12 January 2015.

24 Hagyományok Háza, Folklórdokumentációs Könyvtár, http://www.hagyomanyokhaza.hu/main/mediatar/.

25 Zalai Táncegyüttes, http://www.zalaite.hu/index.php?ugras=statikus&statoldal=2915, 12 January 2015. For camp information see Vajdaszentiványi tábor, Selyei tábor, and Szászcsávási tábor.

Camp'.[26] And the 'Kalotaszeg Folkdance Ensemble' organizes the annual 'Kalotaszegi Vándor Folkdance Camp'.[27] In addition to these camps, others are more accessible to the general public and encourage amatures to participate in the folk revival. For example, The 'Kallós Zoltán Foundation' (Kallós Zoltán Alapitvány) organizes at least two yearly camps: the 'International Kalotaszeg Folk Music and Dance Camp' and the 'International Meszőség Dance Camp'.[28]

Many summer music and dance camps, however, are also frequently organized and run by Hungarian *táncház* bands. These musicians are considered experts in Transylvanian folk music themselves, therefore eliminating the need to hire musicians from Transylvania to teach or entertain camp participants. The fact that they are touted as *táncház* bands, and not necessarily a band from a specific village, gives them the freedom to teach music from a different village each year. This change in repertoire helps to keep the camp experience fresh and exciting for folk music and dance enthusiasts. Well-known bands from the Budapest area such as Téka, Méta, and Dűvő, among others, have run camps to great success.

Hungarian music and dance camps that teach Transylvanian repertoire in the United States began with the energy and vision of American and Hungarian-American folklore enthusiasts. The first Hungarian music and dance camp in the US, Barátság, ran for almost 20 summers, beginning in 1982 in Mendecino, California.[29] Ti Ti Tábor in Washington state began ten years after the first Barátság camp in 1992 (and is still going strong), and Aranykapu Tábor, also in California, ran from 2002 to 2006. These camps were dedicated to learning Transylvanian folk music and dance via the *táncház* movement model and, therefore, the organizers hired *táncház* teachers from Budapest rather than Transylvanian performers and teachers. However, the Michigan-based Csipke Tábor, organized and run by the Hungarian dance ensemble Csipke, has recently hired Transylvanian musicians as guest artist teachers and performers. Violinists István Varga from Méra, Florin Codoba from Pălatca and Cluj, and the Transylvanian *táncház* band Heveder have helped to draw large numbers of attendees to the camp.

In addition to the weeklong training camps, Hungarian influence on Tranylvanian music and musicians extends beyond its own political borders to the United States, Canada, Australia, Japan and Western European countries via year-round weekend workshops, lectures, concerts, and festivals. Transylvanian musicians often travel to these countries to participate in these events organized under the banner of the Hungarian nation.

---

26 Háromszék Táncegüttes Sepsiszentgyörgy, Roma (Gypsy) Folklore Camp from Kommandó, http://www.hte.ro/category/9-kommandoi-ciganyfolklor-tabor/, 12 January 2015.

27 Facebook, Kalotaszegi Vándor Néptánctábor, https://www.facebook.com/kalotaszegitabor/timeline, 12 January 2015.

28 Kallós Zoltán Alapitvány, http://www.kallos.org.ro/index.php/hu/home.html, 12 January 2015. For camp information see táborok.

29 History of Barátság, http://www.baratsag.com/History_of_Baratsag.html, 17 August 2014.

The Romanian government is also active in supporting folk culture, but from a different angle than that of the Hungarian complex. While the Hungarian *táncház* movement strives to preserve village folk music, the Romanian cultural officials largely understand village folk music as the prototype of an ideal national folk art. Instead of understanding village musical performances as art or entertainment in its own right, Romanian folk projects are often focused on developing the music into a polished artistic expression, performed by institutionally trained musicians. With that said, there are preservationist activitities happening in Cluj, for example, by Mircea Câmpeanu, director of the Center for Popular Arts (Centrul Creatii Populare). Câmpeanu is instrumental in providing organizational support to Transylvanian village musicians, especially in Frata and Soporu.[30] The County Center for Preservation and Promotion of Traditional Culture (Centrul Județean pentru Conservarea şi Promovarea Culturii Tradiționale) in Cluj, along with the city of Gherla, is also responsible for the promotion and encouragement of amature, semi-professional, and professional folk musicians across Transylvania through festivals like the annual Transylvanian Trio Festival in Gherla.[31] A video of Florin Codoba performing at this festival in 2012, along with Pălatca natives Mihai Radac (three-stringed contra) and Mircea Covaci (bass), is posted on Câmpeanu's individual professional website, along with a number of other Transylvanian string ensembles.[32]

Patronage of Transylvanian musicians also comes in the form of professional audio recordings funded by various government or government-allied agencies. The record label Electrecord, established in 1932, was the only record lable in communist Romania. Electrecord sub-labels that focused on Romanian folk music included Trésors Folkloriques Roumains and The Romanian National Collection of Folklore.[33] Today the label's involvement in folk music tends to focus on re-releases of previous material. However, Romanian ethnomusicologist Speranța Rădulescu directed and released the 2002 CD project called 'Romanian and Hungarian music from Central Transylvania' through Electrecord, which spotlights the music and musicians from and near the village Buza.[34] Centrul Județean pentru Conservarea in Cluj has recorded and released recordings of amateur, semi-professional, and professional musicians from Transylvania.[35] Recently Câmpaeanu has been instrumental in this endeavor as the project director for recent recordings of Transylvanian string musicians.

---

30 Mircea Cimpeanu, doctor in muzica, http://www.mirceacimpeanu.ro, 12 January 2015.

31 Centrul Județean pentru Conservarea şi Promovarea Culturii Tradiționale [The County Center for Preservation and Promotion of Traditional Culture], http://www.traditiiclujene.ro/index.php, 12 January 2015. For the folk music calendar, musicians list, and archival audio see Folclor Muzical.

32 Cimpeanu, Video: Grupa II.

33 Discogs, Electrecord, http://www.discogs.com/label/11624-Electrecord, 12 January 2015.

34 Romanian and Hungarian music from Central Transylvania, Fundația Al. Tzigara-Samurcaş, Electrecord, compact disc liner notes.

35 Centrul Județean pentru Conservarea. See arhiva audio.

Hungarian institutions, however, have funded the majority of professional recordings of Transylvanian village musicians available to the general public. Most impressively, a number of Hungarian-sponsored recordings were conceptualized and produced as sets or series, organized by village, in separate volumes. One such collection is the popular Új Patria Series, a selection of recordings released for public sale that derived from a larger project called the Final Hour program.[36] Of the 50 CDs released between 1997–2001, 23 are recordings of Tranysylvanian musicians while the remaining 27 CDs are recordings divided between musicians from Slovakia, various regions within present-day Hungary, and Voivodina. Other noteworthy folk music series that include Transylvanian musicians and funded by Hungarian organizations are the Dance House Association's Élő népzene [Live Folk Music] and Új élő népzene [New Live Folk Music] series, and the Kallós Archivum series.[37] [38]

These various organizations and their activities are creating history. By determining who to hire and not to hire as representatives, they are shaping Transylvanian folk music's narrative and amplifying their particular point of view of history. For example, in 2013, the Smithsonian Institute's Folklife Festival in Washington, D.C., was called 'Hungarian Heritage: Roots to Revival'. A number of important Transylvanian musicians participated, including Florin Codoba, who was invited to perform as a traditional artist. Each participant's biography was included on the Folklife Festival's official website. Florin's biography introduces him as the lead fiddler of the Magyarpalatka Folk Ensemble, but from there, it slips past him to focus on the Magyarpalatka musicians as a general group of tradition bearers:

> 'Florin Codoba ("Kodoba Florin") is the lead fiddler of the Magyarpalatka Folk Ensemble, one of the most popular and widely known bands in the Hungarian Dance House Movement, playing Hungarian, Romanian, and Roma music. The musicians, most of whom are related to each other, maintain the tradition of passing down musical knowledge from generation to generation.
>
> The musicians of Magyarpalatka are among the last representatives of Transylvanian instrumental folk music. [...] The younger generations of Roma musicians in Palatka have preserved much of this musical treasure, which they play with their parents and uncles.'[39]

36 Heritage of Our Future, XX–XI, http://utolsoora.hu/en/final-hour, 12 January 2015. For a list of the CDs see Új Patria Series.

37 For information on the Élő népzene series, see the the Dance House Association's website: http://tanchaztalalkozo.hu/hun/index.php?option=com_content&task=view&id=497&Itemid=930, 12 January 2015.

38 Information on the Kallós Archivum series can be found on the Kallós Zoltán foundation's website: http://www.kallos.org.ro/index.php/hu/home/kiadvanyok.html?showall=1, 12 January 2015.

39 Smithsonian, Hungarian Heritage, http://www.festival.si.edu/past-festivals/2013/Hungarian_Heritage/participants.aspx#martin_florin_kodoba, 15 September 2014.

The biography is not about the artist Florin Codoba. It is a story about a Transylvanian community that has been preserving music as if it were a delicate artifact. Instead of describing Florin as a musician who 'makes' Pălatca folk music happen in the immediate sense, the narrative makes Florin disappear. The image that emerges is a Hungarian village in Transylvania that owns treasure, an object of value that is shared, inherited, accounted for, catalogued, played with, and protected by Roma musicians.

In reality, every tradition-bearing musician has had to recreate what they hear within the mold of their individual bodies. By separating Florin from the music he makes, the Smithsonian biography implicitly perpetuates the story that Florin's success as a musician has nothing to do with his daily practice, exquisite attention to detail, problem solving skills, and leadership abilities. Instead their story is that his success rests entirely on his family's long connection to Pălatca, his adherance to his father and grandfather's performance practices, and the successful passing, from one generation to the next, a collection of objectified musical gestures and sounds – described as 'musical treasure' – that somehow took shape in the distant, unspecified past.

Florin Codoba as a Tightrope Walker: Navigating Folk Music Practice and Patronage

Although Florin's ethnic background is Rom, his preferred identity is as a Hungarian musician. This story is often accepted by others, but at various other times it has been negotiated, ignored, or negated through competing stories. As a hereditary musician from Pălatca, Florin's identity is also bound up in emodied movement, gathered through years of intensive training with his father Márton and uncle Béla. Bourdieu refers to this as *habitus*, and it allows for an interplay between explicit stories and embodied, tacit knowledge in the development of human action and identity creation.[40]

Florin began learning how to play the violin at the age of three. In an early video that was later posted on YouTube, a young Florin is playing next to his uncle Béla and periodically self-correcting his bow strokes to match his uncle's.[41] Béla's teaching method, as evidenced in the video, was the apprenticeship model. He taught the correct sequence of notes, the direction and duration of bow strokes, and other appropriate, nuanced violin-playing techniques such as melodic ornaments by example. He also taught how to lead a band of musicians and interact with the music collectors who recorded the video by way of example. As a student, Florin had a difficult job. For an extended duration, he had to be intensely focused

40 Pierre Bourdieu, Outline of a Theory of Practice, Cambridge 1977.

41 V. Hegedü-VII.Brácsa-I.Bögő Iskola: Magyarpalatkai szökős [V. Violin-VII.Viola-Bass School: szökős from Magyarpalatka], https://www.youtube.com/watch?v=9W8jFwigN_4.htm, 16 February 2014.

on two bodies, his uncle's and his own, and intuit every motion and sound his uncle was about to make. While Florin was playing the violin, he was also playing with perception, complex time, and movement.

The first time the author met Florin Codoba was in Cluj, Romania, in the summer of 2008. Over the span of two weeks, they met three times so that she could video record him playing the violin. She paid him money, and he, staring into the camera, absorbed with what his limbs were doing, played melodies that he learned from his father and uncle. Dozens of these melodies would pour from his fingertips before he would stop to take a break. The author was drawn to record Florin because others interested in Transylvanian string band music – friends she had met at Hungarian folk music and dance camps in the United States – had already recorded him and had told that he was highly regarded as a source of special information. In the folk music world, growing up in a musical family in a village and taking part in an apprenticeship model of musical training is a sign that implies a deep bodily knowledge of musical style, as if, by mere saturation, Florin's limbs held the knowledge of his father and uncle's limbs.

The next meeting in person was the summer of 2014, at the Csipke Hungarian Music and Dance camp in Sauk Valley, Michigan. For seven consecutive days, six hours a day, Florin taught the music students, including the author, by playing the same set of songs over and over again. He modeled exquisite Pălatca violin technique as we stumbled along. Although the students played wrong notes, rhythms, and bow directions, Florin never stopped playing the violin in order to correct them. In fact, even though they had a translator, he never verbally instructed the class. Instead, Florin instructed by modeling and gesturing. If a student asked how to play a specific part of a melody, he would simply answer by playing on the violin.

Florin often pulls his fingers off the strings in a distinctive lateral motion while playing. This motion creates the melody, but it also creates ornamental 'ghost notes', a specific and uncommon type of 'melodic floricele', that evoke the playing styles of his late father and uncle and is widely identified with the music of Pălatca. He seamlessly combines this movement with other left hand motions such as the 'trills' and 'turns' that lace his melodies. The author wanted to know how Florin understands these extra-melodic 'ghost notes'. When he was interviewed, the author asked him to demonstrate Pălatca ornaments instead of using the Romanian term 'melodic floricele'. Therefore, he responded to the author's request by demonstrating a musical practice that was unrelated to the 'ghost notes' that the author had in mind. Instead, he played a short eight-bar melody that is not a complete song and is not meant to be played by itself. It is a musical stock-phrase, a thinking or resting melody that is inserted, like a bridge, in-between two songs. Its purpose is to allow the bandleader a few moments to think of a new song to play without stopping the music. Although the author had made a translation mistake, the resulting conversation revealed an interesting conundrum for Florin. After his demonstration, Florin offered a multi-lingual, tangled web of terms about the music that he plays:

'That was a *csárdás – joc țigănesc.*
In Hungarian you say *csárdás*; in Romanian you say *țigăn* [gypsy] dance.
That's the ornament. Dance which [...]
[pauses] [...] there is no normal [...] [pauses]
There is no way to say it in Romanian.
In Hungarian it's: *koziatek.*
In Romanian, you can't say it; I don't know the translation.'[42]

Because one dance set can last up to an hour without a pause in the music, these thinking melodies are important tools for the lead violinist. However, although the thinking melody has a very specific and important function, Florin did not offer a specific term for it. Instead he offered a collection of terms that he has heard other people use. First he used the word *csárdás*, a Hungarian word that refers to the Hungarian-specific dance and dance rhythm. The only Romanian correlate Florin knew of was *joc țigănesc* [gypsy dance]. This surprised the author since the terms, *csárdás* and *joc țigănesc*, links the melody to two distinctive groups: Hungarians and Roma, respectively. Florin more or less finally settled on the Hungarian word *koziatek*, which translates as 'in-between,' and is commonly used by Hungarian *táncház* musicians.

The conversation continued a little while later when Florin pulled the author aside to tell that sometimes Hungarians use the word *cifra* in place of *koziatek. Cifra* is an adjective that means 'gaudy' or 'flashy'. This surprised the author. When the author had asked Florin to demonstrate Pălatca-style ornaments, the author used the English word 'ornament', expecting that he would play examples of trills and the 'ghost note' technique that is specific to Pălatca folk music. Instead, Florin demonstrated a series of thinking melodies, or *cifra-s*. His knowledge of the Hungarian musical term *cifra* helped him to make sense of the author's English term *ornament*.

Florin's job is not to theorize and define his music, but to recreate Pălatca music as closely as possible to how his father and uncle had performed it. As a budding researcher, the author wanted an immediate verbal explanation for something that took Florin about 20 years of intensive apprenticeship training to learn. By inventing a way to try to understand the author and her question and then offering this multi-lingual collection of terms for something that did not have a name in the first place, Florin was performing his expertise as a master musician and teacher of Pălatca folk music in a way that was expected of him at a Hungarian *táncház* camp.

But although he sets the standard for how Pălatca music should be played, Florin's playing and teaching style elicited some critical feedback from at least one veteran *táncház* musician who is intimately familiar with Transylvanian folk music history and practice. Janos, a man about 20 years older than Florin, had lear-

42 Florin Codoba, personal interview, 2 July 2014. Translation from the original Romanian into English by the author.

ned some Pălatca melodies from Kozak Csiga, a violinist who was influential in Transylvania in the 1960s and 1970s.[43] Csiga was not from Pălatca, but had taken a wife from there, and over time had exchanged music with Florin's father and uncle.[44] After class one day, Janos recalled Csiga's version of a song that we were learning and realized that it was different from how Florin was teaching it. Janos reasoned that since he had learned this song before Florin was born, he must be recalling older melodic information, which for him meant more authentic, and thus correct.

Later, when the author spoke with him privately, Janos also expressed frustration about Florin's teaching style. For him, the non-verbal teaching method was a sign that Florin did not fully understand his own abilities or the art of teaching how to play the violin. Although he respected Florin's position as the son and nephew of great Pălatca violinists, Janos simply did not buy the story that Florin himself is a master Pălatca musician and expert violin teacher in his own right.[45]

The camp organizers also hired a professional Hungarian *táncház* band from Transylvania called 'Heveder'. Throughout the week, whenever the band played music from Pălatca, Florin would lead them. His instrument was louder than the other musicians: he used every inch of his bow and dug it deep into the string, breaking multiple strings throughout the week. But Florin only played music from Pălatca, unlike 'Heveder', who were required to play music from various villages and regions. A large Transylvanian repertoire is a basic requirement to be hired by *táncház* organizers anywhere in the world so that *táncház* dancers have the chance to dance a wide variety of styles throughout the week. Commonly played at most *táncházok* is music from the Hungarian regions of Transylvania including Kalotaszeg, Székélyföld, Gyimes, and Mezöség, where Magyarpalatka is located. The genre has become so specialized that different villages within these regions have their own cycle, or set of dances and music, that they are identified with. While there are some melodies and dances that appear in multiple villages, specifying differences between village practices is fetishized in the *táncház* community, as demonstrated at camp workshops, *táncház* events, and the large number of village-specific recordings produced by Hungarian organizations.

On one hand, the fetishization of music and dance differences between villages in Transylvania is good business for Florin. His highly specialized ability for playing music from Pălatca means that his presence at Csipke lends the camp relevancy in the world-wide *táncház* market. Florin teaching at Csipke also signals to the global *táncház* community that this is a serious camp with serious intentions of supporting Transylvanian musicians with Hungarian patronage. On the other hand, Florin did not participate in all of the week's revelries. There was a *táncház* very night after dinner that started at eight pm and lasted well into the morning

43 Janos is not his real name. Janos, personal interview, 2 July 2014.

44 Florin Codoba and Janos, combined interview, 2 July 2014.

45 Janos, interview 2 July 2014.

hours. There was a large, wooden dance floor, and in the back, was a *kocsma* [bar]. Depending on the mood of the party-goers, the dancing would shift from the dance floor to the *kocsma,* and sometimes back again. In all of these scenarios, the musicians were always at the center of the excitement. But Florin's role was very limited within this ebb and flow of improvised party making. Not only did Florin not know the vast musical repertoires that the *táncház* band could play, he could not speak fluent Hungarian or English to always engage with non-musicians.

Conclusion

Florin's identity as a Pălatca folk musician is an ongoing process that he negotiates via stories about his family and musical upbringing, working within the Hungarian *táncház* movement, and being a Romanian citizen. Contradictions surrounding his ethnic identity abounds. Although he is a Romanian citizen who speaks fluent Romanian, he identifies most readily as a Hungarian musician. On the pretense of his tradition-bearing Roma status, Hungarians have allowed him to claim a secondary Hungarian ethnic identity, albeit one he must work at to maintain. And even though he has changed the spelling of his family name from the Hungarian 'K' to the Romanian 'C' spelling of Codoba, his insistence that he is Hungarian, and his regular participation in Hungarian sponsored events, aligns him with his family's history of involvement with Hungarian folk music patrons, as well as Pălatca's history as a multi-ethnic, Romanian-Hungarian-Roma, village.

The geo-political history of Transylvania and the activities of Transylvanian folk music patrons are mosaic pieces that contribute to Florin's identity as a Pălatca musician. Starting with Bartók's ethnographic work through the *táncház* movement, Hungarians have established the norms of ethnic or national identification of folk music in Transylvania. The sheer amount of funding devoted to village folk music, in terms of the numbers of recordings, concerts, festivals, and camps, lends great framing power to the Hungarian folk music network, and amplifies a Hungarian viewpoint of Transylvanian history. On the one hand, they sometimes hire Roma musicians from Transylvanian villages to teach their music under the banner of Hungarian folk music. On the other hand, some Hungarian sponsored events, such as Hungarian music and dance camps, forego hiring Transylvanian musicians altogether, and instead, hire Hungarian musicians from Budapest to teach music from Transylvanian villages. These alignments frame and define musical activity in terms of a national music evolution, regardless of the biological background of the individual performer producing that music.

The ethnographic sections in this paper that depict the author's own experience working with, observing, and interviewing Florin, are examples of his creative navigation of a western hegemonic musical system, within which he had to match the demands of the international Transylvanian folk music and dance market. There is a great difference between how Florin knows Pălatca music and how others know Pălatca music. The difference has to do with the difference between explicit knowledge and tacit knowledge: those who reflect on and define musical and cultural 'facts' versus Florin's embodied knowledge. In his employment, Florin must function in a system that champions explicit, definable knowledge. But what makes Florin highly sought after is his tacit, embodied knowledge of what it means to be a musician from Pălatca, which is thus far indefinable, and unrelated to strict ethnic labels.

Lukáš Motyčka

Die homoerotische Camouflage im literarischen Werk Josef Mühlbergers

Palacký Universität Olmütz

Josef Mühlberger und die Mühlberger-Forschung

Der, aus einer deutsch-tschechischen Familie stammende Josef Mühlberger (1903–1985) wurde im ostböhmischen Trutnov [Trautenau] geboren. Er machte als Mitherausgeber der Zeitschrift *Witiko* auf sich aufmerksam, betätigte sich in den 1930er Jahren als Vermittler zwischen (Sudeten-)Deutschen und Tschechen, setzte sich für die Werke jüdischer Autoren (etwa für Franz Kafka) ein. Die Publikation der Novelle "Die Knaben und der Fluß" (1934) im renommierten Insel-Verlag bedeutete für Mühlbegers Karriere einen Höhepunkt, der jedoch nie mehr übertroffen werden sollte. Er beteiligte sich – etwa mit dem historischen Roman "Huss im Konzil" (1931) – an der zugespitzten Diskussion in der politisch und national polarisierten Tschechoslowakei der Zwischenkriegszeit. Im politisch zunehmend extremen Mitteleuropa standen Mühlbergers Emporkommen zwei schier unüberwindbare Hindernisse im Weg, nämlich sein politisches Lavieren und seine Homosexualität. Nachdem Mühlberger Anfang der 1940er Jahre auf eine sexuelle Provokation hin verhört und inhaftiert wurde, meldete er sich freiwillig zur Wehrmacht. Den Krieg verbrachte er an mehreren Fronten. 1946 verließ er unter passablen Bedingungen die Tschechoslowakei und ließ sich – seinen eigenen Worten nach '[vertrieben] in ein Paradies'[1] – in Schwaben nieder. Hier wirkte er als Journalist lokaler Zeitungen, Übersetzer und Propagator (nicht nur) tschechischer Literatur und Kultur. Er publizierte in mehr als zwanzig Verlagen Romane, Erzählungen, Gedichte sowie landeskundliche bzw. (literatur-)historische Essays. Diverse Preise, die meistens von den Institutionen der Vertriebenen (Sudetendeutschen) verliehen wurden, konnten dem Autor zu keiner breiteren Rezeption verhelfen. Mühlberger starb in beinahe völliger Vergessenheit in Eislingen bei Stuttgart.[2]

1 Josef Mühlberger, Leben an Grenzen, in: Josef Mühlberger, Türkische Novelle. Erzählung, Bad Wörishofen 1948, 71–79, hier 78.

2 Näher zu Mühlbergers Biographie siehe z. B. Michael Berger, Josef Mühlberger (1903–1985). Sein Leben und Prosaschaffen bis 1939. Ein Beitrag zur Geschichte der deutschböhmischen Literatur in den 20er und 30er Jahren des 20. Jahrhunderts. Dissertation Berlin 1989; oder Susanne Lange-Greve, Leben an Grenzen. Josef Mühlberger (1903–1985). Eine Veröffentlichung zu seinem 100. Geburtstag, Schwäbisch Gmünd 2003.

Das Leben und Werk dieses Autors lassen sich in mancherlei Hinsicht als exemplarisch betrachten. Er ist keineswegs ein welt- bzw. europabekannter Autor, der in 'keinerlei Literaturgeschichte fehlen darf [und] dem Bibliographien, historisch-kritische Ausgaben und Handbücher gewidmet [werden]'.[3] Es handelt sich auf der anderen Seiten jedoch durchaus nicht um einen Autor, dessen Bücher 'in den Regalen größerer oder regionaler Bibliotheken [verstauben], wenn sie es denn überhaupt bis dorthin geschafft haben'.[4] Mühlberger ist vielmehr einer dritten Gruppe von Künstlern zuzuordnen, denen – wie Jörg Krappmann in seinem Buch "Allerlei Übergänge" darlegt – '[letzteres] Schicksal erspart, [ersteres] verwehrt blieb'. Diese Schaffenden genossen 'zeitweise einen gewissen Rang im literarischen Leben', 'ihr Name [figuriert oft] in Lexika und anderen Nachschlagewerken'.[5]

Auch Josef Mühlberger, der eine zweifellos wichtige Rolle in der mitteleuropäischen Literaturgeschichte des 20. Jahrhunderts spielte, dessen Bücher immer noch neu aufgelegt und rezipiert werden[6], zu den Vernachlässigten. Allerdings weniger in Anbetracht der Quantität der Forschungsliteratur, sondern vielmehr ihrer Qualität.[7] Die Mühlberger-Forschung weist bei näherem Hinsehen eine Reihe von Mythen,

---

3 Jörg Krappmann, Allerhand Übergänge. Interkulturelle Analyse der regionalen Literatur in Böhmen und Mähren sowie der deutschen Literatur in Prag (1890–1918), Bielefeld 2013, 9.

4 Krappmann, Allerhand Übergänge, 9.

5 'Kennzeichnend für diese Autoren ist, dass zu ihnen meist ein bis zwei monographische Studien vorliegen, die an speziellen Instituten erarbeitet und in einschlägigen Verlagen publiziert wurden. In aktuellen Diskursen fungieren sie als Querverweise im Fußnotenapparat. Kennzeichnend ist auch, dass Anstrengungen unternommen werden, das Werk dieser Autoren durch die Publikation einzelner Romane oder Erzählungsbände wiederzubeleben. Ins Bewusstsein einer breiteren wissenschaftlichen oder publizistischen Öffentlichkeit rücken sie jedoch nicht mehr, so dass sie hinsichtlich des Bearbeitungsniveaus der "großen" Autoren als Vernachlässigte zu bezeichnen sind.' (Krappmann, Allerhand Übergänge, 9f.) Mühlbergers Status im literarhistorischen Kanon wurde auch etwa durch dessen Miteinbezug in den Kontext des renommierten 'Prager Kreises', vgl. Ludvík Václavek, Zu einigen Autoren des weiteren "Prager Kreises": Uffo Daniel Horn, Josef Mühlberger, Ludwig Karpe und Franz Carl Weiskopf, in: Klaas-Hinrich Ehlers – Steffen Höhne – Václav Maidl – Marek Nekula (Hgg.), Brücken nach Prag. Deutschsprachige Literatur im kulturellen Kontext der Donaumonarchie und der Tschechoslowakei. Festschrift für Kurt Krolop zu 70. Geburtstag, Wien 2000, 419–427.

6 2003 erschien im Insel-Verlag die Novelle "Die Knaben und der Fluß" mit dem Nachwort von Peter Härtling, 2006 wurde Mühlbergers "Geschichte der deutschen Literatur in Böhmen 1900–1939" ins Tschechische übersetzt, 2009 konzentrierte sich die ganze Nummer der Zeitschrift *Germanoslavica* auf das Leben und Werk des Autors.

7 Dies bezeugt eine zusammenfassende Betrachtung von Bernd-Ulrich Hergemöller, der Mühlberger ein Lemma in seinem Lexikon "Mann für Mann" widmete und keineswegs zu den Insidern der Mühlberger-Forschung gehört: 'Bis heute fehlen: eine historisch-kritische Gesamtausgabe seiner Werke, eine wissenschaftliche Darstellung seines Lebens auf dem Hintergrund der politischen Verhältnisse sowie literaturwissenschaftliche Untersuchungen jeder Art.' (Bernd-Ulrich Hergemöller, Josef Mühlberger, in: Bernd-Ulrich Hergemöller (Hg.), Mann für Mann. Biographisches Lexikon. Zur Geschichte von Freundesliebe und mannmännlicher Sexualität im deutschsprachigen Sprachraum, Berlin 2010, 852f., hier 853) Und in ihrer komparatistischen Studie zu Mühlberger und Torberg beklagte sich Helga Abret, die Literaturforscher hätten Mühlberger 'bis zum heutigen Tag stiefmütterlich behandelt.' (Helga Abret, Zwei Prager Geschichten aus "finsteren Zeiten" – Josef Mühlbergers Der Galgen im Weinberg (1951) und Friedrich Torbergs Golems Wiederkehr (1968), in: Stifter Jahrbuch 15, München, 2001, 42–69, hier 48.)

Verdrängungen und Leerstellen auf.[8] Mühlberger war sein ganzes Leben lang im Visier national gesinnter Kulturinstitutionen: Vor dem Zweiten Weltkrieg wurde er als ein höchst suspekter Judenfreund, ein lauer Sudetendeutscher, darüber hinaus als ein halbseidener Erzähler von Knabenfreundschaften öffentlich diffamiert, nach dem Zweiten Weltkrieg von derselben Seite hochgelobt, unterstützt.

Der erste Mythos der Mühlberger-Forschung rankt sich um das politische Profil des Schriftstellers: Mühlberger wurde nach dem Zweiten Weltkrieg – und wird bis heute von der sudetendeutschen Sparte der Forschung – unkritisch zum integren Antifaschisten, Antimilitaristen usf. stilisiert.[9] Die Tatsache, dass Mühlbergers Einstellungen und Handlungen gegenüber dem Nationalsozialismus vielmehr als problematisch anzusehen sind, wird in diesen Kreisen bis heute ausgeblendet.

Der zweite heikle Punkt im Umgang mit Josef Mühlberger ist die Homosexualität des Autors. Während aus der biographischen Tatsache – unter dem Einfluss der allgemeinen Liberalisierung der Literaturwissenschaft – in der Mühlberger-Forschung inzwischen kein Hehl gemacht wird, gab es bis unlängst keine wirkliche Studie über die Auswirkung der historisch langfristig diskriminierten und pönalisierten Variante der Sexualität[10] auf die Texte des Dichters. Nach genauer Analyse von Mühlbergers Œuvres zeigt sich, dass sein gesamtes Werk von einem Camouflageverfahren geprägt wird und dass der Gegenstand der indirekten ästhetischen Kommunikation die mann-männliche Intimität ist.

Die homoerotische Camouflage als ästhetisches Phänomen

Dass im literarischen Diskurs manche Gegenstände, besonders wenn sie zu dem jeweiligen Zeitpunkt sozial-politisch tabu sind, auf indirektem Weg dargestellt und diskutiert werden, ist eine Binsenwahrheit. Die Themen solch einer indirekten Kommunikation können politischer, ethnischer, sexueller Provenienz sein. Die Sexualität ist traditionell ein gesellschaftliches Tabu; die Ängste und die Tendenzen, Sexualität anthropologisch in Griff zu bekommen, sie ferner politisch zu instrumentalisieren, lassen sich auch im 'System Literatur' verfolgen und anhand von

8 Vgl. den ausführlichen Bericht über die wissenschaftliche Rezeption Mühlbergers: Lukáš Motyčka, Der "sudetendeutsche" Dichter Josef Mühlberger – ein Rückblick auf die Mühlberger-Forschung und ein Ausblick, in: Stifter-Jahrbuch Neue Folge, München 2011, 123–142.

9 'Dabei hätte eine genauere Auseinandersetzung mit Mühlbergers Schaffen einem Schriftsteller gegolten, der kaum wie ein anderer den Gedanken der Vermittlung, Aussöhnung und Freundschaft zwischen Deutschen und Tschechen zum Hauptanliegen seiner vielfältig differenzierten, in über 70 selbstständigen Buchveröffentlichungen ausgebreiteten literarischen Tätigkeit erhob. Mühlberger hat dieses Anliegen in allen Phasen seiner dichterischen Entwicklung verfochten, *unbeirrt von politischen Wandlungen und Brüchen und mit einer geradezu hartnäckigen Konsequenz*, deren Intensität ihm bis zuletzt die schmerzlich erfahrene Rolle eines einsamen Außenseiters im jeweils vorherrschenden zeitgenössischen Literaturbetrieb zuwies.' Frank-Lothar Kroll, Josef Mühlberger. Bemerkungen zu Leben und Werk, in: Josef Mühlberger, Ausgewählte Werke, 1. Bd., Bonn 2004, 17–28, hier 17f., Herv. LM.

10 Vgl. Gisela Bleibtreu-Ehrenberg, Tabu Homosexualität. Die Geschichte eines Vorurteils, Frankfurt am Main 1978.

literarischen Produkten analysieren. Die minoritären Varianten der Sexualität (wie z.B. das Gleichgeschlechtliche) unterliegen bekannter Weise einer verstärkten Tabuisierung, welche – des Öfteren in der Gestalt diverser Pathologisierungs- und Kriminalisierungsversuche – strafrechtliche Konsequenzen mit sich brachte. Begreiflich nur, dass sich das Ausleben und Kommunizieren der gleichgeschlechtlichen Intimität unter solchen Koordinaten seit je auf den Bereich der Kunst, v.a. der Dichtung konzentrierte, die schon *per definitionem* aus dem Zusammenspiel der direkten (pragmatischen) und indirekten (ästhetischen) Kommunikation besteht.

Seit den 1970er Jahren haben sich im deutschsprachigen Raum mehrere Forscher bemüht, diesen Kommunikationsmodus literaturwissenschaftlich systematisch zu erfassen. Wahrscheinlich die erste wichtige, jedoch folgenlose Monographie zum Thema der indirekten literarischen Kommunikation des Tabuisierten (am Beispiel des Gleichgeschlechtlichen, des Jüdischen und der Frauen) war Hans Mayers Buch "Außenseiter" (1975). Neben vielen Fall- und komparativen Studien verdienten Volker Otts Buch "Homotropie und die Figur des Homotropen in der Literatur des zwanzigsten Jahrhunderts" (1979), Wolfgang Popps "Männerliebe" (1992) bzw. Keilson-Lauritz' Monografie über Stefan George "Von der Liebe die Freundschaft heißt" (1987) Erwähnung. Die Autoren der (nicht nur erwähnten) Publikationen wurden auf jedem Schritt mit der theoretisch-methodologischen Herausforderung konfrontiert, was sich bereits in den Titeln ihrer Studien eindeutig widerspiegelt. Einen nachvollziehbaren, terminologisch disziplinierten und zur Anwendung und Weiterführung einladenden Ansatz bot jedoch erst Heinrich Detering in seinem bahnbrechenden Buch "Das offene Geheimnis" (2002).[11] Nach soziologisch, historisch, anthropologisch bzw. diskursanalytisch ausgerichteten Studien schuf Detering als erster einen komplexen Ansatz, der sich in einer hermeneutisch-strukturalistischen Tradition bewegt und sich mit Zugriff auf die Errungenschaften des Dekonstruktivismus der genauen Analyse literarischer Texte widmet. Detering geht von einer Auffassung der Literatur als Kommunikation aus, die eine mehr oder weniger klare Autorenintention voraussetzt. Das Bestreben, das Verpönte literarisch darzustellen und dadurch an der seit der Antike andauernden, sozial akzeptablen, weil indirekten Diskussion über das intime Mann-Männliche teilzuhaben, manifestiert sich laut Detering in dem Phänomen der literarischen, ästhetischen Camouflage. Er resemantisiert den Begriff der Camouflage: Sie bestünde nun nicht darin, restlos zu tarnen, sondern im dialektischen Zusammenspiel zwischen gleichzeitigem Kaschieren und Dekuvrieren (die Hauptverfahren werden als Camouflieren und Signalisieren, bzw. als Maske und Signal bezeichnet). Auf diesem Hintergrund definiert Detering die Camouflage als '*intentionale Differenz* zwischen (unanstößi-

11 Zur verknappten Darstellung der sog. homoerotischen Camouflage vgl. Heinrich Detering, Das offene Geheimnis. Zur literarischen Produktivität eines Tabus von Winckelmann bis zu Thomas Mann. Durchgesehene und mit einer Nachbemerkung versehene Studienausgabe, Göttingen 2002.

gem) Oberflächentext und (hier: homoerotischem) *Subtext*.'[12] Hiermit wird nicht unbedingt eine Ästhetik des Homoerotischen' postuliert, wie dies etwa Gerhard Härle beabsichtigte, sondern eine allgemeine Ästhetik des Defizitären, die sich diverser Inhalte bedienen kann und die v.a. auf der festzustellenden und zu beschreibenden textlichen Doppelbödigkeit basiert. Detering ließ in seiner Monographie begreiflicherweise manche Fragen offen, er schuf jedoch ein ausbaufähiges Konzept und illustrierte im analytischen Teil seiner Arbeit (Kapitel Winckelmann, Platen, Kleist, Chamisso, Andersen, Bang und Th. Mann) seine hohe Anwendbarkeit. Woran es jedoch auch Deterings Studie mangelt, ist eine systematische Auseinandersetzung mit den konkreten kommunikativen und imaginativen Verfahrensweisen im literarischen Diskurs über das intime Mann-Männliche, welcher nicht selten mit dem allzu vagen Begriff 'homoerotische Literatur' vereinfachend bezeichnet wird. Eine ähnlich konzipierte Monographie in der Literaturwissenschaft, welche sich mit der Präsenz des Gleichgeschlechtlichen in literarischen Werken beschäftigt, bleibt immer noch ein Desiderat. Sie wird es wohl noch lange bleiben, denn für ihre Realisierung ist nicht nur ein theoretisch und methodologisch luzider und anwendungsfähiger Ansatz sowie der Mut, alle für die Ziele der Arbeit marginalen literatur- bzw. kulturwissenschaftlichen Auseinandersetzungen zu ignorieren (wie sie sich etwa in dem grundsätzlichen Konflikt zwischen dem Essentialismus und Konstruktivismus zeigt, bzw. wie sie etwa die 'queer studies' fabrizieren), sondern auch ein immens umfangreicher Materialfundus vonnöten. Bedenkt man, dass sich die oben erwähnten Publikationen meistens auf einen oder höchst wenige Autoren, auf eine bestimmte literarische Gattung oder einen eng abgesteckten Zeitraum konzentrierten, erklärt sich ihre Lückenhaftigkeit von selbst.

Die homoerotische Camouflage im literarischen Werk von Josef Mühlberger

Das umfangreiche und vielgestaltige, von der Intention, das Mann-Männliche zu kommunizieren, durchzogene Werk von Josef Mühlberger – einem Lyriker, Prosaisten, Dramatiker, Essayisten, Historiker, Übersetzer und passionierten Leser – eignet sich außerordentlich gut für den Versuch, eine relativ komplette und strukturierte Hierarchisierung der Verfahren der literarischen homoerotischen Camouflage zusammenzustellen und zu belegen. Die Analyse seiner Texte ermöglicht eine relativ komplette und in hohem Maße strukturierte Typologie dieser Mittel aufzustellen, ihre genaue Funktion in dem jeweiligen Text sowie im Allgemeinen ins Auge zu fassen, sie ferner etwa epochen-, gattungsgemäß u.a. zu kontextualisieren. Neben dem Ziel, Mühlbergers Werk in Anbetracht der sein Werk dominierenden Camouflage des Gleichgeschlechtlichen zu reinterpretieren, war das Anliegen der Dissertation 'Die homoerotische Camouflage im Werk Josef Mühl-

12 Detering, Das offene Geheimnis, 30. Herv. im Original.

bergers'[13] auch, ein komplexes Modell vorzulegen, das – bei einer möglichst geringen Modifikation – der textanalytischen Befragung möglichst vieler literarischen Werke auf die Präsenz des Gleichgeschlechtlichen den Weg ebnet.

Das Anliegen verfolgend, alle grundsätzlichen Textebenen des literarischen Werkes abzudecken, wurden folgende grundsätzlichen Strategienbündel festgestellt[14]:

1. Strategie des intertextuellen Rekurses

Auf die Relevanz der Strategie des intertextuellen Rekurses einigen sich beinahe alle Forscher, die sich mit dem Konnex von Gleichgeschlechtlichem und Literatur bzw. Kunst auseinandersetzen.[15] Intertextualität – dieser 'schillerndste [...] Begriff zeitgenössischer Textforschung'[16] wird in der Forschung bekanntlich unterschiedlich breit aufgefasst: Die auf Julia Kristeva zurückzuführenden Konzepte des Intertextuellen, die unter dem vagen Begriff 'letztendlich *alles*, oder doch zumindest jedes kulturelle System und jede kulturelle Struktur'[17] zusammenfassen und jeden Text also 'nur [als] [ein] Teil eines *texte général*'[18] verstehen, wobei die auktorielle Intentionalität relativiert und die Funktion der Autorinstanz selbst bestritten wird[19], erwiesen sich für die Zielsetzung der Dissertation als unbrauchbar. Daher wurde mit der enger angelegten Auffassung von Intertextualität gearbeitet, wie sie etwa Ulrich Broich vertritt, für den Intertextualität dann besteht, wenn 'ein Au-

---

13 Der Beitrag ist eine Zusammenfassung der Dissertation des Autors: Lukáš Motyčka, Die homoerotische Camouflage im Werk Josef Mühlbergers, Olomouc 2010, sowie seiner Studien zu einzelnen Problematiken im Werk Josef Mühlbergers, auf die an den jeweiligen Stellen verwiesen wird. Dieser Beitrag ist im Rahmen des Projektes 'Podpora vytváření excelentních výzkumných týmů a intersektorální mobility na Univerzitě Palackého v Olomouci' (reg. č.CZ.1.07/2.3.00/30.0004) entstanden.

14 Bei der folgenden Besprechung der jeweiligen Strategiebündel schränkt sich der Autor auf die Aufzählung und knappe Kontextualisierung ein. Aus Platzgründen werden keine Belege/Zitate aus Mühlbergers Texten angeführt werden, der Anmerkungsapparat ist ferner auf das Minimum beschränkt. Alle Einzelheiten lassen sich in der Dissertation nachlesen sowie die Belegstellen in Mühlbergers Texten und weitere Hinweise.

15 Vgl. etwa: 'Intertextualität läßt sich also vom Autor offenbar dazu instrumentalisieren, mit einer besonderen Zielgruppe auf diskrete Weise zu kommunizieren und ihr gesellschaftlich anstößig empfundene Inhalte mitzuteilen, ohne daß das Lesevergnügen des allgemeinen Publikums beeinträchtigt wird.' (Claudia Gremler, "Fern im dänischen Norden ein Bruder". Thomas Mann und Herman Bang. Eine literarische Spurensuche, Göttingen 2003, 34.) Allgemein zur Intertextualität-Forschung vgl. etwa Ulrich Broich – Manfred Pfister (Hgg.), Intertextualität. Formen, Funktionen, anglistische Fallstudien, Tübingen 1985; Susanne Holthuis, Intertextualität. Aspekte einer rezeptionsorientierten Konzeption, Tübingen 1993.

16 Zit. nach Gremler, "Fern im dänischen Norden ein Bruder", 15.

17 Manfred Pfister, Konzepte der Intertextualität, in: Ulrich Broich – Manfred Pfister (Hgg.), Intertextualität. Formen, Funktionen, anglistische Fallstudien, Tübingen 1985, 1–30, hier 7.

18 Gremler, "Fern im dänischen Norden ein Bruder", 16. Herv. im Original.

19 Vgl. etwa Gremler, "Fern im dänischen Norden ein Bruder", 16. 'In Kristevas Konzept andererseits kann die Intentionalität von Intertextualität verständlicherweise keine Relevanz erlangen. Das ist darin begründet, daß Intertextualität ihrer Ansicht nach ja gar nicht vermieden werden kann und es daher keiner besonderen Absicht bedarf, intertextuelle Bezüge herzustellen. Hinzu kommt, daß ein Subjekt, dem diese Absicht unterstellt werden könnte, das heißt eine Autoreninstanz, in Kristevas Konzept gar nicht existiert.' (Gremler, "Fern im dänischen Norden ein Bruder", 18.)

tor bei der Abfassung seines Textes sich nicht nur der Verwendung anderer Texte bewußt ist, sondern auch vom Rezipienten erwartet, daß er diese Beziehung zwischen seinem Text und anderen Texten als vom Autor intendiert und als wichtig für das Verständnis seines Textes erkennt'.[20] Ein grundlegender Unterschied zu Kristevas Auffassung ergab sich daraus, dass unter Intertextualität nicht jedes Rekurrieren auf bereits Vorhandenes verstanden wurde, sondern ein Aufgreifen von 'textlichen' oder 'vertextlichten' Versatzstücken.

Es wird in der sog. homoerotischen Literatur zuhauf von der Technik des *name dropping*s Gebrauch gemacht.[21] Die Skala beim Übernehmen von Aussagen reicht vom exakten Zitieren bis zur vagsten Paraphrase. Unter dem Label der Intertextualität lassen sich auch das Nennen oder bedeutungsträchtige Platzieren von vertextlichten Namen realhistorischer Persönlichkeiten, das Nennen von fiktiven Gestalten, von Werken und Tatsachen aus den Biographien bekannter, ikonologisch instrumentalisierter realhistorischer und fiktiver Persönlichkeiten unterbringen. Nicht zu vergessen sind die textgewordenen Versatzstücke aus diversen mythologischen bzw. religiösen Kontexten.

- Als eine erste Großgruppe lassen sich Verweise auf traditionelle Topoi, Stoffe, Motive des Diskurses über mann-männliche Intimität identifizieren. Zu den 'Highlights' gehört seit je die 'Norden-Süden-Imagination'. Sie hat viel mit Wunschprojektionen zu tun, die des Öfteren als menschliche Universalie, als 'Ausdruck allgemein-menschlicher Paradiessehnsucht'[22] aufgefasst werden. Mühlbergers Werk wird von der Norden-Süden-Dialektik dominiert, es ist v.a. das insistierende 'Thematisieren des mediterranen Raumes', v.a. der 'Italien- und Griechenland-Sehnsucht'.[23] Neben der Rezeption dieses Topos dürfte als Impuls für eine Süden-Obsession bei Mühlberger auch der biographische Hintergrund betrachtet werden.[24] Die Süden-Sehnsucht wird jedoch zugleich eindeutig instrumentalisiert, um die Ambivalenz des Homoerotischen (d.h. die Verknüpfung der Attraktion mit der Gefährdung) zu artikulieren. Der Süden gilt als Signal für das lockere mann-männliche Beisammensein. Konkrete Ma-

20 Ulrich Broich, Formen der Markierung von Intertextualität, in: Ulrich Broich – Manfred Pfister (Hgg.), Intertextualität. Formen, Funktionen, anglistische Fallstudien, Tübingen 1985, 31–47, hier 31.

21 'Die Verwendung von Namen als Intertextualitätssignale ist eine auffällige und in ihrer Aussagekraft explizite Möglichkeit der Markierung von Intertextualität.' (Gremler, "Fern im dänischen Norden ein Bruder", 20.) Vgl. ferner bei Marita Keilson-Lauritz, Von der Liebe die Freundschaft heißt. Zur Homoerotik im Werk Stefan Georges, Berlin 1987, 127.

22 Ludwig Ammann, Östliche Spiegel. Ansichten vom Orient im Zeitalter seiner Entdeckung durch den deutschen Leser 1800–1850, Hildesheim 1989, 58f.

23 Zur Präsenz des Griechentum-Topos in der homoerotischen Literatur vgl. Marita Keilson-Lauritz, Geschichte der eigenen Geschichte. Literatur und Literaturkritik in den Anfängen der Schwulenbewegung am Beispiel des *Jahrbuchs für sexuelle Zwischenstufen* und der Zeitschrift *Der Eigene*, Berlin 1997, 226–228.

24 Mühlbergers Vater kämpfte im Ersten Weltkrieg an der Südostfront, Mühlberger selbst bereiste den Balkan und Griechenland.

nifestationen dieser 'überlieferten Sehnsucht' bieten die Topoi 'Florenz, Neapel, Venedig, Insel Capri' u.a.; der Rekurs auf sie lanciert bei Mühlberger oft die v.a. in der Literatur der Jahrhundertwende forcierte Dekadenzmotivik bzw. -kritik. Andere homoerotisch besetzten Territorien bei Mühlberger sind Griechenland, Dalmatien, Südfrankreich, der Nahe Osten, welcher abermals bekanntlich traditionell mit 'homosexueller und heterosexueller Libertinage [assoziiert]'[25] wird, so dass viele Homoeroten, im Orient ihre 'private Glücksutopie'[26] erblickten. Neben den räumlich fixierten Imaginationen seien weitere homoerotisch grundierten Topoi genannt, auf welche Mühlberger rekurriert und welche er in seinem Werk implementiert wie etwa den Stern-, Schatten- bzw. der erkenntnistheoretisch und existenziell flankierten 'Spiegeltopos'. In Mühlbergers Texten ist eine differenzierte 'phallische Symbolik' vorzufinden: Neben die auf die Antike zurückzuführenden 'Symbole der Flöte, der Eidechse, des Horns' treten bei Mühlberger auch innovierte/originäre Symboliken (Baum, Pistole, Distel, Angelzeug u.a.).

- Eine andere große Gruppe von Verweisen bilden die 'Rekurse auf realhistorische Persönlichkeiten', die im 'literarischen Homokanon' figurieren. Mit der fast kränklichen Imitierung Goethes bei Th. Mann lässt sich Mühlbergers unaufhörliches Rekurrieren auf Thomas Mann vergleichen. Der Repräsentationsstatus von Thomas Mann und der Signalwert des Rekurrierens auf dessen Werk, in dem 'das ungelebte Leben eines der zentralen Themen'[27] ist, wurde in der Forschung oft referiert[28]: Bei Mühlberger lassen sich neben narrativen Analogien Rekurse finden, die als gedankliche Auseinandersetzungen mit der Vorlage zu interpretieren sind. Verweise auf den 'ersten offen homosexuellen' Dichters in Deutschland, August Platen[29], diese Konstante, 'Chiffre'[30] des homoerotischen literarischen Diskurses, durchzieht Mühlbergers Werk, so-

25 Andrea Fuchs-Sumiyoshi, Orientalismus in der deutschen Literatur. Untersuchungen zu Werken des 19. und 20. Jahrhunderts, von Goethes *West-östlichem Divan* bis Thomas Manns *Joseph*-Tetralogie, Hildesheim 1984, 15.

26 Ammann, Östliche Spiegel, 66.

27 Jan Steinhaußen, "Aristokraten aus Not" und ihre "Philosophie der zu hoch hängenden Trauben". Nietzsche-Rezeption und literarische Produktion von Homosexuellen in den ersten Jahrzehnten des 20. Jahrhunderts: Thomas Mann, Stefan George, Ernst Bertram, Hugo von Hofmannsthal u.a., Würzburg 2001, 198.

28 Vgl. etwa Hermann Kurzke, Thomas Mann. Das Leben als Kunstwerk. Eine Biographie, Frankfurt am Main 2001; Gerhard Härle, Die Gestalt des Schönen. Untersuchung zur Homosexualitätsthematik in Thomas Manns Roman "Der Zauberberg", Königstein im Taunus. 1986.

29 Zu Platens Leben und Werk und der Platen-Rezeption vgl. etwa: Peter Bumm, August Graf von Platen. Eine Biographie, Paderborn u.a. 1990; Hans Mayer, Außenseiter, Frankfurt am Main 1975, 207–209; Hans-Joachim Teuchert, August Graf von Platen in Deutschland. Zur Rezeption eines umstrittenen Autors, Bonn 1980; Paul Derks, Die Schande der heiligen Päderastie. Homosexualität und Öffentlichkeit in der deutschen Literatur 1750–1850, Berlin 1990, 479–613.

30 Steinhaußen, "Aristokraten aus Not" und ihre "Philosophie der zu hoch hängenden Trauben", 307. Vgl. auch Friedhelm Krey, Hans Henny Jahnn und die mannmännliche Liebe, Frankfurt am Main 1987, 80: 'Kaum ein gebildeter Homosexueller, der sich nicht irgendwann auf Platen beruft.'

wie die Erwähnungen von Autoren, deren ambivalente Auffassung des Erotischen in der Forschung bereits Aufmerksamkeit erregte wie etwa Hölderlin, Winckelmann, Nietzsche, Hofmannsthal, Rilke, George, Schiller. Die Anspielung auf den führenden tschechischen Symbolisten und Homosexuellen Ottokar Březina in Mühlbergers Novelle "Die Knaben und der Fluß" stellt einen immens wichtigen Moment bei der Interpretation des Werkes dar. Der Fundus von deutschsprachigen bzw. tschechischen Autoren ist bei Mühlberger um die 'homoerotischen' Stars der Weltliteratur (Shakespeare, Wilde, Whitman, Rimbaud, Verlaine, Andersen, Bang, Hafiz u.a.), der bildenden Kunst und Musikgeschichte (da Vinci, Donatello, Cellini, Schubert, Tschaikowski) sowie um Verweise auf andere Persönlichkeiten (Friedrich II. von Preußen, Ludwig II. von Bayern, der letzte Staufer Konradin) ergänzt. Mühlberger beteiligt sich in seiner Novelle "Casanovas letztes Abenteuer" sogar an der psychoanalytischen grundierten Diskussion des Casanova-/Don-Juan-Syndroms als einer unbewussten psychischen Transformierung der homoerotischen Ängste und thematisiert somit unterschwellig die heteronormative Kraft, die die Konstituierung dieses Typus fördert.[31]

- Die antike mythologische Welt als Projektions- und Bezugsfläche bildet ein weiteres Reservoir für intertextuelle Verweise im homoerotischen Diskurs. 'Noch bis weit ins 19. Jahrhundert hinein war die Darstellung von Homosexualität in Kunst und Literatur nur über den Umweg über die Antike möglich'[32], sodass die Instrumentalisierung der antiken mythologischen Welt, welche die Androgynität noch positiv aufwerten konnte[33] und die vor den homoerotischen Liaisons mancher Götter und Helden nicht zurückschreckte, wahrscheinlich das wichtigste und zugleich vagste Mittel für die Artikulation homoerotischer Inhalte und eine Möglichkeit zur Legitimierung des Gleichgeschlechtlichen darstellte. In Mühlbergers Werk lassen sich eher verklausulierte Anspielungen an bekannte antiken Paare (Orest-Pylades, Achill-Patroklos, Castor-Pollux), Erwähnungen mancher sexuell ambivalenter Götter (Zeus, Apoll) sowie anderer mythologischen Figuren (Pan und Daphnis, Ganymed, Narziss, Ado-

31 In ihrer Studie über die literarische Darstellung der Casanova-Gestalt in der modernen deutschen Literatur behandelt Carina Lehnen auch Mühlbergers Novelle (vgl. Carina Lehnen, Das Lob des Verführers. Über die Mythisierung der Casanova-Figur in der deutschsprachigen Literatur zwischen 1899 und 1933, Paderborn 1995, bes. 295–300). Auch wenn die Autorin den homoerotischen Subtext nicht reflektiert, muss sie abschließend feststellen, dass 'Casanova [...] in diesem Stück [...] konsequent seiner Identität beraubt' (Lehnen, Das Lob des Verführers, 300) wird. Das Besondere der Verfremdung besteht bei Mühlberger jedoch nicht nur in der Tatsache, dass der berühmte Frauenliebhaber und -liebling bei und an den Frauen wegen seines Alters scheitert, sondern gerade auch in der parallel vorgenommenen Unterwanderung von Casanovas exklusiver Heterosexualität.

32 Goodbye to Berlin? 100 Jahre Schwulenbewegung. Katalog zur Ausstellung des Schwulen Museums und der Akademie der Künste, 17. Mai bis 17. August 1997, Berlin 1997, 24.

33 Vgl. Lutz S. Malke, Weibmann und Mannweib in der Kunst der Renaissance, in: Androgyn. Sehnsucht nach Vollkommenheit, Berlin 1986, 33–56.

nis) finden. Mit dem Zugriff auf den fabelhaften Sänger Orpheus partizipiert Mühlberger an der verwickelten und folgenreichen Rezeption dieser Figur: Von der konkreten Zurückführung der antiken Homosexualität auf Orpheus (laut Ovids Überlieferung)[34], der Aufwertung und Transzendierung der Orpheus-Gestalt in den orphischen Kulten und im Neoplatonismus[35], über die Vereinnahmung der Sängergestalt im frühen Christentum (David-, Jesusparallelen) und die damit unausweichliche Transformation der homosexuellen Konnotationen[36], bis zur modernen sinnbildlichen Gleichsetzung Orpheus' für die Dichterinstanz, ja Wortkunst überhaupt, die Funktion des Mythos bei Ausgestaltung der Poetologien moderner Dichter (Benn, Trakl, Rilke u.a.)[37], ferner der Initiationsrolle des Orpheus-Mythos bei der Entstehung der modernen Oper[38], dem konkreten Signalwert der Orpheus-Gestalt im homoerotischen Diskurs[39], bis letztlich zu postmodernen theoretischen Ansätzen, welche das 'orphische Moment', das libidinöse Mann-Männliche zum Motor des Kreativen überhaupt erklären.[40]

- Die Bibel und der jüdisch-christliche Kontext bieten ebenso eine geeignete Projektions- und Bezugsfläche für intertextuelle Rekurse. Neben den Topoi, wie etwa der kulturologischen Konstante des 'Paradieses' oder der inflationären 'Schlangen-Symbolik', ließe sich auch das Berufen auf biblische bzw. in der christlichen Ikonographie verwurzelte Figuren nennen (David und Jona-

34 Zu den zwei wichtigen, unterschiedlichen Versionen des Mythos bei den antiken Dichtern und der Rezeption dieser Überlieferungen siehe etwa: Manuela Speiser, Orpheusdarstellungen im Kontext poetischer Programme, Innsbruck 1992.

35 Zur neoplatonischen Annexion des Orpheus-Mythos, v.a. in der bildenden Kunst vgl. Andreas Sternweiler, Die Lust der Götter. Homosexualität in der italienischen Kunst. Von Donatello zu Caravaggio, Berlin 1993, 105, 133–135, 188 u.a.

36 Vgl. etwa Steinhaußen, "Aristokraten aus Not" und ihre "Philosophie der zu hoch hängenden Trauben", 35: 'David wurde seit der Spätantike mit Orpheus in einen typologischen Zusammenhang gebracht.' Vgl. ferner Detlef C. Kochan, Literarische Spuren einer Symbolfigur: Orpheus zum Beispiel, in: Werner Wunderlich (Hg.), Literarische Symbolfiguren. Von Prometheus bis Švejk. Beiträge zu Tradition und Wandel, Bern 1989, 37–64, hier 53.

37 Vgl. etwa Speiser, Orpheusdarstellungen im Kontext poetischer Programme; Eva-Maria Knittel, Orpheus im Horizont moderner Dichtungskonzeptionen, Münster 1998, 69–92.

38 Heinz Hofmann, Orpheus, in: Heinz Hofmann (Hg.), Antike Mythen in der europäischen Tradition. Tübingen 1999, 153–198, hier 177.

39 'Die Orpheus-Sonette [von Ernst Bertram] maskierten Homosexualität. Orpheus stand in einer homosexuellen Tradition. Er galt im Mittelalter als der Urheber und Erfinder der Homosexualität. Herbert Mercuse meinte sogar, daß die klassische Orpheus-Tradition mit der Einführung der Homosexualität begann.' (Steinhaußen, "Aristokraten aus Not" und ihre "Philosophie der zu hoch hängenden Trauben", 35.) Vgl. ferner Christian Klein, "Daß du mir nicht nach Mädchen riechst ...". Neuauflagen und Neuerscheinungen homoerotischer Literatur in Deutschland und der Schweiz 1933–45, in: Dirck Linck – Wolfgang Popp – Annette Runte, (Hgg.), Erinnern und Wiederentdecken. Tabuisierung und Enttabuisierung der männlichen und weiblichen Homosexualität in Wissenschaft und Kritik, Berlin 1999, 125–148, bes. 127.

40 Vgl. Klaus Theweleit, Buch der Könige, Bd. 1: Orpheus und Eurydike, Frankfurt am Main 1977, 49.

than, der Lieblingsjünger Jesu Johannes, Hl. Sebastian, der Lasterbekämpfer Hl. Georg). Ein heikles Moment im Rekurrieren auf die biblische bzw. christliche Ikonologie stellt die Homoerotisierung der Jesusfigur dar, die Mühlbergers Werk stark prägt.

2. Strategie der konzeptuellen Modifizierung des Gleichgeschlechtlichen

Unter diesem Strategiebündel werden sozial-geschichtliche, von der Kunst mehrmals internalisierte Konzepte der Bewältigung des Gleichgeschlechtlichen zusammengefasst. Dass eine rigorose Trennung zwischen den beiden bisher erwähnten Strategien, die mit Hilfe unzähliger Stoffe, Topoi und Motive Gestalt annehmen, zuweilen unmöglich erscheint, darf auf den kulturellen Usus zurückgeführt werden, das Konzeptuelle zu vertextlichen. So lässt sich die Erwähnung des Namen Platons als ein eindeutiger intertextueller Hinweis auffassen, denn sein Name ist kulturell seit jeher zum textähnlichen Signal petrifiziert. Ebenso lassen sich Zitate, Paraphrasen oder teilweise auch Topoi aus seinen Schriften als intertextuelle Hinweise verstehen. Dies trifft auch auf Sokrates und Alkibiades zu, die letztlich als vertextlichte, literarische Protagonisten anzusehen sind. Das diskursive oder imaginative Aufgreifen von der mit Platon zusammenhängenden Tradition der philosophisch erhöhten Knabenliebe wird in der Dissertation jedoch unter der Rubrik der konzeptuellen Modifizierung behandelt.

- Zu einer häufigen Kaschierungsstrategie gehört die Geschlechtsnivellierung bzw. -eliminierung. So schien etwa die 'Verminderung des Alters der Protagonisten, die Verschiebung ins (prä-)pubertäre Alter' oft der einzige Weg, das sinnliche mann-männliche geltend zu machen. In der Geschichte des Entwicklungs- bzw. Erziehungsromans als eine Probatum-Konstante auf dem Lebensweg des männlichen Individuums obligatorisch, galt die Pubertät – lange vor Freuds Analysen der infantilen und adoleszenten Sexualität – als 'Phase eines undifferenzierten Geschlechtslebens'.[41] Auch Mühlberger beteiligt sich intensiv an der Konstruierung einer 'homosexuellen Utopie', indem er den pubertären Knabenkörper – ein Zustand der Vormännlichkeit, der Noch-Nicht-Vollvirilität, einer weichen Männlichkeit[42] und somit die Adoleszenz-Phase zu einem Zeit-Raum der homoerotischen Idylle, zum ontogenetisch sowie phylogenetisch konstruierten Vakuum der erwachenden und immer noch reinen und unbeschnittenen Sinnlichkeit emporhebt. Bei Mühlberger wimmelt es nämlich von Jünglingen und Jünglingsfreundschaften. Zur Aufhebung bzw. Modifizierung der Geschlechterdifferenz dient auch das traditionelle Androgynie-

41 Ulfried Geuter, Homosexualität in der deutschen Jugendbewegung. Jugendfreundschaft und Sexualität im Diskurs von Jugendbewegung. Psychoanalyse und Jugendpsychologie am Beginn des 20. Jahrhunderts, Frankfurt am Main 1994, 233. Vgl. auch bei Wolf Borchers, Männliche Homosexualität in der Dramatik der Weimarer Republik, phil.Diss. Köln 2001, 19.

42 Vgl. Härle, Die Gestalt des Schönen, 133–138.

Konzept.[43] Der weltanschauliche Hintergrund – nämlich die Auffassung vom 'Androgyn[en] [...] als [einem] platonische[n] Ur-Mensch[en]'[44] – wurde in der Neuzeit, v.a. im 20. Jahrhundert oft von den sexual- oder politisch-emanzipatorischen Gedanken in Anspruch genommen.[45] Als religiös verbrämte Manifestation dieses Konzeptes findet sich bei Mühlberger der 'Engel-Topos'; für Engel ließe sich die gleiche Spannung zwischen dem entsexualisierten bzw. geschlechtslosen Wesen auf der einen Seite und dem sinnlich dargestellten Zwitter auf der anderen attestieren.[46] Für Mühlbergers Werk sind ferner das 'Motiv der Vater-Sohn-Liebe'[47] konstitutiv, das ebenso die erwünschte Entschärfung des homoerotischen oder -sexuellen Begehrens ermöglicht (eine Nivellierung durch das Familiäre), das auf der 'christliche[n] Mythologie basiert' und das einen 'inhärenten Skandal'[48] birgt sowie das 'Motiv der erotisierenden Bruderfreundschaft' und der 'libidinösen Beziehung von Mentor und Novize'.

- Die Verschiebung ins Utopische lässt sich als eine weitere Hauptstrategie ausmachen. Dass das utopische Denken auf ein im Sozialen verankertes Defizit zurückzuführen ist, gilt als bekannt, ebenso wie die Tatsache, dass die sog. homoerotische Literatur von dem Problem der 'Unverortetheit/Unverortbarkeit' des Homoerotischen bzw. sexuellen durchzogen ist. Der Halbstatus (eine Existenz zwischen Sein und Nicht-Sein) bringt die Kunst besonders beeindruckend an Hand der Spannung zwischen Sagbarem/Darstellbarem und Unsagbarem/Nicht-Darstellbarem zum Ausdruck. Versinnbildlicht zeigt sich dieser 'noma-

43 Zu der Androgynie-Forschung siehe z.B.: Mechthild Fend, Grenzen der Männlichkeit. Der Androgyn in der französischen Kunst und Kunsttheorie 1750–1830, Berlin 2003; Dorothee Alfermann – Ulla Bock (Hgg.), Quer*elles*. Jahrbuch für Frauenforschung 4: Androgynie. Vielfalt der Möglichkeiten, Stuttgart 1999. Siehe auch Sternweiler, Die Lust der Götter, 106–108; Dominique Fernandez, Der Raub des Ganymed. Eine Kulturgeschichte der Homosexualität. Aus dem Französischen von Verena Vannahme, Freiburg ²1992, 170–173; oder George L. Mosse, Nationalismus und Sexualität. Bürgerliche Moral und sexuelle Normen, München 1985, 123–127.

44 Ralph Tegtmeier, Zur Gestalt des Androgyns in der Literatur des Fin de siècle, in: Ursula Prinz (Hg.), Androgyn. Sehnsucht nach Vollkommenheit. (Neuer Berliner Kunstverein. Ausstellung und Katalog), Berlin 1986, 113–119, hier 115. Vgl. auch Sternweiler, Die Lust der Götter, 109.

45 Julika Funk diagnostiziert die 'Tradition des Androgynie-Motivs und eine zyklisch auftauchende Utopie vom androgynen Menschen' als ein 'immer noch gültiges Emanzipationsideal, ein Ideal der Unabhängigkeit von traditionellen (Geschlechter-)Rollenkonzepten'. (Julika Funk, Die melancholische (Un-)Ordnung der Geschlechter in der Moderne und die Androgynie-Utopie, in: Dorothee Alfermann – Ulla Bock (Hgg.), Quer*elles*. Jahrbuch für Frauenforschung 4: Androgynie. Vielfalt der Möglichkeiten, Stuttgart 1999, 35–54, hier S. 35.) Zur Soziologisierung und Politisierung der Androgynie-Konzepte im Sex-/Gender-Diskurs vgl. etwa: Ursula Prinz, Einführung, in: Ursula Prinz (Hg.), Androgyn. Sehnsucht nach Vollkommenheit. (Neuer Berliner Kunstverein. Ausstellung und Katalog), Berlin 1986, 9–32; Härle, Die Gestalt des Schönen, 133–138.

46 Vgl. Malke, Weibmann und Mannweib in der Kunst der Renaissance, 42.

47 Es wären z.B. Mühlbergers Romane "Bogumil", "Verhängnis und Verheißung", "Das Tal der Träume", und die Erzählungen "Der Galgen im Weinberg" oder "Im savoyardischen Dorf" zu nennen.

48 Beide Zitate Nikolaus Tiling, Hubert Fichte, in: Alexandra Busch – Dirck Linck (Eds.), Frauenliebe – Männerliebe. Eine lesbisch-schwule Literaturgeschichte in Porträts, Stuttgart 1997, 167–171, hier 169.

dische Charakter'[49] an der 'Topik bzw. Topographik des Homoerotischen'.[50] Mühlbergers Utopien des intimen mann-männlichen Zusammenseins werden an Hand vom 'Feld/Erde-Wasser-Komplex' dargestellt: Der 'Bereich der braunen Erde bzw. des braunen Feldes' als Metapher des Heterosexuellen bzw. der offiziellen, vom Staat subventionierten Sexualität wird in endlosen Variationen gegen die 'Wasserwelt' (Fluss, Teich, Bach, Quelle, Meer usf.) ausgespielt. Mit dem Wasserkomplex hängt konzeptuell das 'Motiv des Schwimmens und Badens' als Metapher der (Nicht-)Bewährung. Diese laut Werner Ross althergebrachte komplexe literarische Formel[51] könne eine Reihe von Bedeutungen suggerieren: das Eindringen, die Aneignung, die Eroberung und das Treiben-Lassen, das Sich-Ergeben bzw. Sich-Aufgeben/Auflösen.[52] Die dem Wasser-Bereich inhärente Dialektik des Geborenwerdens und Sterbens illustrieren bei Mühlberger am eindeutigsten die archetypal anmutenden 'Auflösungs- und Einmündungsphantasien'. Das Element Wasser wird 'als Quell des Lebens und als Flut des Todes'[53], als eine die Existenz umrahmende/umarmende Allmacht evoziert. Bei Mühlberger findet sich dieses regressive 'ozeanische Gefühl', ein entgrenzender Zustand (religiöser, sexueller Rausch)[54] meistens im homoerotischen Vorstellungsgeflecht und ist in Verbindung mit den streng polarisierten psychosexuellen Rollen (insertiv vs. perzeptiv) zu deuten. Die 'Metapher des Einmündens' in ein Meer evoziert zugleich die utopische Sehnsucht nach einem Un-Ort bzw. All-Ort. Als weitere althergebrachte und im homoerotischen Diskurs instrumentalisierte Topoi, die in Mühlbergers Texten auszumachen sind, dürfen der 'Garten-Topos' (samt dem 'Gärtner-Beruf' und dem antagonistisch inszenierten 'Treibhaus-Motiv'), der 'Insel-Topos', der *locus amoenus* und das existenzialistisch lancierte 'Brücken-Motiv' betrachtet werden.

---

49 Über den nomadischen Charakter oder eine Grenzidentität des Homoerotischen lässt sich in Hinblick auf die 'wandelnde' Identität mancher Homoeroten der Literatur diskutieren. Gerhard Härle spricht im Zusammenhang mit den Gestalten Thomas Manns über ein 'Modell einer repräsentativen sexuellen Identität, die nicht abgeschlossen, nicht männlich oder weiblich ist, sich nicht vom Körper her definieren und diktieren läßt, sondern die ein "Dazwischen" darstellt, einen Schwebezustand oder einen sich ständig neu wieder aufrollenden Prozeß. Ohne homosexuell sein zu müssen, leben und erleben seine Gestalten doch, *als ob* sie homosexuelle Männer wären.' (Gerhard Härle, Simulationen der Wahrheit. Körpersprache und sexuelle Identität im Zauberberg und Felix Krull, in: Forum Homosexualität und Literatur 14, Siegen 1992, 23–46, hier 43f.)

50 Vgl. etwa bei Jacob Stockinger, Homotextualität – ein Vorschlag, in: Forum Homosexualität und Literatur 2, Siegen 1987, 5–26, 11.

51 Vgl. Werner Ross, Vom Schwimmen in Seen und Flüssen. Lebensgefühl und Literatur zwischen Rousseau und Brecht, in: Arcadia 3/3, Berlin 1968, 262–291.

52 Ross, Vom Schwimmen in Seen und Flüssen, 291.

53 Bernhard Blume, Lebendiger Quell und Flut des Todes. Ein Beitrag zu einer Literaturgeschichte des Wassers, in: Arcadia 1, Berlin 1966, 18–30, hier 20.

54 Vgl. Sigmund Freud, Das Unbehagen in der Kultur, in: Alexander Mitscherlich – Angela Richards – James Strachey (Hgg.), Sigmund Freud. Studienausgabe, Bd. IX: Fragen der Gesellschaft. Ursprünge der Religion, Frankfurt am Main 2000, 191–270.

- Eine häufig vorkommende Strategie im Umgang mit der Darstellung des Gleichgeschlechtlichen ist die Strategie der Ästhetisierung. Manche Forscher fordern sogar eine systematische Darstellung der Geschichte einer 'homoerotisch' grundierten Ästhetik ein. Dies mag wohl tollkühn anmuten, ebenso wie berechtigt, denn trotz aller Bedenken bezieht sich das – vereinfacht gesprochen – Gleichgeschlechtliche produktions- sowie rezeptionsästhetisch auf diverse europäische ästhetische Theoriegebäude, so dass eine 'schwer durchschaubare Verquickung von männlicher Schönheit und "ästhetischer" Argumentation' entstanden ist, 'die sich wegen dieser Undurchschaubarkeit recht gut als Maske strategisch einsetzen l[ässt]'.[55] Die 'Transfiguration des Mann-Männlichen in der Kunst und im Schönen' gilt seit der Antike als Gemeingut. In der 'Geschichte des Schönen' wurde bekanntlich immer aufs Neue versucht, die homoerotischen Begehrensstrukturen an Hand von subtilen Theorien zu camouflieren (d.h. darstellbar zu machen). Diese Tradition beginnt mit 'Platons Erhöhung des Homoerotischen bzw. der Knabenliebe' (Begriff der 'Knabenliebe', bzw. der 'Päderastie'), welche eine folgenschwere, in der 'neoplatonischen Philosophie und Ästhetik' Ficinos und Bembos ('Begriff der platonischen Liebe') nachzuweisende und noch in der 'idealistischen Ästhetik des 19. Jahrhunderts' (Kant, Winckelmann, Schopenhauer, Pater, Vischer) identifizierbare 'Entsexualisierung und gleich verlaufende Transzendierung' der mann-männlichen Sexualität zur Folge hatte, und verschmilzt zu einem nur schwer durchschaubaren Ideen-Konglomerat ('eine ästhetisierte Erotik'[56]), dessen Versatzstücke noch tief im 20. Jahrhundert ihre sozialpragmatische, staatspolitische und moralisch-ethische Anwendung finden. In Mühlbergers Texten lassen sich viele solcher Versatzstücke identifizieren, wie etwa der strapazierte 'Sublimierungsimperativ', er diskutiert auf eine camouflierte und inkonsequente Weise den bei Winckelmann festgestellten 'Entwurf einer spezifisch *homoerotischen Ästhetik*'[57] und 'die Konturen [s]einer *homoerotischen Kunstpädagogik*'.[58] Die 'Formel des Schönen', der 'erotisierende und erotische Blick', das 'Motiv der Betrachtung des schlafenden Freundes'[59], die als ein Kruzifix allem Ausschweifenden sowohl *in politicis* als auch *in eroticis* entgegengehaltene 'Maß-Parole' bzw. 'Keuschheitsvorstellung' lassen sich als konkrete Ausgestaltungen der Ästhetisierungsstrategie betrachten.

55 Keilson-Lauritz, Geschichte der eigenen Geschichte, 250. Diese Konzepte – die schmerzlich erlebte Homosexualität forciere die künstlerische Produktivität und werde als Grundstein der Genialität angesehen – lassen sich auch als Thema in der literarischen Fiktion entdecken, etwa bei T. Mann oder H.H. Jahnn u.a. (Vgl. Krey, Hans Henny Jahnn und die mannmännliche Liebe, 151.)

56 Geuter, Homosexualität in der deutschen Jugendbewegung, 267.

57 *Ibid.* Herv. im Original

58 *Ibid.* Herv. im Original.

59 Gerhard Härle, "Jetzt aber gehst du mir aus dem Gesicht". Klagen um den toten Geliebten, in: Forum Homosexualität und Literatur 50, Siegen 2007, 45–65, hier 53.

- Die in der sog. homoerotischen Literatur allerorts anzutreffende Strategie der Diabolisierung bzw. Utilisierung des Gleichgeschlechtlichen hat mit der 'Geschichte der politisch-sozialen Traktierung des Gleichgeschlechtlichen' zu tun, die eine 'Geschichte der Verfemung' ist. Dass die homosexuellen Künstler und Intellektuellen diese Einstellung allzu oft verinnerlicht haben (und immer noch verinnerlichen) und dadurch zur 'Geschichte des Verschweigens und der Verzerrung' ihren Anteil beitrugen, steht ebenso außer Frage. Die meisten Gründe für die Ablehnung der Homosexualität lassen sich unter dem 'Subversivitätsbegriff' (Stichwort: 'die schwule Internationale') subsumieren. Die Akzentverlegung differierte in den jeweiligen Zeitaltern oder Gesellschaften merklich. Das bis in die Moderne in den Köpfen der Intellektuellen grassierende Bedenken gegen die praktizierte Homosexualität (Stichwort: 'Krise der Männlichkeit') findet seine Anfänge in der Ethik und Moral der späten Antike und ist auf die Unterstellung der alten Griechen zurückzuführen, dass der Penetrierte an Virilität verliere. Sie führte in der patriarchalen Gesellschaftsordnung zur 'allmählichen Desavouierung des Homosexuellen', die sich etwa in der Kunst der Jahrhundertwende in einem fatalen 'Zerrbild der eigenen Homosexualität zwischen Verteufelung einerseits und Vergöttlichung andererseits' manifestiert.[60] Der 'Natürlichkeit-Diskurs'[61], angeheizt von 'Lasterhaftigkeitsvorwürfen' und der 'ästhetischen Prämisse der Undarstellbarkeit des Hässlichen' (der homosexuelle Geschlechtsakt galt im nachantiken Denken als widernatürlich, sprich: teuflisch, hässlich) führten bei den meisten Künstlern zu einer höchst ambivalenten Einstellung zur eigenen Sexualität, die zwischen einer Nicht-Akzeptanz und Selbstbehauptungsallüren oszillierte. Das Gleichgeschlechtliche, v.a. seine sexuelle Ausprägung, wurden mit 'diversen Krankheitssymboliken' belegt, zu der sich das Sprechen über 'Krankheit und Heilung, Verführung, Heimsuchung, Erlösung', aber auch der traditionelle 'Eros-Thanatos-Topos', die 'Darstellung des Todes als schöner Jüngling (Freund Hain)', 'Motiv des Blutens' (Initiationsmoment), der 'Sturm- und Gewittermotiv' u.v.a. zuordnen lässt. Andererseits wird in der Tradition der sog. homoerotischen Literatur eine Gegentendenz registriert, das Gleichgeschlechtliche zu utilisieren und es somit von dem sozialen, moralischen, ökonomischen, politischen Subversivitätsmakel zu bereinigen, indem dessen Akzeptanz für die Gesellschaft als profitabel dargestellt wird.

---

60 Steinhaußen spricht über 'die Ambivalenz homosexueller Seinslage zwischen göttlicher Dignität und Sündhaftigkeit, zwischen Erhabenheit und Verfluchung' (Steinhaußen, "Aristokraten aus Not" und ihre "Philosophie der zu hoch hängenden Trauben",41).

61 Hierzu vgl. Fernandez, Der Raub des Ganymed, 10–24; Ilija Dürhammer, Geheime Botschaften. Homoerotische Subkulturen im Schubert-Kreis, bei Hugo von Hofmannsthal und Thomas Bernhard, Wien 2006, 382; oder Erhard Köllner, Homosexualität als anthropologische Herausforderung. Konzeption einer homosexuellen Anthropologie, Bad Heilbrunn 2001, 415–420.

- Das Utilisierungsbestreben zeigt sich in den historisch variierenden sozialpolitischen Arrangements des Gleichgeschlechtlichen. Die Homosexualität, die zum Sinnbild des jedem Zweck Fremden wurde, gerät zum äußersten Politikum.[62] Die Rhetorik, mit welcher der heikle Gegenstand in der Geschichte behandelt wurde, darf nicht über den wahren Stand hinwegtäuschen: Hinter allen Versuchen, das Gleichgeschlechtliche unter Kontrolle zu bringen, liegt ein kulturalistisches, politisches Interesse. Diese Zügelungsmanöver lassen sich bereits am Beispiel der kulturellen 'Institution der antiken Päderastie' vorzeigen, die durch die strenge Rollenzuweisung (erastes-eromenos) das Ausschweifende zu regulieren versuchte bzw. für Staatszwecke zu nutzen suchte ('pädagogische Kultivierung der Staatselite und kulturpolitische Interessen des Staates' etwa in der Gestalt der Kunst und Philosophie). Der lockere Umgang mit dem Mann-Männlichem im frühen Christentum (bis ungefähr zum 13. Jahrhundert) wurde von dogmatisch restriktiven Methoden abgelöst, welche im Interesse des nun politisch etablierten Konnex von Staat und Religion die Erhaltung der Macht zum Ziel hatten. Die Intoleranz der Kirche dem Gleichgeschlechtlichen gegenüber (dessen Instrumentalisierung) und die folgenden Konsolidierungsversuche (Reformation und Rekatholisierung als Reaktionen auf die Subversivität der neoplatonischen Renaissance) demonstrieren offensichtlich die heikle Position des Gleichgeschlechtlichen im kulturpolitischen Kampf. Die das Doppelleben begünstigende bürgerliche Moral ermöglichte paradoxerweise eine stärkere Ausprägung homosexueller Sub- oder Parallelkultur. Die althergebrachten 'homosozialen Milieus'[63] mit ihrer 'ausgeprägte[n] Ikonologie'[64] (etwa das 'militärische/kriegerische Milieu' mit der 'Ikone des tapferen Kriegers'[65], die 'religiös oder mystisch verbrämten mann-männlichen Gruppierungen des Mittelalters' mit der 'Ikone des Mönchs, Ritters, Templers'[66] u.a.) werden in der Zeit des Bürgertums um weitere Facetten erweitert,

62 Hierzu vgl. ausführlich Keilson-Lauritz, Die Geschichte der eigenen Geschichte; Gerhard Härle, Männerweiblichkeit. Zur Homosexualität bei Klaus und Thomas Mann, Frankfurt am Main 1988, 13–15.

63 Hierzu vgl. z.B. Mosse, Nationalismus und Sexualität, 11–13; u.a.; Steinhaußen, "Aristokraten aus Not" und ihre "Philosophie der zu hoch hängenden Trauben", 257–259 u.a. Zum homosozialen Arrangement im späten Mittelalter vgl. Bernd-Ulrich Hergemöller, Sodom und Gomorrha. Zur Alltagswirklichkeit und Verfolgung Homosexueller im Mittelalter. Überarbeitete und ergänzte Neuausgabe, Hamburg 2000, 58–64, siehe auch Bleibtreu-Ehrenberg, Tabu Homosexualität.

64 Keilson-Lauritz, Die Geschichte der eigenen Geschichte, 270. Keilson-Lauritz sieht die Ikonisierung hauptsächlich im Kontext des Homokanons. Sie bietet auch eine Ikonenliste: 'Ein "Kanon der Gestalten": Grundriß einer schwulen Ikonologie' (Keilson-Lauritz, Die Geschichte der eigenen Geschichte, 344–357, hier 344).

65 Mihály Riszovannij, Männerbilder in der zeitgenössischen Karikatur. Eine kultursemiotische Analyse, Berlin 2008, 79f.

66 Zur Identifizierung der Templerorden mit Ketzerei, Sodomie und Götzendienst und den Templerprozessen im 13. Jahrhundert vgl. etwa Bernd-Ulrich Hergemöller, Krötenkuß und schwarzer Kater. Ketzerei, Götzendienst und Unzucht in der inquisitorischen Phantasie des 13. Jahrhunderts, Fahlbusch 1996.

wie etwa um das als lasterhaft empfundene Proletariat mit der 'Ikone des einfachen, kräftigen Mannes' oder das 'Milieu des Mediterranen' mit den 'Ikonen des Matrosen'[67], 'Italieners', 'Griechen' usw. Das auf das antike 'Konzept des pädagogischen Eros' zurückzuführenden pädagogischen Konzept der Jahrhundertwende sowie der schillernde 'Begriff der intimen mann-männlichen Freundschaft' finden im Werk Mühlbergers eine enorme Resonanz: Sie werden zu einer ambivalenten 'Distanz-Nähe-Figur' entwickelt, die sich in diversen Motiven und Metaphern (z.B. 'Motiv des Geschenkes für den Freund bzw. des Freundschaftsbeweises', die 'Rettung des Freundes', 'Essen-Motiv') konkretisieren. Die kriegerisch-politische (wiederum auf die Antike zurückzuführende) Vereinnahmung des Mann-Männlichen wird des Öfteren in dem von Mühlberger inflationär benutzen 'Motiv der Kriegsfreundschaft' offenbar; auf dem Hintergrund der sog. 'Schützengrabenliteratur' nimmt das intime Mann-Männliche sowohl die (nicht nur bei Mühlberger) politisch akzeptable Form ('Freundschaft zwischen Soldaten aus dem Freundeslager') als auch die politisch subversive Form an ('Liaison zwischen Soldaten aus verfeindeten Lagern'). Die Geschichte der Jugendbewegung (v.a. des Wandervogels) illustriert die 'Instrumentalisierung des Sports' in diesem Kontext: Sportliches Ausleben, ergänzt von Momenten des Kräftigen, Nackten, Sieghaften, wurde nun allzu oft genützt, um das unbekümmerte Gleichgeschlechtliche – vom bloß Kameradschaftlichen bis zum eindeutig homoerotisch fundierten Miteinander – darstellen zu können ('Bademotiv', 'Wandertopos'). Ein weiteres kultursoziales Arrangement stellt die 'Thematisierung der Kunst, Musik und Musikausübung' dar: Musik/Kunst wird entweder zum Medium einer diskursiven Auseinandersetzung mit der Homosexualität, oder aber wird die künstlerische Betätigung der literarischen Figuren zum 'Surrogat für Erotik', vornehmlich Homoerotik. In diesem Zusammenhang wäre auf die unterschiedlich besetzten 'Motive des Improvisierens, der Stimme, des Singens, des Tanzes' aufmerksam zu machen. Als konstanter Bestandteil der homoerotischen Camouflage ist ferner die 'Verschmelzung von Religiösem bzw. Mystischem und Erotischem' zu erwähnen, die sich etwa in der christlich fundierten Wonneerotik[68], in dem bei Mühlberger pietistisch inspirierten 'Programm der "seligsten Pein"' äußert.

3. Strategie der Verbalisierung des Gleichgeschlechtlichen

Die spezifische jahrtausendlange Kommunikationserfahrung der gleichgeschlechtlich Liebenden zeigt, dass die politische Subversivität des Gleichgeschlechtlichen eine gravierende Auswirkung auf dessen verbale Präsenz bzw. Absenz im sozialen Raum hatte. Die künstlerische Rede als Teil der allgemeinen Rede blieb von dem

67 Vgl. etwa Krey, Hans Henny Jahnn und die mann-männliche Liebe, 65.

68 Zur Verschmelzung der Wanderer-Mystik mit der christlichen Wonne vgl. Friedemann Spicker, Deutsche Wanderer-, Vagabunden- und Vagantenlyrik in den Jahren 1910–1933. Wege zum Heil – Straßen der Flucht, Berlin 1976, 93f.

erwünschten Nicht-Status des Gleichgeschlechtlichen begreiflicherweise nicht unbeeinflusst. Über das scheinbar Inexistente sollte nicht gesprochen werden. Der von Seiten der interessierten Machtstrukturen als ideal empfundene Zustand der totalen Verstummung des Nicht-Erwünschten erwies sich jedoch als eine nicht durchführbare Utopie. Vielmehr erlangte das Gleichgeschlechtliche einen – defensiv betrachtet – subversiven Halb- oder Zwischenstatus, produktiv gesehen – einen Vermittler-Status. Die sprachliche Stummheit wäre daher in einem engen Zusammenhang mit dem generellen sozialen Grenzcharakter des Gleichgeschlechtlichen, dessen sozial-politischer Unverortetheit, zu sehen. Wollte ein Sprecher das Gleichgeschlechtliche (verbal) darstellen, musste er sich genötigt fühlen, mit den institutionalisierten Formen der 'künstlerischen Rede' vorlieb zu nehmen und die ihr inhärente 'Dialektik zwischen dem Gesagten/Nicht-Gemeinten und dem Nicht-Gesagten/Gemeinten' zu Gunsten der Erreichung des Kommunikationszieles zu nutzen. Die Rede über Gleichgeschlechtliches musste eine 'periphrastische, aposiopetische, metaphorische, kurzum: eine künstlerische resp. poetische' sein. Die verfremdende poetische Sprache über das 'Konglomerat des Unsagbaren, Unbeschreibbaren, Unbenennbaren' musste noch um 'ein "richtig stellendes" Verbalisierungsinstrumentarium' bereichert werden. Das verhängte Sprachverbot hatte die Ausbildung einer filigranen Geheimsprache zur Folge. Diese Bedingungen hatten in den Augen mancher Kritiker auf die Entstehung vieler Erzstücke der Kunst paradoxer Weise einen positiven Einfluss ausgeübt: Das Sprachverbot wirkte im Falle wahrer Äußerungsnotwendigkeit für die Kunst subventionell.[69] Aus der Sicht der linguistisch fundierten Literaturwissenschaft können sich die Manöver der homoerotischen Camouflage ebenso interessant erweisen, wenn sie nicht direkt als Zeichen einer 'mehr oder weniger gestörte[n] Kommunikation'[70] abgetan werden. Die pragmatisch-rhetorischen '"Vermeidungsstrategien", d.h. entweder gar nichts oder nur einen Teil von dem ursprünglich Geplanten zu sagen'[71], entpuppen sich im Kunst- bzw. Literaturdiskurs m.E. stets als 'Strategien des gleichzeitigen Verschweigens und Mitteilen-Wollens', also als subversive Revision des von außen auferlegten Sprachverbots.

- Auf die Methoden der Distanz durch rhetorische Mittel wurde in der Forschungsliteratur, die sich mit dem Gegenstand der indirekten literarischen Rede über das Gleichgeschlechtliche beschäftigt, zwar mehrmals hingewiesen, sie wurden jedoch m.W. bis dato noch nie systematischer erforscht. Seien es etwa 'Umständlichkeitsformeln', die sich oft an klassische Vorlagen anlehnen,

69 Konsequenterweise scheinen manche Theoretiker die postmoderne Sprachfreiheit fast zu bereuen, denn sie verhülfe zur Banalisierung der künstlerischen Aussage, vgl. etwa bei Fernandez, Der Raub des Ganymed, 20–22.

70 Vgl. Astrid Stedje, Sprechabsicht und Lückenindikatoren. Zur Problematik der Kommunikationsstrategien, in: Zeitschrift für germanistische Linguistik 10, Berlin1982, 156–172, hier 160.

71 *Ibid.* Herv. LM.

wie die 'Lass uns-Formel' bei Mühlberger[72], seien es auf diverseste Weise eingesetzte '[r]hetorische Figuren der Absenz'.[73] Diese sprachlichen Ausblendungsmanöver werden bei Mühlberger just in den Momenten des erotisierten mannmännlichen Miteinanders benutzt; dieses Verstummen wird allerdings an Hand mannigfaltiger rhetorischer Figuren hörbar gemacht (Periphrase, Aposiopese, Paralipse, Ablenkung u.a.). Das 'periphrastische Umschweigen' fordert oft den 'defizitären Charakter des Dialogs' und unterwandert somit seine pragmatische Funktion: Beim Sprechen wird vielmehr verheimlicht als offengelegt.

- Ein häufig genutztes Mittel ist das Switchen zwischen den Sprachcodes, etwa zwischen Sprachen, der Hochsprache und Dialekt bzw. der Einsatz diverser Soziolekte usf. Das jeweils unterschiedliche repressive Ausmaß der betreffenden Sprachen tritt somit krass zutage.[74] Das signalträchtige 'Abgleiten der Figurensprache ins Französische', wenn delikate Inhalte artikuliert werden, darf bei Mühlberger einmal mehr auf die Inspiration durch Th. Mann zurückgeführt werden. Dem restriktiven Deutschen (der Luthersprache!) werden in solchen Momenten (analog zu der Norden-Süden-Topik) die südlichen Sprachen gegenübergestellt, welche 'als Substitut einer "offenen" Liebessprache'[75] fungieren.

- Einen beliebten Modus der Verfremdung stellt das distanzierende Sprechen durch einen Ton dar. In der Geschichte der sog. homoerotischen Literatur wird häufig vom 'ironischen oder generell humorigen Sprechen' Gebrauch gemacht[76] (ausgeprägt etwa bei Th. Mann, Th. Bernhard und terminologisiert als 'erotische Ironie'[77]). Bei Mühlberger hat der Leser eher mit dem kaschierenden 'Pathos' zu tun.

- Eine wichtige Sondergruppe der Verbalisierungsstrategien stellt das Sprechen über das Sprechen vom Gleichgeschlechtlichen. Die Topoi und Motive, die die

72 Vgl. etwa Arie Schippers, Die Knabenpoesie in der arabisch- und hebräisch-andalusischen Literatur, in: Forum Homosexualität und Literatur 31, Siegen 1998, 35–56, hier 54.

73 Vgl. Claudia Benthien, Barockes Schweigen. Rhetorik und Performativität des Sprachlosen im 17. Jahrhundert, München 2006, 140–157, hier 140.

74 Diese Differenz bestand im Mittelalter zwischen Latein und den sich konstituierenden Volkssprachen. Latein fungierte – z.B. im Gegensatz zum Deutschen – als eine gewisse Oase der artikulatorischen Freiheit, vgl. hierzu Sven Limbeck, Plautus in der Knabenschule. Zur Eliminierung homosexueller Inhalte in deutschen Plautusübersetzungen der frühen Neuzeit, in: Dirck Linck – Wolfgang Popp – Annette Runte, (Hgg.), Erinnern und Wiederentdecken. Tabuisierung und Enttabuisierung der männlichen und weiblichen Homosexualität in Wissenschaft und Kritik, Berlin 1999, 15–67.

75 Härle, Die Gestalt des Schönen, 20; Yahya Elsaghe, 'Genre', 'gender' und sexuelle Orientierung in Thomas Manns Erzählwerk, in: Forum Homosexualität und Literatur 41, Siegen 2002, 5–16; Fernandez, Der Raub des Ganymed, 58; Kurzke, Thomas Mann, 331.

76 Vgl. Steinhaußen, 'Aristokraten aus Not' und ihre 'Philosophie der zu hoch hängenden Trauben', 430–432.

77 Vgl. Kurzke, Thomas Mann, 250f.

historische Tatsache der sprachlichen Tabuisierung thematisieren, ließen sich unter dem 'Topos der stummen Sünde'[78] subsumieren, dessen sich noch Oscar Wilde während seines Prozesses bediente, als er über das Gleichgeschlechtliche als über Liebe spricht, 'which dare not say her name', bis zu dessen Variation wie etwa dem 'Topos des Unsagbaren, des Unbenennbaren, der Liebe ohne Namen', welche mit einer Unermüdlichkeit in der homoerotischen Literatur bis tief ins 20. Jahrhundert grassieren.

4. Strategie der erzähltechnischen Signifikanz

Ebenso marginal erforscht wie die Verbalisierungsstrategien sind im Kontext der sog. homoerotischen Literatur die Strategien der narrativen Signifikanz. Es wäre spannend, jedoch umso spektakulärer, der möglichen Absicht des Autors, das Homoerotische an Hand von spezifischen narrativen Modifikationen mitzucamouflieren, nachzugehen – allerdings nicht mit dem Ziel, eine spezifisch homoerotische Schreibweise zu postulieren. Legitim erscheinen solche Überlegungen wohl noch im Kontext der allgemeinen Geschlechterkrise der Jahrhundertwende zu sein, welche sich laut mancher Forscher in der '"Verweiblichung" des Erzählens [...] einer Krise männlicher Autorschaft'[79] äußert. Diese 'Krise des paternalen Erzählens'[80] platterdings auf die Homosexualität der Autoren zurückzuführen, erwiese sich jedoch bestenfalls als unüberlegt.

- Spezifische, zugleich signalisierende und vertuschende Erzählverfahren lassen sich etwa im Aufbau und Ausgang des Plots verfolgen. Es wurde in der Forschungsliteratur mehrmals darauf hingewiesen, dass die homoerotische Literatur von einem beschränkten Repertoire von Konstituenten im Handlungsaufbau und -abschluss beherrscht wird. Bis zur Mitte des 20. Jahrhunderts gab es für gleichgeschlechtlich liebende literarische Protagonisten nur unglückliche Ausgänge. Der 'Verzicht auf das gemeinsame Mann-Männliche'[81] prägt einen erheblichen Teil dieser Literatur. Eine nicht seltene extreme Lösung stellt der 'Selbstmord'[82] oder 'der (natürliche) Tod' dar. Ein Happy-End ist den schwulen Paaren in der modernen Literatur – abgesehen von der Trivialliteratur – bis zur Hälfte des 20. Jahrhunderts nur in Ausnahmefällen beschieden.[83]

---

78 Vgl. z.B.: Mayer, Außenseiter, 176; Limbeck, Plautus in der Knabenschule, 63. Zur Etymologie und zum Ursprung dieses Topos siehe detailliert bei Hergemöller, Sodom und Gomorrha, 19f. und v.a. 97–140.

79 Birgit Dahlke, Jünglinge der Moderne. Jugendkult und Männlichkeit in der Literatur um 1900, Köln 2006, 146.

80 Dahlke, Jünglinge der Moderne, 144.

81 Vgl. Borchers, Männliche Homosexualität in der Dramatik der Weimarer Republik, 19, 63, 117 u.a.

82 "Es will scheinen, als gebe es in dieser Art von Literatur ein 'Muß' des Selbstmordes – um welchen Preis auch immer." (Borchers, Männliche Homosexualität in der Dramatik der Weimarer Republik, 57.)

83 Vgl. auch bei Mühlberger: Alle mann-männlichen Beziehungen in seinem Werk, die zu einer glücklichen, ausgewogenen Partnerschaft werden können, enden letzten Endes mit dem Verzicht

- Die Figurencharakteristik der homoerotisch suggerierten Protagonisten[84] befolgt des Öfteren bestimmte stereotype Vorstellungen: Auf der einen Seite gibt es einen sensiblen, effeminierten, introvertierten, passiven Homoeroten, auf der anderen einen sexuell möglichst nicht festlegbaren Begehrten, der attraktiv, viril, aktiv und oft gefühllos ist. In dieser Disproportion scheinen die beiden üblichen Handlungsabschlüsse (Verzicht, Selbstmord) bereits vorprogrammiert. Zu den wichtigsten Konstituenten der homoerotischen Camouflage gehört die homoerotische Protagonistenkonstellation: Laut Keilson-Lauritz etwa müsse es sich erstens um zwei Personen des gleichen Geschlechts handeln, ferner müssten sie durch Sinnliches verbunden werden (Verlangen, Körperlichkeit, Liebesrede *etc.*).[85] Dass die homoerotische Camouflage sich nicht der expliziten homoerotischen Konstellation bedient, sondern eher die typische heteronormative Paarstellung untergräbt, lässt sich auch an Mühlbergers Texten zeigen.

- Auf ein enorm wichtiges Moment macht wiederum Heinrich Detering aufmerksam, wenn er betont, dass 'heteroerotische und homoerotisch konnotierbare Freundschafts-Beziehung *parallelisiert* werden'.[86] Solche strukturellen Parallelisierungen finden sich häufig auch bei Mühlberger; ihre Funktion ist es, die Beziehung, welche wegen Verbalisierungshemmungen als minderwertig erscheint, wieder indirekt aufzuwerten.

- Ein übliches Manöver, um das verbal in den Hintergrund geratene Mann-Männliche wieder ins Zentrum der Aufmerksamkeit des Lesers zu rücken, ist 'die unterschiedliche quantitative *Gewichtung* der erzählten Ereignisse'.[87] Die quantitative und qualitative Akzentuierung des Mann-Männlichen in der Handlung zu Ungunsten des Heterosexuellen kann dann untergründig auf das Eigentliche verweisen.

- Ein nicht zu unterschätzendes Moment stellt die narrative Unbestimmtheit[88] dar: Mühlberger macht in seinem Werk mehrmals Gebrauch von diesem subtilen Mittel, um den Leser auf die Spur des Homoerotischen zu führen. Er nutzt

---

des einen oder anderen ("Licht *über den Bergen*"; "Das Tal der Träume"; "Bogumil"), mit dem erzähllogisch unabdingbaren Tod eines der Protagonisten ("Die schwarze Perle", "In einem savoyardischen Dorf") oder mit dem Selbstmord ("Die Knaben und der Fluß").

84 Vgl. Borchers, Männliche Homosexualität in der Dramatik der Weimarer Republik, 20, 279–281, 321f.

85 Vgl. Keilson-Lauritz, Von der Liebe die Freundschaft heißt, 62.

86 Detering, Das offene Geheimnis, 230. Herv. im Original.

87 *Ibid.* Herv. im Original.

88 Vgl. Detering, der von 'sprachliche[n] Unbestimmtheiten' spricht (*ibid.*, 231–231). Diese Strategie ist in dieser Arbeit breiter aufgefasst: Auch wenn es sich um im engeren Sinne um 'sprachliche' Mehrdeutigkeit oder Unbestimmtheit handeln kann, üben diese Unbestimmtheiten eine Auswirkung auf die narrative Struktur aus.

v.a. die Möglichkeit der deiktischen Ambiguität bzw. referenziellen Mehrdeutigkeit.

- Neben der deiktischen Ambiguität findet man in den Texten von Mühlberger auch diverse Brüche in der Narrationslogik, welche auf den Subtext aufmerksam machen und zur interpretativen Vorsichtigkeit auffordern.

Schlussbemerkung

Die vorliegende kommentierte Auflistung der Mittel der ästhetischen homoerotischen Camouflage ist aus verständlichen Gründen sehr knapp gehalten. Eine tiefere Einsicht in die Problematik – zusammen mit detaillierten Textanalysen – findet sich in meiner Dissertation.

Das hierarchisierte und an vielen Diskursen partizipierende System dieser Camouflage bietet bei näherem Hinsehen eine nicht zu ignorierende Möglichkeit, politisch und langfristig verzerrte Deutungen mancher Autoren bzw. ihrer Werke mit Hilfe der textanalytischen 'Beweise', d.h. philologisch plausibel, zu revidieren (wie etwa im Falle Josef Mühlbergers) oder die Interpretation mancher Ideologeme und Bereiche bei anderen Autoren zumindest zu erweitern (wie etwa im Falle des Amerika-Ideologems bei dem österreichischen Autor Charles Sealsfield).[89]

89 Hierzu vgl. die Beiträge Lukáš Motyčka, Worüber spricht man in der Cajüte. Charles Sealsfields *Cajütenbuch* neu beleuchtet (erscheint in Germanoslavica. Zeitschrift für germano-slawische Studien 1, Prag 2016); und Lukáš Motyčka, Die Spuren des Diskurses über das Mann-Männliche im Werk Charles Sealsfields (erscheint in: Wynfrid Kriegleder (Hg.), Charles Sealsfields Nordamerika im 21. Jahrhundert. Neue Fragen, neue Antworten, Wien 2015).

Rachel Schaff

Home Is Where the Heart Is: From Family to Nation in Czech Film Melodramas

University of Minnesota

Introduction

In 1998, in its volumes of "Czech Feature Films" ["Česky hrany film"], the National Film Archive (NFA) in Prague [Národní filmovy archiv] retroactively catalogued 69 films made between 1930 and 1944 as melodramas.[1] That the Czech National Film Archive would so classify the films made during the period of the Nazi occupation and its immediate prelude suggests a desire to consign these films to the 'domestic' sphere and, thereby, to remove them from the seemingly charged realms of geopolitics and national politics. Yet, these films are in fact an important litmus test of the ways in which the intimate 'home' lives of ordinary Czechs and Slovaks negotiated cataclysmic political shifts in the public sphere. The project investigates the reception of these film melodramas during four key eras in Czechoslovak history: the interwar period, the Nazi occupation, the aftermath of the Holocaust, and the reimagining of Czechoslovakia as a nationally homogeneous, Socialist state.[2]

The present work links the archival practice of these films' generic classification to the social and historical contexts in which these films were produced, and also in which classification occurred. That is, to look at how popular culture can reveal a great deal about how we view and revise history from specific temporal vantage points. It is argued that popular cinema in particular made history legible to mass Czechoslovak audiences and contributed, in different ways at different times, to the construction of national identity in post-war Czechoslovakia. In doing so, this project engages with scholarship on film melodrama as a mode of conception and expression, a sense-making system that, as literary scholar Peter Brooks points out, emerged in France directly after the French Revolution to make everyday life meaningful within the rebuilding of a nation on newly secular terms.[3] As Brooks

1 National Film Archive, (Ed.), Czech Feature Film II, 1930–1945, Prague 1998.

2 While Czechoslovakia was officially a state of the Czechs and Slovaks who were referred to collectively as Czechoslovaks, the vast majority of citizens identified as either Czech or Slovak. Here I focus specifically on Czechs.

3 Peter Brooks, The Melodramatic Imagination, New Haven, 1995.

and others (including, notably, film scholars Linda Williams and Christine Gledhill) have suggested, melodrama is characterized by hyperbolic representation and an intensity of moral appeal, evoking the essential conflicts between good and evil that play out just below the surface of everyday life.[4]

In post-war Czechoslovakia, this powerful mode of representation became a crucial form through which popular film helped address the country's recent past. In the immediate post-war years, before (or after) the Communist authorities developed policies to minimize any serious public discussion of the Holocaust, melodrama normalized, and made morally legible, the tumultuous events of the period 1930–1944 – including the Nazi occupation, the Holocaust, and the lead-up to the country's 1945 expulsion of its German citizens – by pointing to daily life. Further, the article explores how changes in the historical context of the films' dissemination, and how particularly their re-viewing after their initial release through various channels, including their theatrical re-release in the 1970s and television broadcast in the 1980s and 1990s modified their reception, and thus their moral legibility. Through this investigation, the author offers a crucial study of both melodrama as a film genre within Czech cinema and how these films play a role in East Central European history.

The Five Volumes of "Czech Feature Films" ["Česky hrany film"]

The research is grounded in theoretical and historiographic questions presented by the five volumes of "Czech Feature Films" ["Česky hrany film"], which were compiled and distributed by the National Film Archive in Prague (NFA) starting in the mid-1990s. These volumes, which span from 1898 to 1993, attempt to provide a comprehensive 'official' guide in both the Czech and English languages to feature-length Czech fiction films. Each film title is supplemented with production information including the film's release date, director, screenwriter, editor, producer, cast, crew, shooting location, and even a brief narrative summary. Additionally, each film is classified by genre.[5] In these volumes, the genre classification 'melodrama' is attributed to 69 films made between 1930 and 1944. With the exception of two films from the 1980s, 'Oznamuje se láskám vašim' ('Announced to Your Loves', dir. Karel Kachyňa, 1988) and 'Na brigádě' ('On the Brigade', dir. Thomas Vorel, 1989), no other films are categorized as melodrama; rather, the genre simply disappears.

The project asks why. What happened during these crucial mid-century years to bring melodrama into focus in Czechoslovakia? This period is marked by the 1938 Munich agreement in which France and Great Britain allowed Nazi Germany

4 For more see: Christine Gledhill, Rethinking Genre, in: Christine Gledhill – Linda Williams (Eds.), Reinventing Film Studies, London, 2000, 219–243; Linda Williams, Melodrama Revised, in: Nick Browne (Ed.), Refiguring American Film Genres, Berkley 1998, 42–88.

5 Among the genres classified within the five volumes of "Czech Feature Films" are comedy, drama, tragic comedy, romance, *etc.*

to annex the largely German-speaking western borderlands (the Sudetenland) and spans the entirety of Nazi occupation, which began in March 1939. These events produced fundamental reconfigurations of social, political, and cultural life in Czechoslovakia, the effects of which would be felt throughout the post-war period. As historians of East Central Europe have pointed out, at the end of World War II, Czechoslovakia was left in a state of uncertainty; the material effects of the war forced Czechs and Slovaks to re-think traditional notions of Czech and Slovak national identity (as previously, Czechoslovakia had been a multinational state, comprising multiple national groups) through de-Germanification. Yet the generic categorization of the films produced during this period – the archive at the core of the project – belies these momentous social and political occurrences, for melodrama's tendency to privilege domestic themes – love, sex, marriage, motherhood, jealousy, loss – has positioned it historically as a 'low genre', with melodrama films often dismissed as cliché: as 'women's films', 'weepies', or 'tearjerkers'.

The article is based on the assumption that the domestic may inadvertently reveal political assumptions about personal life, and thus lend insight into both political and historical experience. Critical to this approach to melodrama are the economic, political, social, and cultural changes that Czechoslovakia faced at this moment, as it grappled with the end of the multinational interwar First Republic and the advent of a new, ethnically homogeneous identity. If, as Brooks and others write, melodrama allows for binaries like good and evil or moral and amoral to be recognized so as to confront, combat and expel evil – to purge the social order – then how, I ask, do these films engage with the problems that attended the formation of a Czechoslovak nation and national identity? How do they engage with the Czechoslovak experience of the Holocaust? Indeed, the excess of emotion associated with melodrama allows for the expression of what scholars of the Holocaust such as Dominick LaCapra and Saul Friedländer associate with the 'unrepresentable' representation of the Holocaust.[6] From the perspective of this research, then, the melodramatic maxim 'home is where the heart is' moves away from the family and invites reinterpretation as an overtly nationalist sentiment.

But asserting that a film is a melodrama does not necessarily point us to a single, definitive meaning or method for its classification. Even within the discipline of Film Studies, there are many different understandings as to what the term 'melodrama' means and what type of films it evokes. One of the criticisms of the term by film historians and scholars is that melodrama is particularly ambiguous and can be invoked to describe a wide range of aesthetics, gestures, themes, and so on. From this criticism emerged efforts to produce a more coherent field of investigation, which can be characterized by two key methodological approaches: Film Studies' standard approach to melodrama, best exemplified in the work of film

6 Dominick LaCapra, Trauma, Absence, Loss, in: Neil Levi – Michael Rothberg (Eds.) The Holocaust Theoretical Readings, New Brunswick 2003, 199–205; Saul Friedländer, Trauma, Memory, and Transference, in: Geoffrey H. Hartman (Ed.), The Holocaust Remembrance. The Shapes of Memory, Oxford 1994, 252–263.

scholars Linda Williams and Christine Gledhill, and the Film Studies' revisionist Reception Studies approach advocated by film scholars Ben Singer and Steve Neale.[7] These two approaches present a clear divide: Whereas Film Studies' standard approach to melodrama analyzes film form through the lenses of Neo-Marxism, psychoanalysis, and feminism to identify melodrama as a modality (that is, a narrative formula), stressing the role of film critics and historians in its formation and ongoing interpretation, its' Reception Studies looks instead to publicity materials, press advertisements, reviews and journalistic articles to historicize precisely how the initial reception and distribution of a film created and popularized the genre (a thematic and aesthetic classification system).

Neither approach is without problems. For example: Reception Studies' aim to establish a fixed meaning for melodrama (traceable through genre cycles) can be understood as a reaction to the shortcomings of Film Studies' standard version of melodrama to provide a more specific meaning. In Film Studies' standard version, melodrama can be a 'woman's film' or even more problematically, it can be an all-encompassing 'umbrella genre' – and these inconsistencies leave room for misreadings. However, as film historian Rick Altman points out in his response to Steve Neale's study of the American Trade Press[8] to form a 'precise' historical account of melodrama as it was originally used in Hollywood: 'genres are not democratically elected representatives of like-minded texts.'[9]

The research adopts aspects of each approach in an attempt to formulate a new methodology for understanding how melodrama functions within specific national cases. It takes two assumptions as its starting points: First, melodrama is an essential narrative form for understanding historical phenomena. It is particularly helpful here for making sense of the Czechoslovak situation, which is characterized by constant instability, with linguistic and political divides enabling certain aspects of the affective world of popular culture to be expressed – and forcing others to go under cover. That is, despite its popular nature, melodrama is a genre that has a historical validity and that plays a role in the construction of a national sensibility. Second, and more specific to the East Central European context, melodrama is a mode that enables an understanding of how the Holocaust became part of a national cultural experience. It is melodrama's particular investment in the private and domestic sphere that has enabled this negotiation. This point stresses how important melodrama is for the representation of the Holocaust, especially in the years that followed.

---

7 For more on debates concerning the conception – and re-conception- of melodrama in Film Studies see: John Mercer – Martin Shingler, Melodrama. Genre, Style, Sensibility, London 2004.

8 Here the author is following dialogue between Steve Neale and Rick Altman: Steve Neale, 'Melo Talk'. On the Meaning and Use of the Term 'Melodrama' in the American Trade Press, in: Velvet Light Trap 32, Austin 1993, 66–89; Rick Altman, Reusable Packaging. Generic Products and the Recycling Process, in: Nick Browne (Ed.), Refiguring American Film Genres. History and Theory, Berkeley 1998, 1–41.

9 *Ibid.*, 5.

In effect, what I am arguing for is a redefinition of melodrama through what I call 'historicized pathos'.[10] My original concept of historicized pathos considers that we are conditioned by our consciousness of history (ies) to both set up and anticipate historical events as narrative events. To be clear: In our recognition of the historical film's narratological and temporal functions, historicized pathos stipulates that in any historical film narrative pathos is produced by the 'condition of history' (it is 'too late' to relive the historical event, but through film it can be reproduced), and varies based on the film's 'historical condition' ('shared' historical action). By merit of the historical film's position within the past, 'our pre-learned knowledge' of the underlying historical events (based on 'national' of cultural specific memory) – the historical condition – produces the nostalgia for pre-experienced emotions, creating a framework of expectations, and changing both how we approach and how we experience a film.

Historicized pathos thus addresses us within the limitations of representing the past. It acknowledges the demands of the historical film narrative, of the expectations – or moral legibility one brings to a 'pre-experienced' historical event (or events). If historicized pathos can only exist within the conditions of history, its possibilities lie in the acknowledgement of the historical condition – or how we know ourselves affectively.[11] Without our noticing, we have learned (inherited) these historical events and historical timelines, and have been structured to react – to feel – to be moved – to be historically affected by history. Since then, we have been structured by history, the formal aspects of these historical films; both narrative and visual, only help to supplement these affective frameworks. However, this falsely implies that there is one specific type of reaction for each historical event. How we feel towards history – it is intrinsically pathetic, because it is 'too late' to re-live the historical event – may be the condition of history. But history – as a se-

---

10 In the 1970s, 1980s and 1990s, as melodrama theory grew into a valid critical practice, several film scholars including Linda Williams and Steve Neale adopted literary theorist Franco Moretti's [Franco Moretti, Kindergarten, in: Signs Taken for Wonders. On the Sociology of Literary Forms, London 2005, 157–181] understanding of the 'pleasure of pathos and how it works with action' as a 'too late' sensation [Linda Williams, Playing the Race Card, Princeton 2002, 69f.]. Although these tears cannot turn back time, they do at least recognize that something important has been lost. The feeling of loss – of a time, a person, or a place – is critical to understanding the relationship between melodrama and tears. This loss produces a 'too late' sensation, contingent on time and timing. Linda Williams builds upon these existing theories, writing, 'melodrama does not always move, then toward a new future; very often it moves to restore some semblance of a lost past. To this degree melodrama can be considered an inherently conservative and backward looking form even as it progressively tackles basic problems of social inequity' [*ibid.*, 36f.]. According to Williams, 'melodrama involves a dialectic of pathos and action – a give and and take of "too late" and "in the nick of time"' [*ibid.*, 69f].

11 According to Richard Dyer [Richard Dyer, Pastiche, New York 2007], our ability to 'know ourselves affectively as historical beings' can be attributed to pastiche [*ibid.*, 180.]. Dyer asserts that pastiche 'imitates formal means that are themselves ways of evoking, molding and eliciting feeling, and thus in the process is able to mobilize feelings even while signaling that it is doing so. Thereby it can, at its best, allow us to feel our connection to the affective frameworks, the structures of feeling, past and present, that we inherit and pass on' [*ibid.*, 180f.].

ries of happenings subject to national and culturally specific memory of individual historical action – is subject to a historical condition. These two factors both feed into our anticipation of how these historical films work on us.

In this way, historicized pathos is important for understanding not only how we are moved by history, but of how and why the narratives of history are formed, remembered, and re-experienced. Studying the emotional force of melodrama in historical terms enables us to see the way its spectators know history from specific subject positions. By combining the methodologies of Film Studies and Reception Studies, I aim to forge new connections and open potential avenues for further research into melodrama as a particular genre and a universalized mode that occupies a privileged position vis-à-vis the most intimate subjectivity of the nation.

Ultimately, my understanding of melodrama positions it as a foundation of possibilities that gesture towards shared memory-meanings, as well as the limitations of national and historical imaginaries. The Czech National Film Archive's classification of only these 69 films from 1930–1944 as melodramas thus positions the genre as a helpful tool to understand how Czechs self-fashioned their national identity through popular film culture throughout Nazi occupation.

Classifying/Identifying Melodrama: A Case Study

Despite several moves by film scholars towards challenging how melodrama has been applied and read onto various national cinemas through transnational film discourse, these challenges have done little to solidify the slippery boundaries that position melodrama globally. These studies are rooted in Linda Williams's's[12] argument that melodrama is the dominant mode of Classical Hollywood Cinema, and so they engage specific national cases in comparative studies with Hollywood cinema (primarily concerning the aesthetic melodramatic excess found in mise-en-scène). This, coupled with Miriam Hansen's contention that the 'language' of classical Hollywood cinema spread worldwide and took 'vernacular'[13] forms in each

12 See: Williams, Playing the Race, 42, 47f.

13 In her essay "Vernacular Modernism. Tracking Cinema on a Global Scale" [Miriam Hansen, Vernacular Modernism. Tracking Cinema on a Global Scale, in: Nataša Ďurovičová – Kathleen Newman (Eds.), World Cinemas, Transnational Perspectives, New York/London, 2010, 287–314] film scholar Miriam Hansen supplements her original understanding of the term vernacular modernism as a post-modern concept that stipulates that classical Hollywood cinema became a global cinematic language through modernity to reflect its role in establishing a transnational cinema. In order to demonstrate vernacular modernism's transnational abilities, Hansen [*ibid.*, 288f.] offers the films 'Madame X' (Dir. Sam Wood, USA, 1937), 'Applause' (Dir. Rouben Mamoulian, USA, 1929), 'Blonde Venus' (Dir. Josef von Sternberg, USA, 1932) and 'Stella Dallas' (Dir. King Vidor, USA, 1937) as examples of a variant of melodrama that she calls the 'trope of prostitute-with-a-heart-of-gold.' She goes on to trace this trope across Japanese and Chinese cinema in order to prove that it functions within different film traditions, and she notes that it is often foregrounded through performances and mise-en-scene. Although these films are destined to elicit different interpretations and responses based on location of reception, Hansen realizes that through 'filmic representation, they gesture towards a modernist, non-anthropocentric aesthetics of contingency, even as they mobilize material objects to create pathos and critical reflections'. As a result, Hansen

local context to which it spread, has invited scholars to read melodrama as a transnational film discourse.[14] I will take this research a step further by developing a new methodology for understanding the melodramatic impulses and functions of melodrama specifically in Czech film. The following is a comparative case study of two Czechoslovak films: The first, 'Sobota' ['Saturday'] (Václav Wasserman's 1944), has been classified by the Czech National Film Archive as a melodrama; the second, 'Daleká cesta' ['The Long Journey'/'The Distant Journey'] (Alfréd Radok's 1949), has not.

There are countless Czech films that are melodramas that have beenover looked over by the Czech National Film Archive's approach to classifying the genre. In this paper, I want to look at a film that has been catalogued as a melodrama alongside a film that I would argue 'should be' identified as a melodrama to understand why and how they might be recognized, as well as why and how they might not. I want to argue that 'Sobota' and Alfréd Radok's 1949 film 'Daleká cesta' can both be distinguished on a basic level – by which I mean visual style, narrative theme and narrative structure – as melodramas, suggesting a flaw in the Czech National Film Archive's approach to identifying the genre. But the issues presented by identifying how melodrama might be recognized are less obvious routes to my main concern: the role that history – as the historical time of a film's production and release, as a narrative theme, and also as a subject of reflection or response to negotiating a recent past – plays in this recognition. How did this specific 14-year period from 1930 to 1944 come to represent the total presence of melodrama in Czech film? And, at what expense has the term 'melodrama' taken on other meanings in Czech films outside of this period, if it has taken on other meanings at all?

'Sobota' ['Saturday']

Before addressing these questions, the following paragraph wants to start by considering the ways in which 'Sobota' might be identified as a melodrama, beginning with an analysis of the film to establish how melodrama is its operative genre, and ending with the problems presented by this notion of melodrama as a genre.

The film 'Sobota' opens in the home of its protagonist, Helena, a young housewife, as she prepares breakfast for her husband. As she does this, she moves constantly throughout her small-yet-comfortable house; as she moves through the kitchen and to the dining room, the camera pans on a 360-degree axis to follow her, and we watch as she pours hot water, makes coffee and butters toast for her husband's breakfast. When her husband finally leaves for work, she breathes a sigh of relief.

---

concludes that film language and especially genre conventions retain their original intent even after the translation process to 'construct a space and time in spectatorial subjectivity [*ibid.*, 313f.].

14 Miriam Bratu Hansen, The Mass Production of the Senses Classical Cinema as Vernacular Modernism, in: Christine Gledhill – Linda Williams (Eds.) Reinventing Film Studies, London 2000, 332–350.

It is clear that Helena is bored by her marriage and that she feels stifled by the limitations of her domestic life, and soon, for a change of pace, she takes a job outside of the home as a shop girl in her brother's flower shop. At her workplace she meets Richard Herbert, a wealthy older businessman, who is immediately taken with her. Richard returns to the shop daily and showers her with expensive gifts to express his interest. After a brief courtship, he convinces Helena to abandon her husband and her old life to start anew with him – and she soon moves in with him – into his large, luxurious apartment. However, the true nature of Helena's new life and position is revealed when she spots Richard out in the city with another woman. Helena quickly learns that this woman is Richard's wife. After coming to terms with this initial shock, Helena uneasily resumes her new life as a 'kept woman'. But her ability to live this life – and this lie – does not last long, even despite its lavish gifts, stylish clothing, and sparkling jewels. Helena gives in and confronts Richard's wife. This confrontation does not have the desired effect; Richard's wife admits to knowing about her husband's affairs and tolerating them to keep their marriage in tact. Helena realizes the impossibility of her situation and agrees to never see Richard again. The film closes after presenting the audience the reunion of the seemingly happy couples: Richard with his wife and Helena with her faithful and loving husband.

Perhaps then, to understand why 'Sobota' has been identified as a melodrama, one should think about how this genre may have been distinguished (by critics, spectators, and the National Film Archive in Prague) – and also how it can be distinguished. By this the author wants to suggest that both methodological approaches – reception and theory – can lead toward establishing what this genre classification might mean. As we have seen, even despite their methodological differences, these approaches are in dialogue with each other. Certainly, reception studies can be used to inform a theoretical approach and theory can be used to engage reception (and vice-versa). If we look at a sample of 'Sobota's' reception, we can get at the question of what methodologies or materials might have informed its classification as a melodrama. More importantly, this will position the film within Czechoslovak history, leading us towards thinking about the historical conditions of this 14 year-period.

The Czech film periodical *Filmový přehled* [Film Review] provides us with a starting point to thinking about 'Sobota's' reception. The periodical was established in 1939 to provide cinema managers and operators with detailed information on all films in Czech distribution. Like the volumes of "Czech Feature Films", each film title in *Filmový přehled* is supplemented with the film's production information including release date, director, screenwriter, editor, producer, cast, a 'short assessment', and a brief narrative summary.[15] Although this periodical does not include any material from 'Sobota's' initial release in 1944, it does provide an article from the film's re-release in 1970. This retrospective review positions 'Sobota'

15 *Filmový přehled* [Film Review], http://www.nfa.cz/filmovy-prehled1.html), 25 December 2012.

within its original 1944 reception by noting that the film was 'shot during occupation'. It goes on to explain that the film 'served as temporary escape from difficult war' because it was 'light', 'uncomplicated' and 'superficial.' Strangely, the term 'melodrama' does not appear in the article. Rather, the film is called 'comedy' and 'kitsch' suggesting that it is popular, lowbrow – or more precisely, generic. Perhaps then, the term 'melodrama' was adopted as a popular pejorative term to describe it as a generic film?

This makes sense if one considers that the term 'melodrama' can be – and has been – applied to an expansive and diverse body of films throughout each decade. From this point of view, the diversity of forms designated as 'melodrama' effectively reduces the term's critical value. Nevertheless, the Hollywood family melodrama has taken on a credible form for generic categorization, which enables melodrama to be studied as a genre. In his groundbreaking article "Tales of Sound and Fury. Observations on the Family Melodrama", Thomas Elsaesser asserts that the 'characteristic feature of melodrama' is 'the point of view of the victim'.[16] Within the context of his argument, Elsaesser favors the fifties family melodrama as the 'genre's quintessential form because there is a tendency for these films to "present all the characters convincingly as victims'.[17] This follows what, in the early 1980s, Thomas Schatz set out as a clear history of melodrama from the silent era to 1960, providing a list of family melodramas from 1954–1960, which were subdivided into a number of subgenres and variants.[18] If one looks at Schatz's foundation for the basic model for the family melodrama, we can easily identify 'Sobota' within the sub-genre of the 'widow/lover melodrama,' since the film follows Helena's romantic relationship with Richard. The narrative of 'Sobota' is motivated by the sub-theme of the 'intruder-redeemer'. Helena's boredom with the domestic sphere of life gives her the motivation to venture out into the world. Once Helena abandons the domestic space of the home, she meets Richard, an 'intruder redeemer' figure, who pulls her even further away. However, when Helena learns that he is an adulterer, she reflects on her own situation and returns home. In the end, the home – and Helena – is redeemed.[19]

On a basic level, Schatz's foundation of the family melodrama helps us to identify 'Sobota' as a generic melodrama, but it also points out the problems inherent with the notion of melodrama as a genre. These ambiguities and contradictions have effectively created what can be thought of as an all-encompassing umbrella genre, which restricts it from becoming 'a single cinematic form' like the west-

16 Thomas Elsaessar, Tales of Sound and Fury. Observations on the Family Melodrama, in: Christine Gledhill (Ed.), Home is Where the Heart Is. Studies in Melodrama and the Women's Film, London 1987, 43–69.

17 Elsaesser, Tales, 51f.

18 Thomas Schatz, The Family Melodrama, in: Marcia Landy (Ed.), Imitations of Life. A Reader on Film and Television Melodrama, Detroit 1991, 148–167.

19 Schatz, The Family, 155f.

ern or film noir.[20] This also leaves us with the overwhelming (and over-brimming) conception of melodrama as a hybrid of various sub-genres and film cycles.[21] As Christine Gledhill explains, the construction of melodrama as the family melodrama as a specific Hollywood genre has 'made it difficult to pursue its connection with 19th century melodramatic traditions'.[22] Further, she asserts that it is not useful for to describe a specific group of films to label 'melodrama', rather it is more helpful to approach melodrama through a 'melodramatic rhetoric' that a range of films of different genres can utilize.[23]

'Daleká cesta' ['The Long Journey'/'The Distant Journey']

Unlike 'Sobota', Radok's 'Daleká cesta' is not categorized as a 'melodrama' in the volumes of "Czech Feature Films". Rather, the film is classified as occupying the genre of 'occupation drama'. Surely 'Daleká cesta' presents the historical events of the occupation, but I want to suggest that it can also be considered a melodrama – that the film has a clear a melodramatic sensibility. The reasons why it has not been categorized as a melodrama are quite obvious; 'Daleká cesta' explicitly represents the historical events of the Holocaust, which is typically viewed as a 'high theme' incompatible with melodrama – a 'low' genre. In other words: if 'Daleká cesta' were to be classified as a melodrama, it would then decrease its value as a historical object that faithfully adheres to the representation of events as-they-really-happened.

The film's distinct visual style may be another factor for this classification. 'Daleká cesta' intercuts what is immediately recognizable as a glossy and stylized studio melodrama with documentary footage. To achieve this effect, the studio melodrama is not merely grounded in reality, but is framed within the real of the documentary. Several times throughout 'Daleká cesta' the still active frame of the studio melodrama shrinks down into the lower right corner within the larger frame of the screen; it is then superimposed through a picture-in-picture effect within this 'reality' to create a historical framework. In other words: through editing, the 'documented past' is intertwined with a type of 'present' to produce a narrative within two separate times – the time of the studio narrative, and the time of World War II and the Holocaust.

Melodrama, as Linda Williams describes it, is an aesthetic and epistemological mode that 'involves a dialectic of pathos and action – a give and take of "too

20 Mercer – Shingler, Melodrama, 5f.

21 Films that fall in the category of melodrama include the romantic drama, historical costume drama, psychological thrillers, gothic thrillers, woman's weepies, domestic dramas, juvenile delinquency films, crime thrillers, *etc.*

22 Christine Gledhill, The Melodramatic Field. An Investigation, in: Christine Gledhill, (Ed.) Home is Where the Heart Is. Studies in Melodrama and the Women's Film, London 1987, 5–42.

23 Gledhill, The Melodramatic 12f.

late" and "in the nick of time".'[24] One can argue then, that one must understand melodrama as a foundation – a narrative formula contingent on 'dual recognition of how things are and how they should be' to produce pathos – that can be translated across geographic and cultural boundaries through a shared understanding of narrative 'types' – that is to say, films categorized by similar narrative settings and events.[25] According to Christine Gledhill, this is made possible because melodrama is always grounded in realism, and, 'taking its stand in the material world of everyday reality and lived experience, and acknowledging the limitations of the conventions of language and representation, it proceeds to force into aesthetic presence identity, value and plentitude of meaning'.[26] Williams expands on this, writing that melodrama is grounded in the 'social problems of reality' and lists 'problems such as illegitimacy, slavery, racism, labor struggle, class division, disease, nuclear annihilation, even the Holocaust' as potential narrative subjects.[27]

The opening montage of 'Daleká cesta' introduces black-and-white shapes marching against a brick wall – soon recognizable as newsreel footage from Nazi Germany – intercutting footage from Leni Riefenstahl's 'Triumph of the Will' (1935)[28] with newsreel footage, and ends on a formal title card, setting the film's narrative in Prague 1941. This sequence situates the film in Prague after the enactment of Protectorate's anti-Semitic laws. These laws have an immediate effect on the film's protagonist, Hana Kaufmannová, a Jewish doctor, for she is soon dismissed from her position for being Jewish. As time passes, the anti-Semitic laws become increasingly oppressive. Signs appear on buildings that read, 'Jews, keep out!' Then, Jews are forced to identify themselves by wearing Jewish stars. At one point, her family has the opportunity to immigrate to America, but she decides that she cannot leave her home and fiancé, Dr. Antonín Bureš (a Czech), so her family abandons this option in order to remain in Prague with their daughter. Hana and Antonin quickly marry so that she can avoid deportation. However, entering a mixed marriage transforms Antonin into a second-class citizen; he soon loses his position at the city hospital and must begin to work as a laborer in a factory. Several weeks later, Hana's family is deported to Terezín. In an attempt to save his wife's family from being transferred to a death camp, Antonín infiltrates the transit camp, but he arrives too late to save them. Eventually, even Hana and Antonín's time runs out, and they are shipped to separate camps. When she arrives at Terezín, Hana learns that her parents are likely dead. Horrified by with the camp's conditions, she begins to work as a doctor, treating patients in the camp's typhus ward. Finally, the Red Army defeats the Nazi forces and liberates the camp. The Jews and other prisoners celebrate their freedom – and Hana defiantly rips the

24 Williams, Melodrama, 69f.

25 Williams, Melodrama, 48.

26 Gledhill, The Melodramatic, 29.

27 Williams, Melodrama, 53.

28 Triumph des Willens [Triumph of the Will] Dir. Leni Riefenstahl, 1935, DVD.

yellow Star of David from her shirt. The film ends with a wide shot of Hana and Antonín as they walk through a field of unmarked graves. As the reunited couple walks into horizon and their future, a voice-of-god voice over narrator speaks the names of the death camps, noting 'only a few survived', just before the film fades to black.

The ending of 'Daleká cesta' is a happy ending, and yet it is uneasily so. While both the Jews and the Czechs have been liberated, they can never return to a point of origin (to before the occupation – or perhaps more appropriately, to the mythical nation of the First Republic), and the lives that have been lost can never be reproduced. Out of a nuclear family of at least five, only Hana survives. In the end, it is too late for the Kaufman family to be reunited; the surviving family members can never return to their point of origin, because the events of the events of World War II destroyed everything they once had. Here it is clear that the events of the war and the Holocaust are associated with the destruction of an entire people. Yet it is, above all, associated with the death of the domestic sphere of social life. In another way, this final image can also be interpreted as an anticipatory image directed towards a better future; Hana and Antonín, reunited, represent the future of the family. This displacement of the home is echoed through Hana's final gesture – as she rips off her yellow Star of David, she asserts, 'I am not a Jew, I am a Czech'.

Reading History: Moral Context and Moral Legibility

Significantly, the five brief years between the 1944 release of 'Sobota' and the 1949 release of 'Daleká cesta' represent the shifts from occupation, liberation, and the 'Czechoslovak road to socialism'. At the end of World War II, Czechoslovakia was left in a state of uncertainty; the material effects of the war brought immediate economic, political, social, and cultural changes that forced Czechs and Slovaks to re-think traditional notions of 'national identity'. As historian Bradley Abrams explains in "The Struggle For the Soul of the Nation", his intellectual history of the rise of communism in post-war Czechoslovakia by way of intellectual leaders: 'the experiences of 1938 to 1945 ripped the fabric of the interwar societies, reconfigured social hierarchies, reorganized economies, reshuffled political allegiances, caused a reevaluation of both foreign and domestic political priorities, triggered a rethinking of the meaning of the nations involved, and catalyzed forces aiming at the fundamental restructuring of the states of the region.'[29] These experiences forced Czechs to reflect back on their recent past to negotiate the crisis of their post-war national identity – to reinforce a nationalist image by reclaiming these recent historical events as 'their own' and re-imaging them to make these events morally legible.

---

29 Bradley Abrams, The Struggle for the Soul of the Nation. Czech Culture and the Rise of Socialism, Cambridge 2004, 10f.

This directly relates to the dominant ideology of the melodramatic mode; for in melodrama, the discovery of moral legibility is key. In melodramas, moral legibility is typically characterized by polarizing forces and takes form in the recognition of binaries like good and evil or moral and amoral it works towards recognition and confrontation of the evil or amoral, to combat and expel it, to purge the social order. It asks the questions, 'how to live, who is justified, who are the innocents, where is villainy at work now?'[30]

The question of moral legibility is particularly relevant when we consider how the post-war expulsion of ethnic Germans from the Czech lands helped to reinforce a 'nationalist image of an essentially democratic Czech ethnicity'.[31] The 1945 expulsion of close to three million ethnic Germans from the Czech lands relied upon remembering Nazism as 'forced denationalization'. This 'forced denationalization' recognizes the action of forcibly stripping away national identity and positions the Germans as Czech oppressors. In order to provide a moral context, Czech nationalists conflated 'Germanification' with 'Nazification' to rationalize that 'Czech families would never be safe from the pervasive threat of Germanization as long as they were forced to share their communities or their state with German-speakers'.[32] Furthermore, these discourses were accepted by Czech Left and Right, Communist, Socialists, and feminists, who justified the acts as 'protect[ing] the ethnic purity of Czech children they were simultaneously contributing to a greater struggle to defend democratic values and promote social justice'.[33]

For Abrams, the Prague Uprising on 5 May 1945 against the Nazi regime represents the articulation of a formerly illegible morality derived from additional pressures to transform national consciousness. The moralization of the Prague Uprising reconfigured the dominant strategy of the Czech nation during the war from collaboration to 'an attempt to punish an oppressive occupier and regain a measure of self respect'. Abrams attributes the contradictions presented by this historical inaction to the psychological effects of the Munich Accords and the problem of 'smallness'[34] that forced Czechs into the role of onlookers as the fate of their nation was being decided. By making the uprising the struggle for 'true independence', it offered an opportunity for collective affective healing. This struggle for 'true independence' was proliferated by young Czechs who viewed themselves as a determined generation whose defining moment was the Uprising and positioned the date as an alternative Czechoslovak Independence Day. Abrams goes on to highlight several writings by Communist party members and intel-

---

30 Gledhill, Rethinking Genre, 234.

31 Tara Zahra, Kidnapped Souls. National Indifference and the Battle for Children in the Bohemian Lands, 1900–1948, Ithaca 2008, 539f.

32 *Ibid.*, 539.

33 *Ibid.*, 540.

34 Bradley Abrams notes that 'One of the communist recipes for relieving the psychological burden of this "smallness" was to define the nation in terms of its ties to a resurgent and powerful Slavism that had the victorious Soviet Union at the head' [Abrams, The Struggle, 145f.].

lectual allies that describe the uprising in nationalist terms: 'transformed from an anti-German military action intending to secure the physical liberation of the nation into the first act of the national and democratic revolution', the 'brilliant rehabilitation of the Czech Nation', and 'simultaneously an act of liberation and a moral purification'.[35] Further, he links the Czechs' wartime collaboration, the Prague Uprising, and the Communist Party's rise to total power by tracing post-war Czech culture's demand for moral certainty to 'ideological allure to the certainty that Marxism embodies'.[36]

Conclusion

It can be resumed that the question of moral legibility is particularly relevant in any discussion of how melodrama relates to any representation of history.

To return to Peter Brooks's understanding of melodrama – not as a theme or genre, but as a 'mode of conception and expression' – a sense-making system through the act of interpretation – the melodramatic mode searches 'to locate and to articulate the moral occult' – the 'domain of operative spiritual of values which is both indicated within and masked by the surface of reality'.[37] In other words, the melodramatic form developed in a 'post-sacred' culture, where society needed a secular system of ethics to make everyday life meaningful. Brooks has described this feeling as a longing for a 'still-sacred universe' – for a return to a space of innocence – a point of origin.[38]

Melodrama may require a 'home' to represent a 'space of innocence', but it also requires the visual suffering of a victim to prove virtue. This is because 'melodrama focuses on victim-heroes and on recognizing their virtue. Recognition of virtue orchestrates the moral legibility that is key to melodrama's function'. The visual recognition of the victim is crucial to the melodramatic mode, because 'if virtue is not obvious, suffering – often depicted as the literal suffering of an agonized body – is'.[39] This suffering can be mental or physical, male or female.

So it can be assumed that the melodramatic mode takes over for the genre as it takes on the function of distinguishing moral context of a historical subject or experience. For example, in both 'Sobota' and 'Daleká cesta' the home as the sacred point-of-origin is threatened, but the stakes of the sacred changes with its historical context. Released during the occupation, 'Sobota' follows a bored young housewife with an absentee husband as she ventures outside of the home to work, has an affair with a wealthy man, is betrayed, and returns to her husband. From a very different position – post occupation, post-war, on the 'Czechoslovak road to social-

35 *Ibid.*, 155.

36 *Ibid.*

37 Brooks, The Melodramatic, xvii–5.

38 *Ibid.*, 15.

39 Williams, Playing the Race, 29.

ism' – 'Daleká cesta' explicitly addresses the historical events of World War II by following a young Jewish doctor's experiences of the Nazi occupation, her deportation, and survival at Terezín. In the aftermath of World War II, what Brooks refers to as the 'still-sacred' has been wiped out.[40] But this re-imaging of the sacred is no longer the home – the post-war reflection re-imagines the nation in terms of the 'sacred'. From this perspective, home is where the heart is moves away from the family to become an overtly national sentiment.

40 Brooks, The Melodramatic, 15.

About the authors

Arnold Suppan, born 1945 in Carinthia, studies at the University of Vienna, PhD 1970, 1971 assistant, 1984 associate, 2000 full professor of East European History at the University of Vienna; visiting professor at Leiden, Fribourg, Stanford, and Budapest; Head of the Austrian Institute of East and South-East European Studies (1988–2002); Head of the Department for East European History at the University of Vienna (2002–2008); Corresponding (1998), Full member (2003) of the Austrian Academy of Sciences/AAS, Chairman of the Historical Commission of the AAS (2003–2011), Secretary General (2009–2011) and Vice President of the AAS (2011–2013); Honorary member of the Hungarian Academy of Sciences; 8 monographs (Die österreichischen Volksgruppen im 20. Jahrhundert, Vienna, 1983; Jugoslawien und Österreich 1918–1938, Vienna–Munich, 1996; Zwischen Adria und Karawanken, Berlin, [2]2002; Hitler – Beneš – Tito: Konflikt, Krieg und Völkermord in Ostmittel- und Südosteuropa, Vienna, [2]2014), 30 volumes (Nationen, Nationalitäten, Minderheiten, 1994; Osteuropäische Geschichte in Wien, Innsbruck, 2007), 11 editions (Außenpolitische Dokumente der Republik Österreich 1918–1938, 10 vols.); Scientific Award of the University Ljubljana 1999, Silver medal of the Faculty of Philosophy of the Charles University, Prague 2001, Austrian Honorary Cross for Science and Art first class 2001, Wacław Felczak and Henryk Wereszycki Prize, Kraków 2014.

Nir Barak is a PhD Candidate at the Department of Political Science at the Hebrew University of Jerusalem and a fellow in the 'Human Rights-Under Pressure' dual program with the Freie Universität Berlin. In his doctoral research, he is developing a normative-political framework termed 'urban ecologism' which is an attempt to urbanize environmental theory and philosophy and to rethink its implications for urban political institutions and human rights. Additional research interests include political philosophy, critical theory and philosophy of space.

Colleen Bertsch is a PhD candidate in Musicology/Ethnomusicology at the University of Minnesota. She holds degrees in violin performance from Concordia College, Moorhead, and music education from the University of Minnesota. Her dissertation research focuses on the co-articulation of violin playing techniques and identity formation among Hungarian, Romanian, and Roma folk violinists living in Transylvania. She is a 2015/2016 US Fulbright Student Research Fellow to Romania.

Andra-Octavia Drăghiciu is a PhD candidate at the doctoral school of Central European Studies at Andrássy University Budapest. She studied History at the University of Vienna and was awarded a Herder scholarship in 2010/2011. Her research interests are Central and Eastern European microhistory, youth (sub)culture, and Oral-History.

Ferdinand Kühnel is a PhD fellow at the Institute of East European History at the University of Vienna. He studied History and Political Science at the Universities of Vienna and Warsaw. His research focuses on Austrian History of the 20th century, contemporary history (cultures of remembrance & politics of memory), and East Central European History of the 20th century (Polish History).

Lukáš Motyčka, studied Czech and German Studies in Olomouc, where he also obtained his PhD in German Literature. Since 2012, he has been the organizational leader of The Research Center for German Moravian Literature. He does research on regional literature from Bohemia and Moravia, homoerotic literary camouflage, modern German and Austrian literature, and theory and criticism of translation. He is a co-editor of Literarische Wanderungen durch das deutsche Olmütz (2012) and Anthologie der deutschmährischen Literatur (2014).

Noémi Nagy is a PhD Candidate at the Faculty of Law, University of Pécs, and a Doctoral Research Fellow at the Wirth Institute for Austrian and Central-European Studies, University of Alberta. Since 2010 she has been affiliated with the Research Institute for Linguistics, Hungarian Academy of Sciences. She holds university degrees in law and psychology. Her research interests lie in the field of language rights and minority protection.

Giovanni Matteo Quer is post-doctoral fellow at the European Forum of the Hebrew University of Human Rights. He holds a law degree from the University of Trento, Italy, and a PhD in International Studies from the School of International Studies (Trento). His research focuses on diversity management, human rights policies and contemporary antisemitism.

Ricarda Rindlisbacher is a PhD candidate and a researcher at the Department of Geography and Regional Science at the University of Graz. Her research work focuses on juvenile crime in combination with urban planning and geospatial technologies. Research stays both in Maynooth/Ireland at the National Centre of Geocomputation (NCG) and in Louisiana/USA at the Louisiana State University (LSU) have contributed to deepening her knowledge within the fields of crime, spatial statistics, (multimedial) cartography, and other geospatial technologies.

Adéla Rossípalová is a PhD candidate of German Literature at Palacký University Olomouc. She has been awarded various scholarships to study abroad and to conduct her research (University of Vienna, University of Bamberg, University of Salford and University of Innsbruck). In her dissertation she analyzes novels written by Prague German authors and explores whether these works can be characterized as novels influenced by *Neue Sachlichkeit*. She regularly participates in the Summer School of Slavonic Languages where she gives presentations about Prague German Authors.

Rachel Schaff is a PhD candidate in the Department of Cultural Studies and Comparative Literature and Moving Image Studies at the University of Minnesota. Schaff holds a B.F.A. in Film and Television Production from New York University – Tisch School of Arts and a M.A. in Film Studies from Columbia University. She is currently a Fulbright Research Scholar in the Czech Republic.

Sebastian Sparwasser is a PhD candidate at the doctoral school of the Faculty for Central European Studies at Andrássy University Budapest. He studied Modern History and European Ethnology in Freiburg, Budapest, and Basel. His research focuses on migration and cultural identity in post-war Europe.

Michał Wiącek is a PhD Candidate in International Relations at the Faculty of Social Sciences, University of Wrocław and a 2014/2015 Doctoral Research Assistant at the Wirth Institute for Austrian and Central European Studies, University of Alberta. He received his master degrees in European and International Law at the University Paris-Dauphine. His areas of interest include contemporary history, European integration and history of Polish émigré press.